All Things Hold
Together in Christ

# All Things Hold Together in Christ

## A Conversation on Faith, Science, and Virtue

EDITED BY

JAMES K. A. SMITH

AND MICHAEL L. GULKER

**Baker Academic**
a division of Baker Publishing Group
Grand Rapids, Michigan

© 2018 by The Colossian Forum

Published by Baker Academic
a division of Baker Publishing Group
P.O. Box 6287, Grand Rapids, MI 49516-6287
www.bakeracademic.com

Printed in the United States of America

Library of Congress Cataloging-in-Publication Data
Names: Smith, James K. A., 1970– editor.
Title: All things hold together in Christ : a conversation on faith, science, and virtue / James K.A. Smith and Michael L. Gulker, eds.
Description: Grand Rapids : Baker Academic, 2018. | Includes index.
Identifiers: LCCN 2017020095 | ISBN 9780801098987 (pbk. : alk. paper)
Subjects: LCSH: Church. | Christianity and culture. | Public worship. | Virtues. | Spiritual life—Christianity. | Religion and science.
Classification: LCC BV600.3 .A44 2017 | DDC 261—dc23
LC record available at https://lccn.loc.gov/2017020095

Each chapter in this book has been reproduced by the permission of its original publisher. For the sake of consistency there have been alterations to punctuation and documentation. Cross-references that appeared in the original version, but are not pertinent in this context, have been removed herein.

18   19   20   21   22   23   24        7   6   5   4   3   2   1

# Contents

# Preface

Talk to anyone who tracks how the church engages our culture today and you'll likely hear that the church in America has a *brand problem*. This problem is seen most readily in the shrinking of the church, its declining positive contribution to the wider culture, and millennials' flight from organized religion. One crucial part of our brand problem is that the church so often fails to engage divisive issues like origins, sexuality, immigration, or race in ways that "smell like Jesus." For a people claiming to follow the Prince of Peace, the polarization, fragmentation, and endless infighting seem especially problematic. It's tempting to think the "nones" and "dones" exiting the church may just be right.

Against this temptation, The Colossian Forum exists as witness to the belief that God has given us everything we need to be faithful. This is especially true in the midst of conflict. Whether one begins, as we do, with the cosmic hymn of Colossians 1:17—"In him all things hold together"—or with Jesus's prayer for unity in John 17, Paul's declaration that the dividing wall has been broken down in Ephesians, or 1 Corinthians 12 on unity amid difference, Christians have enormous theological warrant for believing that in times of conflict and polarization we, as the body of Christ, offer something to the world that can be found nowhere else. In the practices, confessions, worship, and traditions of the church, God in Christ has provided his church with all that we need to be faithful *if only* we would be faithful to what we've been given.

Thus, The Colossian Forum was launched to remind the body of Christ that *how* we seek the truth is integral to our witness. Called to pursue the truth in love, Christians must learn to engage controversial cultural issues in ways that are rooted in the gifts God has given us in Christ, mindful of the fact that "in him all things hold together" (Col. 1:17).

In order to grapple with difficult questions that can often divide the body of Christ, it is crucial that we first "clothe" ourselves with those virtues that will enable us to have such conversations *well*: compassion, humility, patience, forgiveness, and above all, love (Col. 3:12–15). The Colossian Forum equips churches and other Christian communities such as Christian colleges, universities, and high schools to create the productive, formative spaces in which to put on these virtues.

Attending to the formation of virtue creates the platform and hospitable space we need to then deal with difference and disagreement. And, as Jamie Smith has argued in *Desiring the Kingdom*, putting on the virtues takes practice. Most important, it requires being immersed in the practices of Christian worship (Col. 3:16).

For this reason, The Colossian Forum has sought to create spaces to practice the faith in the face of conflict as one way to faithfully receive these gifts, thereby equipping Christian leaders to transform messy cultural conflicts into opportunities for discipleship and witness. The goal: that the church become a place people run *to* rather than *from* in the face of conflict.

By situating cultural conflicts where they belong—in the presence of God and amid the worship practices of his church—we find that conflicts, like those between faith and science, can become gifts, a crucible by which Christ is formed in us. After all, what better way to cultivate the fruit of the Spirit like patience and forbearance than by spending time with another believer who tests your patience, whom you think may very well be leading the church off a cliff!

For the past five years, The Colossian Forum has had the privilege of spending time with such believers—saints holding vastly different theological perspectives while at the same time demonstrating deep patience and forbearance with one another in the midst of those differences. Saints who willingly place those differences at the foot of the cross to see what the Spirit might do with them—arguing vigorously yet doing so with the explicit goal of building up the church.

We've engaged believers of different ages and ideologies, on a variety of divisive topics. We've worked with high school and college students, faculty, administrators, college trustees and presidents, pastors, elders and youth, public intellectuals both famous and infamous. While there have been plenty of bumps and bruises along the way, we've repeatedly encountered stunning surprises—friendship where there was animosity; delight where there was anger; light where there had been only heat; and new avenues for exploration and investigation where there had been only deadlocks.

Of course, we've not overcome conflict in the church. Fear not, there's still plenty of opportunity to receive conflict as a gift! However, we have regularly encountered the power of the gospel right at the heart of conflict and experienced the truth that God has, indeed, given us everything we need to be faithful. For a church with a brand problem, this is good news indeed.

Because of these positive experiences, we have invested significant time and energy recovering and refining concrete practices of engaging, teaching, and reflecting on divisive issues in ways that display the truth of Colossians 1:17 as seen in the following initiatives:

- Through a partnership with Calvin College's Kuyers Institute for Christian Teaching and Learning, The Colossian Forum engaged high school teachers through the Faith and Science Teaching (FAST) Project, including creation of a website (www.teachFASTly.com) with resources developed by teachers to offer practices of teaching that cultivate virtue at the intersection of faith and science.
- A partnership with Bill Cavanaugh and Jamie Smith allowed The Colossian Forum to host scholarly colloquia rooted not in the competitive practices of the academic guild but in the prayers of Christ's church. This effort produced a volume of essays entitled *Evolution and the Fall* (Eerdmans, 2017) by top theologians, biblical scholars, historians, and scientists that display new possibilities for progress in a debate that has been gridlocked since the 1925 Scopes Trial.
- Through multiple partnerships with national and local leaders, pastors, scholars, and youth, The Colossian Forum developed *The Colossian Way* (www.colossianway.org)—a small group leaders' training program utilizing curricula on key topics like origins or sexuality to invite Christians into *a way* of using the practices of the faith in the midst of conflict to encourage spiritual growth and witness.

As the work of The Colossian Forum has taken root in churches, colleges, and high schools, there has been an increasing demand for us to share the theological undergirding that makes our work possible. Therefore, I am delighted that Jamie agreed to edit this volume as well as provide context for each section, shedding light on how The Colossian Forum has managed to turn conflict into opportunity.

But this volume contains more than information on the faith and science conversation. Each essay comes from a scholar who exemplifies theology as a practice rooted in the worship of the church. They display the kind of practice-based reflection The Colossian Forum exists to encourage—that form of theological reflection which takes up a contemporary conundrum in ways that don't simply update the faith by discarding those bits "outdated" by the latest cultural up-and-comer (science in this case), but instead extend the gift of faith we received from those who came before us into the present so that it might be received as a gift by those who come after us. It is our hope that, by us pointing to a practice done well, others may not only know our minds, but come to imitate those master practitioners who have helped make our lives possible.

We believe this anthology could be productively put to use in a variety of ways:

- in undergraduate and seminary settings where concerned believers are looking for not only a robust theological frame, but also productive practices for engaging faith and science more effectively;

- by FASTly high school teachers seeking continuing education on how to teach at the often tense intersection of faith and science; and
- by church leaders following the Colossian Way and looking for a deeper understanding of how the practices of the church inform how we engage today's most divisive topics.

Special thanks to Jamie Smith for making this project possible and for all he has done to frame and further the work of The Colossian Forum over the past five years. Thanks also to Bob Hosack, our editor at Baker. Our gratitude also goes to The Colossian Forum team (past and present) as well as Brian Mattson, who helped pull this anthology together.

Michael Gulker
President, The Colossian Forum

# Introduction

## Taking Theology and Science to Church

. . . . . . . . . . . . . . . . . . . . . . . . . . . . . . .

### JAMES K. A. SMITH

This book is an invitation to join a conversation between theology and science, between the way of life that is following Jesus and the creaturely curiosity that propels us to understand the natural world. But since this book invites you to a very different *kind* of conversation between theology and science, it is also an invitation to a pilgrimage of sorts. Think of the sources collected in this anthology as an itinerary for reframing your imagination about *how* to navigate the interactions between theology and science. But doing so requires a *radical* reboot of this dialogue, asking fundamental questions at the *root* (*radix*) of the encounter between science and Christianity—questions too often left unasked and uncritically assumed in most cases. This book is like a course in how to work out, in fear and trembling, the conviction that in Christ "all things hold together" (Col. 1:17)—whether heaven and earth, or science and faith, or church and creation.

## Science Takes Practice

The impetus to articulate an understanding of the natural world that resonates with (and is informed by) Scripture and revelation is as old as Christianity itself. For any community whose credo begins, "I believe in God the Father, Creator of heaven and earth," there is a properly *theological* desire to understand the creation in which the Creator has placed us as his image-bearers. And thus, in many ways, the "theology and science" conversation is as old as Paul's sermon on Mars Hill, in which the apostle proclaims an intersection between Greek metaphysics and

Christian confession: that in Christ we know the Creator in whom we live and move and have our being (Acts 17:28).

But the challenges and pitfalls of this endeavor are as old as the endeavor itself. As long as there has been a "theology and science" conversation, there have been tensions, missteps, temptations, and the necessity for careful discernment.[1] Natural philosophies and scientific theories are ambitious projects that can easily bleed into worldviews and rival confessions. Our empirical accounts of the penultimate can take on a tenor of ultimacy. That these tensions and rivalries have been amplified in modernity—in the wake of Darwin especially—is a point that hardly needs demonstration. We are all familiar with the way science and religion are construed as competing armies in a culture war.

This is why so many Christians have rightly sought to be peacemakers in the "science" theater of the culture wars. Recognizing that any posited dichotomy between the natural world and Christian confession is a rending of the Creator-creature relationship, and hence a denigration of the doctrine of creation itself, these reconcilers of science and theology have tried to quell the doubts of both scientists and theologians. But sometimes our well-intentioned reconciliation efforts end up (unwittingly) endorsing problematic understandings of both science and theology. Too often reconciliation projects accept a dichotomy that is itself part of the problem.

This anthology, which offers a set of paradigm-shifting sources to change this conversation, is animated by a conviction that, in many ways, the theology-science dialogue operates on the basis of a category mistake—that the regnant paradigms in science-and-religion or science-and-theology discourse have been playing with loaded dice such that the house (science) always wins. Or, to employ a different metaphor, we could say that the dominant paradigm in the theology-science dialogue has set up an uneven playing field that has put theology in the position of having to play uphill.

The primary category mistake stems from the fact that much of the science-theology conversation has operated on the basis of a certain positivism vis-à-vis "science," and taken the "findings" of science as if they were pristine disclosures of "nature."[2] Thus we constantly encounter familiar tropes: "we now know ... ," "science shows us ... ," "what science says," and so on. This is the case whether we're talking about "new atheists" like Dawkins and Dennett or theological voices like

---

1. In positing this long history of a conversation between "theology" and "science," I am using the terms broadly and somewhat anachronistically. As Peter Harrison has carefully argued, in some ways the categories "science" and "religion" are relatively recent (i.e., modern) inventions. See Peter Harrison, *The Territories of Science and Religion* (Chicago: University of Chicago Press, 2015).

2. This is why theological claims generated by the theology-science dialogue tend toward versions of a "natural theology." For two robust—but very different—Christian critiques of the very project of natural theology, see Alvin Plantinga, "The Reformed Objection to Natural Theology," *Proceedings of the American Catholic Philosophical Association* 15 (1980): 49–63; Stanley Hauerwas, *With the Grain of the Universe: The Church's Witness and Natural Theology* (Grand Rapids: Brazos, 2001).

Polkinghorne and McGrath. On both ends of the continuum, there is a similar assumption about the nature of science: it is either the pristine deliverer of the cold, hard, secular truth or the crystal-clear lens for disclosing the "message" in the book of nature.[3] "Science" is too often reduced to its *products*, to its conclusions and findings. As such, it is taken to be an odd sort of transparent black box which simply discloses the "objective" features of *nature*. So while the "dialogue" is purportedly between "science" (roughly, a constellation of academic disciplines) and "theology" (roughly, another academic discipline), *in fact* or *functionally* the dialogue tends to assume that theology is a kind of human cultural product whereas science is merely the conduit for disclosing the cold, hard realities of "nature"—to which theology must answer, demur, or affirm. After all, who's going to argue with "nature"?

So, like a schoolchild of years ago, we have to suck it up, lay out our hand, and bear the brunt of the strap. Theology needs to be *disciplined* by the findings of science and submit itself to the cold, hard realities of nature. If this turns out badly for some traditional or "fantastic" theological claims, then theologians have to take that as part of their whipping, and leave the principal's office grateful that they've been chastised since this will make them more intellectually responsible. Science is a stern tutor, but also just a civil servant, since all he does is force the theologian to face up to the realities of "nature." On this (admittedly cartoonish) account, the theologian brings his work to the desk of the scientist, who then determines what is acceptable and what is unacceptable, given the "realities" of nature, and the theologian leaves, hat-in-hand, grateful for whatever scraps of theological claims remain after the tutor's red ink has shredded the student's paper.

Framed this way, the theology-science dialogue is an asymmetrical relationship because of an equivocation about the nature of "science." While the conversation claims to be a dialogue between "science" and "theology," *functionally* it is taken to be a confrontation between *nature* and *culture*.

**science :: theology**
**nature :: culture**

But that is a category mistake. In fact, a dialogue between "science" and "theology" is always already a dialogue between "culture" and "culture," both of which are confronted by, are constrained by, and answer to a certain "givenness" that we often describe as "nature."

**science :: theology**
**culture :: culture**
**nature**

3. For a critique of the "hermeneutics of immediacy" that characterizes both of these efforts, see James K. A. Smith, *The Fall of Interpretation: Philosophical Foundations for a Creational Hermeneutic*, 2nd ed. (Grand Rapids: Baker Academic, 2012).

In other words, the theology-science conversation has tended to ignore the fact that *science* is a *cultural* institution. By a "cultural institution" I mean first of all an institution that is a *product* of human *making*.[4] Culture is the unfolding of potentialities that are latent or implicit in "nature," as it were. So aspects of "culture" are the fruit of human making and unfolding; they are not "natural kinds." A painting by Picasso, an elementary school, a Boeing 747, and a political constitution are all examples of "culture," of human making. They are not "naturally occurring" entities that one would bump into if there weren't human agents that unfolded them and brought them into being. Cultural institutions are networks of practices, habits, and material environments that are the product of human making. So a hospital is a cultural institution that is "unfolded" by a human community and is composed of both a particular built-environment (ER and ORs, ambulances and CAT scan machines, etc.) and networks of practices and traditions which are learned by apprenticeship (e.g., the "disciplines" of surgery and medicine, the traditions of care that define nursing, etc.). Hospitals don't fall from the sky, nor do they simply crawl up from the lagoon in the La Brea Tar Pits. They emerge as products of human making—which means that they are essentially historical and contingent. They unfold over time, and they could have unfolded otherwise (or not at all).

Now, it seems to me that the science-theology conversation happily acknowledges that *theology* is a cultural institution. How could one not? Theology is a product of religious traditions and communities, which are themselves paradigmatic instances of "cultural institutions" that are historical, contingent, and certainly not "natural." They have unfolded over time, have unfolded differently in different places, could have unfolded otherwise, and might even have not unfolded at all. Thus "theology," as a cultural institution, is recognized as a kind of "hermeneutic" reality—it offers interpretations of the world, is shaped by different traditions and presuppositions, and represents a "take" on things. From the perspective of the regnant paradigm in the theology-science conversation, this means that theology is sort of one step back from "reality." It is a cultural institution that ascribes "meaning" to reality/nature, whereas "science" is a conduit for disclosing the reality of nature *as such*.

But this is exactly where the conversation has gone off course. It has failed to appreciate (even if it might officially concede) that science is also a cultural institution. "Science" is not a naturally occurring entity like igneous rocks or sea horses; that is, science is not something that either emerges from the swamp or falls from the sky apart from human making. Rather, science is a network of material practices, built environments (including laboratories, instrumentation, etc.), traditions of apprenticeship, and learned rituals that emerged over time, in particular configurations, in different places.[5] So any conversation between

4. This should be a relatively noncontroversial claim. For a discussion of culture in terms of *making*, see James K. A. Smith, *Desiring the Kingdom: Worship, Worldview, and Cultural Formation* (Grand Rapids: Baker Academic, 2009), 71–73; and Andy Crouch, *Culture Making* (Downers Grove, IL: InterVarsity, 2008).

5. See Stephen Gaukroger's magisterial history, *The Emergence of a Scientific Culture: Science and the Shaping of Modernity, 1210–1685* (Oxford: Oxford University Press, 2009).

"science" and "theology" is never going to be simply a matter of getting theology to face up to "nature"; rather, it is always already a *cross-cultural* dialogue. It is a conversation between two different cultural institutions, each with its own traditions, practices, built environments, and meaning-systems. Because of its lingering positivism, the theology-science dialogue—at least as I've seen it—tends to operate in isolation from a vast (and growing) literature on science *as* culture, such as the social history of experimentation, the politics of the Royal Society, the material dynamics of apprenticeship, the economics of instrumentation and technological developments, the cultural embeddedness of medicine, and so on.

The point here is *not* a debunking project. The goal isn't to point out that science is a cultural institution in order to dismiss it. Rather, the point is to situate science *as* a cultural institution in order to clarify the category mistake and thus level the playing field for reconnoitering the science-theology dialogue in a way that yields new possibilities.

One important implication of recognizing science as culture is a leveling of the playing field in the theology-science dialogue. While it might be the case that theology must rightly be constrained by the "givenness" of nature—the world that pushes back on our claims—that is not the same as saying that theology must bow at the feet of *science*. We need to recognize a distinction between science and nature, a distinction too often erased in the theology-science conversation. Science is not just a transparent magnifying glass or pristine conduit that delivers nature "as it really is." Science is a cultural institution (or, better, a constellation of cultural institution*s*) that is, of course, especially attentive to nature, is interested in describing and perhaps even explaining nature, and exposes itself to nature's pushback through the rigors and disciplines of experimentation and observation. But that doesn't make science "natural." It remains a cultural layer of human making. And in this respect it is in the same boat as theology (and literature and sociology and . . .).

Therefore theology should no longer feel that it has to defer to science *as if* it was thereby subjecting itself to nature or "reality" (as in, "science tells us . . ."). While theological claims are rightly disciplined by the ways in which the givenness of the world "pushes back" on our claims, this is not synonymous with being disciplined by science. In the vein of John Milbank's manifesto regarding theology's deference to the social sciences, we might also suggest that theology ought to drop the false humility and reassert itself as a cultural voice with the same epistemic standing as science.[6] The asymmetry of the conversation so far has been predicated on a privileged place of science as a veritable divine postman, as the deliverer of nature's truth who sets the rules of the game. But science is a player, not referee or judge.

6. See John Milbank, *Theology and Social Theory: Beyond Secular Reason* (Oxford: Blackwell, 1990), 1: "The pathos of modern theology is its false humility. For theology, this must be a fatal disease, because once theology surrenders its claim to be a metadiscourse, it cannot any longer articulate the word of the creator God, but is bound to turn into the oracular voice of some finite idol, such as historical scholarship, humanist psychology, or transcendental philosophy. If theology no longer seeks to position, qualify or criticize other discourses, then it is inevitable that these discourses will position theology."

The theology-science conversation should also stop thinking of "science" as a static body of *findings* and instead consider science as a dynamic process of *finding*. The way the theology-science dialogue is usually conducted, one would almost guess that "science" existed only in journals. The "science" in the theology-science dialogue is a remarkably disembodied phenomenon—as if there were no laboratories, instruments, or communities. But science is not just the *results* of science, the data sets or images that get produced at the end of a very long process. Nor is science just a matter of *theory*. Rather, "science" is perhaps best identified as the *practices* that yield such fruit. This will require that we give up lingering perceptions of science as itself mechanistic or technicistic, along with theory-centric conceptions of science as the sort of thing best pursued by brains-in-vats. Science is a deeply social, communal project, composed of material practices and rituals that are handed on as traditions, absorbed as habits, and enacted in experimental performance that, literally, creates worlds.

How might the theology-science dialogue look different, if we not only recognize science *as* culture, but recognize it as a *community* with a set of cultural practices? This will require appreciating the central role of experimentation, along with all the rituals and traditions that inform it. Thus Robert Crease suggests that experimentation is a kind of "performing art."[7] Theories can't do the work that experimental "art" does. This is because

> a scientific entity does not show up in a laboratory the way an airplane shows up on a radar screen, a fully formed thing out there in the world whose presence is made known to us by a representation. Nor is a scientific entity like a smaller version of the airplane, which could be perceptible if only scaled up large enough. Nor, finally, is a scientific entity like some distant and unknown object on the radar screen that when closer becomes perceptible. A scientific entity becomes perceptible only in performance.[8]

So experimentation "is not merely a *praxis*—an application of some skill or technique—but a *poiēsis*; a bringing forth of a phenomenon."[9] While science seeks to be disciplined by nature, there is also a sense in which science *creates* its own phenomena. It constitutes its world through experimental performance which is a *learned* performance requiring its own set of virtues and skills, deft employment of instrumentation, and a kind of "know-how" that is not theoretical, and perhaps not even "intellectual."[10]

Hans-Jörg Rheinberger, in his stunning philosophical history of the protein synthesis, notes the way in which the "stuff" of science—"epistemic things" or

---

7. Robert P. Crease, *The Play of Nature: Experimentation as Performance* (Bloomington: Indiana University Press, 1993), esp. 74–102. My thanks to Arie Leegwater and Matt Walhout for pointing me to this resource.

8. Ibid., 85–86.

9. Ibid., 82.

10. The point is that such know-how is more on the order of what Heidegger describes as the "understanding" or preunderstanding, or what Charles Taylor calls a "social imaginary."

"research objects"—in some ways emerges because of experimental conditions that are created by "technical objects" (such as instruments). The epistemic things "articulate" themselves "through" a "wider field of epistemic practices and material cultures" which include both instruments and theories.[11] In important ways, the "epistemic things" that will emerge "usually cannot be anticipated when an experimental arrangement is taking shape."[12] (So there are a lot more surprises in science than one would guess from the picture we get from the theology-science dialogue.) Thus "experimental systems are necessarily localized and situated *generators of knowledge.*"[13] What science *finds* is determined not just by what science goes looking for but by *how* it looks. And that "how" is not primarily a theory but a constellation of practices that constitute an experimental system. As these systems build up over time and generate linkages with other experimental systems, there emerges what Rheinberger calls "experimental cultures" which "share a certain material style of research" or "laboratory style." At that point, experimental systems begin to take on a life of their own.[14] They generate epistemic things by generating microworlds—which are responses to nature but should not be identified with nature. Hence, once again, we see the importance of not mistaking science for nature. We also note Rheinberger's concluding caveat:

> To characterize science as practice and as culture does not amount, as far as I apprehend it, to determining the social influences hindering or furthering the sciences. It does not amount to a critique of ideologies of science in the traditional sense. Rather, it amounts to characterizing the sciences themselves as cultural systems that shape our societies and all the while trying to find out what makes the sciences different and confers on them their peculiar drive, not privileging them with respect to other cultural systems.[15]

This is not a rejection or diminishment of science, but it does reposition science. This reframes the theology-science dialogue by leveling the playing field. But that is only the beginning of our journey.

## Discernment Takes Practice

The science-theology dialogue will look different if we appreciate that science is a constellation of practices. But the dialogue will also look different if we stop reducing Christianity to "theology." What if Christianity is not just a set of ideas or body of doctrines or system of beliefs but a *way of life*? What if we also appreciated

11. Hans-Jörg Rheinberger, *Toward a History of Epistemic Things: Synthesizing Proteins in the Test Tube* (Stanford: Stanford University Press, 1997), 28–29.
12. Ibid., 74.
13. Ibid., 76, emphasis added.
14. Ibid., 138–39.
15. Ibid., 140.

that religion takes practice—and that before religious communities ever generate theologies and worldviews they engage in worship and prayer? How might we imagine the science-religion dialogue differently if, instead of seeing it as a confrontation of belief systems, we considered both as cultural institutions animated and defined by sets of practices? What if the resources we need for discernment are not just the knowledge and information that comprise "Christianity" but the practices and habits that comprise the church?

Here lies the other fundamental animating conviction of this anthology: faithful wrestling with challenging issues at the intersection of theology and science will not be settled by more information; rather, what's needed is the *form*ation of requisite virtues in order to enable us to discern what matters. You might call this "the Colossian way."

The Colossian Forum was launched to remind the body of Christ that *how* we seek the truth is integral to our witness. Called to pursue the truth in love, Christians must learn to engage controversial cultural issues in a way that is rooted in the gifts God has given us in Christ, mindful of the fact that in Christ "all things hold together" (Col. 1:17). In order to grapple with difficult questions that can often divide the body of Christ, it is crucial that we first "clothe" ourselves with those virtues that will enable us to have such conversations *well*. These include the Christlike virtues of compassion, humility, patience, forgiveness, and above all love (Col. 3:12–15), which are so crucial for the community of faith when working through matters that could divide us. Attending to the formation of virtue creates the platform and hospitable space we need to then deal with difference and disagreement. Certainly of late "science" has been a catalyst for disagreement— whether it's matters of human origins, genetics, climate change, or technology. Over the past generation, science has often been a catalyst for vitriolic debates within the body of Christ. Too often we assume we disagree just because the "other side" lacks the information that "we" have. And thus we tacitly assume that that disagreement is caused by ignorance and will be solved with knowledge. But many of our disagreements are more intractable than that, and what's lacking is not some bit of information but the spiritual formation we need to learn to live with difference in the body of Christ. That's why, in this book that is ostensibly about "theology and science," we devote significant space to talking about the virtues that characterize a community of Jesus followers who reflect compassion, forgiveness, and patience. A lot of the debates in the theology-science conversation are less about theology or science and more about what and Whom we love.

But we also need the requisite intellectual virtues—humility, patience, discipline, creativity—in order to imagine constructive ways forward. In short, we need the requisite virtues that make *discernment* possible. Otherwise we end up *confusing essentials and nonessentials*: Some individuals and organizations, burdened by the problems above, have rightly begun to address the perceived conflict between Christianity and science by showing that this is only a *perceived* conflict—that Christian faith need not be opposed to careful empirical attention to God's creation and that "science" does not conflict with the essentials of Christian faith. The problem, however, is that such approaches can quickly become hampered by a very narrow agenda, fixated on demonstrating and proving one particular scientific position as if it were *the* necessary and only viable Christian position on faith and science (particularly on issues of creation and evolution). Indeed, some confuse their particular position on scientific matters *as* orthodoxy—as a matter essential to salvation. Others, desiring intellectual respectability, defer too easily to regnant paradigms in science. They make hasty concessions to the supposed authority of "what science says" and thus treat rather flippantly the historic commitments to Christian orthodoxy, thereby trivializing the deeply held faith of the church and alienating believers. The result has been hostility between Christians in the name of minimizing the perceived hostility between science and Christianity.

On the other hand, Christians concerned about these issues can fall into *culture-war agendas*. Because issues of science and religion have become political footballs of both the left and right in American politics, Christians engaged in these discussions have sometimes fallen prey to partisan agendas. Thus, for example, the project of scientifically establishing "design" has been seen as a way of securing a particular *moral* agenda which could then be legislated. The perhaps unintentional result of such culture-war approaches to science and faith has been to advance particular political (and partisan) agendas rather than to serve the church. The result, in fact, is that the particularity of *Christ* tends to disappear from view and instead we get the more deistic "creator" of natural law, who seems more universally palatable. In such invocations of creation, we lose the cross.

The sources gathered in this volume reflect The Colossian Forum's conviction that it is crucial to locate the center of gravity for these conversations in the nature and mission of the church as the body of Christ, rather than letting the center of gravity shift to the cultural issues and various "positions" associated with them. If the church has been unable to carry out constructive internal conversations about these hot-button cultural issues, it's not simply because we lack correct beliefs or adequate information; it's also and more importantly because we have treated the church as irrelevant to such "academic" issues. But the issue isn't whether there can be a dialogue between faith and science; the issue is whether the body of Christ has the requisite *virtues* to sustain such a conversation.

So this volume is not primarily a conduit of more scientific information. This is because we believe that the church doesn't need to *know* more, it needs to *be* differently, *act* differently. And we believe our actions flow from our character, from those habits and dispositions that we acquire. This is why the center of The Colossian Forum's vision is an *ethical* conviction that resonates deeply with my argument in *Desiring the Kingdom*: we don't need more information deposited in our heads that will help us come up with the answers; rather, we need to first undergo the *formation* of the Spirit, who, by grace and through practice, *makes* us the kind of people who are characterized by Christlike virtue—including the intellectual virtues that enable us to pursue the truth.[16] And we believe it is primarily in the community of practice which is the church that the Spirit forms us in this way.

What characterizes this "Colossian Way" is the conviction that *in Christ* "all things hold together" (Col. 1:17). Science, then, is not an autonomous sphere that has to be correlated to or reconciled with faith; rather, Christ is Lord of creation just as he is the head of the church. Christ is "firstborn over all creation; for by him all things were created." Indeed, "all things were created through him and for him" (Col. 1:15–16). So the stuff of scientific investigation—the earth below us and the starry heavens above, the intricacies of our nervous system and the regularity of the water cycle—are features of *Christ's* creation. As Lord of creation, Christ is also Lord of the world that science seeks to investigate.

In the same context as this claim, the apostle Paul immediately points out that Christ "is the head of the body, the church" (Col. 1:18). Church and creation are not two separate realms; indeed, it is not the case that Christ rules over the church while nature is an independent reality. *Both* subsist or hold together in Christ. And this is why God's work of redemption also aims at a kind of unity—a *reconciliation* that reflects the unity of all things "in Christ." The gospel announced by Paul is the message that God, in Christ, has reconciled all things to himself (2 Cor. 5:19; Col. 1:17).

Any constructive dialogue about science and Christian faith needs to be rooted in and formed by this "holding together." In other words, the dialogue does not need to bring together (or integrate) Christianity and science. Instead, we need to begin with the unity that already exists in the lordship of Christ—which is incarnate in the church as the body of Christ. We will only begin to reconcile faith and science when we recognize that church and creation are *already* one in Christ. This anthology of readings is intended to exhibit a different way—a completely new paradigm for carrying out the dialogue between science and Christian faith.

The book is organized in four parts, reflecting the core themes of The Colossian Forum. The parts are organized with a *pedagogical progression* in mind: before students can begin to engage substantive matters at the intersection of faith and science, we need to first attend to more fundamental issues. (And material within each section of the book is also organized with a pedagogical progression in mind, beginning with more accessible selections, progressing to more advanced discussions.)

Part 1 demonstrates how and why the church and worship are the only proper seedbed for a distinctly Christian reflection on the world, including the natural world. Part 2 then shows the importance of the virtues for the pursuit of truth, and hence the need to consider the importance and nature of virtue formation— with a specific view to those virtues which are necessary for the church to have a

16. See Smith, *Desiring the Kingdom*. For a more recent, more accessible articulation of the same argument, see Smith, *You Are What You Love: The Spiritual Power of Habit* (Grand Rapids: Brazos, 2016).

constructive, charitable conversation about difficult issues in a way that does not compromise our witness to Christ. Part 3 builds on this to articulate an account of "tradition-based rationality," drawing on the work of Alasdair MacIntyre but taking this specifically in the direction of considering how the Christian confessional tradition is both a gift and resource for contemporary conversations. This section will specifically consider the theological interpretation of Scripture as an expression of tradition-based rationality for the Christian tradition. Finally, only after that preparation, part 4 turns explicitly to matters of science, illustrating how this different frame leads us to ask different questions and pursue different goals. In particular, this framework recontextualizes science as itself a "tradition-based" form of rationality, which then reframes how we consider its relationship to theology and Christian faith. This final section will sketch the implications of a specifically *christological* engagement with science.

We're looking for pilgrims to accompany us on this journey. Won't you join us?

# PART ONE

# Creating a Community for the Conversation

*Ecclesiology and Worship*

JAMES K. A. SMITH

We tend to assume that the conversation between science and theology is an "academic" concern, and therefore, by default, we assume that it should be conducted in the environs of the university. But this hasty assumption misses a fundamental point: any wise, discerning, faithful work at the intersection of faith and theology requires participants with the requisite virtues to pull it off. And the incubator of such Spirit-given virtues is the church. So this first, and fundamental, section of the book—and hence our argument—begins in the body of Christ. We will be equipped to carry out a constructive conversation, and will know how to disagree *well*, just to the extent that we've been apprenticed to Jesus in those practices of worship that Craig Dykstra describes as "habitations of the Spirit."

Mark Twain once quipped: "He who carries a cat by the tail learns something he can't learn in any other way." Twain's point is that there is an irreducible know-*how* one acquires from the actual experience of carrying a cat by the tail. It doesn't matter how many books about cat-carrying you might have read, or how many lectures you've heard from other cat-by-the-tail carriers, there is something about this you can only know by doing. So too with the body of Christ: there is an understanding of the gospel that can only be "caught" in the body of Christ. Thus faithful scientists and faithful theologians should not only be attentive to the information they acquire in their disciplines; they should be equally concerned about the imagination formation they absorb in the practices of Christian worship and the unique apprenticeship to Jesus that is discipleship in the body of Christ. The chapters in this first part of the book unpack a picture of the church as a school of virtue.

In chapter 1, Rodney Clapp lays out the basis of a robust ecclesiology, particularly sensitive to explain this historic understanding of the church for those who find themselves in "free church" traditions, which tend to have a "lower" view of church. As Clapp explains, drawing on John Howard Yoder, Stanley Hauerwas, and others, the church is not just a club of Christians who gather to express their praise and worship of God. Rather, the church is a called people, gathered to encounter and be shaped by God into a "peculiar people."

This picture of a deeply communal endeavor in which others—even those we disagree with—are gifts given to us by God to mold us and (re)shape us is deepened in chapters 2 and 3 by Samuel Wells and David Burrell, respectively. The church is an invitation to friendship—to the remarkable, unthinkable vocation of being friends of God (John 15:15) and friends with God's friends. Such friendship, Aristotle points out (and Burrell reminds us), is essential to the life of virtue and wisdom. Created as social beings, there are no lone rangers of virtue, no lone wolfs of wisdom. Friends are gift givers that bind us to the Good. So any advancement in knowledge and wisdom about thorny questions of science and religion is going to take communities of friends bound to God and one another.

Chapter 4, by James K. A. Smith, shows the intimate link between the ideas of a Christian "worldview" and the practices of Christian worship. In a sense, Smith argues, we pray before we know; we worship before we worldview. What will eventually be articulated as theology and doctrine begins as the practices of prayer, confession, praise, and sharing the meal that is the Lord's Supper. And there remains a unique understanding of the gospel that is "carried" in the practices of Christian worship. Therefore, Christian worship is the "imagination station" that fuels faithful thinking and equips us with the understanding we need to discern what really matters.

Finally, chapter 5, a selection from *Common Prayer: A Liturgy for Ordinary Radicals* (Grand Rapids: Zondervan, 2010) serves a twofold purpose. It provides an introduction to the historic discipline of "fixed hour" prayer, especially for those unfamiliar with this practice. This way of praying the Scriptures with the church suffuses the mission and habits of The Colossian Forum precisely because we believe this is a way to baptize our imagination in God's Word. That's why we also hope the selection whets your appetite and serves as an invitation to take up the practice yourself.

# 1

## The Church as Church

*Practicing the Politics of Jesus*

Rodney Clapp

Now that the long Constantinian age has all but passed, we Christians find ourselves in a situation much more closely analogous to that of New Testament Christians than to the Christendom for which some nostalgically long. The Bible, it turns out, offers abundant resources for living in a wildly diverse and contested world. With Constantine finally buried, theologians and biblical scholars find themselves able to reclaim, and present again to the church, the politics of Jesus.[1]

### Jesus's World

Perhaps the main reason that the Bible has, at least in recent centuries, seemed to offer scarce political or cultural guidance is that Christians have read a "rank

Originally published as "The Church as Church: Practicing the Politics of Jesus," in Rodney Clapp, *A Peculiar People: The Church as Culture in a Post-Christian Society* (Downers Grove, IL: InterVarsity, 1996), 76–93. Copyright © 1996 by Rodney Clapp. Used by permission of InterVarsity Press, PO Box 1400, Downers Grove, IL 60515. www.ivpress.com.

1. Obviously I borrow this chapter's subtitle from John Howard Yoder's influential work *The Politics of Jesus: Behold the Man! Our Victorious Lamb*, 2nd ed. (Grand Rapids: Eerdmans, 1994).

anachronism" back into its text. The strict split between "religion" and "politics" belongs to centuries much later than the first. As N. T. Wright remarks, "No first-century Jew . . . could imagine that the worship of their god and the organization of human society were matters related only at a tangent."[2]

Even the most rank anachronizer will not deny that there is much of the political, the physical, the social and economical throughout the Old Testament. Israel, after all, is a nation, an irrefutably political entity. And it is a political entity born of social, not merely psychological, rebellion—the revolt of slaves against what was then the world's most powerful empire, Egypt. The story of the nation Israel is, like that of all nations, one of conquest (the vanquishing of Canaan), of hierarchy and its power plays (the kingdom of David), of hope and striving for justice as well as security. Israel's story, furthermore, does not become apolitical the moment it loses its capital and its land and is sent into exile. The nation is scattered but still a nation, and now a nation whose prophets hope strenuously for the restoration of that capital and land. Isaiah, Jeremiah, Joel, Micah, and Zechariah all cite Zion as the place of God's climactic (and clearly political) saving act.[3] So: "Hear the word of the LORD, O nations, and declare it in the coastlands far away; say, 'He who scattered Israel will gather him, and will keep him as a shepherd a flock'" (Jer. 31:10).

Yet even if all this is recognized, there remains a strong tendency to imagine that the political and social dimensions of faith fell away at, or with, the birth of the church. A moment's pause reveals how untenable this assumption is. To make the earliest church asocial and apolitical is to suppose that suddenly the Jews of Jesus's day ceased worshiping a God that, for hundreds of years, their people had considered eminently involved with history and politics.

In fact, Jesus proclaimed his message and gathered his disciples in a politically charged context. His was a society grinding under the oppression of a distant, colonizing empire, that of Rome. The Jews of Jesus's day and place, although they were regathered in Palestine and had rebuilt the temple in Jerusalem, considered themselves still in exile, "since the return from Babylon had not brought that independence and prosperity which the prophets foretold."[4] The Pharisees and other parties vying for control were in no sense "religious" in such a manner that their aims excluded the political, the social, and the economic. The political agendas of Jewish parties ranged from the most "conservative" (the Sadducees, most nearly allied with the occupying Romans and so least

2. N. T. Wright, "The New Testament and the 'State,'" *Themelios* 16, no. 1 (October/November 1990): 11.

3. See Ben F. Meyer, *The Early Christians: Their World Mission and Self-Discovery* (Wilmington, DE: Michael Glazier, 1986), 61.

4. Roman occupation was "simply the mode that Israel's continuing exile had taken. . . . As long as Herod and Pilate were in control of Palestine, Israel was still under the curse of Deuteronomy 29." N. T. Wright, *The Climax of the Covenant* (Minneapolis: Fortress, 1991), 141. See also his *The New Testament and the People of God* (Minneapolis: Fortress, 1992), 268–72.

desirous of significant change) to the most radical (the dispossessed Zealots, who advocated violent revolution).[5]

To make good, faithful, and biblical sense of Jesus, we simply must take into account the world in which he lived and the problems he (or any other religious figure) was expected to address. Wright summarizes the situation: "Jewish society faced major external threats and major internal problems. The question, what it might mean to be a good and loyal Jew, had pressing social, economic and political dimensions as well as cultural and theological ones."[6] It is perhaps only the most affluent, socially stable people who can ignore social, economic, and political questions and concentrate on their abstracted inner well-being. Christian Science and other mind-cure groups so popular in the nineteenth century made no converts in Naples or Calcutta. Outside the United States, they appealed only to the English upper middle class. I doubt that Christian Science, or for that matter Christianity as it is now profoundly psychologized by many liberals and evangelicals alike, would have found many converts—or even have made any sense—among first-century Palestinian Jews. You might just as well have entered into an argument with them that the world was really round or that the earth was not the center of the cosmos. The anachronism, whether drawn from our physical sciences or our preoccupation with individualistic psychology, is equally rank.

Wright emphasizes that "the pressing needs of most Jews of the period had to do with liberation—from oppression, from debt, from Rome." None of this is to suggest for a moment that Jewish (and Jesus's) faith was exclusively political, whatever that might mean. But it does suggest that other issues "were regularly seen in this [political] light." This context—the actual context of Jesus's life and work—renders incredible Ernst Troeltsch's confident assertion that the "values of redemption" preached by Jesus were "purely inward" and led "naturally to a sphere of painless bliss."[7] The hope of Israel was, as Wright puts it, not for "disembodied bliss" after death "but for a national liberation that would fulfill the expectations aroused by the memory, and regular celebration, of the exodus. . . . Hope focused on the coming of the kingdom of Israel's God."[8]

5. For a helpful survey of these options as theological and political, see Yoder, *Politics of Jesus*. Meyer comments that much theology (I would note pietistic evangelicalism and existentialist neo-orthodoxy) has misconceived the career of Jesus "as an individualistic call to decision, in almost complete abstraction from its Jewishness and from the intra-Jewish historical context of religious competitors for Israel's allegiance (Pharisees, Zealots, Sadducees, Essenes, Baptists . . .)." Meyer, *Early Christians*, 43–44.

6. Wright, *New Testament and the People of God*, 169.

7. Ernst Troeltsch, *The Social Teaching of the Christian Churches*, trans. Olive Wyon (New York: Macmillan, 1931), 1:40.

8. All quotations from Wright in this paragraph are from *New Testament and the People of God*, 169–70.

## Language Matters

Indeed, given such blatantly political language as *exodus* and *kingdom*, it can be difficult to comprehend how we have managed to so thoroughly privatize the New Testament faith. Of no less political provenance than *kingdom* is the term *gospel*, or *evangel*. In the Greco-Roman world from which the early church adopted it, "gospel" was a public proclamation of, say, a war won, borne by a herald who ran back to the city and, with his welcome political news, occasioned public celebration.[9] Christian ethicist Allen Verhey suggests that Mark, in calling what he had written a "Gospel," was meaning to evoke *evangel* as it was used within the Roman cult of emperor to refer to announcements of the birth of an heir to the throne, of the heir's coming of age, accession to the throne, and so forth. If so, the writer of the Gospel is comparing the kingdom of God come in Jesus to the quite this-worldly and political kingdom of Caesar.[10] It would not be amiss to translate "The Gospel according to Mark" as "The Political Tidings according to Mark." In short, if Mark in his world had wanted to convey a privatistic and individualistic account of Jesus's life and death, he could have thought of many better things to call it than a Gospel (Mark 1:1).

No less political is the language used to describe the church's worship. Our word *liturgy* comes from the Greek meaning "work of the people," or, as we might put it now, a "public work." In Roman society, "to build a bridge for a public road across a stream on one's private property would constitute a liturgy." Military service at one's own expense was an act of liturgy. The wealthy sought favor by sponsoring lavish "liturgies"—huge dramas for the entertainment of the citizenry. *Leitourgoi*, or, very roughly, "liturgists," in the secular Greek usage of the time referred to government officials.[11] To modern, privatized Christian ears, *worship* too easily connotes escape from the world (we worship, after all, in a "sanctuary"), a removal from the political and the social. Yet inasmuch as we read such connotations onto the word in its New Testament context we are saying something oxymoronic like the "private public work" of the church. The New Testament Christians themselves, I submit, were not so confused.

No less cultural and political is the very word used to describe the new community of God. *Church* (the Greek *ekklēsia*) from the fifth century BC onward referred to an assembly of citizens called to decide matters affecting the common welfare.[12] The Hebrew *qahal* denotes a solemn, deliberative assembly of Israel's tribes. The assembly par excellence, for example, was at Mount Sinai, where the Law was received (Deut. 9:10; 18:16). When the ancient Jews translated the Old Testament into Greek, *qahal* was rendered *ekklēsia*. This is the term Christians seized

9. Yoder, *Politics of Jesus*, 28.

10. Allen Verhey, *The Great Reversal* (Grand Rapids: Eerdmans, 1984), 74.

11. Charles P. Price and Louis Weil, *Liturgy for Living* (New York: Seabury, 1979), 21; Yoder, *Politics of Jesus*, 206–7.

12. Robert Banks, *Paul's Idea of Community* (Grand Rapids: Eerdmans, 1988), 34.

on to describe their own assemblies. Thus the *"Ekklēsia* of God" means roughly the same thing as what New Englanders might call the "town meeting of God."[13]

Given all this, it is unsurprising that early observers of Christianity were not struck by its "religious" (in our privatized sense) qualities. What struck outsiders, says Wright, was the church's "total way of life"—or in my terms, its culture.[14] The Romans called Christians "atheists" (they refused cultic emperor worship) and classified Christianity as a political society. This classification meant that Christianity was under a ban on corporate ritual meals, much as many governments down to the present ban the "free assembly" of those considered subversive. Christians, says Wright, "were seen not just as a religious grouping, but one whose religion made them a subversive presence within the wider Roman society."[15] There can be no doubt that Rome consistently saw Jews and early Christians as a social and political problem and treated them accordingly.

Of course we know that the Romans misunderstood both Jews and Christians on many counts. Did they also grossly misconstrue their intentions here? The thoroughly political language adopted by the church suggests otherwise. The clincher is that if the early church had wanted itself and its purpose to be construed in privatistic and individualistic terms, there were abundant cultural and legal resources at hand for it to do just that. The early church could easily have escaped Roman persecution by suing for status as a *cultus privatus*, or "private cult" dedicated to "the pursuit of a purely personal and otherworldly salvation for its members," like many other religious groups in that world.[16] Yet instead of adopting the language of the privatized mystery religions, the church confronted Caesar, not exactly *on* his own terms but *with* his own terms. As Wayne Meeks summarizes the matter, early Christian moral practices

> are essentially communal. Even those practices that are urged upon individuals in the privacy of their homes . . . are extensions of the community's practice—indeed they are means of reminding individuals even when alone that they are not merely devotees of the Christians' God, they are members of Christ's body, the people of God. That was how the Christian movement differed most visibly from the other cults that fit more easily into the normal expectations of "religion" in the Roman world. The Christians' practices were not confined to sacred occasions and sacred locations—shrines, sacrifices, processions—but were integral to the formation of communities with a distinctive self-awareness.[17]

13. Wayne Meeks, *The Origins of Christian Morality: The First Two Centuries* (New Haven: Yale University Press, 1993), 45.

14. Wright, *New Testament and the People of God,* 120.

15. Ibid., 350.

16. See John H. Westerhoff, "Fashioning Christians in Our Day," in *Schooling Christians,* ed. Stanley Hauerwas and John H. Westerhoff (Grand Rapids: Eerdmans, 1992), 280.

17. Meeks, *Origins of Christian Morality,* 110.

The original Christians, in short, were about creating and sustaining a unique culture—a way of life that would shape character in the image of their God. And they were determined to be a culture, a quite public and political culture, even if it killed them and their children.

### Biblical Faith on the Ground

What I am suggesting is that the Constantinian church, for many centuries, responded to the world in such a manner that it lost sense of itself as an alternative way of life. Most immediately, the late Constantinian and modern belief in some (preeminently scientific) truths as acultural and ahistorical made it seem as if there was a neutral, nonperspectival viewpoint available to anyone, anywhere who was rational and well-meaning. In that atmosphere, much of the church thought it necessary to divide Christianity into (1) private truths, or values, to be confirmed by individuals apart from any communal and political context, and (2) public truths, or facts, which consisted of Christianity translated into acultural and ahistorical truths, "essences" more or less instantiated in all viable cultures.

But this was distorting, since Christianity, like Judaism, is historically based. It concerns what has happened with a particular people, namely ancient Israel, and through a particular man who lived and died in a specific time and place, namely Jesus the Nazarene, "crucified under Pontius Pilate." It is true that most religions posit a god who in no way can be pinned down or identified by time and place. But not so the religion of the Israelites. As Robert Jenson observes,

> Other ancient peoples piled up divine names; the comprehensiveness of a god's authority was achieved by blurring his particularity, by identification of initially distinct numina with one another, leading to a grandly vague deity-in-general. Israel made the opposite move. Israel's salvation depended precisely on unambiguous identification of her God over against the generality of the numinous.[18]

The God of Israel simply is he who led Israel out of Egypt, established it in the promised land, abandoned it to exile, and promised someday, somehow, to end that exile. Thus Israel's God can only be identified narratively, by the telling of this story. That is why "in the Bible the name of God and the narration of his works ... belong together. The descriptions that make the name work are items of the narrative. And conversely, identifying God, backing up the name, is the very function of the biblical narrative."[19]

Accordingly, when those not born into the heritage of Israel later come to know and worship Israel's singular God, they can do so only through this same story—but now extended and made more encompassing by the life, teachings,

18. Robert W. Jenson, *The Triune Identity* (Philadelphia: Fortress, 1982), 5.
19. Ibid., 7.

death, and resurrection of the Jew Jesus. Put bluntly, Christians "*know how* to pray to the Father, daring to call him 'Father,' because they pray with Jesus his Son."[20]

In modernity, this particularity was such a scandal that many Christians acted as if (and sometimes outright argued that) everyone of all and sundry faiths worshiped the same "God" and that the story of Israel and Jesus was secondary to knowing this "God." Now in post-Constantinian postmodernity, all communities and traditions (including the scientific) are called back to their inescapable and particular histories.[21] Christianity no longer need worry about its "scandal of particularity," since it is recognized that particularity "scandalizes" everyone. The upshot for Christians is that the church does not have to aspire anymore to a supposedly neutral language and story; now we can freely speak our own language and tell our own story.

To phrase it only slightly differently, we can now embrace, more wholeheartedly than we could under the modern regime, what might be called the Bible's narrative logic. Modernity pushed us toward a logic, or way of seeing and thinking, concerned to find "universal" and "reasonable" principles that could be embraced apart from any historical tradition. Modern "logic" is at work in Matthew Arnold's eagerness to think that Greek philosophy, Jewish faith, and indeed "all great spiritual disciplines" move toward the same goal. All alike, says Arnold, now quoting Christian Scripture, aim for the final end "that we might be partakers of the divine nature."[22] Yet there have been and are many divinities worshiped and admired by humanity. What divine nature do we aspire to? Will we partake of Zeus's caprice? The Mayan god's lust for human blood? And how do "great spiritual disciplines" that claim no divinity (such as Buddhism) then partake of this selfsame divine nature?

Biblical logic, by contrast, does not search for disembodied, abstracted essences. It is historical through and through. It deals with particular characters and events unfolding over time, and as such it is narrative, or story based. Hence the God who will later elect Israel creates the heavens and the earth, then suffers its rebellion (Gen. 1–3). Spiritual, political, familial, and economic division and alienation ensue (Gen. 4–11). Now this specific Creator God decides to reclaim the world. Yet this God is not a very good modernist and so aims to reclaim the world not by calling the divided peoples to "principles" or "essences" that somehow reside within all of them. Instead God chooses a particular man, Abraham, and promises to make of him a "great nation" through which "all the families of the earth shall be blessed" (Gen. 12:2–3).

The rest of the Old Testament is the story of this God's refusal to give up on a chosen, if often fickle and unfaithful, people. Israel is that strange and great nation

20. Ibid., 47, emphasis original.
21. For a fuller account on this point, see my *Families at the Crossroads* (Downers Grove, IL: InterVarsity, 1993), 9–26, 174–79.
22. Matthew Arnold, *Culture and Anarchy: An Essay in Political and Social Criticism* (Ann Arbor: University of Michigan Press, 1965), 164.

elected to wrestle with the strange and great God Yahweh down through the centuries. This election is often not such an appealing privilege, since the God who has chosen Israel will judge Israel when it departs from its covenant (Isa. 7:9). Yet God, even if God sometimes judges, will not relinquish a sure grip on the descendants of Abraham and Jacob. As Ben Meyer writes, "Though any generation in Israel might fall victim to catastrophic judgment, Israel itself will never go under."[23] Once again biblical narrative logic is relentlessly particular. Thus most of Israel may stray, but God will snatch a remnant from the lion's mouth (Amos 3:12) and make it "the new locus of election and the seed of national restoration."[24]

Ultimately confident in God's election, Israel suffers its national ups and downs but persists in looking ahead to a new reign like glorious David's (Isa. 11:1–9; Jer. 30:8–9; Amos 9:1–5). It hopes in a new and paradisal Zion (Isa. 2:2–4; 28:16), a new covenant (Jer. 31:31–34), and vindication in the teeth of its national enemies (Ps. 137). So:

> Listen to me, my people,
>   and give heed to me, my nation;
> for a teaching will go out from me,
>   and my justice for a light to the peoples.
> I will bring near my deliverance swiftly,
>   my salvation has gone out
>   and my arms will rule the peoples. (Isa. 51:4–5)

As N. T. Wright memorably puts it,

> This is what Jewish monotheism looked like on the ground. It was not a philosophical or metaphysical analysis of the inner being of a god, or the god. It was the unshakeable belief that the one god who made the world was Israel's god, and that he would defend his hill against all attackers or usurpers. To the extent that Israel thought of her god in "universal" terms, this universal was from the beginning made known in and through the particular, the material, the historical.[25]

## The New Testament in the Light of Jewish Politics

It was according to the rules of this narrative logic that Jesus understood his mission and the early church interpreted its Lord and its life.[26] Exactly twelve disciples, one for each of the tribes of ancient Israel, were chosen. This is but one sign that the church saw itself as Israel's seed restored and that a crucial aspect of its early

---

23. Meyer, *Early Christians*, 46.
24. Ibid., 47.
25. Wright, *New Testament and the People of God*, 247–48.
26. Meyer: "Neither the primitive Christian proclaimer nor the point and function of his proclamation is intelligible in historical terms apart from this biblical and ecclesial legacy." *Early Christians*, 47.

mission was to call on all Israel to claim its heritage.[27] The disciples were a flock (Luke 12:32) destined to be scattered (Mark 14:27; John 16:32) much as Israel had been scattered. But like Israel they would be regathered (Mark 14:28; John 16:17, 22) and enjoy kingly rule when God drew the world's drama to its end (Matt. 19:28; Luke 12:32).[28]

Following the Bible's narrative logic, Israel and the disciple remnant within it are saved in even more specific terms. Everything depends on the single man Jesus, who takes onto himself the history and destiny of Israel. Thus, like Israel, Jesus was the one called out of Egypt (Matt. 2:15). Like Israel, Jesus wanders, is tempted, and is fed by God in the wilderness. Like Israel, Jesus cares for the poor, the orphaned, and the stranger.

Jesus of Nazareth, as he apparently understood himself and certainly as he is interpreted by the New Testament documents, was a living recapitulation of Israel's history. More precisely, Jesus did not merely copy the history of Israel but realized it afresh in terms of his own life and obedience. By so doing, he re-presented not only Israel's past but also its future, what it would come to be through Yahweh's mighty consummating works.[29] Hence Jesus (with and through his disciples) will build a new and unsurpassable temple.

Now it is crucial to recall how important the temple was to the biblical story. Within Israel the temple bore manifold social, spiritual, political, economic, and cultural importance. In contemporary America it would be the equivalent of the entire range of our iconic political and cultural institutions: the White House, Capitol Hill, the National Cathedral, Wall Street, and Hollywood.[30] More than this, Jerusalem, in a profound theological sense, was considered the center of the earth—the hill Yahweh would defend against all attackers. And at the center of Jerusalem was the temple, in whose inner chambers the King of the Universe was known to dwell with an especially awesome presence. To this temple's courts all the world would someday stream, bearing offerings and worshiping the earth's one true God—Israel's Lord (Ps. 96:8–10).[31]

In this light it is hard to overstate the significance of Jesus's climactic few days in Jerusalem. His entry on a donkey identifies him with the lowly and peaceable king of Zechariah 9:9. His attack on the temple, if so it may be called, simultaneously critiques Israel theologically, culturally, politically, socially, and economically. And since the temple was the center not only of Israel but indeed of the universe, the cleansing of the temple purifies not only Israel but the entire cosmos.[32] Jesus and

27. Ibid., 38–39.
28. Ibid., 65.
29. See E. J. Tinsley, *The Imitation of God in Christ* (Philadelphia: Westminster, 1960), 177. As Tinsley eloquently puts it on the same page, Jesus was not simply "a copyist, but a creative artist, in relation to his nation's history."
30. Wright, *New Testament and the People of God*, 225n29. I have added Hollywood to Wright's list.
31. See Meyer, *Early Christians*, 60–61.
32. Ibid., 64. See also Wright, *New Testament and the People of God*, 306–7.

the church together, furthermore, are the new temple, a temple whose splendor will exceed that of any built with human hands (Mark 14:58; compare 2 Sam. 7:4–17; Hag. 2:9). •

But the new temple will be built in three days—the span of time between Jesus's crucifixion and his resurrection—which means it can be built only through Jesus's death. So Jesus proceeds to his death. Under covenantal dynamics, Israel is blessed when it responds obediently to God and cursed when it strays. Roman-occupied Israel, as I have noted, still considered itself in exile, under the curse. But Jesus the Christ (Messiah-King) represents Israel and so can take on himself Israel's curse and exhaust it.[33] He perishes as King of the Jews, at the hand of the Romans, whose oppression is "the present, and climactic, form of the curse of exile itself. The crucifixion of the Messiah is, one might say, the *quintessence* of the curse of the exile, and its climactic act."[34]

Narrative logic, then, reveals the significance of Jesus's resurrection. As David Hume was to observe many centuries later in impeccable modern terms, if Jesus was raised from the dead, that *in and of itself* proves nothing except that a first-century man in a backwater country somehow survived death. It is only within the context of Israel's story that Jesus's resurrection assumes its supreme significance. For this was not just any man who died, but a man who took onto himself Israel's story. And within Israel's story, resurrection had long functioned as a symbol for the reconstitution of Israel, the return from exile, and the crowning redemption. In the Israel of Jesus's day, resurrection was seen as the divine reward for martyrs, particularly those who would die in the great and final tribulation and bring Israel to its own divine reward. The prophet Ezekiel, for instance, saw the return of Israel in the figure of bones rising and taking on flesh (37:1–14). Since at least Ezekiel, the symbol of corpses returning to life not only denoted Israel's return from exile but also implied a renewal of the covenant and all creation. So Jesus's resurrection was nothing less than the monumental vindication (or justification) of Israel's hopes and claims. Israel has claimed throughout its history that its God is the single Creator God, and Jesus's resurrection at last redeems that claim.[35]

Recall one more time the Bible's narrative logic. Israel's God is universal, but is known as such only through the particular, the material, the historical. God elects Abraham, and from Abraham a nation, and from that nation Jesus. Now from Israel and Jesus flow God's blessings on all the world. God restores Israel; then, building on this event, God seeks the Gentiles. As Meyer writes, "This scheme is recurrent in Acts. First, the word is offered to the Jews, who split into camps of believers and unbelievers. The believers by their faith constitute restored Israel,

33. God "sees that the only way of rescuing his world is to call a people, and to enter into a covenant with them, so that through them he will deal with evil. But the means of dealing with evil is to concentrate it in one place and condemn—execute—it there. The full force of this condemnation is not intended to fall on this people in general, but on their representative, the Messiah." Wright, *Climax of the Covenant*, 239.

34. Ibid., 151.

35. On the significance of resurrection, see Wright, *New Testament and the People of God*, 328–34.

heir of the covenant and promises. Now and only now may gentiles find salvation, precisely by assimilation to restored Israel."[36]

The early Christians saw themselves as continuing Israel's story under new circumstances. The church "understood itself now as messianic Israel covenanted with her risen Lord" (Acts 2:38; 5:30–32).[37] It, with Jesus's headship, is the new temple, the sanctuary of the living God. It in fact is nothing less than the firstfruits of a new humanity, reborn in the last Adam named Jesus. Thus the church was seen, by itself and others, as a "third race," neither Jew nor Gentile but a new and holy nation or people (*ethnos hagion*, 1 Pet. 2:9). Narrative logic drives home to a theological conclusion that is unavoidably cultural and political.

Consider Ephesians 2:11–22. Here the Gentile addressees of the letter are reminded that before Christ they existed in the political status of "aliens from the commonwealth of Israel" and as a consequence were "strangers to the covenants of promise, having no hope and without God in the world" (v. 12). But now by the blood of Christ the Gentiles—we members of disparate nations among whom Israel was sent as a light and an example—have been made part of the same humanity as Israel (vv. 13–15). Christ has broken down the dividing wall between the Hebrews and the Gentiles, for "he is our peace" (v. 14). This is not a peace of mere inner, psychological tranquility; it is the peace of two reconciled peoples, a peace made possible by the change wrought "through the cross" (v. 16), a change of nothing less than the political and cultural status of the Gentiles from "aliens" to "*citizens* with the saints" (v. 19).

Christian faith, far from being a matter solely between the individual and God, amounts to being grafted into a new people. For the apostle Paul, those who are justified are justified because they believe the gospel and through it become God's covenant people. Gentiles, through baptism, are incorporated into the body and life of God's particular, historical people. Baptism is initiation into a new culture, a culture called church that now, exactly as a political and social entity, is poised at the pivot point of world history. As theologian John Milbank puts it, "The *logic* of Christianity involves the claim that the 'interruption' of history by Christ and his bride, the Church, is the most fundamental of events, interpreting all other events." The church claims to "exhibit the exemplary form of human community," and as such "it is *most especially* a social event, able to interpret other social formations, because it compares them with its own new social practice."[38]

In short, the church understands itself as a new and unique culture. The church is at once a community and a history—a history still unfolding and developing, embodying and passing along a story that provides the symbols through which its people gain their identity and their way of seeing the world. The church as a culture has its own language and grammar, in which words such as *love* and *service*

---

36. Meyer, *Early Christians*, 96. See also Wright, *New Testament and the People of God*, 93, 96; Wright, *Climax of the Covenant*, 150–51.

37. Meyer, *Early Christians*, 43.

38. John Milbank, *Theology and Social Theory* (London: Basil Blackwell, 1990), 388, emphasis original.

are crucial and are used correctly only according to certain "rules." The church as a culture carries and sustains its own way of life, which includes

- a particular way of eating, learned in and through the Eucharist
- a particular way of handling conflict, the peculiar politics called "forgiveness," learned through the example and practice of Jesus and his cross
- a particular way of perpetuating itself, through evangelism rather than biological propagation

In its existence as a culture, the church is eminently Jewish. Only in certain Constantinian, and peculiarly modern, terms could it regard its mission as acultural, its gospel as ahistorical, its existence as apolitical. Instead, what political scientist Gordon Lafer says of the Jewish nation and its witness is true as well of the church:

> [The Jewish emphasis on] social solidarity . . . helps to make sense of the concept of a "chosen people," which will be a "light unto the nations." The example that Jewish law seeks to set is one aimed not at individuals but specifically at other "nations." The institutions of solidarity that mark off Jews' commitments to one another from their more minimal obligations to outsiders are not designed to be applied as universal law governing relations among all people, but rather to be reiterated within each particular nation. This, then, is the universalist mission of Judaism: not to be "a light to all individuals," . . . but *rather to teach specific nations how to live as nations.*[39]

### The Individual: A Modern Mystification

So, the church as what I am calling a culture is a manner and mode of church that is, as George Lindbeck says, "more Jewish than anything else. . . . It is above all by the character of its communal life that it witnesses, that it proclaims the gospel and serves the world." And such is why "an invisible church is as biblically odd as an invisible Israel."[40] Biblical narrative logic simply demands a specific, visible people, a society or societal remnant, a *polis*.

I realize all this will strike many readers as exceedingly strange. I too, after all, have been reared and shaped in late modernity, taught to conceive of persons and Christianity in liberal, individualistic terms. So I understand that what I am calling for is an arduous retraining of the imagination, the learning and practice of a new grammar or logic. But perhaps it will ease the difficulty to remember that much of this grammar is new only to us. In historical perspective, it is our individuated, isolated self that is exceedingly strange.

---

39. Gordon Lafer, "Universalism and Particularism in Jewish Law," in *Jewish Identity*, ed. David Theo Goldberg and Michael Kraus (Philadelphia: Temple University Press, 1993), 196, emphasis added.

40. See George Lindbeck, "The Church," in *Keeping the Faith*, ed. Geoffrey Wainwright (Philadelphia: Fortress, 1988), 193, 183.

As rhetorician Wayne Booth notes, the self as "in-dividual" (literally "un-divided one") is barely more than two centuries old. The in-dividual was invented by a succession of Enlightenment thinkers and became, in its most extreme but perhaps also its most widespread interpretations, a view of the self as "a single atomic isolate, bounded by the skin, its chief value residing precisely in some core of in-dividuality, of difference." Thus it remains popular—almost second nature—to think we get at our "true self" by peeling away social ties like the skin of an onion. The "real me" is not my membership in the worldwide church, my shared kin with Clapps around the country, nor my connection—with three million other people—to the geography and culture of Chicago. The "real me" is my unique, in-dividual, core self. The in-dividual self values itself most for what is supposedly utterly different and unconnected about it. But, objects Booth, such an understanding of self is incoherent. Can we really believe that we are not, to the core, who we are because of our kin, our occupations, our political and social situations, our faith or philosophical associations, our friendships? And if our "true self" is whatever stands apart from those around us and is altogether unique about us, most of us are in trouble. The bizarre modern, liberal notion of the self means even the greatest geniuses have only minimal worth. "Goethe," says Booth, "was fond of saying that only about 2 percent of his thought was original."[41] Truly, as Philip Slater remarks, "the notion that people begin as separate individuals, who then march out and connect themselves with others, is one of the most dazzling bits of self-mystification in the history of the species."[42]

In fact, Booth continues, "people in all previous cultures were not seen as *essentially* independent, isolated units with totally independent values; rather, they were mysteriously complex persons overlapping with other persons in ways that made it legitimate to enforce certain kinds of responsibility to the community." In these settings, persons were not "'individuals' at all but overlapping members one of another. Anyone in those cultures thinking words like 'I' and 'mine' thought them as inescapably loaded with plurality: 'I' could not even think of 'my' self as separated from my multiple affiliations: my family, my tribe, my city-state, my feudal domain, my people."[43]

Are the biblical cultures part of the "previous cultures" Booth here remarks on? Scholars have again and again noted the Hebrew conception of "corporate personality," the understanding that families, cities, tribes, and nations possess distinctive personalities and that individuals derive identity from and so might represent these social bodies.[44] We need no new frame when we extend this picture.

41. Wayne Booth, "Individualism and the Mystery of the Social Self," in *Freedom and Interpretation*, ed. Barbara Johnson (New York: Basic Books, 1993), 81, 87–88.

42. Quoted from Philip Slater's *Earthwalk* (New York: Anchor, 1974) without further attribution in Lawrence Stone, *The Past and the Present Revisited* (London: Routledge and Kegan Paul, 1987), 325.

43. Booth, "Individualism," 78, 79.

44. For a classic statement, see H. Wheeler Robinson, "Hebrew Psychology," in *The People and the Book*, ed. A. S. Peake (London: Oxford University Press, 1925), 353–82.

Writing on the concept of personhood in New Testament times, Bruce J. Malina notes, "The first-century Mediterranean person did not share or comprehend our idea of an 'individual' at all." Rather, "our first-century person would perceive himself as a distinctive whole *set in relation* to other such wholes and *set within* a given social and natural background."[45]

When Paul spoke of the church as a "body," he borrowed the metaphor from a fable widely used in several cultures of antiquity. Just as "Israel" could serve as the name either of an individual (Jacob) or of a community (the nation), so could Paul use "Christ" to refer to an individual (Jesus of Nazareth) or a community (the church). In the words of New Testament scholar Charles Talbert, "'Members' . . . is Paul's term for the parts of the body through which the life of the body is expressed (1 Cor. 12:12, 14–26; Rom. 6:13). Paul is saying then that individual Christians in their corporeal existence are the various body parts of the corporate personality of Christ through which the life of Christ is expressed."[46]

It is no simple matter to "translate" ancient understandings of self (or anything else) into our later, quite different setting. Yet I think this is another task that is made more feasible by our post-Constantinian, postmodern setting. As Booth comments, the in-dividuated self has been criticized from its beginning, and "it has been torn to pieces and stomped on by almost every major thinker in this century."[47]

Furthermore, freed from its distorting Constantinian "responsibility," the church no longer must support a view of the self as in-dividuated and able to determine the good apart from all "accidental" ties of history or community. We can reaffirm that just as there can be no individual Americans apart from the nation America, so can there be no Christians apart from the church. We can be like the apostle Peter, who "did not learn God's will by Socratic questioning and rational reflection, but as the member of a group who had been with Jesus 'from the beginning in Galilee.'"[48] We can be like the early followers of Christ the Way, who trained fresh imaginations and became a new humanity by devoting themselves "to the apostles' teaching and fellowship, to the breaking of bread and the prayers" (Acts 2:42). After Constantine, on the other side of modernity, we can regard and embrace the church as a way of life.

---

45. Bruce J. Malina, *The New Testament World: Insights from Cultural Anthropology* (Atlanta: John Knox, 1981), 54, 55, emphasis original.

46. Charles Talbert, *Reading Corinthians: A Literary and Theological Commentary on 1 and 2 Corinthians* (New York: Crossroad, 1987), 31.

47. Booth, "Individualism," 79.

48. Meeks, *Origins of Christian Morality*, 6.

# 2

# Friends of God and Friends of God's Friends

Samuel Wells

## Sharing Peace

Christians prepare to hear the Word by being reconciled with God. They make their confession and receive absolution before they share the Scripture. Likewise Christians prepare to share food by being reconciled with one another. Just as Scripture and sacrament are two parts of a liturgical whole, two aspects of the one meeting with God, so being reconciled with God and being reconciled with one another are two dimensions of the one movement of forgiveness.

Like the intercessions, much of the significance of the sharing of the peace may be disclosed by its location in the liturgy. Perhaps most significantly, it comes after the congregation have already confessed their sin and been reconciled with God. In other words, those present have been shaped by the virtues of mercy and forbearance, virtues that depend on the knowledge that they too have sinned and been forgiven, that they too have grown through constructive criticism, that they too have moods and quirks and prejudices. They grow in the virtues of humility and honesty, virtues that rest on the realization that the Christian life is not about arriving at perfection, but about making interesting mistakes on the way. Being

Originally published in "Responding" and "Sharing," in Samuel Wells, *God's Companions: Reimagining Christian Ethics* (Malden, MA: Blackwell, 2006), 174–214, here 184–91, 195–214. Reprinted with permission.

prefaced by reconciliation with God means that corporate reconciliation is conducted in a spirit of humility. The members of the congregation seek peace with one another in order to embody the peace they have found with God. They do not have a leg (of their own) to stand on; they do not make peace from a vantage point on the moral high ground; they stand only as sinners forgiven by God, and thereby inspired to extend and experience that grace with one another.

One local congregation had a parish away day during which a litany of complaints, anxious frustrations, and a sense of helplessness about one aspect of the church's ministry rained down upon those responsible. That day, when the time came for the Holy Communion, the peace was shared without words—the simple handshake and holding of eye contact were a statement of trust and commitment and reconciliation after perhaps too many words had been said. In being able to share the peace after such a traumatic day, the congregation discovered that it was possible to name the truth without fear.

Sharing the peace also takes place after the hearing of the word in Scripture and sermon. The word proclaims that reconciliation is fundamentally the act of Christ, and that Christ has definitively brought about that reconciliation.

> So if anyone is in Christ, there is a new creation: everything old has passed away; see, everything has become new! All this is from God, who reconciled us to himself through Christ, and has given us the ministry of reconciliation; that is, in Christ God was reconciling the world to himself, not counting their trespasses against them, and entrusting the message of reconciliation to us. So we are ambassadors for Christ, since God is making his appeal through us; we entreat you on behalf of Christ, be reconciled to God. For our sake he made him to be sin who knew no sin, so that in him we might become the righteousness of God. (2 Cor. 5:17–21)

The word tells a story that is full of setbacks rooted in human shortcomings and alienation stemming from cruelty, jealousy, and bitterness. But the story teaches Christians that they have nothing to fear from the truth. The worst thing that could happen has already happened, and yet God has nonetheless transformed the worst thing into a source of life and hope: that is what the resurrection means. Knowing this truth sets Christians free (John 8:32).

In speaking the Creed Christians have learned how to live in the light of revealed truth. The sharing of the peace comes after the confession of faith. This enables them to realize that protecting others from the truth is seldom a statement of faith. If the truth sets them free, they may develop the habit of not letting the sun go down on their anger, of seeing the naming of resentment as the first step in the forming of a new relationship based on healing and forgiveness rather than tolerance and turning a blind eye. Perhaps the most vivid recent example of this form of liberation is the work of the Truth and Reconciliation Commission in South Africa. This commission has been engaged in "the difficult but ultimately rewarding path of destroying enemies by turning them into friends."[1] Healing and rehabilitation, a new sense of a transformed story, are necessary for both victims and perpetrators. The Commission used slogans to attract people to meetings where they would tell their stories and hear others', seek redress for injustices and healing for memories, have lies acknowledged and animosities addressed, and move toward reconciliation. The slogans included "Revealing is Healing," "Truth, the Road to Reconciliation," and "The Truth Hurts, but Silence Kills."[2]

Sharing the peace comes after the intercessions. This shapes the practice of peacemaking with the character of compassion. Interceding clarifies distinctions between pain and sin, healing and forgiveness, need and want. But in the light of the sharing of the peace, the intercessions also illuminate the distinction between the better (or worse) and the merely different—the wrong and the odd. Is a given problem primarily attributable to alienation from God, a breakdown in forms of communication and relationship between people—or is it primarily a matter of intolerance or of incomprehension of difference? This is the kind of question that is reformulated by the regular practice of confession, intercession, and sharing peace in the liturgy. Proximity to the intercessions sets the sharing of the peace in the context of compassion—of recognition of another's story, of another's pain, of another's "love not knowing how to love well." It helps to distinguish between malice and misunderstanding. And it affirms to the members of the congregation that reconciliation is not in their own strength.

But if the sharing of the peace comes after reconciliation with God, the hearing of the word, the confession of faith, and the intercessions, it comes before the sharing of food. And here are perhaps its deepest resonances.

> So when you are offering your gift at the altar, if you remember that your brother or sister has something against you, leave your gift there before the altar and go; first be reconciled to your brother or sister, and then come and offer your gift. (Matt. 5:23–24)

This is a significant way in which the Eucharist constitutes the church. It is not just that in the broken body of Christ the church finds its peace with God. It is not just that the Eucharist makes the church one body. It is that the church cannot eat one body unless it is one body. Otherwise, it eats and drinks judgment against itself (1 Cor. 11:29). This creates a significant urgency. There is a very limited time to address the points of conflict within the community. Either the sacrament will not continue or the unreconciled parties risk incurring judgment on themselves. Christians discover here that they cannot stand before God's judgment without being called to account for those others who are or should be standing with them.

---

1. Desmond Tutu, *No Future without Forgiveness* (London: Rider, 1999), 138.
2. Ibid., 81; Duncan Forrester, "Violence and Non-Violence in Conflict Resolution: Some Theological Reflections," *Studies in Christian Ethics* 16, no. 2 (2003): 64–79.

For sharing peace is principally about becoming one body. This is epitomized in Elias Chacour's account of the early days of his ministry in Ibillin, a village in Galilee, and the day he tried the locked-door trick. In 1966, Father Chacour became the Melkite priest of this village. What he found was a community racked with divisions and riven by feuds. When he faced the congregation to offer them God's blessing, he rediscovered how deeply divided and embittered they were. There was so much spite, hatred, and gossip among the people, there seemed nothing he could do. So one day, when the service was concluded, and the large congregation was preparing to leave, he walked down the aisle and locked the church doors, placing the keys in his pocket, and said, "You've got three options. You can kill each other—and I'll take your funerals for nothing. You can kill me. Or you can work out how you are going to live together from now on." Ten minutes of silence followed. No one moved. Then the local policeman, who worked for the Israeli police force, stood up, wearing his uniform. He admitted how much he had hated and hurt his three brothers. He begged forgiveness. His brothers embraced him. Then one after another people stood and recalled how they had hurt, cheated, and slandered one another. After an hour the people burst out of the church and started making peace with neighbors, colleagues, and old foes. It was Palm Sunday, but Father Chacour declared that it would be celebrated as Easter Day, because that community had risen from the dead.[3]

Another celebrated account, that of Vincent Donovan, clarifies why the sharing of the peace takes place at this precise moment in the liturgy. Donovan describes in vivid detail his experience of evangelizing the Masai in Tanzania in the 1960s and 1970s, and of how they rediscovered the significance of the Mass as it shaped their common life. The Mass would begin when the priest drove his Land Rover into the village, as children swarmed for a blessing, elders looked up from their cattle herding, and mothers stirred from their milking. But long before, the consciousness of the coming Mass had begun to permeate the village. It was not confined to a specific building: it started from a spot where some elders had lit a small fire before the priest arrived. Before he entered the village, Donovan would stoop to scoop up a handful of grass, ready to present to the first elders who came to greet him. Grass was sacred to the Masai because their cattle depended on it, and they in turn depended on their cattle. So grass indicated peace and happiness and well-being. If an argument erupted, the offer and reception of a tuft of grass would guarantee that no violence would ensue. So Donovan would begin by offering a tuft of grass to the first elder who met him, and this elder would pass it to his family, and they would pass it to neighboring elders and families, and thence all through the village. This was the peace of Christ.

Donovan describes how the Mass would take place all over the village. A woman repairing the mud roof of her house would see this work as part of her offering.

3. Elias Chacour and Mary E. Jenson, *We Belong to the Land: The Story of a Palestinian Israeli Who Lives for Peace and Reconciliation* (San Francisco: Harper, 1992), 30–33.

A local elder would brief him on the people he was instructing for Baptism. They would then perhaps visit a woman sick with fever, lay hands on her, and promise to return with the Eucharistic bread later. The dancing group would be getting going. Donovan would sit down with the core Christian leaders in the village, light a lantern, and teach them from the Bible. By the time they finished, it would be getting chilly and the crowd would move near the fire, to be joined by the singers. A woman once gave an account of her faith and, since no one could improve on it, that was their Creed for the day. Another woman might pray for the sick person, and her prayers would incorporate the dry season, herding, and carrying water. One of the leaders would explain the lesson they had received earlier, and everyone would join in the discussion. But it was never certain whether the Eucharist would emerge from all of this. Was it really an offering of their whole lives—family, milking, herding, singing? Had there been selfishness or hatefulness or unforgiveness—had the tuft of grass stopped, had someone refused to receive it? These were the questions that determined whether there would be a Mass. And yet sometimes there was a will to overcome the community's shortcomings, and call on the Holy Spirit to transform it into the Body of Christ, so they could see all of what lay before them—people, flocks, fields, homes, and the whole life of the village as Christ's body.[4]

Chacour's and Donovan's accounts both display how sharing peace is about being one body. And whenever the language of body is used, the practices of Baptism and marriage become significant. When marriage or Baptism takes place in the context of the Eucharist, this is the point where they belong: for sharing peace, marriage, and Baptism are each different ways in which the church is embodied. Baptism and marriage are key ways in which a Christian community may practice patience and courage. Such virtues not only lead the people to perceive all relationships through the lens of death and resurrection, gift rather than possession, but also help them to try once more with challenging relationships and risk rejection by attempting to reconcile.

Sharing peace grounds the practice of reconciliation in a specific moment in the liturgy. But reconciliation is by no means limited to the congregation present. This act of peacemaking is a token of a far more wide-ranging reconciliation. It incorporates not just personal animosities, but corporate enmities. This is the moment when the call to love enemies is rehearsed.

> If you love those who love you, what credit is that to you? For even sinners love those who love them. If you do good to those who do good to you, what credit is that to you? For even sinners do the same. But love your *enemies*. (Luke 6:32–33, 35, emphasis added)

The practice of sharing peace embodied and learned in the liturgy is to be extended into a whole range of relationships, near and far. Each member of the

4. Vincent Donovan, *Christianity Rediscovered: An Epistle from Masai* (London: SCM, 1982), 124–28.

congregation asks how they can be a reconciling presence in the life of their neighbor and thus transform the need and lack of the intercessions into the abundance and plenty of the shared meal. And, in the context of the sharing of food to follow, this is also the moment when the love of strangers is embodied.

> When you give a luncheon or a dinner, do not invite your friends or your brothers or your relatives or rich neighbors, in case they may invite you in return, and you would be repaid. But when you give a banquet, invite the poor, the crippled, the lame, and the blind. And you will be blessed, because they cannot repay you. (Luke 14:12–14)

Wider still than that, this is a proclamation of the peaceable kingdom, of humanity at peace with its environment and the whole of creation. The sharing of peace, together with the offering of gifts that follows, is a celebration of the right ordering of creation in preparation for participation in the heavenly banquet. It is the bride prepared to meet her bridegroom. James Jones points out that Matthew's Gospel alone tells of twenty-seven animals: the sharing of the peace embodies the harmony prophesied in Isaiah 11:

> The wolf shall live with the lamb,
>     the leopard shall lie down with the kid,
> the calf and the lion and the fatling together,
>     and a little child shall lead them.
> The cow and the bear shall graze,
>     their young shall lie down together;
>     and the lion shall eat straw like the ox.
> The nursing child shall play over the hole of the asp,
>     and the weaned child shall put its hand on the adder's den.
> They will not hurt or destroy
>     on all my holy mountain;
> for the earth will be full of the knowledge of the LORD
>     as the waters cover the sea. (Isa. 11:6–9)[5]

The location of the sharing of the peace directly before the offering of the gifts makes clear not just that if there is no peace, the offering should be left until there is. In one local church, the priest was troubled by the degree of bitterness and unacknowledged grief that festered under the surface of the worship. It was a church where the person leading was accustomed to wear a chasuble when presiding. One person suggested that the priest leave the chasuble on the altar until the peace had been shared, and only put the vestment on and continue with the thanksgiving prayer if the peace was genuine. Although it was decided that communion was always a gift, and therefore should not be at the mercy of the moment, the congregation was moved by the suggestion.

---

5. James Jones, *Jesus and the Earth* (London: SPCK, 2003), 50.

The timing of the peace also demonstrates that the gift that the church offers to the world—the distribution of the gift received from God—is its peace, God's peace. For

> now in Christ Jesus you who once were far off have been brought near by the blood of Christ. For he is our peace; in his flesh he has made both groups into one and has broken down the dividing wall, that is, the hostility between us. He has abolished the law with its commandments and ordinances, that he might create in himself one new humanity in place of the two, thus making peace, and might reconcile both groups to God in one body through the cross, thus putting to death that hostility through it. So he came and proclaimed peace to you who were far off and peace to those who were near; for through him both of us have access in one Spirit to the Father. So then you are no longer strangers and aliens, but you are citizens with the saints and also members of the household of God. (Eph. 2:13–19) ♦

The peace between members of the congregation and one another, between them and strangers, between them and enemies, and between them and the whole creation, is but an emblem of the overarching peace between God and his people, brought about in Christ. This is God's gift to the church, and, through the church, to the world—and it is embodied at this moment in the liturgy.

The kiss of peace is widespread in the New Testament—five of the epistles conclude with it—but in one place it takes the vital, salvific, and almost liturgical dimensions outlined above.[6] And that place is in the story of the loving father and his two wayward sons. "But while he was still far off, his father saw him and was filled with compassion; he ran and put his arms around him and kissed him" (Luke 15:20). Many features of this story are relevant here—the way the father, like the Suffering Servant, goes outside the village, and undergoes public humiliation (running was considered indecent) for the sake of the sins of another. But two features stand out for our present purposes about the father and his kiss. One is that a kiss (with arms around, as the story makes clear), like a handshake, is the interaction of two equals. In either case, both must be standing, or at least of equivalent posture. The reconciliation that is the sharing of peace is a restoration to harmony of status—regardless of whether a third party might say that such restoration were deserved. The second is that throughout this story the father exudes abundance. Despite having his property removed from him at the outset of the story and divided in two so half was lost and gone; despite living through a famine; despite sharing a home with the meanest of sons; despite undergoing not only the private humiliation of one son's demand for the property but also the public humiliation of the other son's refusal to join the party; despite even slaying the fatted calf, and throwing a banquet for hundreds of people—despite, in other words, giving away his property, his pride, and his heart, the father epitomizes abundance from beginning to end. The younger son's profligacy contrasts with

6. Kenneth Bailey, *Poet and Peasant* (Grand Rapids: Eerdmans, 1976), 158–206.

his father's abundance, but only in that he spent all those resources on trifles; the story narrates the way his sin is redeemed—and thus redeemable. By contrast the elder son's meanness poisons every relationship he has—in making up a story to explain his refusal to come to the party, he has to fabricate a tale about his brother (that he wasted the money on Gentile harlots), another about himself (that the property does not already belong to him), and a third about his father (that he wants the service of a slave, rather than the love of a son). The story narrates that even this sin is redeemable—but it does not narrate that it is redeemed. The heart of the elder son's sin is that he does not trust that, even in his father's house, there will be enough—even though everything in the story makes it plain that where his father is, there is always more than enough.

The kiss is the symbolic center of the story because it embodies the moment when the father *finds* his lost son, and it is this finding—rather than the son's return—that is the reason for the party. The tension at the end of the story is whether the elder son will be reconciled, will accept the father's kiss—and thus come to the banquet. The kiss is the entrance to the banquet, just as the peace is the entrance to the Eucharistic feast. But the kiss simply displays what the story proclaims throughout—that God abundantly offers everything his people need to follow him: and that offer is never more present than in the sharing of the peace.

## Lifting Hearts

At the beginning of the Eucharistic Prayer the person leading the service enjoins the congregation to lift their hearts. This has a twofold significance in shaping the life of the Christian community. One dimension is that of feeling, the other is that of the kind of participation being invited.

This is the only point in the liturgy when the members of the congregation are instructed to maintain a particular quality of feeling. To participate in the thanksgiving, celebration, and transformation that is to follow, they *must* lift their hearts. Just as in the offering the congregation discovered that they had to bring every aspect of their lives to the altar, so at the "Sursum Corda" the congregation discovers that it must bring its heart and soul under the same discipline. And the logic is similar. Why must humanity have the correct relationship with the created order? In order that human beings might bring the fruits of creation to their fulfillment at the altar—and thus fully celebrate the Eucharist. Why therefore must God's people learn to discipline their hearts, sculpt their souls, mold their feelings so as not to give in to malevolent moods, malign passions, or maudlin emotions? In order that when they come to the central moment of transformation in the Eucharist, they will be able to lift their hearts without inhibition. Participating in the Eucharist requires heart and soul and mind and strength. It is not simply "going through the motions"—it is "going through the wondering," "going through the pondering," and "going through the passions" as well.

An ethic of the senses is rooted at this moment in the liturgy. The education of desire belongs first of all in lifting hearts together to the Lord. This is a corporate process, and counselors who help other disciples lift their hearts may perceive the purpose of their ministry here. The consumption of toxic substances to excess is wrong in great part because it pollutes the temple of the Spirit that is the human body, but primarily because it weakens the disciple's ability to lift the heart to the Lord at this vital moment. The lustful glance, the wandering eye, the furtive photograph, are wrong in great part because they train the soul for adultery and treat the beauty of another as an object of coveting and possession, but primarily because they weaken the disciple's ability to focus every sense on the thanksgiving, celebration, and transformation of the Eucharist. But likewise the eradication of desire, the iron-fisted discipline of the will, the imposition of listless compliance, are wrong when they mean that the disciple can find inside no surge of passionate longing at the moment in the liturgy when God is about to give his people everything they need to follow him. Hearts were made with one purpose above all: to be lifted to the Lord when he comes in transforming grace.

The second significant dimension of this moment in the liturgy relates to the conviction that when disciples respond to Jesus's command to "Do this," his will is done in heaven as it is on earth. It is an act of discipline, if not a fulfillment of longing, for the members of the congregation to lift their hearts; but the point of doing so is that this is a moment of entry into heaven, a moment when God makes his people alive together with Christ, and raises them up with him, and makes them sit "with him in the heavenly places in Christ Jesus" (Eph. 2:5–6). Those congregations who articulate the words of both Revelation 4 ("Holy, holy, holy, the Lord God the almighty") and Matthew 21 ("Blessed is the one who comes in the name of the Lord!") during the Eucharistic Prayer identify specifically that God's people are raised to heaven just as God's Son came to earth.

This moment in the liturgy is a rehearsal of heaven on earth. All God's purposes are fulfilled—his people worship him, are his friends, and are about to eat with him. And all that God's people need to be able to be God's friends and eat with him has been provided. They have become one body, with sins forgiven, reconciliation made, peace restored, God's word proclaimed and discerned, faith affirmed, and needs heard. God's purpose has been fully communicated to his people, and it has been fully embodied in their life. The veil between earth and heaven is being drawn aside, and the simple actions of sharing food anticipate the beautiful simplicity of life with God forever. This is a moment of revelation, for the true life of the saints is "hidden with Christ in God" (Col. 3:3), and now it is made plain. Christ is being revealed through the taking, breaking, and sharing of bread and wine, and "When Christ who is your life is revealed, then you also will be revealed with him in glory" (Col. 3:4).

If this glimpse of heaven is the moment of greatest desire, then it is also the moment of greatest aching. For this is where the location of the church, still in exile from heaven, is most acute. Christ is about to come among them through the

Holy Spirit, but the true communion, the true reunion of the body of Christ with its head, lies in heaven. So this lifting of hearts is both a transportation to heaven and also a rehearsal for heaven. It is a taste of the firstfruits and an anticipation of the full banquet. It reminds the church that it is like a football team playing away from home, with perhaps a hostile crowd and a host of pitfalls to be encountered; but also that it will one day come to its home turf and to the saints and angels singing their name as they at last find their true seamless fluency. These moments in the liturgy name the location of the church, in a world pervaded by God, which can yet not be called home. The fact that the Eucharist can be celebrated there describes what it means to call the world good; the fact that no Eucharist can be everything the heavenly banquet will be names the ways in which the world cannot be called home.

The church aches not only because it is away from home, but also because it is not one. It cannot fully lift its heart because its heart is broken. The scandal of the disunity of the church is fundamentally a Eucharistic matter. If the church cannot be one before God, it cannot fully receive everything God has to give it through the Eucharist. God wants his people to worship him, to be his friends, and to eat with him. But when they cannot eat together, they cannot fully be friends and thus they cannot fully worship. Nonetheless, since heaven is one, lifting hearts to heaven must be one way in which Christians seek to restore unity. If they truly hope to sit and eat with God, they prepare to be placed beside some unexpected companions.

### Giving Thanks

Once again the summary of the gospel is rehearsed—after the introduction to confession, the sermon, and the Creed, now in the thanksgiving, the grand narrative of salvation is summoned to surround the vital moments of transformation. The people of God are gathered around a table, ready to eat with him. Now, in this final rendition of the heart of God's story, they are in an attitude not so much of penitence, or of truth-seeking, or of faith (although none of these is absent), but of glory and praise.

This part of the liturgy continues what was begun in the offering. If the offering reassembles creation around the table where God's people eat with him, then the thanksgiving reorders those people's lives so they see this as the fundamental work that defines all other work. Everything the church does is designed to bring all humankind, indeed all creation, into companionship with God, epitomized in the sharing of food at his table. And thus all work is an analogy of this definitive work. It is not that work is co-creation, it is that work is appropriate participation in finding a place and a role and a fulfillment as God's companion—worshiping God, being his friend, and eating with him—and enabling others to do the same. Giving thanks does not exhaust what needs to be said about work. For it is not until the dismissal that the question of vocation, of *what* work, specifically arises. But the question that finds its definition in the Great Thanksgiving is not so much the question of *what* as the question of *how*.

Such an understanding of work begins in gratitude. It is an honor to participate in the Eucharist, it is an honor to have an analogous role to play in serving people and communities in relation to their mental and spiritual (worship), emotional (be his friends), and physical (eat with him) needs. To have mental, spiritual, emotional, and physical abilities that may find expression, purpose, and fulfillment in helping people and communities to flourish—this is to discover in oneself very precious qualities that are to be treasured as gifts. Just as in the Eucharist Christians discover that their definitive form of work is to give thanks, so in return in every aspect of life a significant form of thanksgiving is to work. To work is to develop and discipline the gifts of God to attend to the mental, spiritual, emotional, and physical needs of others and thereby to meet a good number of one's own similar needs meanwhile.

And what are those needs? The Eucharist is likewise a training for what those needs are—they are, narrowly, for worship, friendship, and food, and, more broadly, for community, for forgiveness, for joy, for silence, for truth, for a place in a truthful story, for faith, for hope, for love and reconciliation, for a way of offering one's gifts, for an ordering of desire—in other words, for all the things the Eucharist brings. The Eucharist trains Christians to see need as God sees it. The congregation gets used to what God provides, and comes over time to need what God faithfully gives, and to shape all other wants and desires around this perception of this definitive ordering of needs. And in the paradigm of eating together, the Eucharist offers a goal for all work—a goal of plenty, of harmony, and of relationship with God and one another. By such a goal may the worth of specific kinds of work be judged.

In return work clarifies what it means to be church. Work is always praise and thanksgiving, but calling the life of the church "work" reminds Christians that they should expect church to be hard. It is hard because it requires discipline, to the task, to the agreed method, and to the colleagues—those to whom one gives orders, those from whom one receives orders, and those with whom one works as a team—with whom the task is to be attempted. Although it is hard, task-oriented discipline is still a gift, because aimless freedom is seldom experienced as a gift (any more than purposeless discipline). Discipline arises from necessity—whether the difficulty of dealing with raw materials, the difficulty of overcoming logistical obstacles, the difficulty of engaging the frailty of human character, or the difficulty of confronting outright hostility and opposition. Such necessity constitutes all human activity—the praise and thanksgiving of the Eucharist as much as the marketing of new computer software or the harvesting of the cash crop before the onset of the rains. Although for many the Eucharist is an expression of the life of the Sabbath, if it is to be the transforming social practice on all the levels I have described, it is bound to be hard, to require discipline, and to take on other characteristics generally associated with work. Work—and the Eucharist—will not always be an experience purely of resurrection. There are times when both may be an ordinary, less exalted experience of incarnate humanity. And there are times when both may be an experience of the cross. It is this that keeps the Eucharist human, and thus a celebration of the humanity of Christ.

The thanksgiving prayer within the Eucharist governs Christians' attitudes to work in two further ways. On the one hand, the Great Thanksgiving counterbalances work when work becomes too much. Work may, for example, become a substitute for family, when a person displaces real family relationships, and invests their entire emotional well-being in their continued employment by a particular organization. Work may become an alternative church, when it seeks to epitomize an ideal community, or demands the soul of its members, or sets itself the task of putting the whole of society straight. Work may become a rival gospel, when an ideology takes over the minds of a staff team or a whole profession, creating new nostrums whose efficacy no one can challenge. Or work may become a god—when it really does become everything, the defining and controlling force in a person's life. The Great Thanksgiving identifies all of these perversions as kinds of idolatry—for thanksgiving allows Christians to align their deepest needs with the gifts God abundantly gives, and thus it brings freedom, whereas these distortions are each a response to need that leads a person into slavery.

On the other hand, the Great Thanksgiving challenges Christians when work becomes not too much, but too little. Work becomes too little when a member of an organization has little or no respect for where the organization is going or how it is run. Such a sentiment may constitute a healthy skepticism about whether the organization contributes to the spiritual, emotional, mental, or physical needs of the world in any significant way—or even contributes to heightening those needs by worsening people's lives rather than enhancing them. Staying in such an organization without working for change quickly leads to a cynicism that corrodes the body and poisons its bloodstream. Work also becomes too little when a member of an organization, while respecting the system, has little respect for colleagues and thus fiddles expenses or subverts the structure in some other hidden way. Work becomes too little when a person experiences unemployment. While there are things worse than unemployment, it is rare that other ways of serving entirely replace work as a key aspect of the expression of human thanksgiving and thus fulfillment. The Great Thanksgiving, by portraying the definitive work of the Christian, addresses the flawed thankfulness that arises when work becomes too little. For the unemployed person, it reasserts that their true identity is found as God's companion, around God's table, worshiping, being his friend, and eating with him. For the person skeptical about their organization or their role in it, it displays the glory and goal of true work, by which God, through sacrament and story, gives his people everything they need to follow him, when they thankfully offer to him all the gifts they have received for him to use in reordering the lives of communities and persons. If this sacrifice of thanks and praise is not really made in the sacrament, it is scarcely a Eucharist; and if a sacrifice of thanks and praise is not properly made in the workplace, work disintegrates from an analogy of the Great Thanksgiving into a parody of idolatry or exploitation.

## Remembering

Remembering is about actions and words. In the Eucharist, God's people recall the saving events that transformed the world and their place in it, and they reenact those events. Both the words and the actions are significant.

The *words* of remembering locate the church in time. The words recall the Last Supper, and thus identify the hinge of history, the events of the passion and resurrection of Christ. In recalling the Last Supper these words remember that that meal itself recalled a previous meal, the Passover, and its corresponding saving events, the exodus and the establishing of the covenant. God acted in delivering his people from slavery and bringing them to freedom in the promised land, assuring them of his presence and faithfulness and giving them a guide for keeping their freedom. Now, in Jesus, God has acted again, this time decisively, to deliver his people from all that held them in slavery and to offer all the peoples of the world life with him forever.

So remembering means first of all acknowledging that the key events of history have already happened. This simple statement has enormous importance for ethics. For it locates the heart of ethics in particular events with universal significance. This differs in a number of ways from the way ethics is frequently understood. Ethics is not primarily about what is being discovered—it is about what has been revealed. It is not primarily about now—it is primarily about then (those events that constitute the hinge of history, which took place in the first century). It is not primarily about our actions—it is primarily about God's actions displayed in Jesus. It is not primarily about likely consequences of our present decisions—it is primarily about ultimate implications of God's eternal decision. It is not primarily about us acting now lest the worst might happen—it is about how God acted when the worst (the rejection and death of his Son) did happen. It is not about understanding the nature of things and acting rightly or wrongly in relation to their inherent quality—it is about seeing the nature of all things transformed by Christ. It is not about being effective in a world of givens—it is about being faithful in a world where all has been made gift.

The Eucharist locates the church after the decisive events of history—creation, covenant, Christ—have happened, but before the full consummation has come about. It remembers and anticipates. It embodies heritage and destiny. "On the night before he died . . ." signals the looking back; "I will never again drink of the fruit of the vine until that day . . ." signals the anticipation. It thus epitomizes the way every action of the church or the Christian is similarly located between the decisive and the ultimate, between the historically definitive and the transcendentally unknown—between the revealed character of God and the final glory of his company.

Ethics names the ways the church seeks to embody the transformation brought about by Christ and to point to the consummation promised in final glory, and the definitive paradigm of this embodiment is the Eucharist itself. This is what it means to seek to make the whole world a Eucharist: it means to strive to order every aspect of creation in the light of the transformation in Christ and the consummation in heaven.

Remembering the words of institution, the words in which Jesus identified his future presence in the church, defines the way Christians think about memory. The Last Supper becomes the prism through which Christians perceive the past. This means the church's memory can never become detached from its intimate bond with the Jews, for the Last Supper is characterized by the recollection of God's saving purpose in the exodus, his faithfulness to the Sinai covenant, and his promise to bring their long exile to an end. It means the church's memory can never overlook its bond with suffering, for the body of Christ is no sooner identified than it is broken. It means the church's memory can never forget its own sin, for the agony of Judas's betrayal and the quickly broken promises of Peter and the other disciples ripple through the narrative. The defining moment of memory is a body of flawed Jewish people discovering the identity and mission of Christ and realizing that in his suffering lay the renewal of God's covenant and the transformation of their status before him. Every moment in history is thereafter defined by the degree to which it discloses the identity and mission of Christ, the nature and embodiment of God's covenant through him, the transformation of suffering and sin in relation to the paradigm of the cross, and the new life and community made possible through these saving events.

These are among the ways the words of remembering shape the ethic of the church. As for the *actions* of remembering, I refer to the fourfold gestures of taking, blessing, breaking, and giving.[7] These, of course, reenact Jesus's fourfold action at the Last Supper:

> While they were eating, he took a loaf of bread, and after blessing it he broke it, gave it to them, and said, "Take; this is my body." Then he took a cup, and after giving thanks he gave it to them, and all of them drank from it. He said to them, "This is my blood of the covenant, which is poured out for many." (Mark 14:22–24)

The significance of these four actions becomes clearer in the light of Jesus's own story. For he took human nature in his incarnation, and his human flesh bore the divine character in material form. In his ministry, through words of wisdom, question, and command, and through gestures of compassion, challenge, and miracle, he blessed humanity and the whole creation. In his agonizing death and the harrowing exposure of human sin that it entailed, he was broken for the life of the world. And in his resurrection and perhaps most especially in the coming

7. Gregory Dix, *The Shape of the Liturgy* (London: Dacre, 1945).

of his Holy Spirit, he gave and shared new life with all who trusted in him. Thus the fourfold action epitomizes the way Jesus's life is made present in the church.

There are strong hints in the resurrection appearances—at Emmaus, in the upper room, by the Galilean lakeshore—that it was in this fourfold action in relation to food that the identity of the risen Jesus was made known to the dumb-founded disciples. This then becomes the definitive series of actions that identi-fies the birth, ministry, death, and resurrection of Christ and affirms his presence with the church as its living Lord. Thus this series of actions comes to define what the church understands by prophecy. Prophecy is the practice of drawing on the revelation of God in the past to identify his action in the present. "Therefore every scribe who has been trained for the kingdom of heaven is like the master of a household who brings out of his treasure what is new and what is old" (Matt. 13:52). The prophet brings out of the treasure house of God's story the fresh discoveries of his revelation for today. This may be in the form of words, but it may even more vividly be in the form of actions or gestures. The Eucharist is the definitive prophetic action, because it identifies the whole life and work of Christ in such a way that it declares Christ's living presence today. It is a demonstration of how God gives his people everything they need: for everything is taken, blessed, broken, and given. This is how everything is made new.

Whenever a community acts in such a way that their gestures point back to the transforming events of Christ's death and resurrection and point forward to the eschatological fulfillment of God's promises, their actions may be described as prophetic. The point of a prophetic action is not to change the world but to display the manner in which the world is changed by God. Thus, for example, during the Vichy regime in France during the 1940s, villagers in Le Chambon-sur-Lignon took in Jewish escapees from across central Europe, gave them hospitality, and found ways to spirit them along the perilous journey to Switzerland. The point was not that such actions would end the Holocaust or win the war, but that such gestures demonstrated the self-giving love of God revealed in Christ and offered a foretaste of the fellowship to be perfected in heaven.[8] Likewise, under the Pinochet regime in Chile, members of the Sebastian Avecedo Movement against Torture took to performing impromptu street liturgies, in which they would gather outside a known place of torture and recite names of the torturers and their victims. Again, the point was not directly to end the torture or bring down the regime, but to identify the courage of the oppressed, express the anger of God against their oppressors, and to point to the truthfulness of the day when all secrets would be revealed.[9] On a rather more modest level, one local church in a deprived neighborhood in Britain found that it was attracting four times as many children as adults—in a culture where the children were accustomed to appearing without the company

8. Samuel Wells, *Transforming Fate into Destiny: The Theological Ethics of Stanley Hauerwas* (Carlisle: Paternoster, 1998), 134–40.

9. William T. Cavanaugh, *Torture and Eucharist: Theology, Politics, and the Body of Christ* (Oxford: Blackwell, 1998), 273–77.

of their parents. So the church decided to give over its principal worship area to the children and take the adults into a side room. Again the point was not to solve the social problems of the area by educating (or converting) the children, but gently to alert the neighborhood, and other churches in the area, to the God who displaces the mighty and exalts the humble.

The prophetic claim of the Eucharist is that there is no part of life—no part at all—that may not be brought within this saving cycle of taking, blessing, breaking, and giving. This claim derives from the more familiar claim that there is no aspect of life that is not incorporated in Christ's birth, ministry, death, and resurrection. Prophecy demonstrates the ways in which this incorporation takes place. The significance of the Eucharist in relation to prophecy is that it keeps prophecy embodied in action—rather than simply, for example, verbal critique—and that it keeps prophecy christological—in that the fourfold action focuses entirely on the person and work of Christ. So the "Eucharistic" test of all prophecy is whether that prophecy points to an embodied social practice, and whether that prophecy is shaped entirely around the pattern of God disclosed in Christ.

### Inviting

If the words and actions of remembering enable the church to identify the presence of Jesus in the Eucharist, the corresponding moment of invocation enables Christians to identify the activity of the Holy Spirit. This is a defining moment for companionship with God, because it is the moment when the three understandings of the body of Christ—Jesus, the church, and the Eucharistic bread—coalesce. The church meets to discover Jesus in the transforming practice of sharing food. This is the moment when the past, present, and future of the church are united. The Last Supper, the eschatological banquet, and the local celebration are made one as the Holy Spirit makes the incarnate Jesus and the coming Lord present in the sharing of food.

The prayer of invocation asks that the Holy Spirit will do among the congregation what Jesus did at Cana. At Cana, in transforming water into wine, Jesus took the simple and earthy and made it extraordinary and heavenly; he drew back the veil of mortality and for a moment offered a glimpse of divine glory; he saved his people from lack and scarcity and offered them abundance; he anticipated the marriage of heaven and earth and revealed God's purpose of saving the best till last. He epitomized everything that is meant by "Emmanuel"—God with us. The invocation asks that the Holy Spirit will do all these things, and bring heaven to earth in the form of bread and wine and in the sharing of food in companionship with God.

This is the place where Christians discover what is meant by holiness. The definition of holiness involves a number of dimensions, each of which may be derived from this moment in the Eucharist.

Holiness is not a quality in the self, it is the gift of the Holy Spirit. It is not a static condition, but the manifestation of God through the material of flesh and blood, just as the coming of the Holy Spirit in the liturgy is the manifestation of God through the material of bread and wine. Holiness does not define itself, but takes its meaning from its relation to the events of Christ's life, ministry, death, and resurrection, as disclosed in the Eucharist. Just as Christ took, blessed, broke, and shared the bread, so he took and blessed human nature, was broken, and thus gave his life for the world; likewise the holy life is one that God has taken in order to bless and broken in order to give for the life of the world. Holiness, as defined by the Eucharist, is not a momentary state, but a gift that is received through the repeated faithful practice of joining in confession, praise, Scripture study, intercession, reconciliation, peacemaking, thanksgiving, and remembrance, as well as being open to the transformation of the Holy Spirit. Its goal is not so much good actions as good people. It is not an individual pursuit, but one of companionship; just as the Eucharist gathers together an assembly of disparate people, so in the prayer of invocation the longing is that the Holy Spirit will make holy not just the elements of bread and wine but the people who receive them, so that holiness may be revealed through the unity of the church in the bond of peace. Holiness is not just an inner condition—the prayer of invocation is that the congregation become a kingdom of priests, a corporate witness that participates in the reconciliation of the world to God. And finally, the Eucharist defines holiness in that it offers a specific practice, the sharing of food, to embody the longing for life with God. Holiness is fundamentally about abundance, because it is about disciples forgetting their narcissistic self-fascinations in the sheer glory of God's goodness.

This is also the place where Christians discover what is meant by power. If holiness perhaps represents a caricature of the "pious" understanding of Christian ethics, power perhaps epitomizes the "realist" understanding of the discipline. While the distinction may be illegitimate, the significant point here is that both find their paradigm at this point in the liturgy.

The defining moment in a theological understanding of power is the day of Pentecost. The disciples are enjoined to "stay here in the city" until they have "been clothed with power from on high" (Luke 24:49). At Pentecost they are indeed clothed with power from on high. The disciples are given everything they need to worship God, to be his friends, and to eat with him. This moment defines what Christians understand by power, in that it comes from God, and it is the capacity to achieve what God intends. It is not a quality in the self, and it is not a quality that enables the self's aggrandizement; it is the capacity to realize God's reign in present circumstances, to swathe materiality with the life-giving Spirit, to infuse communities and peoples with the ways of justice and peace. In other words, it is the ability to live without the constraint of sin, death, and evil—to embody the life made possible by the death and resurrection of Christ. This is exactly what the Holy Spirit offers—an infusion of all that is made possible in Christ.

The gifts of the Spirit clothe the people of God with this transforming power. And the gift of the Spirit whose regular reception becomes the practice through which all other gifts are understood is the Eucharist. At the Eucharist the Holy Spirit is invited to come down, in a reenactment of Pentecost, to make the process of sharing food the means of receiving all the gifts of the Spirit—all the benefits of Christ. This prayer is an elaborate definition of power. It is, first of all, a prayer. All intercessory prayer is an invocation of God; prayer is an act of recognition of God's sovereignty, a demonstration that all power comes from God. The prayer is an invitation, not an instruction. It is an embodiment of the relationship of creature to Creator, in no position to apply force but confident that asking will lead to receiving—when power lies in the hands of grace. Second, the prayer is directed initially toward the common food—bread and wine. Control over the production and distribution of food constitutes one of the most significant forms of power. This moment in the liturgy is a proclamation that God has control over the food that meets the deepest needs of his people. As at Cana, as at the feeding of the five thousand, what began as a modest offering was transformed into abundant, overflowing bounty, so at this moment the prayer asks that God show his power in flooding the world with grace. Next, this demonstration of power through the distribution of food is for the building up of the church. This epitomizes the purpose of all power, which is a gift intended to strengthen the agents of God's glory in the world. All gifts are to be evaluated by whether they build up the church: this gift builds up the church in a definitive way. This is a gift that liberates, rather than destroys. Just as the manna was a gift to liberate the children of Israel from fear for their own survival and to guarantee the presence of God among them, so this moment in the liturgy expresses the way God is present in the church today, giving his people everything they need and delivering them from fear. As a gift of God, power is therefore good. The exercise of power is not to be avoided as inherently corrupting. However, any power that is not exercised as demonstrated through this moment in the liturgy—is not attributed to God, is experienced as force rather than authority, is not intended to build up the people subject to it, does not liberate but destroys, creates fear rather than plenty—such power enslaves, and this enslavement engulfs not just the people but the powerful too.

One aspect of the power defined at the Eucharistic table remains to be noted. This power is vested in a humble loaf (or wafer) of bread, an item about to be broken in two. If the elements—the people and the world—are about to be clothed with power from on high, that power is the power proclaimed by a crown of thorns, a scourged Savior, a broken body. The power of the cross is a power revealed in weakness. The power demonstrated in the Eucharist proclaims that when the Holy Spirit comes upon disciples, they have everything they need, but they are invariably broken before those gifts can be fully shared for the life of the world. This is where the power of the saint differs from the power of the hero.[10]

---

10. Samuel Wells, *Improvisation and the Drama of Christian Ethics* (Grand Rapids: Brazos, 2004), 42–44.

## Breaking Bread

If this is the moment in the liturgy when the Lord's Prayer is said, then the Lord's Prayer becomes like a collect, focusing all the work of the preceding prayers. And this is very appropriate, because the Lord's Prayer is a proclamation that God gives his people everything they need to worship him, to be his friends, and to eat with him.

The prayer's first petition is for present needs: "Give us." It is a prayer for manna, for daily bread. Provision of daily bread frees the church from one kind of slavery, the slavery of hunger. It is a statement that bread fundamentally comes from God, that anxiety over "your life, what you will eat or what you will drink, or about your body, what you will wear" (Matt. 6:25) is a matter of faith, and that this kind of prison is a prison of one's own making. Placing this prayer for food in the context of the Eucharist expresses once again the way, through the Eucharist, God gives food, and through the giving of food, gives his people everything they need. So the prayer becomes, "May we receive every day what you give us today." Eating with God, being God's companions, is not just the eschatological aspiration of the church, not just the direction of the Eucharist—it is the aim and purpose of every Christian's life every day. "Give us each day the presence and friendship of a companion at table" is a prayer for "bread" to symbolize everything Christians need and desire from God.

The prayer's second petition is for the healing of past wounds: "Forgive us." This is deliverance from a second kind of slavery, the slavery of sin. To be short of food is a pitiful condition. But how much more miserable is to have abundant food but not to be able to eat it because of social division. This is the predicament from which the Lord's Prayer in the context of the Eucharist seeks definitive salvation. If eating with God and one another requires bread, then being God's friends and the friends of one another requires forgiveness. The Eucharistic Prayer defines the way Christians think about memory: but if memory is going to yield the trust that is necessary for friendship, it needs to be accompanied by reconciliation. And just as food fundamentally comes from God, so forgiveness fundamentally springs from God. It is God who forgives his companions, and it is only in the strength and liberation of that forgiveness that they can ask for a second blessing, the blessing to forgive one another. The Eucharist embodies the purpose of forgiveness: for without reconciliation it is not possible to be friends, and without being friends it is not possible to eat together—with one another or with God. If disciples want to eat with God, they have to be able to eat with one another. That is the lesson of the Eucharist.

The prayer's third petition is for disarming the unknown: "Deliver us." The slavery in question here is the slavery of fear. And the church's response to fear is worship.

> If our God whom we serve is able to deliver us from the furnace of blazing fire and out of your hand, O king, let him deliver us. But if not, be it known to you, O king,

that we will not serve your gods and we will not worship the golden statue that you have set up. (Dan. 3:17–18)

The church has abundant food and corresponding gifts for today; it has been liberated from the oppression of past sins committed by and inflicted upon it. Does it dare to take up the offer of companionship, of being God's friends and eating with him? Temptation, testing, evil—these name the forces that may still be stronger than the community that has abundant gifts and is released from the curse of sin. These are the shadows that overawe Christian ethics, the fighting within and fears without that make the ethical task seem so daunting. And the central response to these mighty forces is to name and proclaim a mightier one—to worship the God of Jesus Christ, to invoke the power of the Spirit. Here, in the Lord's Prayer, it is shown that in Jesus, the church, and the Eucharist, God gives his people everything they need to worship him, to be his friends, and to eat with him. They find food through calling on God to meet their present needs, they find friendship by calling on God to forgive their sins and empower them to forgive others', and they find faith by calling on God to manifest his power within and without in worship. Thus they become God's companions.

In one local congregation, there was a profound sense of striving for personal holiness, but a more inhibited air when it came to the corporate identification of shared faith. On one occasion the person presiding at the Eucharist described how she had on many occasions worshiped in France. She told how at this moment in the Mass, she had invariably noticed how all the members of the congregation held hands to say the Lord's Prayer. She commented how sporting heroes in big matches would stand in a line with arms around each other's shoulders to sing the national anthem. This was a way of showing they were a team—that they stood or fell together—that they were one body. "So let's hold hands together to say the Lord's Prayer," she said. "Because we are one body. And the Lord's Prayer is our national anthem."

Having been taken and blessed, the bread is now broken. The breaking of the bread is celebrated in the Emmaus story as the moment of revelation, the moment when two lost souls became God's companions. Just as on the road the two disciples had listened as Jesus explained how the Messiah must suffer, and then at supper they had perceived their companion as that same suffering servant, now resurrected, so at the Eucharist the congregation first rediscovers the true nature of Jesus's person and mission, and then sees the crucifixion and resurrection vividly portrayed in the breaking and sharing of bread.

This is the moment in the liturgy where wrath and mercy meet. On the one hand this is the bread of scarcity—of limited resources, of selfish greed, of cruelty, of breaking the bodies of others, of misusing the gifts of creation, of murder, of raging hatred and bitter enmity: of sin. On the other hand this is the bread of abundance, of limitless love, unending forgiveness, ceaseless forbearance, steadfast endurance, relentless delight, the tender embrace of the beloved child: of grace. The bread of sorrow and the bread of joy. At this moment the anger and the love of God break his heart, as they did on the cross. And this is how God's people come to share his life: they enter the broken heart of God. They become his companions in the breaking of the bread.

Here is the moment that defines Christians' understanding of violence. Violence has no definition in and of itself: it receives its definition by analogy to all that Christ endured. In the background to the passion are the paths that Jesus rejected: collusion with the Roman and Jewish authorities, the gentle path of persuasion and half-truth and postponed integrity, and withdrawal to the desert, a quest for righteousness removed from a personal encounter with political power. In the foreground are the forces that put Jesus to death: the short-term calculations and temptations of militarily dominated government, the pleadings and manipulations of institutional religion, and the sharp edge of bigotry, the ebb and flow of nationalism and the insidious appeal of racism, the fear and frenzy of the mob, and the consequent trampling of justice.[11] And at the center lies the broken body of Christ.

The broken body of Christ crystallizes both the manner of God's sovereignty over his creation and the ultimate purpose of that sovereignty. If God's sovereignty genuinely is the grain of the universe, the whole orientation of creation, then God's love, notably his love of enemies, is the most powerful force of all: thus the power of violence and the power of money are revealed for what they really are, not dominant but ultimately weak. The love displayed on the cross—enacted in the breaking of the bread—is the most powerful force in the universe, because it is the way the sovereign God chooses to make his character known. Meanwhile the portrayal of this sovereign love in the breaking of the bread at the Eucharist discloses the ultimate purpose of that sovereign power expressed in love: and that purpose is to share food with his people—to call them to worship him, be his friends, and eat with him. This key moment in the liturgy displays the church's understanding of violence, of God's character, and of the ultimate purpose of creation: it portrays the method, results, and conclusion of salvation.

At the two defining moments in Jesus's life, his birth and his death, he is utterly powerless—so powerless that he cannot use his arms. At his birth, his arms are strapped to his sides by swaddling clothes—Luke's Gospel relates this twice, and the angels tell the shepherds that this will be the "sign." And later at Jesus's death his two hands are nailed to either end of a horizontal beam, and as he dies in agony he cannot even wipe his own brow or scratch an itch or waft away a fly or mosquito. These are the most intimate moments in Jesus's life, and at both moments, by nails and by swaddling clothes, he is, literally, disarmed. Jesus is God disarmed. The disarmed and disarming love of God. This is the sovereignty disclosed at the breaking of the bread. This is the heart of the church's perception of violence.

11. John Howard Yoder, *The Politics of Jesus: Behold the Man! Our Victorious Lamb*, 2nd ed. (Grand Rapids: Eerdmans, 1994).

## Sharing Food

All the preceding elements of the liturgy meet their consummation in the sharing of food. The significance of gathering is disclosed in the practice of eating together. The goal of reconciliation with God and one another is manifested in the common meal. The anticipation of heaven conveyed in the glory of praise and lifting of hearts is embodied in the banquet of the kingdom. The understanding of Scripture, as for the Emmaus disciples, is made plain in the context of the breaking of the bread. The confession of faith is given its climax in the enactment of the goal of revelation—that God's people might worship him, be his friends, and eat with him. The offering of need and gift is transformed through the prism of the Eucharistic Prayer so that those who have offered their differences receive—and digest—the same things. And most of all, the prayer that Christ in his life and death, his resurrection and exaltation might live in and through the elements of bread and wine finds its true purpose in the ingestion of those elements by the church, so that the members of the congregation may become the Body of Christ, and he might live in and through the church.

Sharing food is a proclamation and a practice, a witness and a discipline. I shall consider its role as revelation before going on to examining its significance as gift.

As revelation, sharing food offers Christians the discovery that God gives them everything they need. This is a proclamation of abundance. The discovery is that the more food is shared, the more food there is: like the sorcerer's apprentice, the congregation finds that breaking bread in two means twice as much bread, not half as much. The inspiration for such a discovery is the feeding of the five thousand, where the role of the disciples was to ensure everyone received the abundant bread available and to collect up the leftovers so that nothing was wasted. And there were twelve baskets of bread that no one could eat.

Thus the sharing of food is the way the church comes to understand economics. Integral to the church's understanding of economics is the practice of hospitality and the virtue of generosity. Generosity is the assumption that, since one has freely received, therefore one may freely give. And the embodiment of this pattern of giving and receiving is, once again, in the Eucharist. The members of the congregation have handed over the firstfruits of their labor and have received back the firstfruits of the resurrection. What reason is there not to be generous?

Sharing food proclaims the abundance of food. But it also proclaims the abundance of places at the table. As Christians gather around the table, they learn to look around them as they eat, and speculate on whether these are the people with whom God predicts they will spend eternity, or whether he has other people in mind, and if so, why those people are not present now. Just as Christians discover when reading Scripture that they need to be a diverse and rainbow congregation if they are truly to hear everything Scripture has to tell them, so now at the distribution of food they discover that they need to incorporate a great number and range of people—especially the hungry—if they are to be able to eat all the food that God has given them.

Everyone is called to a place around the table, whatever their gender, their race, their class, whatever their orientation, their physical health or ability, their mental health or ability, whatever their social or criminal history. And this is not because everyone has a *right* to be there. It is because the church *needs* everyone to be there. The church does not need everyone to be there so as to ensure Christ will be present: the Holy Spirit is not dependent on human cooperation. The reason the church needs everyone to be there is first so that it can hear the Scripture fully; second so that it can offer all of creation, not just a small segment, in thanksgiving; and third so that it can eat and drink all that has been given to it so that *nothing is wasted*. The crisis of the church is the crisis not of scarcity but of abundance: the church is not thirsty but drowning. It is not that God has withheld his gifts, but that the church has been given too much. Thus the church is desperate, not to find sources of nourishment when God's Spirit falls short, but to share and distribute and offer God's superabundant gifts universally so that nothing is wasted.

This is the picture of society enacted at this moment in the liturgy: that the abundant gifts of God should ensure that everyone, every created being, should receive enough, and that every being should be so stirred by receiving that they in turn give generously, give everything. This thoroughgoing pattern of offering and receiving, this spinning spiral of mutual enjoyment and treasuring, this virtuous circle of never-ending provision—this is the embodiment of God's call to his people to worship him (the offering), to be his friends (the sharing), and to eat with him (the receiving). It is not so much that God desires Christians to match his sacrifice with their sacrifice; it is more that he moves Christians to respond to his fulsome pouring-out with their own kenotic imitation. This is the economics of generosity, the politics of love.

One local congregation found it difficult to decide whether they should sit, stand, or kneel to receive communion. Kneeling seemed appropriate to some, because it embodied humility. But some said that, without an altar rail, it asked too much of people with disabilities. It seemed that sitting was the posture that stressed equality, because everybody looked and felt much the same. But it was felt that, besides being too comfortable, remaining in one's seat suggested that God made the whole journey, with almost no response from his people. Standing in a circle became the norm. It stressed the differences of height, age, and physical ability, and it made it necessary for some to rest on the strength of others. Though some said they felt unworthy to stand, others pointed out the Christ had enabled, even commanded, them to stand, and that standing was a symbol of resurrection. By standing in a circle, the congregation realized they did not just eat of one body—they were one body.

If sharing food is revelation, it is also gift. It is gift because it is a practice that shapes a community. Just as parents learn to love the children they have been given, so the community learns to want the gifts God gives it. And if the proclamation of sharing food is about economics, the gift of sharing food is about unity.

This gift of unity is expressed in the single word "communion." Communion embodies the way Christians perceive they are invited to become and remain one. Communion means most importantly that Christians share a belief that they have *a place at God's table*. Communion means being God's intimate friend—and this is characterized by eating with him. Christians make the bold claim that they are invited to occupy the fourth place at God's table, along with the members of the Trinity itself. Communion secondarily involves a shared sense of the importance of sitting at table *with one another*. When Christians eat together they act on the commission of the Son and in the company of the Spirit—and their worship is present to the Father. A further, third understanding is a shared sense of the *discipline and order* required for this special act—Baptism, the faithfulness of the participants, the training, character, and order of those leading the liturgy, the vertical reconciliation of the confession, and the horizontal reconciliation of the peace. And finally there is a fourth common understanding of the *practices* of this special act—greeting, celebrating in praise, giving thanks, listening to Scripture, preaching, confessing the faith through the Creed, interceding, sharing God's gifts, being blessed, and being sent out.

The Eucharist offers a pattern of unity through a perception of the hierarchical and sequential nature of these four shared understandings. For most problems that arise in a community touch on one or more of these shared understandings of communion. A problem with one of the elements does not invalidate the others— on the contrary, it is probably only through a shared understanding of the others that a problem in one of the elements can be overcome. It is only when there is no shared understanding in any of the four areas that communion seems lost. For example, in churches where the person and character of the leader is regarded as especially significant, issues such as the ordination of women and the acceptance of homosexual relationships in clergy households stretch some people's perception of some aspects of the third understanding, that of discipline and order. But a greater grasp of what is shared through having a place at God's table, sharing that place with one another, and engaging together in a transforming pattern of practices ought to put these differences in perspective. Likewise, a difference on the question of the divinity of Christ may seem to make communion impossible due to the significance of sitting at table with the Trinity, but a remarkable fellowship in regard to the other three understandings—sitting with one another, discipline and order, and transforming practices—may still be found.

It is very important to remember that the first understanding, the invitation to eat with God at God's table—communion with God the Trinity—is the point of creation and redemption. It is what the universe was made for, what Christ died for. But there is a clear warning that if Christians cannot meet the terms of the second understanding—sitting at table together—they have little chance of enjoying the fellowship of God eternally. The purpose of the third and fourth understandings of communion—discipline and order and an agreed pattern of practices—should help Christians carry out the second one—sitting and eating together—not make it more difficult. Communion is impaired if it is simply not possible to carry out the whole pattern of shared practices, the fourth understanding; for example, greeting is impaired if the church condones the exclusion of some on racial grounds, and sharing God's gifts may seem absurd if the church is meanwhile condoning grotesque economic inequalities. But the severing of communion is a grave and drastic matter, and should only be accepted if all communication on all four levels has proved impossible.

After sharing food, for the third time the congregation lapses into silence. The first time, after the glory of praise, the members of the congregation pondered how far they had come since the service began—gathered, made into the church, forgiven, transported by worship. The second time, after the proclamation of the word, the members of the congregation sought to discern God's voice now that the past, present, and future of the world and their lives had been renarrated through Scripture and sermon, such that they were now no longer strangers and aliens, but companions and friends. And now, a third time, silence reigns, and the members of the congregation digest the significance and relish the wonder of entering God's life and eating with him. They have been given everything they need. What will they now be asked to do? That is the perennial question of ethics, and that is the burden of the final part of the liturgy.

# 3

## Friendship and the Ways to Truth

DAVID BURRELL

### The Specter of Relativism

It is crucial to note how Enlightenment presuppositions about reason and truth gave that very specter its stature as a threat. For they presume a normative set of rational criteria available to all, against which any claim to other sets of criteria is utterly unsettling. That is what we mean by "relativism": there are no longer any operative norms across human discourse, so power or even violence will have to arbitrate. Yet like earlier debates over "natural law," there may be other ways of thinking about those criteria which are not laden with specific beliefs but which have to do with the fact that believers formed in quite diverse traditions can discourse with one another. Once the idol of "pure reason" has been shattered, and we can learn to accept diverse ways of arriving at conclusions, we will also find that we can employ the skills learned in our tradition to follow reasoning in another. Traditions, in other words, may indeed be *relative* to one another in ways that can prove mutually fruitful rather than isolating. Those traditions which prove to be so will be those which avail themselves of human reason in their development, and the patterns of stress and strain in their evolution will display their capacity for

Originally published as "The Role of Dialogue and Friendship in Cross-Cultural Understanding," in David Burrell, *Friendship and Ways to Truth* (Notre Dame, IN: University of Notre Dame Press, 2000), 37–65. Copyright © 2000, University of Notre Dame Press. Reprinted with permission of University of Notre Dame Press.

exploiting the resources of reason.[1] In short, "relativism" gives way to the human fact that all inquiry takes place within a tradition, and the specter which it evoked turns out to be the shadow of our faith in "pure reason," that is, in the possibility of human inquiry outside any tradition.

The discovery (on the part of reason) that every inquiry employs presuppositions which cannot themselves be rationally justified opens the way to self-knowledge on the part of Enlightenment philosophy, which can then take its place among the traditions.[2] And once that has been accomplished, the specter of "relativism" dissolves in the face of developing the skills needed to negotiate among traditions, which can be negotiated because they can be seen to be related to one another. Since we have become accustomed to associating *faith* with *tradition*, we must then renounce the normative Enlightenment view which represented faith as an "addendum" to the human condition. If that view itself reflects a tradition whose account can be rendered in historical terms (as a reaction to the devastating religious wars in Europe), then it too will have a recognizable convictional basis, and faith will once more emerge as part of a shared human legacy. The intellectual task, and the part of reason operative in any tradition which survives the test of time, becomes one of learning how such traditions develop and how one might learn from the other. *Reason*, in other words, becomes a functional notion displayed in practices which cut across traditional boundaries, rather than a set of substantive beliefs which must be adhered to *in those very terms* before discourse can be undertaken. *Rationality* will show itself in practices which can be followed and understood by persons operating in similar fashion from different grounding convictions.[3]

What they have in common is the need to talk about what they believe. Here emerges the analogy with debates about "natural law": what is so shared and common as to be dubbed "natural" is not necessarily substantive norms regarding human actions so much as the demand that any normative "law" must express itself in a coherent discourse. That very activity, which displays the fruitfulness of human ingenuity, also contains operative parameters whose function can be tracked by astute participant-observers prepared to recognize analogies across traditions of inquiry. Socrates's assembling of linguistic reminders for Thrasymachus made him abandon his projected discourse, without Socrates having to exert any force at all.[4] For those reminders had to do with the possibility of any discourse at all and thus governed the tradition Thrasymachus was defending as well as the totally opposed one which Socrates had set out to elaborate. Book 1

1. Alasdair MacIntyre, *Whose Justice? Which Rationality?* (Notre Dame, IN: University of Notre Dame Press, 1989), chaps. 18–19.

2. Ibid., chap. 17.

3. Here the reference is usually to the work of Ludwig Wittgenstein, notably the *Philosophical Investigations* (New York: Macmillan, 1956) and the extensive elaboration of reason as a human practice which that seminal work spawned.

4. Plato, *Republic* 1.

of the *Republic* does not defend Socrates's own positions so much as it displays the terms for any debate.

Yet dialogue can only take place among persons; systems cannot converse with one another. And even dialogue between persons can degenerate into a "dialogue of the deaf" if each one comes as a "representative" of a position. The prerequisite for dialogue among persons seems to be a shared interest in pursuing the truth of the matter, no matter how deep and shaping are one's convictions on the subject. If those very convictions presume that the path one is traveling is the only way to arrive at truth in such matters, then the goal has already been circumscribed, and dialogue is rendered nugatory. We see that *truth* must transcend any given conceptuality, and that each participant must be committed to questing after it. Yet, as we have just remarked, what once seemed an obvious path is no longer available to us: namely, that philosophy, or untrammeled rational inquiry, represents a neutral achievement accessible to those willing to renounce their particular paths. In this sense, we cannot consistently espouse a "pluralism" which retains the modern presumption that we philosophers can survey diverse religious traditions from a superior vantage point.[5] The alternative to presuming such "objective" neutrality is to turn to an intersubjective encounter with persons prepared in the way we have described: willing to search together for the truth to which they are singly committed, yet which they may name quite differently. Such a commitment is uncannily close to a classical view of friendship first articulated by Aristotle.

## Augustine: Friends Along Can Show the Way

What we are seeking for here is what one might call an "embodied understanding."[6] Augustine's *Confessions* was intended to offer us just that, as he mined his memory to discover for himself and also to show us the ways in which God had led him to the point where he could begin to return all that he had so freely been given. Much has been and should be made of book 7, where he discovers how to negotiate the two outstanding questions which stood between him and an assent of faith: how properly to conceive of God, and how to think about evil. The celebrated ladder of ascent in 7.17 gave him an idiom for speaking of God as the "light of the light of my soul." That allowed him to see "that all finite things are in you, not as though you were a place that contained them, but . . . they are in you because you hold all things in your truth as though they were in your hand" (7.15). Discovering the order in his own reasoning powers, as he ascended "from the consideration

5. This would be my critique of John Hick's *particular* presentation of "pluralism": "Religious Particularity and Truth," in *Hermeneutics, Religious Pluralism, and Truth*, ed. Gregory D. Pritchard (Winston-Salem, NC: Wake Forest University, 1989), 35–49, followed by an exchange with John Hick and Ninian Smart.

6. I have argued that this is precisely the kind of "foundation" which Lonergan calls for, which quite removes him from any "foundationalist" position, in David Burrell, "Method and Sensibility: Novak's Debt to Lonergan," *Journal of the American Academy of Religion* 40 (1972): 349–67.

of material things to the soul, . . . and then to the soul's inner power . . . beyond which dumb animals cannot go, [and thence] to the power of reason, [and finally to] judgment" (7.17), he was able to experience a nonspatial realm and so gain access to a language for "the God who IS" (7.17).

Yet this is far from the end of the road. In fact, Augustine is dismayed at this point to find that "I had no strength to fix my gaze on the [One who IS, but] recoiled and fell back into my old ways" (7.17), so "I began to search for a means of gaining the strength I need to enjoy you" (7.18). This, he avers, "I could not find . . . until I embraced the *mediator between God and men, Jesus Christ, who is a man, like them* (1 Tim. 2:5) yet also *rules as God over all things, blessed forever* (Rom. 9:5). He was calling to me and saying *I am the way; I am truth and life* (John 14:6)." This will come as he reaches out to others, and becomes willing to place his life in their hands to the extent that he lets himself be guided by their witness. This is one more place where we can note how the *Confessions* is pointedly crafted to show us the way beyond "the Platonists" to whom Augustine has just acknowledged his indebtedness.[7] At the end of book 7, he already sees how he has to move beyond them: "None of this [about Jesus] is contained in the Platonists' books. Their pages have not the mien of the true love of God. . . . It is one thing to descry the land of peace from a wooded hilltop; . . . it is another to follow the high road to that land of peace, the way that is defended by the care of the heavenly Commander" (7.21). That journey will be motivated and undertaken on the strength of others' witness.

Book 8 begins with reference to his "heart," which seemed to be the proper focus of attention once the intellectual obstacles had fallen away.[8] Whereupon he notes: "By your inspiration it seemed to me a good plan to go and see Simplicianus, who, as I could see for myself, was a good servant of yours" (8.1). And Simplicianus tells him "about Victorinus, whom he had known intimately when he was in Rome" (8.2). So we have a tableau of imbedded witness, to whom Augustine looks for the courage to take the step which he knows is the right one for him. All this seems quite opposed to the inner journey of intellectual warrant which had given him a language for speaking of God as a nonmaterial being. That rendition laid bare his capacities for understanding and judgment, and while these led him beyond themselves to their source, it was nonetheless an intellect aware of its own capacities which evoked that experience and that idiom. Here is a person all too aware that he lacks the strength to act what he has seen, who seeks out the witness of fellow

7. For the way in which Augustine structures the *Confessions* to carry us with him beyond Neoplatonism, see John Cavadini, "Time and Ascent in *Confessions* XI," in *Collectanea Augustiniana 2: Presbyter Factus Sum*, ed. J. Lienhard, E. Muller, and R. Teske (New York: Peter Lang, 1993), 171–85.

8. I have presented a reading of the *Confessions* in which the odd-numbered chapters offer an intellectual articulation of a particular issue, which will only be fully resolved in the subsequent even-numbered chapter, where the steps will have to be taken to realize in a person's life what they have come to understand: David Burrell, "Augustine: Understanding as a Personal Quest" in *Exercises in Religious Understanding* (Notre Dame, IN: University of Notre Dame Press, 1973).

travelers. Not that *their* actions can simply be made his; he spontaneously seeks God's help in the wake of his encounter: "Come O Lord, and stir our hearts. Call us back to yourself" (8.4). Then begins the celebrated reflection on will: "When your servant Simplicianus told me the story of Victorinus, I began to glow with fervor to imitate him . . . , but I was held fast . . . by my own will, which had the strength of iron chains" (8.5). And that dilemma will not be resolved until the moment in the garden, when he returns to the language of "heart," noting how, "in an instant, as I came to the end of the sentence, it was as though the light of confidence flooded into my heart and all darkness of doubt was dispelled" (8.12).

We have focused on the crucial passage of the *Confessions*, a passage from mind to heart, which is recorded as a personal transformation intimately connected to Augustine's relations with others who shared the faith to which he felt called but which he felt unable to embrace. There is no opposition between others and self here, when those others are already living in the relationship with God which he desires for himself. It is as if that relationship of friendship with God in Christ, which will bind the pilgrims together as friends, is one into which others are invited to enter. We can only learn how to be friends with God from those who have learned already, and it turns out that they have learned from others as well. That is the crosshatching of friendships which makes for community. The finale of Augustine's story invites us to reread it with an eye for friendship, noting how the pear tree incident teaches him that buddies are not always friends (2.6–10), as well as how a friend's embrace of the faith and subsequent death brought Augustine up short in the life project in which he was engaged: "My heart grew somb[er] with grief, and wherever I looked I saw only death" (4.4–8). This event and its aftermath evoked an explicit reflection on friendship and its poignancy without a sustaining envelope of faith, by contrast with "those who love you, O God, and love their friends in you" (4.9).

The quest for understanding some things may be able to be carried out alone. But for those things too close to us to be able to discern, like our own hearts, or so intimately sustaining of us that we cannot gain an independent purchase on them, like God properly conceived, we find that we need the context of a community of friendship to get our own bearings. As paradoxical as this sounds, since such things are apparently more intimately connected with our very selves than more "objective" situations, Augustine felt he had made a signal advance when he came to appreciate how much he "believed on the word of friends or doctors or various other people. Unless we took these things on trust, we should accomplish absolutely nothing in this life" (6.5). Here he deftly distinguishes the role of friends, who will help him become accustomed to this affront to his erstwhile autonomy as well as teach him how to go on in this newfound grasp of the ways of human understanding, from a conviction which he finds will not leave him: "In all the books of philosophy which I had read no misleading proposition, however contentious, had been able, even for one moment, to wrest from me my belief in your existence and in your right to govern human affairs; and this despite the fact that I had no knowledge of what you are" (6.5). This observation is particularly valuable for appreciating how a quest for understanding contrasts with the need for certitude. He continues: "My belief that you existed and that our well-being was in your hands was sometimes strong, sometimes weak, but I always held to it even though I knew neither what I ought to think about your substance nor which way would lead me to you or lead me back to you" (6.5).

Here we have three levels carefully distinguished: a sustaining faith ("my belief that you existed and our well-being was in your hands"), a current set of conceptual tools ("[how] I ought to think about"), and a wholehearted response ("lead *me* to you"). He identifies the first as a mysteriously unyielding fact about himself and his own personal mindset, he is constantly seeking others' help to correct the second, though he undertakes it as his own personal responsibility, while the last (we have seen) inherently requires the assistance of others: their witness and their encouragement—"a friend is as another self" (Aristotle). So a full-blooded understanding, one which engages the entire person in a discriminating and discerning assent to what one has come to regard as true, can never be a solitary endeavor. We are too much in our own way, and are especially led astray by the multiple desires of our wayward hearts. This observation should remind us that, far from being the first autobiography, Augustine's *Confessions* represents antibiography, seeking not for an elusive *self* but for its transcendent source, which is nonetheless closer to us than our very selves. And it is more dependable, as being the very truth of ourselves, the "light of the light of our souls." If that sounds like will-o'-the-wisp language, the invitation of the *Confessions* is to entrust our own search for our self to Augustine's tutelage. If we can place that search in his hands, he will attempt to teach us how to displace it altogether, showing how one of our potential friends—himself—let it be transformed into a search for the source of all, including that precious self. Then we will be empowered to spend it in the service of others, as a part of our project of returning to the One who gives it so freely and abundantly.

## From "Objectivity" to "Intersubjectivity"

What may have appeared to be an *excursus* on friendship turns out to show us that commitment to truth may be barely intelligible in other than personal terms. And attempting to understand the shaping convictions of other persons becomes the best access we can have to a view of truth as personal. It will take a tradition shaped by revelation to give proper voice to truth as personal, where God *speaks* in a language accessible to us. Significantly enough, those traditions which are so shaped invariably speak of a *path* and a *journey* of faith. God's word presents a challenge to understanding rather than a certitude made easily available. Our location in a world where diverse traditions become aware of their mutual presence to one another invites us precisely "on a voyage of discovery stripped of colonizing pretensions: an invitation to explore the *other* on the way to discovering ourselves."[9] I have suggested that the optimum way of responding to this invitation, so eloquently framed by the French Islamicist Roger Arnaldez, is by cultivating friends among those "others," who can then become companions along the way, without ceasing to be the *other*. The precise manner in which explicitly diverse paths become a way defies logic, much as translating knows no firm rules. Yet the challenge to render another's convictions intelligible to oneself without making them over into one's own embodies the act of translating, which requires subtle judgments of similarity-cum-difference, thus exploiting to the full those analogous expressions which structure properly religious discourse.[10]

Philosophers habitually tend to shy away from analogous discourse, preferring the *terra firma* of univocity. Yet the quality of exchange among friends, which can allow for a common pursuit along different paths, requires the capacity inherent in analogous terms to let similarities retain their differences. Otherwise, communication will always presuppose agreement, requiring us to frame our convictions in a common language before we can be said to share them. What is peculiar about faith convictions, however, is precisely the way in which attempting to understand other paths can enrich our journey along our own. From this fact, like the practice of translating, we can counter the philosopher's penchant for univocal speech with an experience which requires another kind of language and reminds us how frequently we have recourse to it in conversations which engage our own convictions with others who may differ, even radically. Since it is unlikely that we should engage in such conversations in an unthreatening way except with friends, I have focused on friendship as a prerequisite for the quality of intersubjectivity which can come to substitute for *objectivity* in a postmodern context. Yet even more internally, as we have seen, the journey shared with friends becomes a paradigm of that quest for truth which displays to us the ubiquity and necessity of analogous discourse in negotiating the way set out before us.

---

9. Roger Arnaldez, *Three Messengers for One God*, trans. Gerald Schlabach (Notre Dame, IN: University of Notre Dame Press, 1994), vii, emphasis original.

10. On the role of judgment in using analogous expressions properly, see my *Analogy and Philosophical Language* (New Haven: Yale University Press, 1973). For an application to central questions of philosophical theology, see the essay by Nicholas Lash, "Ideology, Metaphor and Analogy," in *Philosophical Frontiers of Christian Theology*, ed. Brian Hebblethwaite and Stewart Sutherland (Cambridge: Cambridge University Press, 1982), 68–94; and David Burrell, "Aquinas and Scotus: Contrary Patterns for Philosophical Theology," in *Theology and Dialogue: Essays in Conversation with George Lindbeck*, ed. Bruce Marshall (Notre Dame, IN: University of Notre Dame Press, 1990), 105–29.

# 4

. . . . . . . . . . . . . . . . .

# Worship Is Our Worldview

*Christian Worship and the Formation of Desire*

. . . . . . . . . . . . . . . . . . . . . . . . . . . . .

JAMES K. A. SMITH

## The Primacy of Worship to Worldview

Human persons are not primarily thinking things, or even believing things, but rather imaginative, desiring animals who are defined fundamentally by love. We are embodied, affective creatures who are shaped and primed by material practices or liturgies that aim our hearts to certain ends, which in turn draw us to them in a way that transforms our actions by inscribing in us habits or dispositions to act in certain ways. In short, being human takes practice—and implicit in those practices is a social imaginary that orients, guides, and shapes our desire and action. A social imaginary is an understanding of the world that is precognitive and prereflective: it functions on an order before both thinking and believing, and it is "carried" (according to Charles Taylor) in images, stories, myths, and related practices. Thus we have suggested that it might be more helpful to talk about a Christian social imaginary than to focus on a Christian worldview, given that the latter seems tinged with a lingering cognitivism. By focusing on social imaginaries,

Originally published as "From Worship to Worldview: Christian Worship and the Formation of Desire," in James K. A. Smith, *Desiring the Kingdom: Worship, Worldview, and Cultural Formation*, Cultural Liturgies 1 (Grand Rapids: Baker Academic, 2009), 133–39. Copyright © 2009. Used by permission.

the radar of cultural critique is calibrated to focus on exegeting practices, not just waiting for the blips of ideas to show up on the screen.

The questions we bring to Christian worship are: What is envisioned as the good life? What understanding of the world is carried in these practices? What vision of the kingdom is embedded in Christian worship? What picture of flourishing human community is envisioned by the practices of distinctly Christian liturgy? And how does this vision of the kingdom of God compare to the kingdoms aimed at in secular liturgies?

In other words, what does worship say about Christian faith? Too often we try to define the essence of Christianity by a summary of doctrines. We turn to texts and to theologians in order to discern the ideas and beliefs that are distinctive to Christianity. That's akin to thinking one can understand *Hamlet* just by reading the script; but it is only properly a play when it is performed, and there is a kind of understanding of *Hamlet* that comes from its performance that cannot be found just in the script.[1] So, what if we sought to discern not the essence of Christianity as a system of beliefs (or summarized in a worldview) but instead sought to discern the shape of Christian faith as a form of life? Instead of turning to texts, doctrines, and the theoretical articulations of theologians, we will consider what Christians *do*—or more specifically, what the church *as a people* does together in the "work of the people" (*leitourgos*). To discern the shape of a Christian worldview, we will read the practices of Christian worship in order to make out the shape of a distinctly Christian social imaginary.

Humans are first and fundamentally affective creatures shaped by practices— creatures who love before they think, who imagine before they theorize. We need a corresponding account of the relationship between worship and worldview (or doctrine). This will require undoing some habits we've acquired in theology and philosophy, as well as in discussions of Christian education and the formation of a Christian worldview. In particular, it requires that we reconsider the relationship between practice and belief.[2] In general, we have a tendency to think that doctrine and/or belief comes first—either in a chronological or normative sense—and that this then finds expression or application in worship practices, as if we have a worldview in place and then devise practices that are consistent with that cognitive framework.[3] Such a top-down, ideas-first picture of the relation

---

1. I was prompted to consider this analogy by Ben Faber, "Ethical Hermeneutics in the Theatre: Shakespeare's *Merchant of Venice*," in *Hermeneutics at the Crossroads*, ed. Kevin Vanhoozer, James K. A. Smith, and Bruce Ellis Benson (Bloomington: Indiana University Press, 2006), 211–24.

2. I have addressed the following themes in a more technical way in James K. A. Smith, "Philosophy of Religion Takes Practice: Liturgy as Source and Method in Philosophy of Religion," in *Contemporary Practice and Method in the Philosophy of Religion: New Essays*, ed. David Cheetham and Rolfe King (London: Continuum, 2008), 133–47; and Smith, "How Religious Practices Matter: Peter Ochs' 'Alternative Nurturance' of Philosophy of Religion," *Modern Theology* 24 (2008): 469–78.

3. One can even find someone like Alexander Schmemann falling into the habit of talking this way, as when he says that "worship is . . . the *expression* thus not merely of 'piety,' but of an all-embracing 'world view'" (*For the Life of the World: Sacraments and Orthodoxy*, 2nd ed. [Crestwood, NY: St. Vladimir's

between practice and knowledge, worldview and worship, is often accompanied by a corresponding picture of the relationship between the Bible and worship. According to this model, we begin with the Bible as the source of our doctrines and beliefs and then "apply" it to come up with worship practices that are consistent with, and expressive of, what the Bible teaches.

But there are problems with this picture: First, it doesn't jibe with the historical record. The people of God called out (*ek-klēsia*) to be the church were worshiping long before they got all their doctrines in order or articulated the elements of a Christian worldview, and they were engaged in and developing worship practices long before what we now call our *Bible* emerged and was solidified, so to speak.[4] Thus we can see in the New Testament itself the remnants of early Christian hymns (Phil. 2:5–11) and doxologies (e.g., Rom. 16:25–27) that likely were taken up from worship practices in the early church. In addition, given the oral culture in which the Scriptures emerged and the centrality of their public reading in gathered worship, the letters and documents that came to be the New Testament (in addition to the psalms prayed and sung by the early church) functioned primarily in a liturgical context of worship, not the private context of individual study.[5] And when the Scriptures are heard and read in the context of worship, they function differently. Rather than being approached as a "storehouse of facts" (Charles Hodge), the Scriptures are read and encountered as a site of divine action, as a means of grace, as a conduit of the Spirit's transformative power, as part of a pedagogy of desire. One could say that in the context of worship, Scripture constitutes a different kind of speech act, and thus is heard/received in a different mode.[6] The point here is that just as worship precedes the formation of the biblical canon ("the Bible"), so too does participation in Christian worship precede the formulation of doctrine and the articulation of a worldview. Lived worship is the fount from which a worldview springs, rather than being the expression or application of some cognitive set of beliefs already in place.

---

Seminary Press, 1973], 123, emphasis added)—as if the worldview was in place before worship. But then later he will counsel that we need to recover "the genuine meaning and power of our *leitourgia*" so that it can become "the *source of* an all-embracing world view" (134).

4. For a helpful history on the Bible as, in some significant sense, a product of the church in the Spirit, see Craig D. Allert, *A High View of Scripture? The Authority of the Bible and the Formation of the New Testament Canon*, Evangelical Ressourcement (Grand Rapids: Baker Academic, 2007), esp. 67–130.

5. Much more deserves to be said about this, but for a relevant discussion, see Daniel J. Treier, *Introducing Theological Interpretation of Scripture: Recovering a Christian Practice* (Grand Rapids: Baker Academic, 2008), 42–45.

6. Or, as Daniel Treier elsewhere suggests, we might say that this is a difference between coming to the Scriptures for knowledge and coming to the Scriptures for wisdom—akin to a difference between theoretical and practical reason, *scientia* rather than *sapientia*. (One might say that *sapientia* is akin to Taylor's notion of precognitive "understanding," discussed in James K. A. Smith, "Love Takes Practice: Liturgy, Formation, and Counter-Formation," chap. 2 in *Desiring the Kingdom*, 75–88.) Encountering the Scriptures first and foremost in the context of worship primes us for a *sapiential* engagement with the Word. For relevant discussion, see Daniel J. Treier, *Virtue and the Voice of God: Toward Theology as Wisdom* (Grand Rapids: Eerdmans, 2006).

Second, the common picture of doctrine or a worldview being "expressed" in worship—thus implying that worldview and/or doctrine *precedes* worship—doesn't jibe with the anthropology we've sketched above. This (I hope, biblical) anthropology suggests a different picture—not a top-down, ideas-first picture that prioritizes beliefs and doctrines ("worldview") but rather a bottom-up, practices-first model that prioritizes worship as a practice of desire. As I've been articulating this, I have had two special cases in my mind: children and mentally challenged adults. Both have limited capacities for grasping theological concepts or the sorts of theoretical formulations that characterize even worldview talk. Their ability to process the sorts of abstractions that characterize even beliefs is limited, either temporarily (in the case of children) or chronically (in the case of the mentally handicapped). Does that mean that they cannot achieve fullness in Christ? Do the limits of their cognitive abilities impair the hope of their "growing up" *into* Christ (Eph. 4:15)? Does their inability to traffic in concepts preclude them from being educated? Not according to the anthropology I have sketched above; rather, because we are more fundamentally creatures of love and desire than knowledge and beliefs, our discipleship—our formation in Christ—is more fundamentally a matter of precognitive education of the heart. And Christian worship that is full-bodied reaches, touches, and transforms even those who cannot grasp theological abstractions.[7]

For instance, when our children were quite young, we would sometimes participate in Good Friday services that included a few hymns and an extensive sermon that would focus on the fine points of atonement theory. But sometimes we would have opportunity to participate in Tenebrae, a historic "service of shadows" that revolves around Christ's seven last words from the cross. In the service we have attended, the congregation enters a sanctuary lit only by seven clusters of candles. Through the service, Christ's last words from the cross are read—sometimes with a brief meditation, sometimes with a musical interpretation. After each word, one of the clusters of candles is extinguished (in this case by a person methodically doing so as part of a liturgical dance). The darkness of that dark day increasingly envelops the congregation, until after the final word when the last bit of light is extinguished. After a time of darkened silence, the *strepitus* sounds—a torrent of discordant noise generated by cymbals from a hidden location in the rear of the sanctuary, shuddering through the congregation like a cold wind of desolation. The congregation then departs in somber silence, in darkness, the realities of

7. This is yet another way in which churches need to think of making themselves "accessible" for the handicapped. While we have worried about elevators and barriers, too many Protestant churches continue to offer a (very modern) style of worship that is dominated by quite abstract, heady forms, centering on a sermon that communicates only on a cognitive level (often difficult even for those with college degrees)—rather than adopting historic forms of Christian liturgy that enact the whole person and thus reach those without such cognitive capacities with the story of the gospel. For a developed argument, see Amos Yong, *Theology and Down Syndrome: Reimagining Disability in Late Modernity* (Waco: Baylor University Press, 2007), 203–15.

Good Friday having been enacted in a way that still lingers, almost oppressively. They will not gather again until Easter morn, when the darkened sanctuary will be ablaze with light and lilies in resurrection splendor. But for now they depart in heaviness to endure that dark Saturday between.

As you can perhaps imagine, the Tenebrae service has a much greater impact on my children than the long sermon on atonement. And as you also might expect, it tends to have much more impact on the adults too! Why is that? Because the heavy affectivity of the Tenebrae service—its ability to communicate Good Friday almost directly to our body, as it were—touches our gut, our embodied *kardia*. And *that* is something shared by all of us, including those who are either uninclined or unable to engage in theological abstractions. Historic Christian worship is fundamentally formative because it educates our hearts through our bodies (which in turn renews our mind), and does so in a way that is more universally accessible (and I would add, more universally effective) than many of the overly cognitive worship habits we have acquired in modernity. In this respect, Amos Yong rightly criticizes how Protestant worship has tended to configure Christian initiation and discipleship. "This is especially problematic in Protestantism," he notes,

> with its conviction that salvation is effectively mediated through "knowledge" (of theological or doctrinal content) and that the catechetical process should be focused on cognitively imparting such knowledge to those seeking Christian initiation. However, we have now insisted that this Platonic and Cartesian anthropology is faulty precisely because of its subordination of the body. . . . Insofar as the Hebrew *yada* refers more to the knowledge of the heart than the head, Protestants can now learn from Catholic and Orthodox traditions, especially with regard to how human knowing of God is mediated through formation, imitation, affectivity, intuition, imagination, interiorization, and symbolic engagement.[8]

Because all human beings are more fundamentally affective than cognitive, such is true for all Christian worship. Emphasizing the primacy of worship practices to worldview formation honors the fact that all humans are desiring animals while at the same time making sense of how Christian worship is developmentally significant for those who can participate in rituals but are unable to participate in theoretical reflection. In short, it helps us make sense of the moving testimony of someone like "Judy," a mentally challenged adult who eagerly confessed:

> I want to eat Jesus bread. . . . I can't wait until I can eat Jesus bread and drink Jesus juice. People who love Jesus are the ones who eat Jesus bread.
> . . . Jesus' skin and meat turned into bread and Jesus' blood and guts turned into juice—that's Jesus' bread and Jesus' juice, and I want to eat it and drink with all the other Christians at church 'cause I love him so.[9]

8. Ibid., 208.
9. Cited in ibid., 193.

Responding to such a testimony with a didactic conversation aimed at theological correction would be a colossal adventure in missing the point. A better response would be to worship together at the table, eating Jesus bread and drinking Jesus juice together, opening ourselves up to the Spirit's transformative power.

So if we want to discern the shape of a Christian worldview, it is crucial that we recall the priority of liturgy to doctrine. Doctrines, beliefs, and a Christian worldview emerge *from* the nexus of Christian worship practices; worship is the *matrix* of Christian faith, not its "expression" or "illustration."[10] Just as Taylor emphasized that "humans operated with a social imaginary well before they ever got into the business of theorizing about themselves,"[11] so too did Christians worship before they got around to abstract theologizing or formulating a Christian worldview. And developmentally, our orientation to the world is still more fundamentally shaped by embodied liturgical practices than doctrinal disquisitions (which is precisely why secular liturgies often trump our imaginations). The practices of the church as the gathered people of the coming king precede the formulas and codes that would later emerge from their theoretical reflection. Before Christians had systematic theologies and worldviews, they were singing hymns and psalms, saying prayers, celebrating the Eucharist, sharing their property, and becoming a people marked by a desire for God's coming kingdom—a desire that constituted them as a peculiar people in the present.

10. The argument I'm making here also has curricular import for seminary education: rather than being an addendum or foray in "applied" theology, liturgical training and "practical theology" should be at the center of the theological curriculum, displacing the privileged place of "systematic" theology. "Systematics" should be seen as an explication of the grammar of Christian worship. Something like this intuition is expressed in the structure and logic of *The Blackwell Companion to Christian Ethics*, ed. Stanley Hauerwas and Samuel Wells (Oxford: Blackwell, 2006).

11. Charles Taylor, *Modern Social Imaginaries* (Durham, NC: Duke University Press, 2004), 26.

# 5

## Common Prayer

SHANE CLAIBORNE,
JONATHAN WILSON‑HARTGROVE, AND ENUMA OKORO

There are so many different divisions of Christianity—Greek, Russian, and Serbian Orthodox, Roman Catholic, Anglican, Reformed, Presbyterian, Baptist and Anabaptist, African Methodist Episcopal, Pentecostal, nondenominational, Mennonite, and Quaker. By one count, there are more than thirty-eight thousand Christian denominations. Many people have said that the greatest barrier to becoming a Christian is all the division they see in the church.

God's deepest longing is for the church to be united as one body. In Jesus's longest recorded prayer, he prayed that we would be "one as God is one." As one old preacher said, "We gotta get it together, because Jesus is coming back, and he's coming for a bride, not a harem."

God has only one church.

This prayer book is the result of a collaboration of people from many different branches of Christianity, all of which come from one trunk if you trace the branches all the way back.

Folks are bound to ask if this prayer book is for Catholics or for Protestants. Our answer is, "Yes, it is." We want the fire of the Pentecostals, the imagination of the Mennonites, the Lutherans' love of Scripture, the Benedictines' discipline, the wonder of the Orthodox and Catholics. We've mined the fields of church history for treasures and celebrated them wherever we've found them. We've drawn on some of the oldest and richest traditions of Christian prayer. And we've tried to make them dance.

Our prayer lives connect us to the rest of the body of Christ around the world; at any hour of any day, many of the prayers in this book are being prayed in some corner of the earth. Using these prayers is also a way of connecting ourselves to the past; we're talking about the greatest hits not just from the 1960s, '70s, and '80s but also from the 1800s and the 300s. Many of these prayers and songs are more than a thousand years old.

## A Word about Liturgy

*Liturgy* comes from the Greek word *leitourgia*, meaning "public worship." When we hear the phrase *public worship*, many of us think of large meetings, like Sunday morning services, and while public worship *can* mean that, it doesn't have to take place in a big group. After all, *public* shares the same root word as *pub*, and it really just refers to a gathering of people to share life (and maybe a drink), a get-together that's always open to strangers joining us. Jesus promised that wherever two or three of us gather in his name, he'll be there with us. Jesus will be with us at the "pub" whether there's wine or not (and if not, he might conjure some up, or conjure up grape juice for the Baptists).

For those of us who are new to liturgy, it's noteworthy that, though there are some variations among different traditions, a majority of Christian liturgies around the world share an overall structure—especially the liturgies of Catholics, Anglicans, Lutherans, Presbyterians, and Methodists. It has been said that if the covers were removed from the major worship books of the late twentieth century, it would be difficult to tell which book belongs to which church body. The major traditions follow pretty much the same script.

When we first experience the organized cycle of readings that is a part of liturgical worship—a lectionary, as it's often called—it can seem like magic or a conspiracy. We may hear a pastor preach from the same text we read in morning prayer and think, "How in the world? The Spirit must be moving!" And, in fact, the Spirit is moving, just in a more organized way than we would have guessed. Some liturgical types smile when evangelicals discover the "miracle" of the liturgy. But it is a miracle nonetheless. So lean in and listen as you pray these prayers. Sometimes it may feel like you can hear the church's heartbeat as you pray in a way you never have before.

The readings of the church are arranged in a three-year cycle so that we hear the entire biblical story—creation and fall, the exodus, captivity and return, the promise and advent of the Messiah, the coming of the Holy Spirit, and the promise of the coming kingdom. These cycles are used all over the world, so that on the same day, Christians in Africa are reading the same texts as Christians in Latin America. Since *Common Prayer* is designed to be repeated each year, we have done our best to honor these cycles, though we've squeezed them into only one year of readings.

Participating in the liturgy of the worldwide Christian community, whether on a Sunday morning or at another time, is more than attending a service or a prayer meeting. It is about entering a story. It is about orienting our lives around what God has been doing throughout history. And it is about being sent forth into the world to help write the next chapter of that story.

Wandering the world in search of meaning and purpose, we may not even realize how desperately we need a story. But we know we've found something priceless when we find ourselves in God's narrative.

Liturgy is not about getting indoctrinated. Doctrines are hard things to love.

It's not even really about education. Liturgy at its core is not about learning facts and memorizing phrases.

Liturgy is soul food. It nourishes our souls just as breakfast strengthens our bodies. It's sort of like family dinner. Hopefully you get some nutritious food, but more than nutrition, family dinner is about family, love, community. Liturgy is kind of like family dinner with God. Liturgical theologian Aidan Kavanagh says it well: "The liturgy, like the feast, exists not to educate but to seduce people into participating in common activity of the highest order, where one is freed to learn things which cannot be taught."[1]

While liturgy is a party, it's also about disciplining our spirits like we exercise our muscles. Certainly we are learning as we pray, as we listen to Scripture, as we learn the songs and stories. But we are also participating in the work of God—active prayer, active worship. As we will see, liturgy offers us an invitation not just to observe but to participate. "O Lord, let my soul rise up to meet you" invites us to respond, "As the day rises to meet the sun." When we hear, "God is good," we want to call back, "All the time." Liturgy is a dialogue, a divine drama in which we are invited to be the actors. We become a part of God's story. We sing God's songs. We discover lost ancestors. And their story becomes our story.

## Welcome to a Whole New World

Liturgy is a workout for the imagination, because we are invited to see the reality of the universe through a new lens. Liturgy offers us another way of seeing the world. The liturgical imagination is different from the imagination of films or video games, though every once in a while you catch a film that gives you a hint of another world (like Neo takes the red pill in *The Matrix*).

---

1. Aidan Kavanagh, *Elements of Rite: A Handbook of Liturgical Style* (Collegeville, MN: Liturgical Press, 1990), 28.

In *Common Prayer* we enter a counterintuitive story. *Common Prayer* helps us to see ourselves as part of a holy counterculture, a people being "set apart" from the world around us (and the world inside) to bear witness that another world is possible. We're invited to become a peculiar people, living into a different story, and orienting our lives around a different set of values than those we are taught by the empires and markets around us. In an individualistic culture, liturgy helps us have a communal life. In an ever-changing world, liturgy roots us in the eternal—something that was around long before us and will live long after us, a God who is the same yesterday and today and tomorrow, no matter what happens on Wall Street.

Liturgy's counterintuitive nature may feel a little culturally strange at first. It is weird enough in our culture just to get together to sing songs (unless you are going to a concert or playing Rock Band on the Wii). Singing and praying together can feel awkward, especially if it is not Thanksgiving or Christmas. But liturgy is meant to be an interruption. It disrupts our reality and refocuses on God. It reshapes our perceptions and lives with new rhythms, new holy days, a whole new story.

What we discover is not just a poetic genius behind the words but a community in, with, and under the words. Just as people of the world pledge allegiance to flags or sing national anthems with pride and adoration, these creeds, songs, and prayers are ways that we proclaim our allegiance and sing our adoration not to a nation but to another kingdom altogether. That may sound a little esoteric or ethereal, like heaven is less real than the stuff of earth. But liturgy actually draws us out of counterfeit power and splendor and into another reality. As we pray, this world, with its billboards and neon signs and false promises, becomes ghostlike. We are invited into an ancient and eternal place and time that transcends all that is around us.

Worship is not about God needing us, as if our love and admiration were necessary for God to feel complete. God is not codependent. The beauty of it is not that God needs us but that God wants us. The love of God is so big that it is spilled over into the creation of man and woman. The love of the Trinity is so big that we were created to share in the community of God. And we are in the image of that love. If loving communion is at the core of the Trinity, then it is also the core of who we are. "Who am I?" cannot be answered without asking, "Who are we?" We cannot properly know ourselves until we properly conceive of God and our neighbor.

Liturgy invites us into a new "we." The church reflects the most diverse community in the world—white, black, and all shades in between, rich and poor, all walks of life. We are called to bring our lives and our cultures together to become a new community.

The world the liturgy reveals may not seem relevant at first glance, but it turns out that the world the liturgy reveals is more real than the one we inhabit day by day. It outlasts McDonald's and Walmart, America and South Africa. The songs and readings and prayers of the liturgy are more ancient and true than any culture or empire.

The liturgy presents a form of worship that transcends our time and place. It does not negate culture but creates a new one. Certainly we can see the fingerprints of the cultures from which it has come—Mediterranean, Greco-Roman, North African, German, Frankish, Anglo-Saxon. But we are formed into a people who are singing songs and prayers that transcend place and nation. Though its forms may vary, the liturgy will never grow old. It has been meaningfully prayed by bakers, housewives, tailors, teachers, philosophers, priests, monks, kings, slaves, and revolutionaries for centuries.

This is the story of the Israelites. Their story is our story. The God who saved the Hebrew children saves us today. When we say "Father Abraham," it does not need to feel like artificial words on paper; it can feel like we are discovering lost relatives. Abraham and Sarah are our grandparents. And their God is our God. God is the same yesterday, today, and forevermore. When we say in the Apostles' Creed (one of the oldest declarations of our faith) that we believe in "the communion of saints," we are saying that we are in community with those who have gone before and with those who will come after. We are one in Christ, a union so strong and eternal that nothing can separate us, not even death, and certainly not time or space.

In prayer and worship, we can feel like we are transported to another place, taken into another world. When we say, "O Lord, let my soul rise up to meet you," we are ascending beyond this world and all that is temporary. It is not an escape. Just the opposite—it is a warning not to escape from the eternal into the stuff of earth. In liturgical prayer, we are never alone, because we are surrounded by the thousands of folks who are singing and praying with us around the world. And as we pray, we are lifted up into a place beyond the building or city we are in. We are living in the "city of God," which isn't something you can find with a GPS.

## Welcome to a New Time Zone

Every sturdy society has created its own calendar according to its own values. For some time now, Western civilization has used the Julian and Gregorian calendars, which are influenced largely by the Roman Empire's traditions ("August" referring to Caesar Augustus and "January" referring to the god Janus, etc.). The United States' civil religion uses this calendar, mixing in its own set of holy days, most notably its date of inception (July 4) and its remembrances of human sacrifice (Memorial Day and Veterans Day). Consumer culture always threatens to monopolize the feast days on which the church remembers saints like Nicholas, Valentine, and Patrick, turning them into little more than days to buy stuff in the name of cultural idols such as Santa, the Easter bunny, and green leprechauns. Too often we have forgotten the lives of the people for whom these days are named.

But if we in the church are going to take our citizenship in heaven seriously, we must reshape our minds by marking our calendars differently. We must remember the holidays of the biblical narrative rather than the festivals of the Caesars, and celebrate feast days to remember saints rather than war heroes and presidents. Our inception as the church was on Pentecost, not on July 4. Our fireworks should go off a few months earlier than America's. And instead of commemorating people who sacrifice themselves in order to kill for their country, we find a deeper and more powerful observance on Good Friday, when we remember that Jesus willingly died for everyone in the world, even his enemies, instead of killing them to "change the world."

Or consider our holy season of Epiphany, when the church celebrates the civil disobedience of the magi, who, coming from outside of Caesar's realm, honored a different kind of king and sneaked away from the violent Herod. One of our lesser-known holidays is the Feast of the Holy Innocents (December 28), when the church remembers Herod's genocide of children in his attempt to root out any would-be incumbents. On such a day, we take in the harsh truth that there was and still is a political cost to the incarnation of God's peaceable love. Such a holy feast day of mourning provokes our own political memory and prompts us to communally and publicly remember the Iraqis (around one million) who have died since the US invasion in 2003. On such a day, we don't consider those deaths to be the necessary sacrifice of "collateral damage"; we lament their deaths as acts of our contemporary Herods.

Many of us have learned history by studying wars and violence; we organize it by the reigns of kings and presidents. But in Jesus, we reorder history. We date it from his visit to earth and examine it through a new lens—identifying with the tortured, the displaced, the refugee, and remembering the nonviolent revolutions on the margins of empires.

We enter a new time zone, where it can feel like there is a "cloud of witnesses" surrounding us, praying for us, cheering us on from eternity. It should feel like we are singing "Holy, Holy, Holy" with all the people of God who have come before us. And our own pasts become bigger than ourselves. The day the "world changed" was not September 11 but way back in AD 33. The most significant event in our pasts is not our most shameful transgressions but the death and resurrection of Jesus. Our pasts are defined not by our sins but by Christ's victory. God's story is the lens through which we understand our current world. It affects how we interact with evil and how we hold our possessions. The future, like the past, is no longer held hostage. We are no longer defined by the anxieties of our age. We know how the story ends, and it is beautiful. This is the good news that transcends the nightly news. Even more certain than who the next president will be is the reality that Christ will come again.

Our lives are filled with overlapping calendars and dates. For some folks, football season is the favorite time of year, and everything must give way for *Monday Night Football*. Football has its holy days and landmark moments, its hall of fame (and hall of shame). For those of us who are following the way of Jesus, part of what we do is orient our lives around a different calendar and history. (That's not to say you can't watch a good football game from time to time.)

The worldwide church has its holy days, as you will see in the morning prayers—days such as Presentation, the Annunciation, the Visitation, and the Transfiguration. These are our holidays. We also have our own hall of fame (and hall of shame).[2] There will be days when we highlight different women and men throughout church history (often the days they died). They are exemplary models of Christian discipleship from around the world and across centuries, and they're just really fascinating people who have lived well. It is our hope that their lives and courage will inspire us, and rub off on us, as they point us to Christ. In their imperfect but beautiful lives, we can see our own possibilities and potential.

The church's calendar weaves in and out of the world around us. It is not that we need a "Christian" calendar because we want to separate ourselves from the "secular" world, similar to the way that some Christians adamantly listen only to "Christian" music or have "Christian" T-shirts or bumper stickers or even iPods shaped like a cross. (There really is such a thing as a cross-shaped iPod, by the way!) The point is not to be sectarian or to try to put ourselves at odds with non-Christians. The point is to keep God's story at the center of our lives and calendar. And it is through the lens of Jesus that we read history and interpret whether an event is good or bad. It is important to note that many of the dates on the Christian calendar have their basis in the world's calendar. For instance, the date of Easter has little to do with the actual day on which Jesus rose from the grave, but it is the first Sunday after the first full moon on or after the spring equinox. It's interesting to note too that the natural seasons also teach us about God, even though in Australia it's summer during Advent. (So they go to the beach on Christmas rather than sit by the fire.) But as we build our lives around God's story, we are reminded that this story is the center of the universe.

Much of the church has created a life with common prayer as the center. Our days begin in the evening as we light the Christ candle in darkness, then continue when we greet the morning with resurrection praise and later come back to prayer at noon to center ourselves in the midst of our activity. (And by doing so, we proclaim, "Christ has died. Christ is risen. Christ will come again.") Morning and evening prayer are the touchstones of common prayer, going all the way back to ancient Judaism. The *Didache*, a collection of practical instructions for the early church, instructs believers to say the Lord's Prayer three times a day. But some monastic communities have taken quite literally the psalm that says "seven times a day do I praise thee." They even get up once in the middle of the night to pray together.

The daily cycle of evening, morning, and midday prayer is like a heartbeat for the global church, passing from one time zone to the next each day, so that we as a people can, as the apostle Paul taught us, pray without ceasing. But this daily

2. Because of space limitations, we were not able to include a complete list of saints from every tradition, but we did our best to celebrate the women and men who beautifully represent the faith and global church by their witness. Besides, there are many saints who have not yet been recognized as such and others just being born. Feel free to add your own saints and heroes to the list, and let's keep sharing their stories with one another.

rhythm is but a "wheel within a wheel" of the weekly cycle, which begins on Sunday (Resurrection Day), remembers Jesus gathering the twelve disciples on Thursday, suffers with Christ symbolically on Friday (hence many Christians fast), and makes preparation on Saturday for the great feast after resurrection. And that brings us back to "do, a deer, a female deer." Then we do it all again, and again. *Common Prayer* honors this weekly rhythm in its seven-day cycle of evening prayers.

But the weekly cycle also happens within an annual rhythm of seasons—Advent prepares us for Christ's coming, Christmas celebrates the Prince of Peace, Epiphany to remember the Light (a light outsiders often recognize before we do), Lent to confess our resistance to the Light, Holy Week to remember Christ's suffering, Easter to celebrate resurrection's power, the birthday of the church at Pentecost (a good time for pyrotechnics—be careful), and Ordinary Time to bring us back to the beginning again. These are our seasons in the church.

This peculiar way of counting time teaches us to look at our days differently. No longer do we see dates simply as August 29 or October 4. Now they are John the Baptist's day and St. Francis of Assisi's day. No longer are our seasons simply fall and spring; they are also Advent and Lent. Our history is different from the history told by nations and empires; our heroes are not pioneers of colonialism and capitalism like Columbus and Rockefeller but pioneers of compassion like Mother Teresa and Oscar Romero. And our holy days are different from the holidays of pop culture and the dominatrix of power.

The rhythms of the liturgy are not so much something that has been created as they are something that has been discovered over the centuries. Many of our current patterns of prayer and worship began to take shape as early as the second century. Especially in ancient oral cultures, they were ways of remembering the story. And in a world of Twitter and blogs and text messages, these words and songs and prayers feel more rooted and eternal than the virtual truth that is here today and gone tomorrow.

The church calendar begins not on January 1 but with Advent, four weeks before Christmas (*Advent* means "the coming"), as the world waits, pregnant with hope. So you'll notice our morning prayers begin at the end of the world's calendar year (in December) because we begin with the birth of our Savior Jesus, around whom the entire calendar and world revolve. Everything in the kingdom of God is upside down and backward—the last are first and the first are last; the poor are blessed and the peacemakers are the children of God; and the year begins with Advent rather than with New Year's Day.

The church calendar does not help us remember our meetings, but it aims at nothing less than changing the way we experience time and perceive reality. The church calendar does not help us remember sports events or weather cycles, but it is about the movement of history toward a glorious goal—God's kingdom on earth as it is in heaven.

Select any day of the year and you can find its liturgical significance. In fact, one of the cool things about the Christian calendar is that every day is a holy day.

Holidays are not just days off work but days you remember God's redemptive work in the world.

We also realize that we are not called to be so heavenly minded that we are of no earthly good. We are not to ignore the calendar that the rest of the world lives by, but we are to hold our calendar alongside it and to realize that all of history hinges on the death and resurrection of Jesus two thousand years ago. For this reason, just as we begin morning prayers remembering saints and holy days, we also remember significant dates in world history—dates that mark great strides for freedom or grave injustices we dare not forget.

As we look at the Christian calendar, we are reminded that we are in the world but not of it. We are citizens of the kingdom that transcends time, but we sojourn on a time-bound earth. Without liturgical time, we can easily forget our eternal identity. We can get lost in the hustle and bustle of business and efficiency that shapes our culture and society. Likewise, without the cosmic calendar, we can become so heaven-bound that we ignore the hells of the world around us. And the glorious goal we are headed toward is not just going up when we die but bringing God's kingdom down—on earth as it is in heaven.

### Why *Common* Prayer?

No doubt, we can pray to God ourselves; for centuries both monks and evangelicals (and lots of people in between) have prayed solitarily. There is something beautiful about a God who is personal, who talks face-to-face with Moses, wrestles with Jacob, and becomes fully human in Jesus, a God who needs no mediation, with whom we can speak as a Friend and Lover at any moment and in any place, in a cathedral or an alleyway.

The point is not to take away from the intimacy each of us has with God. Personal or devotional prayer and communal prayer are not at odds with each other. In fact, they must go together. Just as God is communal, God is also deeply personal and intimate.

Certainly one of the unique and beautiful things about Jesus is his intimacy with God as he runs off to the mountaintop or hides away in the garden. Jesus daringly invites us to approach the God of the universe as Abba (Daddy) or as a mother caring for her little chicks. Our God is personal and wildly in love with each of us.

Some friends who have experienced only liturgical worship and prayer are moved to tears by the childlike winsomeness of charismatics and Pentecostals as they pray with such sincerity and honesty, with tears and holy laughter. That kind of prayer is a gift to the church and has much to offer liturgical types, just as liturgy has much to offer Pentecostals.

Just because our prayer lives are personal does not mean they are private. Many of us have grown up in a culture where rampant individualism has affected our prayer lives. When we think about prayer, our imaginations may be limited to evening devotions or a daily "quiet time" with God. As wonderful as these times of solitude can be, prayer moves us beyond what we can do on our own.

It's certainly possible for people to customize their religion, sort of like the "create your own pizza" menu at a restaurant. Ironically, both conservative evangelicals and liberal New Agers often fall into the same temptation to create a religion that is very self-centered—and very lonely. You can be religious and still be lonely. But part of the good news is that we are not alone. If we see prayer only as a private affair, we miss out. To talk with God is to get caught up in conversation with brothers and sisters we didn't know we had.

There is something to this idea that "when two or three of you gather in my name, I will be with you." Prayer is a communal practice.

There is a reason the Lord's Prayer is a communal prayer to "our" Father, asking for "our" daily bread and asking God to forgive us "our" sins as we forgive others. Our God is a communal God. It is not enough to pray for "my" daily bread alone.

The gift of liturgy is that it helps us hear less of our own little voices and more of God's still, small voice (Ps. 46). It leads away from self and points us toward the community of God. God is a plurality of oneness. God has "lived in community" from eternity as Father, Son, and Holy Spirit. God as Trinity is the core reality of the universe, and that means that the core of reality is community. We often live as if the essence of our being is the "I," and as if the "we" of community is a nice add-on or an "intentional" choice. But the truth is we are made for community, and if we live outside of community, we are selling ourselves short. We are made in the image of community.

## Praying with the Saints

To be sure, there is a history in the church of monastic[3] folks who live in caves and monasteries and seek God in solitude. The funny thing is that these holy hermits pray the same prayers, read the same cycles of readings, and sing the same chants as everyone else. Like birds in the forest, monks all sing the same song. In fact, there was an old saying: "If monks stop praying, the world will collapse."

Even when they pray by themselves, they know they are not really alone.

We never pray alone, even when praying by ourselves. The prayers and songs in this book are designed to be prayed together, but if you are not physically with others, rest assured that there are others praying with you around the world. It is

---

3. *Monasticism* comes from the Greek word *monazein*, meaning "to live alone," and often we think of monastics as folks who live in seclusion from the rest of the world in a pious monastery or convent. But correctly understood, monastics are not fleeing the world so much as they are trying to save the world from itself, beginning with what they can change—themselves. The *mono-* at the beginning of *monastic* means "one," and we can think of monastics as folks who have committed their lives to "one thing"—the single-minded pursuit of God, like the person in Jesus's parable who gives everything for the most precious pearl ever seen. That is what it means to be monastic—to will one thing and to run after Jesus as our Lover, saying no to everything that might divide our attention or take our eyes off the Pearl.

impossible to feel alone when we pray these prayers, even when we pray them by ourselves. We are praying prayers crafted not by our lonely piety but by the entire body of Christ throughout her history. We are praying prayers whose origin is in another time and place, going all the way back to the early church, and thus we are mysteriously connected with believers who have gone before us. So while we hope *Common Prayer* is fresh and alive for you, it is not new. It may only seem new because of how much of our history we have lost or misplaced. In this book, we discover lost memories and treasures from the past, digging up amid all the clutter of Christendom old pictures and keepsakes from our ancestors and wiping the dust away.

There is a new "we." If our citizenship is in heaven, this truth should change the way we talk. The word *we*, if a person is truly born again, will refer to the new people into whom a Christian has been born—the church. Christians can no longer refer to "our troops" or "our history" as other people do, because of our new identity. Fabricated boundaries and walls are removed for the Christian. Our neighbor is not only from Chicago but also from Baghdad. Our brother or sister in the church could be from Iran or California—no difference! Our family is transnational and borderless; we are in Iraq, and we are in Palestine. And if we are indeed to become born again, we will have to begin talking like it, changing the meaning of *we*, *us*, *my*, and *our*.

We must connect our prayers to the rest of God's children throughout the world and through all time and space, people who are reading the same Scriptures, singing the same songs, praying the same prayers, and grafting their lines into the same old story of a God who is forming a people who are set apart from the world to be God's light and to show the world what a society of love looks like. Today, more than ever before in history, we have a keen sense of what it means to be a part of a global neighborhood. We are aware of how beautifully diverse and terribly dysfunctional the human family is. As we pray through this book together, we are reminded that we have friends in Sudan and China, Afghanistan and Iraq, Palestine and Israel, whether they are our Facebook friends or not. They are praying with us. And the bond we have in Christ is more real than any virtual social network. This is what it means to be born again. We are a part of a global neighborhood and a beautifully diverse family of God's children.

### What about When You're Not Feeling It?

Sometimes all you have to do is show up. You may not feel like praying. Others will pray, and perhaps their prayers will welcome yours. It is not that others pray for us or that their voices replace our voices, but there is something that can spark in us when we are surrounded by others whose hearts are on fire. Hot coals build a better fire when they are together. There is a harmony that cannot exist when we go solo. To be sure, there is a place for solos and for a cappella, but there is also something about a mass choir or mass prayer that gets our spirits soaring.

Liturgy is public worship, but it is also, more literally, the "work of the people." *Common Prayer* isn't so much an "inspirational" text as it is a workout guide. Liturgy is active. It takes patience (part of the fruit of the Spirit, by the way). And patience is very countercultural. Sometimes we don't feel like working out our bodies, but after the first few steps, we feel our bodies start to breathe, and we can feel our heartbeat, which had grown quiet and lethargic. Liturgy is not simply about watching or listening; it's about participating. You can sit back with a bowl of popcorn and watch all the exercise videos you want, but nothing will happen until you get off the couch and start sweatin' to the oldies.

In many ways, the "official" liturgy can't work for each of us if we're not doing things to stay in shape outside the fixed hours for prayer. Study, discipleship, the works of mercy, and contemplation are the homework assignments that prepare us for the experience of worship and prayer together. Otherwise, it can feel like we are being invited to laugh at a joke we haven't even heard yet. How can you worship unless you have spent some time falling in love? If *Common Prayer* doesn't work for you right away, hang in there and give the divine romance a chance.

But also, a disclaimer: the liturgy is not a magic formula. And you can have liturgy without life in it, just as you can have a nice-looking car that doesn't run. Some of the dreariest services on the planet are rich with liturgy and traditions.

Liturgy is one of the most powerful places to meet and be transformed by God. It is also one of the best places to hide—from God and others. So may it be a doorway into deeper relationship with God and with others. If it's not, may you keep knocking until you find a door that opens.

. . . . . . . . . . . . . . . . . . . . . . . . . . .

# PART TWO

# Putting On Christ

*Formation in Virtue*

. . . . . . . . . . . . . . . . . . . . . . . . . . .

JAMES K. A. SMITH

In the introduction we emphasized that the conversation between science and theology "takes practice." The reason we talk about "practices" is that we also are concerned with *virtue*. Virtues are habits and dispositions (character traits) that dispose us toward certain ends, certain *goods*. Virtues, in short, are good habits that reflect the goods that are modeled by Jesus Christ and admonished in Scripture (see, e.g., Col. 3:12–16). From Aristotle to Aquinas, philosophers and theologians have emphasized that the virtues (good habits) are acquired in two ways. On the one hand, we learn to be virtuous by imitating exemplars, by following the example of those who embody virtue. This is how we can understand Paul's injunctions to imitate him because he imitates Christ (1 Cor. 11:1) or Thomas à Kempis's spiritual classic, *The Imitation of Christ*.

On the other hand, the virtue tradition also emphasizes that we acquire the virtues through practice. It is in this context that we talk about "practices" in the plural: practices are rhythms and routines that inscribe in us those good habits we call the virtues.

Much of the current discussion of practices is indebted to the work of Alasdair MacIntyre, particularly in his now-classic work, *After Virtue*, in which he emphasizes that what counts as a virtue is always relative to the *specification* of "the good," and such specifications of the good are communicated to us through the narratives of particular traditions. In this connection, MacIntyre also emphasizes the storied character of moral traditions by talking about them in terms of a "narrative." As he later puts it, "I can only answer the question, 'What am I to do?' if I can answer the prior question 'Of what story or stories do I find myself a part?'"[1]

Such habits and dispositions are not "natural" in the sense of being inborn capacities or abilities; rather, they are "second nature": acquired dispositions and inclinations that are absorbed over time through the routines and rituals of a tradition, as well as by imitating the models upheld as "exemplars" by the tradition. On this account, a moral "education" is not just a matter of getting the right information about my duties, obligations, and responsibilities; rather, moral education becomes a matter of *formation*—the inscription of good habits (virtue) as the construction of character. And such moral formation happens by means of practice. "Practices" are those social scripts and routines that inscribe virtue in its "practitioners." The most important upshot is that practices are *formative*: they are not just things that we do, they do something *to* us. Chapters 6 and 7 (by Kallenberg and MacIntyre, respectively) provide an introduction to this way of thinking.

It is this formative aspect of practices that has led Christian theologians to appropriate MacIntyre's definition to help us think about Christian worship, spiritual disciplines, and the dynamics of sanctification (becoming holy, becoming Christlike). In chapters 8, 9, 10, and 11 (by Wilson, DeYoung, Griffiths, and Wright, respectively) we see Christian philosophers and theologians fruitfully reframing sanctification and the adventure of becoming Christlike as an apprenticeship in virtue. This kind of ecclesial formation, we suggest, is the condition of possibility for wise, faithful, creative thinking at the intersection of theology and science, as well as a range of other challenging questions that Christians face in what Charles Taylor calls the "cross-pressured" space of our late modern world.

---

1. MacIntyre, *After Virtue: A Study in Moral Theory*, 3rd ed. (Notre Dame, IN: University of Notre Dame Press, 2007), 216.

# 6

## The Master Argument
## of MacIntyre's *After Virtue*

BRAD KALLENBERG

### What's All This Noise?

In September 1995 the Associated Press released a wire photo showing Russian lawmakers of both genders in a punching brawl during a session of the Duma, Russia's lower house of parliament.[1] Is this behavior an ethnic idiosyncrasy? Do only government officials duke it out over matters of great importance? Or have fisticuffs suddenly become politically correct? No, on all counts.

Pick a topic, any topic—abortion, euthanasia, welfare reform, military intervention in the Balkans—and initiate discussion with a group of reasonable, well-educated people and observe the outcome. Chaos ensues. Of course the volume of the debate may vary according to how "close to home" the issue hits the participants. But any moral discussion, given a group of sufficient diversity, has the potential of escalating into a shouting match . . . or worse.

---

Originally published as Brad Kallenberg, "The Master Argument of MacIntyre's *After Virtue*," in *Virtues and Practices in the Christian Tradition: Christian Ethics after MacIntyre*, ed. Nancey Murphy, Brad J. Kallenberg, and Mark Thiessen Nation (Notre Dame, IN: University of Notre Dame Press, 2003), 7–29. Copyright © 2003, University of Notre Dame Press. Reprinted with permission of University of Notre Dame Press.

1. Sergei Shargorodsky, "Russian Lawmakers Do Battle," *The Sun* (San Bernardino, CA), September 12, 1995, A5.

An even more striking feature of moral debates is their tendency *never* to reach resolution. Lines are drawn early, and participants rush to take sides. But in taking sides they appear to render themselves incapable of hearing the other. Everyone feels the heat, but no one sees the light.

Many thinkers are inclined to see *shrillness* and *interminability* as part and parcel of the nature of moral debate. But Alasdair MacIntyre begs to differ. In *After Virtue* he offers the "disquieting suggestion" that the tenor of modern moral debate is the direct outcome of a catastrophe in our past, a catastrophe so great that moral inquiry was very nearly obliterated from our culture and its vocabulary exorcised from our language. What we possess today, he argues, are nothing more than fragments of an older tradition. As a result, our moral discourse, which uses terms like *good*, and *justice*, and *duty*, has been robbed of the context that makes it intelligible. To complicate matters, although university courses in ethics have been around for a long time, no ethics curriculum predates this catastrophe. Therefore, for anyone who has taken ethics courses, and especially for those who have studied ethics diligently, the disarray of modern moral discourse is not only invisible, it is considered normal. This conclusion has been lent apparent credibility by a theory called *emotivism*.

Emotivism, explains MacIntyre, "is the doctrine that all evaluative judgments and more specifically all moral judgments are *nothing but* expressions of preference, expressions of attitude or feeling."[2] On this account, the person who remarks "Kindness is good" is not making a truth claim but simply expressing a positive feeling, "Hurrah for kindness!" Similarly, the person who exclaims "Murder is wrong" can be understood to be actually saying "I disapprove of murder" or "Murder, yuck!"

If emotivism is a true picture of the way moral discourse works, then we easily see that moral disputes can never be *rationally* settled because, as the emotivist contends, all value judgments are nonrational. Reason can never compel a solution; we simply have to hunker down and decide. Moral discussion is at best rhetorical persuasion.

There are sound reasons for questioning the emotivist picture. In the first place, emotivism is self-defeating insofar as it makes a truth claim about the non-truth-claim status of all purported truth claims! To put it differently, if all truth claims in the sphere of ethics are simply expressions of preference, as emotivism maintains, then the theory of emotivism itself lacks truth value, and thus we are not constrained to believe it if we prefer not to. In addition, emotivism muddies some ordinarily clear waters. Any proficient language speaker will attest to the fact that the sense of "I prefer . . ." is vastly different from the sense of "You ought . . ." The distinct uses to which we put these phrases is enabled precisely because the sense of "You ought" cannot be reduced without remainder to "I prefer."

---

2. Alasdair MacIntyre, *After Virtue*, 2nd ed. (Notre Dame, IN: University of Notre Dame Press, 1984), 11–12. Hereafter, page numbers in parentheses in the text refer to this book.

But MacIntyre is not content to offer first-order arguments against emotivism. Stopping there would have made his book simply another ethical theory—just the sort of thing that emotivism so convincingly dismisses. Instead, what MacIntyre is up to has been called *meta-ethics*—an exploration into the conditions (or conditioners) of human ethical thought. As a human enterprise, ethics must be shaped in the same way that language, culture, and history shape the rest of our thinking. By investigating the historical conditionedness of our moral life and discourse, MacIntyre undermines emotivism, making a strong case for its own historical conditionedness. Emotivism as a moral philosophy appears to explain why contemporary moral debates are irresolvable. But it cannot account for the oddity that rival positions within these debates all employ incommensurable concepts. Why cannot the Kantian ("The taking of human life is always and everywhere just plain wrong") concede even a modicum of legitimacy to the Lockean argument ("Abortion is the natural right of women") if both views boil down to "I don't/do approve of abortion"? Nor can emotivism explain the oddity that interminable moral debates are conducted with the expectation that such debates *can be* resolved and, in keeping with this optimism, are conducted in such a way that rival positions appeal to principles presumed to be ultimate. In other words, if all value judgments are expressive, how did this belief in ultimate principles arise? MacIntyre suggests that it makes more sense to look for a source of this optimism, and its belief in ultimates, in a tradition that predates emotivism.

In fact, if one looks closely at the modern moral self, it has the appearance of being dislocated, as if it were missing something. The moral self as conceived by the emotivist is "totally detached from all social particularity" and is, rather, "entirely set over against the social world" (32). This autonomous self has no given continuities, possesses no ultimate governing principles, and is guided by no *telos*. Instead it is aimless, having "a certain abstract and ghostly character" (33). If MacIntyre is correct in asserting that "the emotivist self, in acquiring sovereignty in its own realm, lost its traditional boundaries provided by a social identity and a view of human life as ordered to a given end," then it comes as no surprise that such a self flounders helplessly and endlessly in moral quagmires (33). But how did this catastrophe come to pass, and what exactly are the social identity and *telos* that were lost?

## The Failure of the Enlightenment Project

The catastrophe that left the modern moral world in such disarray was a series of failed attempts to provide *rational* justification of morality for a culture that had philosophy as its central social activity. This eighteenth-century culture was called the Enlightenment, and its misguided agenda MacIntyre dubs the Enlightenment Project.

Among the first attempts to justify morality were those of Denis Diderot (1713–84) and David Hume (1711–76). Diderot tried to make human desire the criterion of an action's rightness or wrongness but failed to answer how a conflict of desires, and hence a conflict between an action's rightness and wrongness, could be resolved. Like Diderot, Hume conceived human passion as the stuff of morality because it is passion, not reason, that ultimately moves the moral agent to act. Hume goes further than Diderot by specifying a ruling passion (he calls it "sympathy"), but he can provide sufficient explanation neither for why this passion ought to predominate nor for why his account of the moral life looks suspiciously like that of the English bourgeoisie he emulated.[3]

Provoked by the failures of Hume and Diderot to ground morality in human passion, Immanuel Kant (1724–1804) strove to ground morality in reason alone. He argued that if morality was rational, its form would be identical for all rational beings. Therefore, the moral thing to do is to follow those principles that can be universalized, that is, to follow those principles that one could consistently wish for everyone to follow. This sounds suspiciously like the Golden Rule. What makes it different, however, is Kant's conviction that the principle of universalizability (also called the *categorical imperative*) gets its punch from the requirement that it be willed without falling into *rational* contradiction.[4] Unfortunately, Kant's system has several large flaws, not the least of which is its ability to "justify" immoral maxims such as "Persecute all those who hold false religious beliefs" as well as trivial ones such as "Always eat mussels on Mondays in March" (46).

Søren Kierkegaard (1813–55) heartily agreed with the content of the morality that Kant defended (middle-class German Lutheran piety), but he also

---

3. Alasdair MacIntyre, *Whose Justice? Which Rationality?* (Notre Dame, IN: University of Notre Dame Press, 1988), 300–325.

4. This can be understood by means of the following illustration. Consider first the case where lying is simply speaking the opposite of the truth. A person faced with the question of whether to lie on a given occasion should easily realize that lying cannot be universalized without rational contradiction. For if everyone lied, then lying would become the normal mode of communication. If everyone always lied, we would simply adjust our expectations and hence could navigate just fine. For example, one day my eight-year-old son declined my offer of a peanut butter sandwich but then reminded me with a grin that Tuesday was "opposite day." Once I knew the plan, we had no trouble communicating because I could bank on the opposite of what he said. ("Do you like it?" "No, it's awful. I hate it!") Similarly, in a world where lying was the universal practice, deception could not exist because lying, in effect, would have become the means of truth telling. Of course, this would fly in the face of what we understand by the term *lying*. So we run headlong into a rational contradiction: lying cannot be universalized because, when universalized, lying ceases to be lying. Therefore, the opposite of lying must be universalizable; or to put it differently, truth telling is the categorical imperative.

Now imagine the case that lying is not simple opposite-saying but distortion of truth—a mixture of truth and error. It should be clear that the sort of confusion that would be produced by universalizing this brand of lying would be on the scale that disables all communication—including deception. In such a world "intent to deceive" has no meaning. So, once again, we run up against a rational contradiction: universalization of lying leads to the state of affairs in which what is universalized, i.e., lying, is logically impossible.

perceived that Kant's *rational* vindication of morality had failed as miserably as its predecessors. According to Kierkegaard, all persons are free to choose the plane of their existence. But this leaves open the problem of how to decide which plane to inhabit, since the criteria for making the decision are internal to the plane under consideration. Shall I inhabit the plane of the pleasure-seeking aesthete or that of the ethical rule-follower? To choose according to passion is to be relegated to the plane of the aesthetic. To choose according to reason is to have already chosen the ethical plane. Hence, neither passion nor reason can be the criterion for making the choice. The choice is a criterionless leap. MacIntyre concludes:

> Just as Hume seeks to found morality on the passions because his arguments have excluded the possibility of founding it on reason, so Kant founds it on reason because his arguments have excluded the possibility of founding it on the passions, and Kierkegaard on criterionless fundamental choice because of what he takes to be the compelling nature of the considerations which exclude both reason and the passions. (49)

So by Hume's standards Kant is unjustified in his conclusions; by Kant's standards Hume is both unjustified and unintelligible. By Kierkegaard's, both Hume and Kant are intelligible, but neither is compelling. The proof of the Enlightenment Project's failure is the stubborn existence of rival conceptions of moral justification.

## Why the Enlightenment Project Had to Fail

The important thing to realize is that the Enlightenment Project didn't simply happen to fail, it *had* to fail. What doomed the Enlightenment Project from its inception was its loss of the concept of *telos*. The word *telos* is borrowed from classical Greek and means "end" or "purpose." When applied to human morality the term signifies the answer to the question, "What is human life for?" In Aristotle's day (fourth century BC), moral reasoning was an argument consisting of three terms. The first term was the notion of the untutored human nature, which so desperately needed moral guidance. The second term was human nature conceived in terms of having fulfilled its purpose or achieved its *telos*. Moral imperatives, the third term, was that set of instructions for moving from the untutored self toward the actualized *telos* (see fig. 6.1). In this way moral precepts weren't snatched out of thin air but got their "punch" or their "oughtness" from the concrete notion of what human life was for.[5]

5. Admittedly, the Aristotelian model of morality makes moral imperatives appear hypothetical—as means to socially conceded ends—but theistic morality has the same basic shape. The primary difference

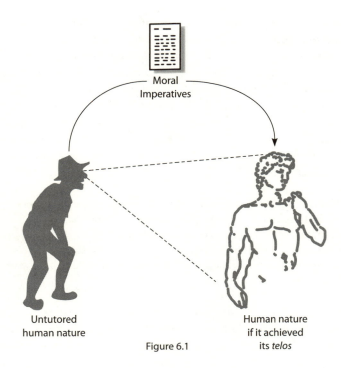

Figure 6.1

The wristwatch is a good example of how this works. If we ask, "What is the wristwatch for?," the usual answer is that watches are for timekeeping.[6] To put it more technically, we could say that the purpose or *telos* of the watch is time-keeping. Or, to put it in still other terms, we can say that the watch is *functionally defined* as a mechanism for keeping time. Knowledge of this *telos* enables us to render judgment against a grossly inaccurate watch as a "bad" watch. Furthermore, our functional definition also allows us to identify the functional imperative for watches: "Watches *ought* to keep time well."

Because the Enlightenment rejected the traditionally shared concept of what human life is for and started, as it were, from scratch by inventing the idea of humans as "autonomous individuals," the concept of *telos*, so very central to morality, was lost. Having rejected the received account of *telos*, the only remaining option upon which moral principles might be grounded was the *un*tutored human nature—the very thing in need of guidance and, by nature, at odds with those guiding principles (see fig. 6.2).

is that the theistic version contends that the human *telos* is divinely determined, a determination that has the effect of bestowing a categorical status on moral imperatives.

6. Of course, it could also be argued that watches make fashion statements, have sentimental value, and so forth. But for the sake of the illustration, let us imagine that watches are useful only for timekeeping.

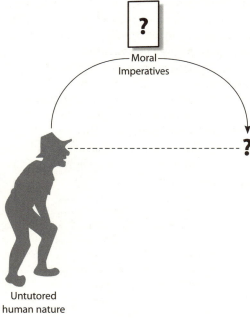

Figure 6.2

The results of the failure of the Enlightenment Project were far-reaching. First, without the notion of *telos* serving as a means for moral triangulation, moral value judgments lost their factual character. And, of course, if values are "factless," then no appeal to facts can ever settle disagreements over values. It is in this state of affairs that emotivism, with its claim that moral values were nothing but matters of preference, flourishes as a theory. Second, impostors stepped in to fill the vacuum created by the absence of *telos* in moral reasoning. For example, utilitarianism can be seen to offer a ghostly substitute when it asserts that morality operates according to the principle of *greatest good for greatest number*. But this principle is vacuous because the utilitarians who assert it cannot adequately define what "good" means.[7] Similarly, Kant tried to rescue the (newly) autonomous moral

7. Please note, however, that the situation in the wake of the Enlightenment Project's failure is far worse than merely a state of being unable to settle disagreements. MacIntyre argues that the disagreements themselves are wrongheaded in the first place. Seventeenth-century empiricists thought themselves adequate to the task of dealing with brute facts, when the truth of the matter is that facts cannot be perceived apart from a conceptual framework that recognizes, sorts, prioritizes, and evaluates the facts. Value-laden theory is required to support observation as much as vice versa. This insight was overlooked when, in the transition to the world of "modern" science, the medieval notion of final cause (i.e., causes that proceed according to *teloi*) was rejected in favor of making efficient causes the whole ball of wax. When this scientistic view becomes adopted by ethicists, what emerges is a mechanistic account of human action framed in terms of "laws of human behavior" with all reference to intentions, purposes, and reasons for action

agent from the loss of authority in his or her moral statements by attempting to provide "rational" justification for statements deprived of their former teleological status. Not only did Kant fail but later analytic philosophy cannot advance Kantian arguments without smuggling in undefined terms such as *rights* and *justice*. MacIntyre's point is that tradition alone provides the sense of terms like *good* and *justice* and *telos*. The presence of this moral vocabulary in debates today only goes to show that "modern moral utterance and practice can only be understood as a series of fragmented survivals from an older past and that the insoluble problems which they have generated for modern moral theories will remain insoluble until this is well understood" (110–11). In the absence of traditions, moral debate is out of joint and becomes a theater of illusions in which simple indignation and mere protest occupy center stage:

> But protest is now almost entirely that negative phenomenon which characteristically occurs as a reaction to the alleged invasion of someone's *rights* in the name of someone else's *utility*. The self-assertive shrillness of protest arises because the facts of incommensurability ensure that protesters can never win an argument; the indignant self-righteousness of protest arises because the facts of incommensurability ensure equally that the protesters can never lose an argument either. (71; cf. 77)

### Nietzsche or Aristotle?

MacIntyre concludes that we are faced with a momentous choice. The present emotivist world cannot be sustained much longer. Nietzsche saw this clearly. He argued convincingly that every time a person made an appeal to "objectivity," it was none other than a thinly disguised expression of the person's subjective will. When we look at post-Enlightenment ethics through Nietzsche's eyes, we can see that insofar as the Enlightenment Project offers putative moral principles (that is, ones that are devoid of the background context that gives them their clout), it creates a moral vacuum which will inevitably be filled by headstrong people asserting their individual will-to-power; and to the victor go the spoils. To put it differently, the emotivist world is neither stable nor self-sustaining. Rather, it is a battleground of competing wills awaiting the emergence of a conqueror. Once the Aristotelian model of morality was rejected and the Enlightenment Project had failed, the danger of an imminent *Übermensch* (who resembles Hitler more than Superman) must be conceded. The only stopper to this danger is the possibility

---

omitted. The "facts" of human behavior are thus construed free from value concepts (such as "good"), and human action is thereafter presumed to be predictable and manipulable like all other physical bodies. This presumption is embodied in the central character of the emotivist era: the bureaucratic manager. Unfortunately for the manager we do not possess lawlike generalizations for human behavior. In fact, human behavior is systematically unpredictable for a number of reasons. Both the expert manager and the attending virtue of "effectiveness" are fictions which expose the poverty of the Enlightenment Project. Cf. *After Virtue*, 93–99.

of recognizing that the Aristotelian model ought not to have been rejected in the first place. We are faced, then, with a momentous choice between Nietzsche and Aristotle. "There is no third alternative" (118).

## In Praise of Aristotle

In order for MacIntyre to make a case that the Aristotelian morality ought never to have been discarded, he must first demonstrate the strength of this moral tradition from its origin in Homeric literature to its full-blown Aristotelian-Thomistic form of the late Middle Ages.

### Heroic Society

Storytelling was the primary tool for moral education in classical Greece. It was for this reason that Homer's epic poems reflect the moral structure of their times. Not only does art reflect life, but literature in particular is the repository for moral stories, stories that have the peculiar ability of becoming embodied in the life of the community that cherishes them. This fact, that human life has the same shape as that of a story, will come up again in our discussion.

The moral structure of heroic society has two other outstanding features. First, morality has a social dimension. The social mobility that typifies our age was entirely absent in Homer's time. Then, one was born into a social structure that was fixed: "Every individual has a given role and status within the well-defined and highly determinate system of roles and statuses" (122). One's social place determined both the responsibility to render certain services to others (for example, it was incumbent on the head of the clan to defend and protect the clan) and the privileges one could expect from others in return. What one lacked in "upward mobility" was compensated by greater security. To know one's role and status in this small social system was to have settled forever the question, "Who am I?" In fact, no one ever thought of asking such existential questions in heroic society because who one was was indistinguishable from what one did. Within this social framework the word *virtue* (*aretē*) describes any quality that is required for discharging one's role. As the clan's warrior-defender, the head of the clan needed courage as well as physical strength and battle savvy. Courage is also intimately linked to another virtue, fidelity. Fidelity and courage become obligatory because the community can survive only if kinsmen can be relied upon to fight valiantly on each other's behalf should the need arise.

This highlights a third feature of the moral structure of heroic societies. Since morality is bound up with the social structure of the clan, questions about moral value are *questions of fact.* Just as what qualifies as a "right" move in the game of chess is predetermined by the agreed-upon object of the game, so, too, the morally acceptable "move" was easily identified for those who participated in the "game."

However, there was no way for a person in heroic society to step outside the moral "game" to evaluate it, as is possible with chess. "All questions of choice arise within the framework; the framework itself therefore cannot be chosen" precisely because the person who does try to step outside his or her given social position "would be engaged in the enterprise of trying to make himself [or herself] disappear" (126).

### Athenian Society

Life in Athens illustrates an important moment in the life of a moral tradition: growth comes through crisis. In large measure, morality was a subject that received a great deal of attention from the Athenians because of a perceived discrepancy between their moral "scriptures" (the Homeric literature) and life as they knew it. No Athenian could conceive of living like an Achilles or an Agamemnon. This does not illustrate that the heroic society had been mistaken about morality's *social* dimension, but rather, that the social structure since the days of Homer had undergone such a drastic change (with the emergence of the city-state, or *polis*) that morality had necessarily changed shape too. The changes in the social world had the effect of broadening the range of application of the concept of virtue. The term no longer denoted excellence in the performance of one's well-defined social roles (where excellence could be understood only from within such a role), but rather *virtues* signified qualities that were applicable to *human life in general* (or, at least, human life in Athens, which in their minds *was* human life par excellence). While the Athenians inherited the vocabulary of the virtues from heroic society, the content of these terms was up for grabs.

For example, the Sophists were inclined to see *virtue* as the generic name for those qualities that ensure successful living, and what counts for success was relative to each different city-state. When in Sparta, do as the Spartans do—treasure physical prowess and warcraft—but when in Athens do as the Athenians do and hanker after beauty and truth. In response to their appalling relativism, Plato charged the Sophists with failing to discern the difference between mundane virtues and "true" virtue. Plato is willing to grant that the virtues are the means to a happy life, but getting clear about the nature of "true" happiness (and "true" virtue) requires shifting one's focus from the earthly *polis* to contemplate instead the "ideal" world. Plato was convinced that this exercise in contemplation would show that true happiness is the satisfaction of having lived in accordance with one's true nature. Human nature, according to Plato, was composed of three parts. The highest part—that which participates most fully in the realm of the ideal—is the intellect and is assisted in its function by the virtue of wisdom. The lowest part—that which is shared with the beasts—is the desiring part and is to be constrained by the virtue of prudence. Between lies a motivational wellspring, or high-spirited part, which is assisted by the virtue of courage. A fourth virtue, justice, refers to the state of affairs when all three are in proper order with respect to each other. This set of four virtues is called *cardinal* (from the Latin *cardo*, which means "door hinge") because they are the qualities upon which the truly happy life hangs.[8]

It is important to remember that these two contemporaneous but varying conceptions of the virtues were attempts to align the concept of virtue with the purpose of life as understood in the newly broadened context—that of the *polis*. This broadening was the first movement toward the belief in a universal moral order, which finds clearer expression in Aristotle.

But Plato did not have the last word even in his own day. His package of virtues, together with the moral order it depicted, was all too neat. The tragic dramatists, such as Sophocles, explored the kinds of real conflicts that might arise *between* virtues or *between* goods. To put it differently, the moral order sometimes makes rival and incompatible claims on a person, which can force him or her into a tragic situation of having to make a choice between two or more socially incumbent duties, each of which entails dire consequences. In grappling with this conflict, the Sophoclean protagonist is forced to transcend his or her society while remaining inescapably accountable to the higher moral order.

Here, then, is not simply an argument over which of two lists of virtues is better (Achilles's courage or Oedipus's wisdom) but rather an argument over which narrative form (Homer's epic poetry or a Sophoclean tragedy) best depicts the form of human living. MacIntyre suggests a general lesson to be learned: "To adopt a stance on the virtues will be to adopt a stance on the narrative character of human life" precisely because narrative and virtues are mutually supporting and "internally connected" concepts (144).

### Aristotle's Model

To defend Aristotle as the apex of virtue theory, MacIntyre must make a characteristically un-Aristotelian move. He must show that Aristotle lies along the historical trajectory that begins with Homeric literature and is, therefore, indebted to and dependent upon his predecessors.[9] Furthermore, MacIntyre must show

---

8. Plato goes on to argue that society is, or ought to be, arranged along the same lines. The bronze class of society are those working folk whose citizenship is assisted by the virtue of prudence. The silver class comprises the warriors, in whom the high-spirited part of the soul dominates. The quality they need above all is courage. The gold class, of course, is made up of the philosopher-kings, whose role in society is not merely to rule but to contemplate truth with the aid of the virtue of wisdom. Social justice, in Plato's view, signified keeping the classes in the proper order, which amounted to maintaining the status quo. In this way Plato's system is by nature conservative: change (including progress) was bad; stability was good.

9. Frederick Copleston notes that Aristotle, like Hegel, saw himself to be systematizing and improving upon previous philosophy. See *A History of Philosophy*, 9 vols. (New York: Doubleday, 1985), 1:371–78. Yet while Aristotle appreciated his Platonic heritage, he conceived his own work in terms of "getting it right" in those places Plato "got it wrong." What is un-Aristotelian, therefore, is MacIntyre's historicist claim that Aristotle's work lies along a trajectory that stretches from Plato to the Middle Ages and beyond, a claim that necessarily relativizes Aristotle's contribution to the conceptual framework he shared with his predecessors. Thus the "new ground" Aristotle broke must be seen as nothing more than intrasystematic improvements.

that Aristotle's formulation of moral philosophy has advanced beyond his predecessors while retaining characteristic features of the overall tradition. To do this
MacIntyre focuses on four features in Aristotle's thought.

First, the concept of a moral order, which began to emerge in Plato's thinking, becomes more explicit in Aristotle. However, unlike Plato's conception of
moral order, which ruled as it were from above, Aristotle sees this moral order as
internal to what it means to be human. Humans are *teleological* beings, which is
to say, human living aims at an end, or *telos*. Some ends are intermediate rather
than terminal. The ship at which shipbuilding aims may in turn be a means for
the practice of warcraft, which itself may be a means to a yet more distant end.
Aristotle reasons that human action consists of means-end chains, which converge
on one ultimate end called the Good. The extent to which humans achieve their
*telos* is the extent to which they participate in the Good. In Aristotle's mind, the
*telos* can be conceived only in terms of a thing's natural function. Similarly, virtues
are function-specific, or more precisely, excellency of function.[10] To illustrate, if
the function of a horse is to run, then the *telos* of a horse is racing, and its virtue
is its speed. Virtues, therefore, are qualities that assist achievement of the *telos*,
and the *telos* of a thing is bound up in the nature of the thing.

The nature of human beings, upon which the notion of the human *telos* depends,
is bound up in the metaphysical structure of the soul. According to Aristotle, while
we may share the vegetative (growth) and locomotive (movement) soul-stuff with
the animals, humans are distinguished in the chain of being by their rational souls.
The end of human life, therefore, is rationality, and the virtues are (1) *virtues of
character* which assist living according *to* reason and (2) *virtues of thought* which
enable proper exercise *of* reason itself.

The notion of a function-specific *telos* represents an advance over earlier formulations of the tradition by providing a clearer account of moral imperatives. As
noted earlier in the wristwatch illustration, it is the concept of *telos* that provides
human beings with moral imperatives. If the function of a watch is timekeeping,
then it *ought* to keep time well. If the function of human beings is rationality, then
humans *ought* to live in accordance with, and in right exercise of, reason.

The second feature of Aristotle's moral philosophy is *eudaimonia*. A difficult
word to translate—blessedness, happiness, prosperity—it seems to connote "the
state of being well and doing well in being well, of man's being well-favored himself
and in relation to the divine" (148). *Eudaimonia* names that *telos* toward which
humans move. Virtues, then, assist the movement toward *eudaimonia*, but *eudaimonia* cannot be defined apart from these same virtues:

> But the exercise of the virtues is not in this sense a means to the end of the good
> for man. For what constitutes the good for man is a complete human life lived at

10. In *Nicomachean Ethics*, Aristotle writes, "Every virtue causes its possessors to be in a good state
and to perform their functions well." *Nicomachean Ethics*, trans. Terence Irwin (Indianapolis: Hackett,
1985), 1106a16.

its best, and the exercise of the virtues is a necessary and central part of such a life, not a mere preparatory exercise to secure such a life. We thus cannot characterize the good for man without already having made reference to the virtues. (149)

The apparent circularity of the relation between *telos, eudaimonia,* and *virtue* is not a mark against Aristotle's system but, rather, an advance over Plato's. For Plato, "reality" not only denoted the world of rocks and doorknobs, it also included the world of intangibles such as "love" and "17"—things whose existence in the realm of Form is every bit as real as the middle-sized dry goods that clutter our sensible world. As Plato saw it, "true virtue" belonged to the realm of Form, and particular human qualities were deemed "virtuous" to the extent that they resembled the "true virtue" of which they were copies. Thus, there could be no inherent conflict or disunity between particular virtuous qualities; any tragic conflict was simply a function of imperfection in copying universal virtue into particular living. In this way, morality was thought to be objective and moral reasoning an exercise of the intellect according to which the mind grasped the Form of "true virtue." Ironically, Plato's doctrine failed even to overcome the relativist claims of the Sophists and tragic dramatists of his own day. Although MacIntyre does not think that Aristotle himself explicitly conquered the problem of what to do when virtues conflict, his model, which defines *telos, eudaimonia,* and *virtue* in terms of each other, does point the way toward conceiving moral reasoning as a *skill* rather than as an exercise of intellect (as Plato and the later Enlightenment thinkers imagined). Such skill could be attained and cultivated only *from within* the form of life in which these concepts were at home.

The third feature of Aristotle's system is the distinction between theoretical reasoning and practical reasoning. Practical reasoning begins with a want, or goal, or desire and always terminates in action. Suppose you are thirsty after a long day of shopping. The major premise of your reasoning process is your (obvious) belief that anyone who is thirsty is well advised to find a drinking fountain. The minor premise of this line of thought is your knowledge that a drinking fountain exists in the northwest corner of this particular department store. Your practical reasoning terminates in your act of walking to the northwest corner of the store and quenching your thirst.

In Aristotle's way of looking at things, moral reasoning is an instance of practical reasoning. It is assisted by virtues of character (which temper, guide, and shape initial desires) and virtues of thought (such as *phronēsis,* which enables the perception of practical reasoning's major premises).[11]

Perhaps the most important use of practical reason is its employment in the balancing of human activities. I cannot spend all my time in theoretical contemplation,

---

11. Since right action follows in straightforward fashion from the initial desire and major premise, and since differences in initial desires as well as differences in major premises boil down to variations in the exercise of the respective virtues, moral quandaries are nonexistent for Aristotle. When in a bind, he can always defer to the maxim "the morally right action is that taken by the virtuous person."

the highest faculty of reason and thus the highest human good (158), because I would soon starve to death. In order to maximize the amount of time I can engage in contemplation, I must balance this activity with work, civic duty, and the like. This mental balancing act is the domain of practical reason. This explanation also sheds light on why virtuous persons make the best civic leaders, since skill in practical reasoning is also what it takes to run the *polis*.

The fourth feature of Aristotle's moral philosophy that MacIntyre emphasizes is friendship. Friendship, of course, involves mutual affection, but for Aristotle, "that affection arises within a relationship defined in terms of common allegiance to and a common pursuit of goods" (156). This is to say, first, that Aristotle's notion on friendship presupposes the existence of the *polis*, which renders common good possible, and second, that this good itself is the health of the *polis*: "We are to think then of friendship as being the sharing of all in the common project of creating and sustaining the life of the city, a sharing incorporated in the immediacy of an individual's particular friendships" (156).

The emphasis on friendship in Aristotle illustrates one aspect of continuity in this historic tradition, namely, that the moral structure is intimately linked with social relationships.

## Obstacles to Be Hurdled

Aristotle is definitely the hero of MacIntyre's account. And at the time *After Virtue* was written (1981, revised 1984) MacIntyre saw Aristotle as the apex of the virtue tradition.[12] However, if MacIntyre is to succeed in rejuvenating the Aristotelian tradition, he must overcome three difficulties in Aristotle's account that threaten to topple the whole project. First, Aristotle's notion of *telos* rests on his distinctive "metaphysical biology." In Aristotle's view, the form guarantees that all humans share a common essence. The essence of humanness is rationality. Rationality is of two sorts, theoretical and practical. The *telos* of human life, then, is actualization of both forms of reason. The goal of theoretical reason is contemplation; the goal of practical reason is life in the *polis*. Aristotle's problem was to give an account of how pursuit of these two forms of rationality could be reconciled. MacIntyre's problem is to provide a replacement for Aristotle's concept of form that will enlighten us as to the *telos* of human life. Traditions provide answers to this question. Second, the virtue tradition sees morality as inextricably enmeshed in the life of the *polis*. What does this do for the applicability of the Aristotelian model today, in view of the extinction of the *polis*? Third, Aristotle retains Plato's belief in the unity of the virtues, which implies that every putative case of tragedy reduces to an instance that is "simply the result of flaws of character in individuals

---

12. In later works MacIntyre becomes convinced that Aquinas had succeeded in surpassing Aristotle on several points. See Alasdair MacIntyre, *Whose Justice? Which Rationality?* and *Three Rival Versions of Moral Enquiry: Encyclopaedia, Genealogy, and Tradition* (Notre Dame, IN: University of Notre Dame Press, 1990).

or of unintelligent political arrangements" (157). As Sophocles dramatized, instances of tragic evil were not inconceivable. Can such real conflicts be interpreted as contributing to the moral life rather than confusing it?

In addition to the three problems internal to Aristotle's account, MacIntyre notes one problem external to it. To identify the trajectory from Homer to Aristotle to Aquinas to the present as a single tradition, something must be done to reconcile the diversity in the lists of virtues taken from every age. Not only have the *lists* changed with each successive formulation of the tradition,[13] but how virtue is defined at one point in history is at odds with the definition explicated in another age.[14] Thus, the fourth problem MacIntyre must overcome is the challenge of demonstrating the kind of continuity between these formulations that makes these disparate accounts a single, unified tradition.

We now turn to MacIntyre's own "metanarrative" to see if he is successful in his endeavors.

## Ethics à la MacIntyre

The disparity between virtue lists and even between the definitions of the term can be reconciled, says MacIntyre, by bringing to light the particular backdrop that each formulation presupposes. The tricky part of his analysis is that each of the central concepts—*virtue, practice, narrative,* and *tradition*—can be defined only, finally, in terms of the other concepts. This does not make the MacIntyrean version guilty of circularity. It simply means that getting a handle on his explanation is not like building a house (which progresses incrementally, brick by brick) but like watching the sun rise—the light dawns gradually over the whole.[15]

### Practices

The cornerstone of this backdrop is the idea of practices. MacIntyre defines a *practice* somewhat tortuously as

> any coherent and complex form of socially established cooperative human activity through which goods internal to that form of activity are realized in the course of trying to achieve those standards of excellence which are appropriate to, and partially definitive of, that form of activity, with the result that human powers to achieve excellence, and human conceptions of the ends and goods involved, are systematically extended. (187)

13. E.g., the early church fathers champion humility as a virtue, while Aristotle repudiates it as a vice (182)!

14. E.g., Aristotle sees virtues as the means to internal ends, while Benjamin Franklin sees virtues as means to external, even utilitarian, ends (184).

15. This illustration comes from Ludwig Wittgenstein, *On Certainty,* ed. G. E. M. Anscombe and G. H. von Wright, trans. Denis Paul and G. E. M. Anscombe (New York: Harper Torchbooks, 1969, 1972), §141.

Attention to the grammar of this sentence reveals four central concepts. First, practices are human activities. However, these are not activities of isolated individuals but socially established and cooperative activities. Such activities cannot be executed alone but require participation by like-minded others. In addition to being social, these activities are also complex enough to be challenging, and coherent enough to aim at some goal in a unified fashion. Building a house is a practice, while taking long showers is not. The game of tennis is a practice, but hitting a backhand is not. Medicine is a practice, while gargling mouthwash is not.[16]

Second, practices have goods that are internal to the activity. Some practices, for example, jurisprudence, have external goods—money, fame, power—which come as by-products of the practice. But true practices are marked by *internal* goods—those rewards that can be recognized and appreciated only by participants.[17] For example, I can bribe my son with pieces of candy to learn the game of chess. But at some point he may begin to enjoy the game of chess for itself. At this point he has become a practitioner and member of the greater community of chess players. He has, furthermore, become hooked on its internal reward—the joy of chess—something to which all players have access.

Third, practices have standards of excellence without which internal goods cannot be fully achieved. The joy of chess is in having played *well*. And what counts for excellence has been determined by the historical community of practitioners. The practitioners have recognized that stalemate is not as desirable an endgame as checkmate. And to execute a queen-rook fork is more satisfying than simple *en passant*.

Fourth, practices are systematically extended. As practitioners have striven for excellence day in and day out over the years, the standards of the practice, along with practitioners' abilities to achieve these standards, have slowly risen. Perhaps no field better illustrates this than medicine. Doctors were no doubt sincere when they once treated fevers with leeches, but contemporary physicians possess skills that far surpass those of their predecessors. Yet the dependence of contemporary practitioners upon their predecessors is unquestionable: it is precisely because previous doctors strove for excellence that the specific advances in medicine that have been made *have* been made. But increase in technical skill does not quite capture what is meant by the notion of systematic extension. It also includes the way technically proficient doctors have come to appreciate how the health of a patient is a function of a larger system. Thus, the practice of medicine is slowly being extended to encompass care for the whole patient in all his or her psychosocial complexity.[18]

16. For an extended discussion of practices see Craig Dykstra, "Reconceiving Practice in Theological Inquiry and Education," chap. 7 in Murphy, Kallenberg, and Nation, *Virtues and Practices*, 161–82.

17. It is often, but not always, the case that internal rewards are shared among all practitioners without diminution.

18. The changing mode of physician-patient relationships is detailed by William F. May in *The Physician's Covenant* (Philadelphia: Westminster, 1983); May, "Images of the Healer," chap. 15 in Murphy, Kallenberg, and Nation, *Virtues and Practices*, 324–42.

Against the backdrop of practices, virtue can be defined as "an acquired human quality the possession and exercise of which tends to enable us to achieve those goods which are internal to practices and the lack of which effectively prevents us from achieving any such goods" (191). The clan leader who *practices* warcraft and the church father who *practices* evangelism are assisted by the qualities of courage and humility, respectively. Against this backdrop many of the discrepancies between virtue lists can be reconciled as a matter of differences of practice.

In our smorgasbord era it is tempting to think of practices as self-contained exercises. In fact, many practices are so complex that they have become an entire tradition in themselves. Medicine, science, and warcraft all have attending epistemologies, authoritative texts, structured communities and institutions, and histories of development. Other practices are parts of clusters that contribute to the identity of a tradition. For example, the Christian tradition defines itself as a socially expanding movement called "the kingdom of God." At its core, therefore, Christianity seems to consist primarily of the practice of community formation. Subpractices that contribute to community formation can be categorized under the rubrics of *witness, worship, works of mercy, discernment*, and *discipleship*.[19] Other schemes can be imagined of course, but my point is that Christianity cannot be explained or understood without reference to a distinctive cluster of practices. In order to participate in the tradition called Christianity one must necessarily participate in these practices. To put it another way, to participate in the community is to participate in practices because communal life is the point at which the practices intersect. Furthermore, knowing the constitutive practices of Christianity tells us a great deal about how Christians ought to live. If virtues are cultivated by striving for excellence in the practice of practices, then we are unable to grow in Christlikeness unless we participate in Christianity's practices.

## Narrative

A second crucial concept that serves as a backdrop to our understanding of the virtues is *narrative*. MacIntyre explains narrative this way. Imagine that a woman approaches you at a bus stop and says, "The name of the common wild duck is *histrionicus histrionicus histrionicus*." Now, what would you make of this person? Truth is, you can't make anything of her, or of her action, without more information. Her act is completely unintelligible. But now suppose it becomes known that this woman is a librarian, and she has mistaken you for the person who earlier had asked for the Latin name of the common wild duck. We can now understand her action because it has been put into a context. The contexts that make sense out of human action are *stories* or *narratives*. To explain an action is simply to provide

19. See Nancey Murphy, "Using MacIntyre's Method in Christian Ethics," chap. 2 in Murphy, Kallenberg, and Nation, *Virtues and Practices*, 30–44. For an alternate list of constitutive Christian practices see Craig R. Dykstra, "No Longer Strangers: The Church and Its Educational Ministry," *Princeton Seminary Bulletin* 6, no. 3 (1985): 188–200; Dykstra, "Reconceiving Practice in Theological Inquiry and Education."

the story that gives the act its context. We can imagine any number of stories that might make sense out of the bus stop incident (for example, perhaps she is a Russian spy whose password is the sentence in question). But we will also say that the explanation of her action is rendered more fully if we can tell the story that takes her longer- and longest-term intentions into account and shows how her shorter-term intentions relate to the longer-term ones. So we might discover that she has rushed out of the library in search of a particular patron because she has been put on a standard of performance under threat of losing her job. Her longer-term intention is to save her job. Her longest-term intention might be uncovered in telling the story of how she is the sole provider for her paraplegic son. MacIntyre reasons that if human actions are intelligible only with respect to stories that contextualize intentions, then that which unifies actions into sequences and sequences into a continuous whole is the story of one's life. My life as a whole makes sense when my story is told.

This has important consequences for the problem of Aristotle's "metaphysical biology." Imagine we had the opportunity to ask Aristotle, "How can I know that I am the same person as the me of ten years ago?" He would likely reply, "Though your body changes through growth and decay, your form, or essence, is immutable." But this answer is not likely to fly very far for a modern audience. In contrast, MacIntyre suggests that *narrative* provides a better explanation for the unity of a human life. The self has continuity because it has played the single and central character in a particular story—the narrative of a person's life. MacIntyre puts it this way: the unity of the self "resides in the unity of a narrative which links birth to life to death as a narrative beginning to middle to end" (205).

Just as practices have a characteristically social dimension, so also do narratives. Humorist Garrison Keillor reminisces about the distinctive characters who populated the Lake Wobegon, Minnesota, of his childhood. But notice how in identifying themselves as "Norwegian bachelor farmers" such folk have immediately linked who they are with others who share these ethnic, gender, and occupational features. I cannot explain who I am without utilizing some social place markers which identify me with certain strata of my community. If pressed to go beyond this first-level answer to "Who am I?," where can one go but to say that I am also someone's neighbor, child, sibling, student, mate, friend, constituent, or employee? In occupying these roles, we simultaneously become subplots in the stories of others' lives just as they have become subplots in ours. In this way, the life stories of members of a community are enmeshed and intertwined. This entanglement of our stories is the fabric of communal life: "For the story of my life is always embedded in the story of those communities from which I derive my identity" (221). Our stories are concretely embedded, or our stories intersect, in those practices in which we are co-participants. For example, the role of ethics professor links the instructor with the rest of the faculty in general and one group of students in particular, within the wider practice of graduate education.

This construction overcomes the fear that the Aristotelian account of the virtues cannot be sustained after the extinction of the *polis*. In MacIntyre's construction, virtues are those qualities that assist one in the extension of his or her story, and, by extrapolation, the extension of the story of his or her community or communities. The question "What ought I to do?" is not a question of one's political duty as it was in Aristotle's day, but it *is* a question whose answer must be preceded by the logically prior question: "Of which stories am I a part?"

Although none of us will ever have the clear moral parameters that were to be had in the well-defined social framework of Aristotle's *polis*, the concept of narrative embeddedness still explains the presence of natural boundaries and moral momentum. In 1994 a US postal worker lost his job and retaliated by going on a killing spree. Our responses to his actions were telling. People reacted by saying he "flipped out," "snapped," "went berserk," or "had gone insane." Our expectation is that postal workers (even unemployed ones) aren't killers, and once a postal worker type, always a postal worker type.[20] This illustrates our deeper belief that *rational* human behavior is action that stays within the boundaries of "character." To step outside these boundaries is not merely to act irrationally but to lose one's sanity. This is because the narrative shape of human life carries with it a certain degree of moral momentum. For example, my wife can bank on the fact that I won't wake up tomorrow morning and say, "Today I think I'll become an ax murderer!" There is a certain momentum in who I am; I will generally stay "in character." The transition from who I was yesterday to who I am today will be a smooth one, marked only by minor changes. A drastic change in character—whether for the better or for the worse—is always taken to be the result of a long-term, preexistent (though perhaps not publicly visible) process.

### Tradition

The third term that forms the backdrop to all the various accounts of virtue is the notion of *tradition*. MacIntyre defines tradition as "an historically extended, socially embodied argument, and an argument precisely in part about the goods which constitute the tradition" (222). This definition has three components. First, MacIntyre's understanding of tradition is really the logical extension of his treatment of narrative. To be "historically extended" is to be narratively extended. Just as the self has the unity of playing a single character in a lifelong story, so too the community has its own continuity—despite loss and gain of members—because the community itself is a character of sorts in a narrative that is longer than the span of a single human life. For example, Christians in the Reformed tradition feel kinship with John Calvin because they can tell the story (recount the history) of the Reformed Church from Calvin's Geneva to their present church community.

20. We would even say that someone who sincerely harbors paranoia that the mail carrier is a killer is mentally maladjusted.

Second, a tradition is "socially embodied" because traditions are lived in community. A tradition has its inception in the formation of the community that is defined by those who have pledged corporate allegiance to the tradition's authoritative voice or text.[21] In that this prophetic word shapes the practices of communal life, the community is said to "embody" the tradition's persona in that age. For example, early Christians prayed because their Scriptures exemplify, illustrate, and command the practice of prayer. Outsiders, who have no access to the authoritative text, can still read the nature of the Christian tradition off the lives and practices of the community's members. Should the community die off or disband, the tradition passes out of existence (at least until another group rallies in the same way around the same text). In this way the tradition has the quality of being "socially embodied." However, because the application of the authoritative text or voice is done afresh in every successive generation, the tradition remains a live option only so long as the discussion about the text's relevance and meaning is sustained. Hence, third, traditions are necessarily long-standing arguments. But let's get clearer on the notion of historical extension because this will help us evaluate the current status of the virtue tradition.

Just as selves and communities are characters in their respective stories, so too traditions are also characters in an even wider narrative. When we recount Christian, Jewish, or Muslim history, we are telling the story of just such a character. The viability of any one tradition is not merely its historical survival, however, but its *historical extension*. MacIntyre uses this term to describe the growth a tradition undergoes through time as it overcomes obstacles raised against it. In his sequel to *After Virtue* called *Whose Justice? Which Rationality?* he defines a tradition as

> an argument extended through time in which certain fundamental agreements are defined and redefined in terms of two kinds of conflict: those with critics and enemies external to the tradition . . . and those internal, interpretive debates through which the meaning and rationale of the fundamental agreements come to be expressed and by whose progress a tradition is constituted.[22]

For example, early Christians faced a crisis when they tried to reconcile three seemingly inconsistent beliefs: God is one, Jesus is divine, and Jesus is not the Father. The well-known "solution" to this quandary came when the Cappadocian fathers borrowed Platonic resources to frame the doctrine of the Trinity. This enabled Christians to believe all three propositions without logical contradiction. The universal adoption of their formulation as orthodoxy at Constantinople (AD 381) freed the Christian tradition to move on to tackle the next obstacle in its

21. For an extended account of how traditions are born and develop see chap. 18 of MacIntyre's *Whose Justice? Which Rationality?*

22. MacIntyre, *Whose Justice? Which Rationality?*, 12.

path.[23] We don't know how long the trinitarian problem might have been sustained had the Cappadocian fathers not entered the debate. We *do* know that by AD 325 the stakes were very high—unacceptable proposals were deemed heretical, and their authors were banished from the community (or worse). Were it not for belief in God's sovereignty over history, it would be tempting to wonder how long Christianity might have lasted had not the trinitarian problem been overcome.

If virtue theory is itself a tradition in the sense just described, then we can see that its viability depends upon overcoming the obstacles that threaten the Aristotelian version. We have already seen how *narrative* overcomes the problem of Aristotle's metaphysical biology and how *practices* overcome the problem of discrepancies in the virtue lists. The extinction of the *polis* is a third crisis that must be overcome. For Aristotle, the *telos* of life, together with the attending virtues, can be expressed only in terms of life in the *polis*. One reason the virtuous person was identical to the virtuous citizen was that without the prosperity and leisure engendered by the shared life of the city-state, the highest *telos* (for Aristotle, metaphysical contemplation) was an impractical and impossible ideal. But by exercise of practical reason the *polis* flourished in such a way that contemplation could be maximized (at least by the elite). However, a more fundamental reason virtue was tied to the *polis* was that the Good, at which human life aims, was thought to be a *corporate* good that could not be possessed by isolated individuals but only jointly in community. The *polis* was the by-product of pursuing this corporate Good together. To put it differently, the Good *was* this corporate life. But now the *polis* is no more. Therefore, in order for the virtue tradition to be extended, there must be an alternative way to understand the social dimension of virtue. Of course, this is ground we have already covered. The narrative shape of human existence—that is, that human sociality is identical to the embeddedness of our respective narratives—shows the way to preserve the sociality of virtue theory even in the absence of the *polis*.

Narrative extends the Aristotelian tradition in another way as well. MacIntyre credits the high medieval age with conceptualizing the genre of our narrativity to be akin to the quest for the Holy Grail: "In the high medieval scheme a central genre is the tale of a quest or journey. Man is essentially *in via*. The end which he seeks is something which if gained can redeem all that was wrong with his life up to that point" (174–75). MacIntyre goes on to say that this move was un-Aristotelian in at least two ways. First, it placed the *telos* of life beyond life, in contrast to Aristotle, who imagined the *telos* of life to be "a certain kind of life." Second, it allowed for the possibility of positive evil in contrast to the Aristotelian scheme, which understood evil as always the privation of good. These two features gave the medieval view an advantage over Aristotle in dealing with the problem of tragic evil. In the eyes of the medieval person, the achievement of the human

---

23. The next major debate was the doctrine of Christ: if Christ was God the Son, how are we to understand the relation of his divine and human natures while preserving the unity of his person?

*telos* counterbalanced all evil, even evils of the tragic sort envisioned by Sophocles. Thus, the fourth objection that threatened *Aristotle* (that is, tragic evil) has been overcome by the Aristotelian *tradition*:

> The narrative therefore in which human life is embodied has a form in which the subject . . . is set a task in the completion of which lies their peculiar appropriation of the human good; the way toward which the completion of that task is barred by a variety of inward and outward evils. The virtues are those qualities which enable evils to be overcome, the task to be accomplished, the journey to be completed. (175)

MacIntyre concludes, therefore, that tragic choices are real but that the inevitability of such choice does not render morality unintelligible or criterionless (as the emotivist claims, thereby concluding that moral choices boil down to matters of preference). Rather such choice plays a central role in the development of character by providing an occasion for moral agents to exercise and build virtue when they sustain the quest for good precisely at the time it is most costly to do so. If "the good life for man is the life spent in seeking for the good life for man, and the virtues necessary for the seeking are those which will enable us to understand what more and what else the good life for man is," then tragic evil is overcome because evil, even evil of the tragic sort, cannot diminish this kind of good (219). Instead of detracting from this kind of goodness, tragic evil can even be thought to *contribute* to the moral fiber of the life so lived. This solution to the problem of tragic evil employs a view of life that has come out of a particular historical cross section of the tradition. Because the medieval period provides them with the resources for overcoming this obstacle, adherents to this tradition are warranted in retaining this feature from their corporate past. So then, not only are practices and narratives sources for understanding the human *telos*, but tradition itself contributes to this understanding.

Identifying the genre of a tradition's narrative also makes sense out of the fractal symmetry that can be seen when we look at the way in which the narrative unity of (1) a life, (2) a community, and (3) a tradition are mutually nested. Individual, community, and tradition, while telling different parts of the master story, nevertheless share equally in the genre of that story. Thus, if the genre of the tradition is that of a quest, the genre of a human life is also that of a quest. And if human life is a quest, then human virtues are those qualities that assist it:

> The virtues therefore are to be understood as those dispositions which will not only sustain practices and enable us to achieve the goods internal to practices, but which will also sustain us in the relevant kind of quest for the good, by enabling us to overcome the harms, dangers, temptations and distractions which we encounter, and which will furnish us with increasing self-knowledge and increasing knowledge of the good. (219)

## Retrospect

Looking back, we can see not only that the virtue tradition that MacIntyre has recounted fits MacIntyre's definition of tradition but that it is one in which MacIntyre represents the most recent advance! He has succeeded in overcoming four important obstacles to the Aristotelian model by elucidating the story about stories, or what has been called the metanarrative about the narrative quality of human life. In so doing he has clarified how the notions of *telos, virtue, practice, narrative,* and *tradition* form a mutually supporting and interlocking web of concepts.

Let us recall now the master argument of *After Virtue*. MacIntyre challenged us to reconsider the emotivist conclusion (namely, that morality is by nature nothing more than matters of preference) by arguing that the Enlightenment Project's move to repudiate all things social (that is, virtues and practices) and all things historical (that is, narrative and tradition) was a major misstep. He argued further that moral imperatives can be derived from an answer to the question, "What is human life for?" In the same way the functional definition of a watch ("A watch is for timekeeping") entails its virtue (accuracy), its functional imperative ("A watch *ought* to keep time well"), and its ground for being evaluated ("This grossly inaccurate watch is a *bad* watch"). To have a grasp on the human *telos* affords us with moral virtues, moral imperatives, and sufficient grounds for moral judgment. Furthermore, because narratives intersect at social practices, and practices constitute traditions, and traditions are historically (that is, narratively) extended, to understand virtue adequately as those qualities that assist pursuit of *telos* at all three levels, virtue itself must be given a threefold definition:

> The virtues find their point and purpose not only in sustaining those relationships necessary if the variety of goods internal to practices are to be achieved and not only in sustaining the form of an individual life in which that individual may seek out his or her good as the good of his or her whole life, but also in sustaining those traditions which provide the practices and individual lives with their necessary historical context. (223)

This relationship might be diagrammed as in figure 6.3.

Aristotle's notion of virtue as "excellency of function" has thus been expanded. Human virtues are learned qualities that assist us in achieving the human *telos*, which can be understood by considering (1) the functional definition of the human person, which is provided by the master story of the tradition, (2) the internal goods of those practices that constitute the tradition, and (3) those roles that arise at the intersection of our life stories. To put it differently, moral imperatives arise from that understanding of the human *telos* that arises within the context of those practices, narratives, and tradition in which we locate ourselves.

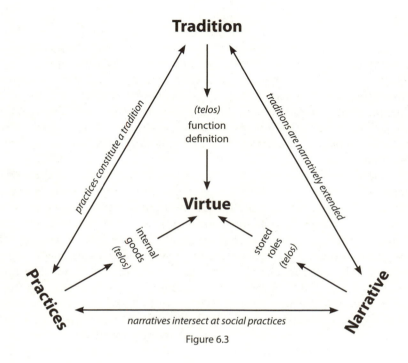

Figure 6.3

## Conclusion

In the end there is much unfinished business. MacIntyre himself bemoans the marked absence of moral communities in the modern world. But this is not the only problem that must be addressed in the wake of *After Virtue*. For example, if the answer to "What is human life for?" is supplied to each of us by our respective practices, narratives, and traditions, doesn't this still leave us with an incurable problem of moral pluralism if not one of downright relativism? Are there some criteria for adjudicating multiple traditions? Further, if MacIntyre's project succeeds, are we in the Western world not faced with the dilemma of being inheritors of at least two conflicting traditions (namely, Aristotelianism and political liberalism)? Or can MacIntyre's thesis possibly succeed if, in fact, the Aristotelian tradition *died* with the Enlightenment? With what resources can it be exhumed and resuscitated?

MacIntyre is not unaware of these perplexities. Some of the objections earned responses in the second edition of *After Virtue* while others he has made the central concern of later books. But the mere presence of these objections does not count against his system because they become the fodder for enlivening the debate by which the tradition is extended. The question, "Is MacIntyre's moral philosophy the *final* word?" is wrongheaded. The better question is, "Is it the best one so far?"

# 7

# The Nature of the Virtues

ALASDAIR MACINTYRE

One response to the history which I have narrated so far might well be to suggest that even within the relatively coherent tradition of thought which I have sketched there are just too many different and incompatible conceptions of a virtue for there to be any real unity to the concept or indeed to the history. Homer, Sophocles, Aristotle, the New Testament, and medieval thinkers differ from each other in too many ways. They offer us different and incompatible lists of the virtues; they give a different rank order of importance to different virtues; and they have different and incompatible theories of the virtues. If we were to consider later Western writers on the virtues, the list of differences and incompatibilities would be enlarged still further, and if we extended our enquiry to Japanese, say, or American Indian cultures, the differences would become greater still. It would be all too easy to conclude that there are a number of rival and alternative conceptions of the virtues, but, even within the tradition which I have been delineating, no single core conception.

The case for such a conclusion could not be better constructed than by beginning from a consideration of the very different lists of items which different authors in different times and places have included in their catalogues of virtues. Some of these catalogues—Homer's, Aristotle's, and the New Testament's—I have already

Originally published as "The Nature of the Virtues," in Alasdair MacIntyre, *After Virtue: A Study in Moral Theory*, 3rd ed. (Notre Dame, IN: University of Notre Dame Press, 2007), 181–203. Copyright © 2007, University of Notre Dame Press. Reprinted with permission of University of Notre Dame Press.

noticed at greater or lesser length. Let me at the risk of some repetition recall some of their key features and then introduce for further comparison the catalogues of two later Western writers, Benjamin Franklin and Jane Austen.

The first example is that of Homer. At least some of the items in a Homeric list of the *aretai* would clearly not be counted by most of us nowadays as virtues at all, physical strength being the most obvious example. To this it might be replied that perhaps we ought not to translate the word *aretē* in Homer by our word "virtue" but instead by our word "excellence"; and perhaps, if we were so to translate it, the apparently surprising difference between Homer and ourselves would at first sight have been removed. For we could allow without any kind of oddity that the possession of physical strength is the possession of an excellence. But in fact we would not have removed, but instead would merely have relocated, the difference between Homer and ourselves. For we would now seem to be saying that Homer's concept of an *aretē*, an excellence, is one thing and that our concept of a virtue is quite another since a particular quality can be an excellence in Homer's eyes, but not a virtue in ours and vice versa.

But of course it is not that Homer's list of virtues differs only from our own; it also notably differs from Aristotle's. And Aristotle's of course also differs from our own. For one thing, as I noticed earlier, some Greek virtue-words are not easily translated into English or rather out of Greek. Moreover consider the importance of friendship as a virtue in Aristotle's list—how different from us! Or the place of *phronēsis*—how different from Homer and from us! The mind receives from Aristotle the kind of tribute which the body receives from Homer. But it is not just the case that the difference between Aristotle and Homer lies in the inclusion of some items and the omission of others in their respective catalogues. It turns out also in the way in which those catalogues are ordered, in which items are ranked as relatively central to human excellence and which are marginal.

Moreover the relationship of virtues to the social order has changed. For Homer the paradigm of human excellence is the warrior; for Aristotle it is the Athenian gentleman. Indeed according to Aristotle certain virtues are only available to those of great riches and of high social status; there are virtues which are unavailable to the poor man, even if he is a free man. And those virtues are on Aristotle's view ones central to human life; magnanimity—and once again, any translation of *megalopsychia* is unsatisfactory—and munificence are not just virtues, but important virtues within the Aristotelian scheme.

At once it is impossible to delay the remark that the most striking contrast with Aristotle's catalogue is to be found neither in Homer's nor in our own, but in the New Testament's. For the New Testament not only praises virtues of which Aristotle knows nothing—faith, hope and love—and says nothing about virtues such as *phronēsis* which are crucial for Aristotle, but it praises at least one quality as a virtue which Aristotle seems to count as one of the vices relative to magnanimity, namely humility. Moreover since the New Testament quite clearly sees the rich as destined for the pains of Hell, it is clear that the key virtues cannot be available to them; yet they *are* available to slaves. And the New Testament of course differs from both Homer and Aristotle not only in the items included in its catalogue, but once again in its rank ordering of the virtues.

Turn now to compare all three lists of virtues considered so far—the Homeric, the Aristotelian, and the New Testament's—with two much later lists, one which can be compiled from Jane Austen's novels and the other which Benjamin Franklin constructed for himself. Two features stand out in Jane Austen's list. The first is the importance that she allots to the virtue which she calls "constancy." In some ways constancy plays a role in Jane Austen analogous to that of *phronēsis* in Aristotle; it is a virtue the possession of which is a prerequisite for the possession of other virtues. The second is the fact that what Aristotle treats as the virtue of agreeableness (a virtue for which he says there is no name) she treats as only the simulacrum of a genuine virtue—the genuine virtue in question is the one she calls amiability. For the man who practices agreeableness does so from considerations of honor and expediency, according to Aristotle; whereas Jane Austen thought it possible and necessary for the possessor of that virtue to have a certain real affection for people as such. (It matters here that Jane Austen is a Christian.) Remember that Aristotle himself had treated military courage as a simulacrum of true courage. Thus we find here yet another type of disagreement over the virtues; namely, one as to which human qualities are genuine virtues and which mere simulacra.

In Benjamin Franklin's list we find almost all the types of difference from at least one of the catalogues we have considered and one more. Franklin includes virtues which are new to our consideration such as cleanliness, silence, and industry; he clearly considers the drive to acquire itself a part of virtue, whereas for most ancient Greeks this is the vice of *pleonexia*; he treats some virtues which earlier ages had considered minor as major, but he also redefines some familiar virtues. In the list of thirteen virtues which Franklin compiled as part of his system of private moral accounting, he elucidates each virtue by citing a maxim obedience to which *is* the virtue in question. In the case of chastity the maxim is, "Rarely use venery but for health or offspring—never to dullness, weakness or the injury of your own or another's peace or reputation." This is clearly not what earlier writers had meant by "chastity."

We have therefore accumulated a startling number of differences and incompatibilities in the five stated and implied accounts of the virtues. So the question which I raised at the outset becomes more urgent. If different writers in different times and places, but all within the history of Western culture, include such different sets and types of items in their lists, what grounds have we for supposing that they do indeed aspire to list items of one and the same kind, that there is any shared concept at all? A second kind of consideration reinforces the presumption of a negative answer to this question. It is not just that each of these five writers lists different and differing kinds of items; it is also that each of these lists embodies, is the expression of, a different theory about what a virtue is.

In the Homeric poems a virtue is a quality the manifestation of which enables someone to do exactly what their well-defined social role requires. The primary role is that of the warrior-king and that Homer lists those virtues which he does becomes intelligible at once when we recognize that the key virtues therefore must be those which enable a man to excel in combat and in the games. It follows that we cannot identify the Homeric virtues until we have first identified the key social roles in Homeric society and the requirements of each of them. The concept of *what anyone filling such-and-such a role ought to do* is prior to the concept of a virtue; the latter concept has application only via the former.

On Aristotle's account matters are very different. Even though some virtues are available only to certain types of people, nonetheless virtues attach not to men as inhabiting social roles, but to man as such. It is the *telos* of man as a species which determines what human qualities are virtues. We need to remember however that although Aristotle treats the acquisition and exercise of the virtues as means to an end, the relationship of means to end is internal and not external. I call a means internal to a given end when the end cannot be adequately characterized independently of a characterization of the means. So it is with the virtues and the *telos* which is the good life for man on Aristotle's account. The exercise of the virtues is itself a crucial component of the good life for man. This distinction between internal and external means to an end is not drawn by Aristotle himself in the *Nicomachean Ethics*, but it is an essential distinction to be drawn if we are to understand what Aristotle intended. The distinction *is* drawn explicitly by Aquinas in the course of his defense of St. Augustine's definition of a virtue, and it is clear that Aquinas understood that in drawing it he was maintaining an Aristotelian point of view.

The New Testament's account of the virtues, even if it differs as much as it does in content from Aristotle's—Aristotle would certainly not have admired Jesus Christ, and he would have been horrified by St. Paul—does have the same logical and conceptual structure as Aristotle's account. A virtue is, as with Aristotle, a quality the exercise of which leads to the achievement of the human *telos*. The good for man is of course a supernatural and not only a natural good, but supernature redeems and completes nature. Moreover the relationship of virtues as means to the end which is human incorporation in the divine kingdom of the age to come is internal and not external, just as it is in Aristotle. It is of course this parallelism which allows Aquinas to synthesize Aristotle and the New Testament. A key feature of this parallelism is the way in which the concept of *the good life for man* is prior to the concept of a virtue in just the way in which on the Homeric account the concept of social role was prior. Once again it is the way in which the former concept is applied which determines how the latter is to be applied. In both cases the concept of a virtue is a secondary concept.

The intent of Jane Austen's theory of the virtues is of another kind. C. S. Lewis has rightly emphasized how profoundly Christian her moral vision is, and Gilbert Ryle has equally rightly emphasized her inheritance from Shaftesbury and from

Aristotle. In fact her views combine elements from Homer as well, since she is concerned with social roles in a way that neither the New Testament nor Aristotle are. She is therefore important for the way in which she finds it possible to combine what are at first sight disparate theoretical accounts of the virtues. But for the moment any attempt to assess the significance of Jane Austen's synthesis must be delayed. Instead we must notice the quite different style of theory articulated in Benjamin Franklin's account of the virtues.

Franklin's account, like Aristotle's, is teleological; but unlike Aristotle's, it is utilitarian. According to Franklin in his *Autobiography* the virtues are a means to an end, but he envisages the means-ends relationship as external rather than internal. The end to which the cultivation of the virtues ministers is happiness, but happiness understood as success, prosperity in Philadelphia and ultimately in heaven. The virtues are to be useful and Franklin's account continuously stresses utility as a criterion in individual cases: "Make no expence but to do good to others or yourself; i.e., waste nothing, Speak not but what may benefit others or yourself. Avoid trifling conversation," and, as we have already seen, "Rarely use venery but for health or offspring." When Franklin was in Paris he was horrified by Parisian architecture: "Marble, porcelain and gilt are squandered without utility."

We thus have at least three very different conceptions of a virtue to confront: a virtue is a quality which enables an individual to discharge his or her social role (Homer); a virtue is a quality which enables an individual to move toward the achievement of the specifically human *telos*, whether natural or supernatural (Aristotle, the New Testament, and Aquinas); a virtue is a quality which has utility in achieving earthly and heavenly success (Franklin). Are we to take these as three different rival accounts of the same thing? Or are they instead accounts of three different things? Perhaps the moral structures in archaic Greece, in fourth-century Greece, and in eighteenth-century Pennsylvania were so different from each other that we should treat them as embodying quite different concepts, whose difference is initially disguised from us by the historical accident of an inherited vocabulary which misleads us by linguistic resemblance long after conceptual identity and similarity have failed. Our initial question has come back to us with redoubled force.

Yet although I have dwelt upon the *prima facie* case for holding that the differences and incompatibilities between different accounts at least suggest that there is no single, central, core conception of the virtues which might make a claim for universal allegiance, I ought also to point out that each of the five moral accounts which I have sketched so summarily does embody just such a claim. It is indeed just this feature of those accounts that makes them of more than sociological or antiquarian interest. Every one of these accounts claims not only theoretical, but also an institutional hegemony. For Odysseus the Cyclopes stand condemned because they lack agriculture, an *agora*, and *themis*. For Aristotle the barbarians stand condemned because they lack the *polis* and are therefore incapable of politics. For New Testament Christians there is no salvation outside the apostolic church. And we know that Benjamin Franklin found the virtues more at home in Philadelphia than in Paris and that for Jane Austen the touchstone of the virtues is a certain kind of marriage and indeed a certain kind of naval officer (that is, a certain kind of *English* naval officer).

The question can therefore now be posed directly: Are we or are we not able to disentangle from these rival and various claims a unitary core concept of the virtues of which we can give a more compelling account than any of the other accounts so far? I am going to argue that we can in fact discover such a core concept and that it turns out to provide the tradition of which I have written the history with its conceptual unity. It will indeed enable us to distinguish in a clear way those beliefs about the virtues which genuinely belong to the tradition from those which do not. Unsurprisingly perhaps it is a complex concept, different parts of which derive from different stages in the development of the tradition. Thus the concept itself in some sense embodies the history of which it is the outcome.

One of the features of the concept of a virtue which has emerged with some clarity from the argument so far is that it always requires for its application the acceptance for some prior account of certain features of social and moral life in terms of which it has to be defined and explained. So in the Homeric account the concept of a virtue is secondary to that of a social role, in Aristotle's account it is secondary to that of the good life for man conceived as the *telos* of human action, and in Franklin's much later account it is secondary to that of utility. What is it in the account which I am about to give which provides in a similar way the necessary background against which the concept of a virtue has to be made intelligible? It is in answering this question that the complex, historical, multilayered character of the core concept of virtue becomes clear. For there are no less than three stages in the logical development of the concept which have to be identified in order, if the core conception of a virtue is to be understood, and each of these stages has its own conceptual background. The first stage requires a background account of what I shall call a practice, the second an account of what I have already characterized as the narrative order of a single human life, and the third an account a good deal fuller than I have given up to now of what constitutes moral tradition. Each later stage presupposes the earlier, but not vice versa. Each earlier stage is both modified by and reinterpreted in the light of, but also provides an essential constituent of, each later stage. The progress in the development of the concept is closely related to, although it does not recapitulate in any straightforward way, the history of the tradition of which it forms the core.

In the Homeric account of the virtues—and in heroic societies more generally—the exercise of a virtue exhibits qualities which are required for sustaining a social role and for exhibiting excellence in some well-marked area of social practice: to excel is to excel at war or in the games, as Achilles does, in sustaining a household, as Penelope does, in giving counsel in the assembly, as Nestor does, in the telling of a tale, as Homer himself does. When Aristotle speaks of excellence in human activity, he sometimes, though not always, refers to some well-defined type of human practice: flute-playing, or war, or geometry. I am going to suggest that this notion of a particular type of practice as providing the arena in which the virtues are exhibited and in terms of which they are to receive their primary, if incomplete, definition is crucial to the whole enterprise of identifying a core concept of the virtues. I hasten to add two *caveats*, however.

The first is to point out that my argument will not in any way imply that virtues are *only* exercised in the course of what I am calling practices. The second is to warn that I shall be using the word "practice" in a specially defined way which does not completely agree with current ordinary usage, including my own previous use of that word. What am I going to mean by it?

By "practice" I am going to mean any coherent and complex form of socially established cooperative human activity through which goods internal to that form of activity are realized in the course of trying to achieve those standards of excellence which are appropriate to, and partially definitive of, that form of activity, with the result that human powers to achieve excellence, and human conceptions of the ends and goods involved, are systematically extended. Tic-tac-toe is not an example of a practice in this sense, nor is throwing a football with skill; but the game of football is, and so is chess. Bricklaying is not a practice; architecture is. Planting turnips is not a practice; farming is. So are the enquiries of physics, chemistry, and biology, and so is the work of the historian, and so are painting and music. In the ancient and medieval worlds the creation and sustaining of human communities—of households, cities, nations—is generally taken to be a practice in the sense in which I have defined it. Thus the range of practices is wide; arts, sciences, games, politics in the Aristotelian sense, the making and sustaining of family life, all fall under the concept. But the question of the precise range of practices is not at this stage of the first importance. Instead let me explain some of the key terms involved in my definition, beginning with the notion of goods internal to a practice.

Consider the example of a highly intelligent seven-year-old child whom I wish to teach to play chess, although the child has no particular desire to learn the game. The child does however have a very strong desire for candy and little chance of obtaining it. I therefore tell the child that if the child will play chess with me once a week I will give the child 50 cents' worth of candy; moreover I tell the child that I will always play in such a way that it will be difficult, but not impossible, for the child to win and that, if the child wins, the child will receive an extra 50 cents' worth of candy. Thus motivated the child plays and plays to win. Notice however that, so long as it is the candy alone which provides the child with a good reason for playing chess, the child has no reason not to cheat and every reason to cheat, provided he or she can do so successfully. But, so we may hope, there will come a time when the child will find in those goods specific to chess, in the achievement of a certain highly particular kind of analytical skill, strategic imagination, and competitive intensity, a new set of reasons, reasons now not just for winning on a particular occasion but for trying to excel in whatever way the game of chess demands. Now, if the child cheats, he or she will be defeating not me, but himself or herself.

There are thus two kinds of good possibly to be gained by playing chess. On the one hand there are those goods externally and contingently attached to chess playing and to other practices by the accidents of social circumstance—in the case of the imaginary child candy, in the case of real adults such goods as prestige, status, and money. There are always alternative ways for achieving such goods, and their achievement is never to be had *only* by engaging in some particular kind of practice. On the other hand there are the goods internal to the practice of chess, which cannot be had in any way but by playing chess or some other game of that specific kind. We call them internal for two reasons: first, as I have already suggested, because we can only specify them in terms of chess or some other game of that specific kind and by means of examples from such games (otherwise the meagerness of our vocabulary for speaking of such goods forces us into such devices as my own resort to writing of a certain highly particular kind); and secondly because they can only be identified and recognized by the experience of participating in the practice in question. Those who lack the relevant experience are incompetent thereby as judges of internal goods.

This is clearly the case with all the major examples of practices: consider for example—even if briefly and inadequately—the practice of portrait painting as it developed in western Europe from the late Middle Ages to the eighteenth century. The successful portrait painter is able to achieve many goods which are in the sense just defined external to the practice of portrait painting—fame, wealth, social status, even a measure of power and influence at courts upon occasion. But those external goods are not to be confused with the goods which are internal to the practice. The internal goods are those which result from an extended attempt to show how Wittgenstein's dictum "The human body is the best picture of the human soul" might be made to become true by teaching us "to regard . . . the picture on our wall as the object itself (the men, landscape and so on) depicted there" in a quite new way.[1] What is misleading about Wittgenstein's dictum as it stands is its neglect of the truth in George Orwell's thesis "At fifty everyone has the face he deserves." What painters from Giotto to Rembrandt learnt to show was how the face at any age may be revealed as the face that the subject of a portrait deserves.

Originally in medieval paintings of the saints the face was an icon; the question of a resemblance between the depicted face of Christ or St. Peter and the face that Jesus or Peter actually possessed at some particular age did not even arise. The antithesis to this iconography was the relative naturalism of certain fifteenth-century Flemish and German painting. The heavy eyelids, the coifed hair, the lines around the mouth undeniably represent some particular woman, either actual or envisaged. Resemblance has usurped the iconic relationship. But with Rembrandt there is, so to speak, synthesis: the naturalistic portrait is now rendered as an icon,

1. Ludwig Wittgenstein, *Philosophical Investigations*, 178e, 205e.

but an icon of a new and hitherto inconceivable kind. Similarly in a very different kind of sequence mythological faces in a certain kind of seventeenth-century
French painting become aristocratic faces in the eighteenth century. Within each
of these sequences at least two different kinds of good internal to the painting of
human faces and bodies are achieved.

There is first of all the excellence of the products, both the excellence in performance by the painters and that of each portrait itself. This excellence—the
very verb "excel" suggests it—has to be understood historically. The sequences
of development find their point and purpose in a progress toward and beyond a
variety of types and modes of excellence. There are of course sequences of decline
as well as of progress, and progress is rarely to be understood as straightforwardly
linear. But it is in participation in the attempts to sustain progress and to respond
creatively to problems that the second kind of good internal to the practices of
portrait painting is to be found. For what the artist discovers within the pursuit
of excellence in portrait painting—and what is true of portrait painting is true of
the practice of the fine arts in general—is the good of a certain kind of life. That
life may not constitute the whole of life for someone who is a painter by a very
long way or it may at least for a period, Gauguin-like, absorb him or her at the
expense of almost everything else. But it is the painter's living out of a greater or
lesser part of his or her life as a painter that is the second kind of good internal to
painting. And judgment upon these goods requires at the very least the kind of
competence that is only to be acquired either as a painter or as someone willing
to learn systematically what the portrait painter has to teach.

A practice involves standards of excellence and obedience to rules as well as
the achievement of goods. To enter into a practice is to accept the authority of
those standards and the inadequacy of my own performance as judged by them.
It is to subject my own attitudes, choices, preferences, and tastes to the standards
which currently and partially define the practice. Practices of course, as I have
just noticed, have a history: games, sciences, and arts all have histories. Thus the
standards are not themselves immune from criticism, but nonetheless we cannot
be initiated into a practice without accepting the authority of the best standards
realized so far. If, on starting to listen to music, I do not accept my own incapacity
to judge correctly, I will never learn to hear, let alone to appreciate, Bartok's last
quartets. If, on starting to play baseball, I do not accept that others know better
than I when to throw a fastball and when not, I will never learn to appreciate good
pitching let alone to pitch. In the realm of practices the authority of both goods
and standards operates in such a way as to rule out all subjectivist and emotivist
analyses of judgment. *De gustibus est disputandum.*

We are now in a position to notice an important difference between what I
have called internal and what I have called external goods. It is characteristic
of what I have called external goods that when achieved they are always some
individual's property and possession. Moreover characteristically they are such
that the more someone has of them, the less there is for other people. This is

sometimes necessarily the case, as with power and fame, and sometimes the case by reason of contingent circumstance, as with money. External goods are therefore characteristically objects of competition in which there must be losers as well as winners. Internal goods are indeed the outcome of competition to excel, but it is characteristic of them that their achievement is a good for the whole community who participate in the practice. So when Turner transformed the seascape in painting or W. G. Grace advanced the art of batting in cricket in a quite new way their achievement enriched the whole relevant community.

But what does all or any of this have to do with the concept of the virtues? It turns out that we are now in a position to formulate a first, even if partial and tentative, definition of a virtue: *A virtue is an acquired human quality the possession and exercise of which tends to enable us to achieve those goods which are internal to practices and the lack of which effectively prevents us from achieving any such goods*. Later this definition will need amplification and amendment. But as a first approximation to an adequate definition it already illuminates the place of the virtues in human life. For it is not difficult to show for a whole range of key virtues that without them the goods internal to practices are barred to us, but not just barred to us generally, barred in a very particular way.

It belongs to the concept of a practice as I have outlined it—and as we are all familiar with it already in our actual lives, whether we are painters or physicists or quarterbacks or indeed just lovers of good painting or first-rate experiments or a well-thrown pass—that its goods can only be achieved by subordinating ourselves within the practice in our relationship to other practitioners. We have to learn to recognize what is due to whom; we have to be prepared to take whatever self-endangering risks are demanded along the way; and we have to listen carefully to what we are told about our own inadequacies and to reply with the same carefulness for the facts. In other words we have to accept as necessary components of any practice with internal goods and standards of excellence the virtues of justice, courage, and honesty. For not to accept these, to be willing to cheat as our imagined child was willing to cheat in his or her early days at chess, so far bars us from achieving the standards of excellence or the goods internal to the practice that it renders the practice pointless except as a device for achieving external goods.

We can put the same point in another way. Every practice requires a certain kind of relationship between those who participate in it. Now the virtues are those goods by reference to which, whether we like it or not, we define our relationships to those other people with whom we share the kind of purposes and standards which inform practices. Consider an example of how reference to the virtues has to be made in certain kinds of human relationship.

A, B, C, and D are friends in that sense of friendship which Aristotle takes to be primary: they share in the pursuit of certain goods. In my terms they share in a practice. D dies in obscure circumstances, A discovers how D died and tells the truth about it to B while lying to C. C discovers the lie. What A cannot then intelligibly claim is that he stands in the same relationship of friendship to both B and C. By telling the truth to one and lying to the other he has partially defined a difference in the relationship. Of course it is open to A to explain this difference in a number of ways; perhaps he was trying to spare C pain or perhaps he is simply cheating C. But some difference in the relationship now exists as a result of the lie. For their allegiance to each other in the pursuit of common goods has been put in question.

Just as, so long as we share the standards and purposes characteristic of practices, we define our relationship to each other, whether we acknowledge it or not, by reference to standards of truthfulness and trust, so we define them too by reference to standards of justice and of courage. If A, a professor, gives B and C the grades that their papers deserve, but grades D because he is attracted by D's blue eyes or is repelled by D's dandruff, he has defined his relationship to D differently from his relationship to the other members of the class, whether he wishes it or not. Justice requires that we treat others in respect of merit or desert according to uniform and impersonal standards; to depart from the standards of justice in some particular instance defines our relationship with the relevant person as in some way special or distinctive.

The case with courage is a little different. We hold courage to be a virtue because the care and concern for individuals, communities, and causes which is so crucial to so much in practices requires the existence of such a virtue. If someone says that he cares for some individual, community, or cause but is unwilling to risk harm or danger on his, her, or its own behalf, he puts in question the genuineness of his care and concern. Courage, the capacity to risk harm or danger to oneself, has its role in human life because of this connection with care and concern. This is not to say that a man cannot genuinely care and also be a coward. It is in part to say that a man who genuinely cares and has not the capacity for risking harm or danger has to define himself, both to himself and to others, as a coward.

I take it then that, from the standpoint of those types of relationship without which practices cannot be sustained, truthfulness, justice, and courage—and perhaps some others—are genuine excellences, are virtues in the light of which we have to characterize ourselves and others, whatever our private moral standpoint or our society's particular codes may be. For this recognition that we cannot escape the definition of our relationships in terms of such goods is perfectly compatible with the acknowledgment that different societies have and have had different codes of truthfulness, justice, and courage. Lutheran pietists brought up their children to believe that one ought to tell the truth to everybody at all times, whatever the circumstances or consequences, and Kant was one of their children. Traditional Bantu parents brought up their children not to tell the truth to unknown strangers, since they believed that this could render the family vulnerable to witchcraft. In our culture many of us have been brought up not to tell the truth to elderly great-aunts who invite us to admire their new hats. But each of these codes embodies an acknowledgment of the virtue of truthfulness. So it is also with varying codes of justice and of courage.

Practices then might flourish in societies with very different codes; what they could not do is flourish in societies in which the virtues were not valued, although institutions and technical skills serving unified purposes might well continue to flourish. (I shall have more to say about the contrast between institutions and technical skills mobilized for a unified end, on the one hand, and practices on the other, in a moment.) For the kind of cooperation, the kind of recognition of authority and of achievement, the kind of respect for standards and the kind of risk-taking which are characteristically involved in practices demand for example fairness in judging oneself and others—the kind of fairness absent in my example of the professor, a ruthless truthfulness without which fairness cannot find application—the kind of truthfulness absent in my example of A, B, C, and D—and willingness to trust the judgments of those whose achievement in the practice gives them authority to judge which presupposes fairness and truthfulness in those judgments, and from time to time the taking of self-endangering and even achievement-endangering risks. It is no part of my thesis that great violinists cannot be vicious or great chess-players mean-spirited. Where the virtues are required, the vices also may flourish. It is just that the vicious and mean-spirited necessarily rely on the virtues of others for the practices in which they engage to flourish and also deny themselves the experience of achieving those internal goods which may reward even not very good chess players and violinists.

To situate the virtues any further within practices it is necessary now to clarify a little further the nature of a practice by drawing two important contrasts. The discussion so far I hope makes it clear that a practice, in the sense intended, is never just a set of technical skills, even when directed toward some unified purpose and even if the exercise of those skills can on occasion be valued or enjoyed for their own sake. What is distinctive in a practice is in part the way in which conceptions of the relevant goods and ends which the technical skills serve—and every practice does require the exercise of technical skills—are transformed and enriched by these extensions of human powers and by that regard for its own internal goods which are partially definitive of each particular practice or type of practice. Practices never have a goal or goals fixed for all time—painting has no such goal nor has physics—but the goals themselves are transmuted by the history of the activity. It therefore turns out not to be accidental that every practice has its own history and a history which is more and other than that of the improvement of the relevant technical skills. This historical dimension is crucial in relation to the virtues.

To enter into a practice is to enter into a relationship not only with its contemporary practitioners, but also with those who have preceded us in the practice, particularly those whose achievements extended the reach of the practice to its present point. It is thus the achievement, and *a fortiori* the authority, of a tradition which I then confront and from which I have to learn. And for this learning and the relationship to the past which it embodies, the virtues of justice, courage, and truthfulness are prerequisite in precisely the same way and for precisely the same reasons as they are in sustaining present relationships within practices.

It is not only of course with sets of technical skills that practices ought to be contrasted. Practices must not be confused with institutions. Chess, physics, and medicine are practices; chess clubs, laboratories, universities, and hospitals are institutions. Institutions are characteristically and necessarily concerned with what I have called external goods. They are involved in acquiring money and other material goods; they are structured in terms of power and status, and they distribute money, power, and status as rewards. Nor could they do otherwise if they are to sustain not only themselves, but also the practices of which they are the bearers. For no practices can survive for any length of time unsustained by institutions. Indeed so intimate is the relationship of practices to institutions— and consequently of the goods external to the goods internal to the practices in question—that institutions and practices characteristically form a single causal order in which the ideals and the creativity of the practice are always vulnerable to the acquisitiveness of the institution, in which the cooperative care for common goods of the practice is always vulnerable to the competitiveness of the institution. In this context the essential function of the virtues is clear. Without them, without justice, courage, and truthfulness, practices could not resist the corrupting power of institutions.

Yet if institutions have corrupting power, the making and sustaining of forms of human community—and therefore of institutions—itself has all the characteristics of a practice, and moreover of a practice which stands in a peculiarly close relationship to the exercise of the virtues in two important ways. The exercise of the virtues is itself apt to require a highly determinate attitude to social and political issues, and it is always within some particular community with its own specific institutional forms that we learn or fail to learn to exercise the virtues. There is of course a crucial difference between the way in which the relationship between moral character and political community is envisaged from the standpoint of liberal individualist modernity and the way in which that relationship was envisaged from the standpoint of the type of ancient and medieval tradition of the virtues which I have sketched. For liberal individualism a community is simply an arena in which individuals each pursue their own self-chosen conception of the good life, and political institutions exist to provide that degree of order which makes such self-determined activity possible. Government and law are, or ought to be, neutral between rival conceptions of the good life for man, and hence, although it is the task of government to promote law-abidingness, it is on the liberal view no part of the legitimate function of government to inculcate any one moral outlook.

By contrast, on the particular ancient and medieval view which I have sketched political community not only requires the exercise of the virtues for its own sustenance, but it is one of the tasks of parental authority to make children grow up so as to be virtuous adults. The classical statement of this analogy is by Socrates in the *Crito*. It does not of course follow from an acceptance of the Socratic view of political community and political authority that we ought to assign to the modern state the moral function which Socrates assigned to the city and its laws. Indeed the power of the liberal individualist standpoint partly derives from the evident fact that the modern state is indeed totally unfitted to act as moral educator of any community. But the history of how the modern state emerged is of course itself a moral history. If my account of the complex relationship of virtues to practices and to institutions is correct, it follows that we shall be unable to write a true history of practices and institutions unless that history is also one of the virtues and vices. For the ability of a practice to retain its integrity will depend on the way in which the virtues can be and are exercised in sustaining the institutional forms which are the social bearers of the practice. The integrity of a practice causally requires the exercise of the virtues by at least some of the individuals who embody it in their activities; and conversely the corruption of institutions is always in part at least an effect of the vices.

The virtues are of course themselves in turn fostered by certain types of social institution and endangered by others. Thomas Jefferson thought that only in a society of small farmers could the virtues flourish; and Adam Ferguson with a good deal more sophistication saw the institutions of modern commercial society as endangering at least some traditional virtues. It is Ferguson's type of sociology which is the empirical counterpart of the conceptual account of the virtues which I have given, a sociology which aspires to lay bare the empirical, causal connection between virtues, practices, and institutions. For this kind of conceptual account has strong empirical implications; it provides an explanatory scheme which can be tested in particular cases. Moreover my thesis has empirical content in another way; it does entail that without the virtues there could be a recognition only of what I have called external goods and not at all of internal goods in the context of practices. And in any society which recognized only external goods competitiveness would be the dominant and even exclusive feature. We have a brilliant portrait of such a society in Hobbes's account of the state of nature; and Professor Turnbull's report of the fate of the Ik suggests that social reality does in the most horrifying way confirm both my thesis and Hobbes's.

Virtues then stand in a different relationship to external and to internal goods. The possession of the virtues—and not only of their semblance and simulacra—is necessary to achieve the latter; yet the possession of the virtues may perfectly well hinder us in achieving external goods. I need to emphasize at this point that external goods genuinely are goods. Not only are they characteristic objects of human desire, whose allocation is what gives point to the virtues of justice and of generosity, but no one can despise them altogether without a certain hypocrisy. Yet notoriously the cultivation of truthfulness, justice, and courage will often, the world being what it contingently is, bar us from being rich or famous or powerful. Thus although we may hope that we can not only achieve the standards of excellence and the internal goods of certain practices by possessing the virtues *and* become rich, famous, and powerful, the virtues are always a potential stumbling block to this comfortable ambition. We should therefore expect that, if in a particular society the pursuit of external goods were to become dominant, the concept of the virtues might suffer first attrition and then perhaps something near total effacement, although simulacra might abound.

The time has come to ask the question of how far this partial account of a core conception of the virtues—and I need to emphasize that all that I have offered so far is the first stage of such an account—is faithful to the tradition which I delineated. How far, for example, and in what ways is it Aristotelian? It is—happily—not Aristotelian in two ways in which a good deal of the rest of the tradition also dissents from Aristotle. First, although this account of the virtues is teleological, it does not require any allegiance to Aristotle's metaphysical biology. And second, just because of the multiplicity of human practices and the consequent multiplicity of goods in the pursuit of which the virtues may be exercised—goods which will often be contingently incompatible and which will therefore make rival claims upon our allegiance—conflict will not spring solely from flaws in individual character. But it was just on these two matters that Aristotle's account of the virtues seemed most vulnerable; hence if it turns out to be the case that this socially teleological account can support Aristotle's general account of the virtues as well as does his own biologically teleological account, these differences from Aristotle himself may well be regarded as strengthening rather than weakening the case for a generally Aristotelian standpoint.

There are at least three ways in which the account that I have given *is* clearly Aristotelian. First, it requires for its completion a cogent elaboration of just those distinctions and concepts which Aristotle's account requires: voluntariness, the distinction between the intellectual virtues and the virtues of character, the relationship of both to natural abilities and to the passions and the structure of practical reasoning. On every one of these topics something very like Aristotle's view has to be defended, if my own account is to be plausible.

Second, my account can accommodate an Aristotelian view of pleasure and enjoyment, whereas it is interestingly irreconcilable with any utilitarian view and more particularly with Franklin's account of the virtues. We can approach these questions by considering how to reply to someone who, having considered my account of the differences between goods internal to and goods external to a practice, inquired into which class, if either, does pleasure or enjoyment fall? The answer is, "Some types of pleasure into one, some into the other."

Someone who achieves excellence in a practice, who plays chess or football well or who carries through an enquiry in physics or an experimental mode in painting with success, characteristically enjoys his achievement and his activity in achieving. So does someone who, although not breaking the limit of achievement, plays or thinks or acts in a way that leads toward such a breaking of limit. As Aristotle says, the enjoyment of the activity and the enjoyment of achievement are not the ends at which the agent aims, but the enjoyment supervenes upon the successful activity in such a way that the activity achieved and the activity enjoyed are one and the same state. Hence to aim at the one is to aim at the other; and hence also it is easy to confuse the pursuit of excellence with the pursuit of enjoyment *in this specific sense.* This particular confusion is harmless enough; what is not harmless is the confusion of enjoyment *in this specific sense* with other forms of pleasure.

For certain kinds of pleasure are of course external goods along with prestige, status, power, and money. Not all pleasure is the enjoyment supervening upon achieved activity; some is the pleasure of psychological or physical states independent of all activity. Such states—for example, that produced on a normal palate by the closely successive and thereby blended sensations of Colchester oyster, cayenne pepper, and Veuve Cliquot—may be sought as external goods, as external rewards which may be purchased by money or received in virtue of prestige. Hence the pleasures are categorized neatly and appropriately by the classification into internal and external goods.

It is just this classification which can find no place within Franklin's account of the virtues, which is framed entirely in terms of external relationships and external goods. Thus although by this stage of the argument it is possible to claim that my account does capture a conception of the virtues which is at the core of the particular ancient and medieval tradition which I have delineated, it is equally clear that there is more than one possible conception of the virtues and that Franklin's standpoint and indeed any utilitarian standpoint is such that to accept it will entail rejecting the tradition and vice versa.

One crucial point of incompatibility was noted long ago by D. H. Lawrence. When Franklin asserts, "Rarely use venery but for health or offspring," Lawrence replies, "Never *use* venery." It is of the character of a virtue that in order that it be effective in producing the internal goods which are the rewards of the virtues it should be exercised without regard to consequences. For it turns out to be the case that—and this is in part at least one more empirical factual claim—although the virtues are just those qualities which tend to lead to the achievement of a certain class of goods, nonetheless unless we practice them irrespective of whether in any particular set of contingent circumstances they will produce those goods or not, we cannot possess them at all. We cannot be genuinely courageous or truthful and be so only on occasion. Moreover, as we have seen, cultivation of the virtues always may and often does hinder the achievement of those external goods which are the mark of worldly success. The road to success in Philadelphia and the road to heaven may not coincide after all.

Furthermore we are now able to specify one crucial difficulty for *any* version of utilitarianism—in addition to those which I noticed earlier. Utilitarianism cannot accommodate the distinction between goods internal to and goods external to a practice. Not only is that distinction marked by none of the classical utilitarians—it cannot be found in Bentham's writings nor in those of either of the Mills or of Sidgwick—but internal goods and external goods are not commensurable with each other. Hence the notion of summing goods—and *a fortiori* in the light of what I have said about kinds of pleasure and enjoyment the notion of summing happiness—in terms of one single formula or conception of utility, whether it is Franklin's or Bentham's or Mill's, makes no sense. Nonetheless we ought to note that although *this* distinction is alien to J. S. Mill's thought, it is plausible and in no way patronizing to suppose that something like this is the distinction which he was trying to make in *Utilitarianism* when he distinguished between "higher" and "lower" pleasures. At the most we can say "something like this"; for J. S. Mill's upbringing had given him a limited view of human life and powers, had unfitted him, for example, for appreciating games just because of the way it had fitted him for appreciating philosophy. Nonetheless the notion that the pursuit of excellence in a way that extends human powers is at the heart of human life is instantly recognizable as at home in not only J. S. Mill's political and social thought, but also in his and Mrs. Taylor's life. Were I to choose human exemplars of certain of the virtues as I understand them, there would of course be many names to name, those of St. Benedict and St. Francis of Assisi and St. Theresa *and* those of Frederick Engels and Eleanor Marx and Leon Trotsky among them. But that of John Stuart Mill would have to be there as certainly as any other.

Third, my account is Aristotelian in that it links evaluation and explanation in a characteristically Aristotelian way. From an Aristotelian standpoint to identify certain actions as manifesting or failing to manifest a virtue or virtues is never only to evaluate; it is also to take the first step toward explaining why those actions rather than some others were performed. Hence for an Aristotelian quite as much as for a Platonist the fate of a city or an individual can be explained by citing the injustice of a tyrant or the courage of its defenders. Indeed without allusion to the place that justice and injustice, courage and cowardice play in human life very little will be genuinely explicable. It follows that many of the explanatory projects of the modern social sciences, a methodological canon of which is the separation of the facts from all evaluation, are bound to fail. For the fact that someone was or failed to be courageous just cannot be recognized as "a fact" by those who accept that methodological canon. The account of the virtues which I have given is completely at one with Aristotle's on this point. But now the question may be raised: your account may be in many respects Aristotelian, but is it not in some respects false? Consider the following important objection.

I have defined the virtues partly in terms of their place in practices. But surely, it may be suggested, some practices—that is, some coherent human activities which answer to the description of what I have called a practice—are evil. So in discussions by some moral philosophers of this type of account of the virtues it has been suggested that torture and sadomasochistic sexual activities might be examples of practices. But how can a disposition be a virtue if it is the kind of disposition which sustains practices and some practices issue in evil? My answer to this objection falls into two parts.

First I want to allow that there *may* be practices—in the sense in which I understand the concept—which simply *are* evil. I am far from convinced that there are, and I do not in fact believe that either torture or sadomasochistic sexuality answer to the description of a practice which my account of the virtues employs. But I do not want to rest my case on this lack of conviction, especially since it is plain that as a matter of contingent fact many types of practice may on particular occasions be productive of evil. For the range of practices includes the arts, the sciences, and certain types of intellectual and athletic game. And it is at once obvious that any of these may under certain conditions be a source of evil: the desire to excel and to win can corrupt, a man may be so engrossed by his painting that he neglects his family, what was initially an honorable resort to war can issue in savage cruelty. But what follows from this?

It certainly is not the case that my account entails either that we ought to excuse or condone such evils or that whatever flows from a virtue is right. I do have to allow that courage sometimes sustains injustice, that loyalty has been known to strengthen a murderous aggressor, and that generosity has sometimes weakened the capacity to do good. But to deny this would be to fly in the face of just those empirical facts which I invoked in criticizing Aquinas's account of the unity of the virtues. That the virtues need initially to be defined and explained with reference to the notion of a practice thus in no way entails approval of all practices in all circumstances. That the virtues—as the objection itself presupposed—are defined not in terms of good and right practices but of practices does not entail or imply that practices as actually carried through at particular times and places do not stand in need of moral criticism. And the resources for such criticism are not lacking. There is in the first place no inconsistency in appealing to the requirements of a virtue to criticize a practice. Justice may be initially defined as a disposition which in its particular way is necessary to sustain practices; it does not follow that in pursuing the requirements of a practice violations of justice are not to be condemned. Moreover, a morality of virtues requires as its counterpart a conception of moral law. Its requirements too have to be met by practices. But, it may be asked, does not all this imply that more needs to be said about the place of practices in some larger moral context? Does not this at least suggest that there is more to the core concept of a virtue than can be spelled out in terms of practices? I have after all emphasized that the scope of any virtue in human life extends beyond the practices in terms of which it is initially defined. What then is the place of the virtues in the larger arenas of human life?

I stressed earlier that any account of the virtues in terms of practices could only be a partial and first account. What is required to complement it? The most notable difference so far between my account and any account that could be called Aristotelian is that although I have in no way restricted the exercise of the virtues to the context of practices, it is in terms of practices that I have located their point and function. Whereas Aristotle locates that point and function in terms of the notion of a type of whole human life which can be called good. And it does seem that the question, "What would a human being lack who lacked the virtues?" must be given a kind of answer which goes beyond anything which I have said so far. For such an individual would not merely fail *in a variety of particular ways* in respect of the kind of excellence which can be achieved through participation in practices and in respect of the kind of human relationship required to sustain such excellence.

His own life *viewed as a whole* would perhaps be defective; it would not be the kind of life which someone would describe in trying to answer the question, "What is the best kind of life for this kind of man or woman to live?" And that question cannot be answered without at least raising Aristotle's own question, "What is the good life for man?" Consider three ways in which human life informed only by the conception of the virtues sketched so far would be defective.

It would be pervaded, first of all, by *too many* conflicts and *too much* arbitrariness. I argued earlier that it is a merit of an account of the virtues in terms of a multiplicity of goods that it allows for the possibility of tragic conflict in a way in which Aristotle's does not. But it may also produce even in the life of someone who is virtuous and disciplined too many occasions when one allegiance points in one direction, another in another. The claims of one practice may be incompatible with another in such a way that one may find oneself oscillating in an arbitrary way, rather than making rational choices. So it seems to have been with T. E. Lawrence. Commitment to sustaining the kind of community in which the virtues can flourish may be incompatible with the devotion which a particular practice—of the arts, for example—requires. So there may be tensions between the claims of family life and those of the arts—the problem that Gauguin solved or failed to solve by fleeing to Polynesia, or between the claims of politics and those of the arts—the problem that Lenin solved or failed to solve by refusing to listen to Beethoven.

If the life of the virtues is continuously fractured by choices in which one allegiance entails the apparently arbitrary renunciation of another, it may seem that the goods internal to practices do after all derive their authority from our individual choices, for when different goods summon in different and in incompatible directions, "I" have to choose between their rival claims. The modern self with its criterionless choices apparently reappears in the alien context of what was claimed to be an Aristotelian world. This accusation might be rebutted in part by returning to the question of why both goods and virtues do have authority in our lives and repeating what was said earlier in this chapter. But this reply would only be partly successful; the distinctively modern notion of choice would indeed have reappeared, even if with a more limited scope for its exercise than it has usually claimed.

Second, without an overriding conception of the *telos* of a whole human life, conceived as a unity, our conception of certain individual virtues has to remain partial and incomplete. Consider two examples. Justice, on an Aristotelian view, is defined in terms of giving each person his or her due or desert. To deserve well is to have contributed in some substantial way to the achievement of those goods, the sharing of which and the common pursuit of which provide foundations for human community. But the goods internal to practices, including the goods internal to the practice of making and sustaining forms of community, need to be ordered and evaluated in some way if we are to assess relative desert. Thus any substantive application of an Aristotelian concept of justice requires an understanding of goods and of the good that goes beyond the multiplicity of goods which inform practices. As with justice, so also with patience. Patience is the virtue of waiting attentively without complaint, but not of waiting thus for anything at all. To treat patience as a virtue presupposes some adequate answer to the question: waiting for what? Within the context of practices a partial, although for many purposes adequate, answer can be given: the patience of a craftsman with refractory material, of a teacher with a slow pupil, of a politician in negotiations, are all species of patience. But what if the material is just too refractory, the pupil too slow, the negotiations too frustrating? Ought we always at a certain point just to give up in the interests of the practice itself? The medieval exponents of the virtue of patience claimed that there are certain types of situation in which the virtue of patience requires that I do not ever give up on some person or task, situations in which, as they would have put it, I am required to embody in my attitude to that person or task something of the patient attitude of God toward his creation. But this could only be so if patience served some overriding good, some *telos* which warranted putting other goods in a subordinate place. Thus it turns out that the content of the virtue of patience depends upon how we order various goods in a hierarchy and *a fortiori* on whether we are able rationally so to order these particular goods.

I have suggested so far that unless there is a *telos* which transcends the limited goods of practices by constituting the good of a whole human life, the good of a human life conceived as a unity, it will be the case *both* that a certain subversive arbitrariness will invade the moral life *and* that we shall be unable to specify the context of certain virtues adequately. These two considerations are reinforced by a third: that there is at least one virtue recognized by the tradition which cannot be specified at all except with reference to the wholeness of a human life—the virtue of integrity or constancy. "Purity of heart," said Kierkegaard, "is to will one thing." This notion of singleness of purpose in a whole life can have no application unless that of a whole life does.

It is clear therefore that my preliminary account of the virtues in terms of practices captures much, but very far from all, of what the Aristotelian tradition taught about the virtues. It is also clear that to give an account that is at once more fully adequate to the tradition and rationally defensible, it is necessary to raise a question to which the Aristotelian tradition presupposed an answer, an answer so widely shared in the premodern world that it never had to be formulated explicitly in any detailed way. This question is: Is it rationally justifiable to conceive of each human life as a unity, so that we may try to specify each such life as having its good and so that we may understand the virtues as having their function in enabling an individual to make of his or her life one kind of unity rather than another?

# 8

. . . . . . . . . . . . . . . .

# The Church
# as a Community of Practice

. . . . . . . . . . . . . . . . . . . . . . . . . . . . . .

JONATHAN R. WILSON

We live today among fragmented worlds. The first half of *After Virtue* identifies the source of this fragmentation by narrating "the failure of the Enlightenment Project." This project seeks a rational justification for morality that is independent of any particular convictions, especially theological convictions. At one level, it may be understood as an attempt to end the conflicts in Europe that were rooted in religious differences. At another level, this project may be read as the rejection of the classical moral tradition. MacIntyre shows that today this project and its failure lies at the root of the problems that both occupy academic philosophers *and* afflict our everyday social life.[1]

## The Culture's Enlightenment Project

After narrating the history of successive attempts to achieve an independent rational justification for morality in the work of Hume (who sought justification in the

---

Originally published as "The Church as a Community of Practice," in Jonathan Wilson, *Living Faithfully in a Fragmented World: Lessons for the Church from MacIntyre's "After Virtue"* (Harrisburg, PA: Trinity Press International, 1997), 39–67. Reprinted with permission.

1. Alasdair MacIntyre, *After Virtue: A Study in Moral Theory*, 2nd ed. (Notre Dame, IN: University of Notre Dame Press, 1984), chap. 4.

passions), Diderot (desire), Kant (reason), and Kierkegaard (choice), MacIntyre argues that these attempts failed, not because they look to the wrong sources for justifying morality, but because they had in common a particular way of characterizing the problem; in short, they were all seeking to achieve "the Enlightenment Project." This project was bound to fail, MacIntyre argues, because it misconstrued the moral tradition that it had inherited.

According to MacIntyre, the moral tradition previous to the Enlightenment depended upon a threefold structure: (1) humanity as we are; (2) humanity as we should be; (3) how we can get from where we are to where we should be.[2] The Enlightenment Project abandoned any notion of "humanity as we should be," because any account of who we should be depends upon a view of the true end of humanity that is rooted in particular convictions—the very thing that the Enlightenment sought to avoid. So the Enlightenment Project abandoned this threefold structure and attempted to justify morality apart from any particular view of what humanity could be if we realized our true end. As a result, the Enlightenment left us with humanity as we are and moral instruction for how to get from where we are to . . . ? Because the Enlightenment abandoned all accounts of where we should be, it could give no description of the purpose of morality. Thus moral precepts lacked the structure that had given them meaning and coherence. Consequently, MacIntyre argues, "the Enlightenment Project had to fail."[3] We still have some of the language and practices of morality, but they exist only in fragments, apart from the overall structure that gave them meaning. This fragmented morality appears to have no justification, for it has been deprived of the very convictions that give it meaning. Increasingly, then, morality seems to be merely a set of (often personal) preferences.

As a result of this history, our culture is largely shaped by emotivism—"the doctrine that all evaluative judgments and more specifically all moral judgments are *nothing but* expressions of preference, expressions of attitude or feeling, insofar as they are moral or evaluative in character."[4] In such a culture

> moral judgments, being expressions of attitude or feeling, are neither true nor false; and disagreement in moral judgment is not to be secured by any rational method, for there are none. It is to be secured, if at all, by producing certain nonrational effects on the emotions or attitudes of those who disagree with mine. We use moral judgments not only to express our own attitudes and feelings, but also precisely to produce such effects in others.[5]

If the church is to live faithfully in the context of an emotivist culture marked by the failure of the Enlightenment Project, then we must learn a number of things from MacIntyre's account.

2. Ibid., 54.
3. Ibid., chap. 5.
4. Ibid., 11–12.
5. Ibid., 12.

## The Church's Enlightenment Project

In order to understand the impact of the Enlightenment Project on the life of the church, we must first attend to ways in which the church is implicated in the Enlightenment Project to achieve an independent rational justification for morality. Certainly, the moral tradition of the Western church, because of our involvement with our culture, has been deeply affected by the failure of the Enlightenment Project.

Of equal significance as a threat to the life of the church is the fact that the church has carried on its own version of the Enlightenment Project in relation not to morality but to the gospel. That is, just as Western culture, in the Enlightenment Project, sought an independent rational justification for morality, so also the Western church has sought independent rational justification for the gospel. And just as the Enlightenment Project to justify morality was bound to fail, for the same reasons the church's version of the Enlightenment Project also had to fail.

The church's quest for an independent rational justification of the gospel has taken a number of forms. It is clearly evident in our apologetics, where there has been considerable debate. It is also the main theme of Hans Frei's influential analyses of hermeneutics and modern theology.[6] Of greatest interest for us is the way that the church's Enlightenment Project has marked our evangelism.

In contrast to the studies of apologetics, rationality, and hermeneutics, the church's language about and practice of evangelism has received little analysis along these lines. In order to initiate some examination of this tendency in evangelism, rather than examine specific practices and programs of evangelism, I will here sketch some general characteristics of the church's Enlightenment Project on evangelism.

The overarching characteristic of this project is the church's attempt to commend the gospel on grounds that have nothing to do with the gospel itself. In this way, the church avoids any convictions particular to the gospel or the church as the basis for justifying or commending the gospel. Two things result from this attempt. First, as with MacIntyre's narrative of the Enlightenment Project on morality, the church seeks various grounds for the gospel. Commensurate with the attempts of Hume, Diderot, Kant, and Kierkegaard on behalf of morality, the church has had its thinkers who have sought to ground the gospel in accounts of the passions, desires, reason, and choice. This has been true of both academic and popular theology. For example, Kant's attempt to ground morality in reason is accompanied by an attempt to ground religion "within the bounds of reason alone." Here an account of reason that is independent of the gospel becomes the putative ground—and boundary—for religion. Likewise, Friedrich Schleiermacher's *On Religion: Speeches to Its Cultured Despisers* may be read as an

---

6. Hans Frei, *The Eclipse of Biblical Narrative: A Study in Eighteenth and Nineteenth Century Hermeneutics* (New Haven: Yale University Press, 1968); Frei, *Types of Christian Theology* (New Haven: Yale University Press, 1992); Frei, *Theology and Narrative* (New Haven: Yale University Press, 1993).

evangelistic presentation of the gospel that seeks to commend the gospel on the basis of the feeling of absolute dependence. Because Schleiermacher's account of the feeling of absolute dependence is developed without reference to the gospel and does not depend upon the gospel for its meaning, his account is an expression of the church's Enlightenment Project.[7]

On a more popular level, we may often hear evangelistic presentations that commend the gospel to its hearers on their terms, rather than seeking to present a coherent account of the gospel's own faithfulness. For example, Robert Schuller's widely known attempt at a "new reformation" based on self-esteem fails, not because self-esteem is the wrong way to translate the gospel for contemporary people, but because Schuller's account develops the notion of self-esteem separate from the structure of the gospel, then makes our quest for self-esteem the ground for commending the gospel.[8] In other words, the fundamental problem with Schuller's appeal is not the notion of self-esteem itself but the structure to which Schuller appeals for the meaning of self-esteem. Of course, if his account of self-esteem were developed within the overall structure of the gospel, then it would change significantly.

Admittedly, this is a difficult point to communicate and to grasp. As MacIntyre reminds us in his much fuller account of our moral situation, if he is right, then "we are in a condition which almost nobody recognizes and which perhaps nobody at all can recognize fully."[9] In the same way, if the church has engaged in its own Enlightenment Project, then we are in a situation that few recognize and that none recognizes fully.

One way for us to begin to recognize our situation is by continuing to learn from MacIntyre's account. MacIntyre argues that the Enlightenment Project on morality had to fail because it rejected any notion of humanity as we could be if we realized our *telos*, and thus it abandoned the very element that gave coherence, meaning, and persuasiveness to our moral precepts. What if the same thing has happened to the gospel in the church's own Enlightenment Project? The church, when it is faithful to the gospel, gives an account of the present human situation, of humanity as God intends us to be, and of the gospel of salvation by grace as the means by which humanity moves (or, more properly, is moved) from where we are to where God intends us to be. When the church abandons the teleological conviction of where God intends humanity to be, then we are left with the project of seeking a ground for the claims of the gospel apart from the gospel itself. As MacIntyre has shown us, such a project is bound to fail.

7. At present a number of theologians are seeking to rehabilitate Schleiermacher's work by overthrowing the traditional reading that I present here. If they succeed, that will not change the force of my argument here, which turns on how Schleiermacher has been read. If he is "revised," then he will become an exemplar of the position I am advocating.

8. Robert Schuller, *Self-Esteem: The New Reformation* (Dallas: Word, 1985).

9. MacIntyre, *After Virtue*, 4. That MacIntyre does not himself fully realize our situation is indicated by the fact that he continues to develop and rewrite his arguments in later works.

Before we move on to consider the consequences of this failure, we should consider an objection, often directed toward MacIntyre, that may be brought against my account. To some, MacIntyre's account, and by extension my account, may appear to give no means for judging among competing convictions and traditions. In other words, our accounts appear fideistic or relativistic. However, as MacIntyre shows in a later work,[10] his position does allow for rational comparison. Moreover, James McClendon Jr. has given an extensive account of evaluating and justifying religious convictions that is compatible with the position I am advocating.[11] What our accounts preclude is the notion that there are grounds for justifying the gospel apart from the gospel itself.

To go beyond MacIntyre's account, the way for the church to justify the claims of the gospel is by living the way of life to which the gospel calls us. This way of life, as it displays the full claims of the gospel, may then be compared to other ways of life. This comparison occurs not from some Archimedean point outside every tradition but from within one's present tradition as one considers the competing claims.[12] In this understanding, the church commends the gospel by living according to the gospel, not by appealing to some ground outside the gospel. For this very reason then, this work is about *living faithfully* in a fragmented world: living faithfully simply *is* the Christian mission in the modern world.

So, one part of the lesson that we learn from MacIntyre's narrative of the failure of the Enlightenment Project is that the church has carried its own version of this project. We will be able to live faithfully in a fragmented world only as we develop our ability to discern how and where we have engaged in this Enlightenment Project that is bound to fail.

## Consequences of the Failure of the Enlightenment Project

We may learn something else from MacIntyre's narrative of the failure of the Enlightenment Project by attending to one of the consequences of this failure. According to MacIntyre, as a result of this failure we live in a culture that is marked by three particular "characters." By characters MacIntyre means social roles that represent the moral nature of a culture. In these characters, role and personality are fused, and possibilities for action are limited by the culture. These characters provide the members of a culture "with a cultural and moral ideal" that "morally legitimates a mode of social existence."[13] As examples, MacIntyre points to the

10. Alasdair MacIntyre, *Whose Justice? Which Rationality?* (Notre Dame, IN: University of Notre Dame Press, 1988).

11. James W. McClendon Jr., *Systematic Theology*, vol. 1, *Ethics* (Nashville: Abingdon, 1986).

12. The best and fullest account of this process may be found in James W. McClendon Jr., *Systematic Theology*, vol. 2, *Doctrine* (Nashville: Abingdon, 1994).

13. MacIntyre, *After Virtue*, 29.

"Public School Headmaster, Explorer and the Engineer" for Victorian England, and the "Prussian Officer, the Professor and the Social Democrat" for Wilhelmine Germany.[14]

In the emotivist culture that results from the failure of the Enlightenment Project, our stock of characters includes the Rich Aesthete, the Therapist, and the Manager.[15] If we consider how these characters mark not only Western culture but also in very particular ways the Western church, we may gain further insight into how the church can live faithfully in a fragmented world.

In MacIntyre's account, the Rich Aesthete, who has a surplus of financial and social resources, seeks to alleviate boredom by manipulating others for the pleasure and good of the Aesthete. MacIntyre rightly warns that not all rich nor all aesthetes live out this character. Nevertheless, our culture is stocked by this "ideal." Even those who do not have the resources to live out this character may aspire to the role: living morally fragmented lives and lacking any clear *telos* for our lives, we may be captured by this character.

In the church, this character of the Rich Aesthete plays itself out in at least two ways. First, in our quest for "converts" we may be motivated more by the manipulation of others to achieve our own ends than by obedience to Christ or the desire to see others find their true *telos* in following Christ. We are especially susceptible to this when our own lives are not oriented toward loving God in obedience. Jesus warns us against this very dynamic in a slightly different setting in Matthew 6:1: "Beware of practicing your piety before others in order to be seen by them; for then you have no reward from your Father in heaven." In our culture, apparently faithful witness may be corrupted by our playing out the role of a religious Rich Aesthete when we seek converts to "add notches" or increase our status before others. Lacking an appropriate *telos*, we manipulate others through the excess of our rhetorical and emotional resources in order to increase our pleasure, alleviate our boredom, and serve our own ends.

We may play out the role of Rich Aesthete in the church in a second way by seeking our own pleasure in worship. It is certainly right for the church to pursue beauty and excellence in worship, but that pursuit must be oriented first toward glorifying and enjoying God. When we orient worship toward giving ourselves pleasure, either through "high" liturgical worship or through "low" informal worship, we are playing out the role of the Rich Aesthete. Many analyses of what is wrong with our worship fasten on a comparison of high and low worship and argue for the superiority of one over the other. Such analyses usually miss the deeper issue of our cultural context and the subtle temptation to adopt the character of the Rich Aesthete that fulfills a (mistaken) moral ideal and legitimates a larger social mode of existence.

14. Ibid., 28.
15. MacIntyre gives his account of these characters primarily in *After Virtue*, chap. 3, "Emotivism: Social Content and Social Context," and chap. 6, "Some Consequences of the Failure of the Enlightenment Project."

The second character that MacIntyre identifies in our culture is the Therapist.[16] This character has received a great deal of critical attention. In L. Gregory Jones's book *Transformed Judgment*, he devotes a chapter to how the character of the Therapist (with the collusion of the Manager, a third character we will consider below) has corrupted our practices of forgiveness.[17] In the previous chapter (of the book in which this chapter originally appeared), I showed how our worship may be wrongly directed toward therapeutic ends. In this chapter, I want to consider briefly the larger problem with the character of the Therapist. As Jones, following MacIntyre, shows, the Therapist plays out our culture's acceptance and reinforcement of "the individualist realm of private feelings and values."[18] That is, as the character of the Therapist is acted out in a morally fragmented culture, the Therapist enables us to adjust our private feelings and values in order to come to terms with that fragmentation. Focusing on technique and lacking any means to question our ends, the Therapist underwrites our moral fragmentation and undermines the possibility of Christian community. Thus the problem with the Therapist, as acted out in our culture, is not that God wants followers of Jesus to be unhealthy and unhappy; rather, the problem is that the Therapist locates health and happiness in the realm of private feelings and values, not in our discovering and living out the proper *telos* of humanity as revealed in Jesus Christ.

It is important for us to recognize that the role of Therapist may be acted out in formal counseling settings in the church, but it may also be more subtly dangerous in less obvious settings, such as preaching and fellowship. When preaching merely helps us to accept the world in its sin and does not call us to the reality of God's work among us that enables faithful living, then the Therapist has triumphed. When our fellowship is a "conspiracy of cordiality,"[19] rather than the communion of the reconciled, the Therapist has triumphed. These triumphs of the Therapist may lead to a growing congregation and apparent success, but they do not lead the Christian community into faithful living.

The third character that MacIntyre identifies in our culture is the Manager. If the Rich Aesthete and the Therapist represent roles in our private lives (as demarcated by our culture), the Manager governs our public lives. According to MacIntyre's analysis, the Manager may be the most pernicious of these characters. For a culture living out the consequences of the failure of the Enlightenment Project, the Manager seeks to achieve maximum bureaucratic efficiency without regard to the end. Thus the Manager's authority is justified in our culture, first, by belief

16. To be fair, we should note that not all therapists play out the character of the Therapist as MacIntyre describes it. However, given the power of a cultural ideal, we must also recognize how difficult it is to resist this role.

17. L. Gregory Jones, *Transformed Judgment: Toward a Trinitarian Account of the Moral Life* (Notre Dame, IN: University of Notre Dame Press, 1990), chap. 2.

18. Ibid., 40.

19. Stanley Hauerwas and William H. Willimon, *Resident Aliens: Life in the Christian Colony* (Nashville: Abingdon, 1989), 138.

in "the existence of a domain of morally neutral fact about which the manager is to be expert." Second, the Manager is believed to know "lawlike generalizations and their applications to particular cases derived from the study of this domain."[20]

The important point about the character of the Manager in our fragmented culture is that the Manager's effectiveness is thought to be morally neutral. That is, the Manager concentrates on mastering "techniques without any evaluation of the ends toward which the techniques are developed."[21] Morality, then, is outside the realm of the Manager's competence and responsibility.

MacIntyre argues that this claim to managerial effectiveness is a "fictitious, but believed-in reality" that is central to our culture. For this reason, he devotes two important chapters to showing the illusory nature of our belief in the domain of morally neutral fact and the predictive power of generalizations in social science to which the Manager claims special access. In this critique, MacIntyre allows modest claims to managerial effectiveness, but disputes the larger claims to managerial power that so often mark our culture. The persistence of those larger claims and our acceptance of them, he shows, depend upon the moral fragmentation of our culture and the histrionic skills of the Manager (whom MacIntyre sometimes labels "the bureaucrat"): "The most effective manager is the best actor."[22] By this claim, MacIntyre means that despite the illusory basis of the Manager's claim to authority, that authority may be maintained by the Manager's ability to sustain the illusion by acting it out convincingly.

As the Western church participates in the consequences of the failure of the Enlightenment Project, it may be infected by the character of the Manager. This infection may be difficult to diagnose, because we do not think of the church as a domain of morally neutral fact ruled by lawlike generalizations from the social sciences. However, in our morally fragmented world, the church may often find itself serving ends other than faithfulness to God. In this situation, the church may appear successful and the Manager may appear effective, but that success and effectiveness can be directed toward wrong ends.

Before continuing, we should note two qualifications. First, it is not success or effectiveness that is problematic. Rather the problem is that in our culture success and effectiveness are determined by the illusory convictions outlined above. Certainly, the church is called to be successful and effective, but it is called to be those things in relation to the mission given by God, not by our culture. Second, as I move on to criticize the church's use of the social sciences, that criticism is directed toward the practice of social science that is divorced from the question of ends and strives merely for maximum bureaucratic effectiveness.[23]

20. MacIntyre, *After Virtue*, 77.

21. Jones, *Transformed Judgment*, 40.

22. MacIntyre, *After Virtue*, 108.

23. In a *tour de force*, John Milbank deconstructs theological reliance on social theory and relocates social questions within ecclesiology. Milbank, *Theology and Social Theory: Beyond Secular Reason* (Oxford: Blackwell, 1990).

The church's capitulation to the authority of the Manager is tied to the centrality of that character in our culture and to the church's attempt to live with its history. Seeking to recover or to maintain our perceived place in the culture, we in the church turn to the Manager for guidance. So today, some of the most powerful leaders of the church are those who know how to manage public opinion and the political process in order to achieve success. If we examine the ends of that management, however, we may well question whether its success is directed toward making disciples.

Although the influence of the Church Growth Movement and its advocacy of the "homogeneous unit principle" is fading, at one time this movement represented a powerful example of the authority of the Manager. Drawing largely on social science, this movement argued that the most effective means for growing churches was through targeting homogeneous units. The social scientific apparatus that accompanied this argument and its apparent effectiveness drew many churches into its orbit. Today, most advocates of this movement have greatly modified their position and propose modest claims more in line with MacIntyre's analysis of managerial effectiveness. Nevertheless, the movement stands as a reminder of the church's capitulation to the character of the Manager.

Finally, drawing on MacIntyre's analysis of the character of the Manager, we can learn to be on guard against the perpetuation of the authority of the Manager through histrionics. In recent years, many sincere followers of Jesus Christ have been made captive to good acting. What else are the televangelists but prime examples of MacIntyre's dictum that "the most effective bureaucrat is the best actor"? Quite apart from these highly visible Managers, many local churches aspire to have pastors who differ from televangelists only in the degree of acting ability they possess and in the private morality they live out. That is, they do not see the pernicious effect of the Manager on the church's faithfulness. They want a pastor who combines managerial effectiveness with private morality.

## Recovering Tradition[24]

### *The Aristotelian Story*

In *After Virtue*, MacIntyre develops his argument by telling two stories.[25] The first story, the failure of the Enlightenment Project, has already given us a number

24. Here we turn to MacIntyre's constructive counterproposal to the Enlightenment Project. This proposal could be characterized in a number of ways, each of which has its limitations. I have chosen "tradition" as a way of faithfully reflecting the development of MacIntyre's proposal beyond his *After Virtue*; see MacIntyre, *Three Rival Versions of Moral Enquiry: Encyclopaedia, Genealogy, and Tradition; Being Gifford Lectures Delivered in the University of Edinburgh in 1988* (Notre Dame, IN: University of Notre Dame Press, 1990).

25. This and the following three paragraphs are adapted from Jonathan R. Wilson, "Living Faithfully in a Fragmented World: Four Lessons from MacIntyre's *After Virtue*," *Crux* 26, no. 4 (December 1990): 38–42, here pp. 40–41.

of lessons. The second story that MacIntyre tells is of the classical tradition of morality. In telling this story, MacIntyre seeks to vindicate and recover a form of the Aristotelian moral tradition. MacIntyre's narrative of this tradition begins with the earliest Greek poets of heroic society and then moves on to the dramatists and philosophers of early Athenian society. After MacIntyre scrutinizes Aristotle's detailed account of this moral tradition, he considers the medieval "dialogue with"—rather than "simple assent to"—the Aristotelian moral tradition.[26] MacIntyre argues that this dialogue brought three improvements to the classical moral tradition: (1) it recognized the inevitability of conflict and met conflict with the Christian virtues of charity and forgiveness, which were entirely missing in Aristotle; (2) its understanding of God's grace meant that neither Aristotle's *fortuna* (the bad luck of ugliness, low birth, childlessness, or other such circumstances) nor evil (provided we do not become complicit) excludes anyone from realizing the human good; (3) it incorporated a fuller understanding of human historicity. Aristotle understood that the moral life is lived in a particular place; the medieval thinkers recognized that the moral life is also lived within a particular history.

This is the moral tradition that the Enlightenment sought to escape. Now that we see the failure of the Enlightenment Project, MacIntyre advocates a recovery of some form of the Aristotelian tradition. His constructive proposal consists of five elements: the conception of a practice, an account of the virtues, a narrative account of the good life (the *telos*) for a human, a living tradition, and a community within which these are set. MacIntyre spends several chapters developing and defending his proposal. He contrasts his position to competitors, defends it against objections, and argues for its viability, even its necessity.

### A Revision of MacIntyre

MacIntyre's proposal provides us with several lessons for living faithfully in a fragmented world. However, before we turn to those lessons, we must consider a weakness in MacIntyre's proposal as it stands in *After Virtue*. MacIntyre has since revised and expanded his argument, most notably in *Whose Justice? Which Rationality?* Nevertheless, to make full use of his proposal for the church, we must revise it.[27]

The weakness in MacIntyre's account in *After Virtue* is that, although he advocates a recovery of the moral tradition, no specific moral tradition is present. He argues for a conception of practices but advocates no specific practices. He argues for virtues but no particular virtues. His proposal, as it stands in *After Virtue*, is a torso without a head, onto which any number of heads may be grafted. John

---

26. MacIntyre, *After Virtue*, 165.

27. Even with this later work, MacIntyre has still received considerable criticism for his neglect of substantive theological convictions in Jones, *Transformed Judgment*; Millbank, *Theology and Social Theory*; and Stanley Hauerwas and Charles Pinches, *Christians among the Virtues: Theological Conversations with Ancient and Modern Ethics* (Notre Dame, IN: University of Notre Dame Press, 1997). The major purpose of my revision of MacIntyre's proposal will be to give some theological direction.

Rawls,[28] for example, has given an account of liberal democracy, the development of which is inextricably tied to the Enlightenment Project that MacIntyre decries, as a tradition with practices and virtues set within a community.[29]

Thus MacIntyre's account in *After Virtue* must be revised. In part, I think this weakness is due to the fact that *After Virtue* represents a stage in MacIntyre's return to Christianity. As I have already noted, MacIntyre himself revises his account in later writings. Nevertheless, his account gives us some guidance for living faithfully in a fragmented world, to which we will add some theological substance.[30] Although the five elements of MacIntyre's proposal fit tightly together, for the sake of clarity we will consider them separately and then weave them back together.

Before turning to our constructive account, I must add one more caveat. If MacIntyre's account of our circumstances is generally accurate, as I believe it is, then this constructive account will lack initial plausibility because we are in a situation in which it has few exemplars. That is, the real force of MacIntyre's constructive proposal rests in its embodiment in the life of a community. Lacking communities that exhibit such force, accounts such as mine can only grope toward living faithfully. In the end, it is not my account but faithful communities that will teach us how to live faithfully in a fragmented world. Nevertheless, drawing on MacIntyre's insights, we may gain some understanding of what we are groping toward, by God's grace.

### The Good Life

In MacIntyre's account, he shows that our moral fragmentation largely results from the loss of the conception of the *telos* of human life. Because this loss is at the heart of our fragmentation, it is helpful to begin our constructive account at this point. In *After Virtue*, MacIntyre provisionally defines the *telos*, or "good life," for humans, as "the life spent in seeking for the good life for man."[31] Although this conclusion is provisional, MacIntyre gives little further explanation in *After Virtue*. In spite of the rather abstract account MacIntyre gives of the good life, he does make clear that we must recover some notion of the *telos* of humanity.

The Christian notion of the human *telos* may be described in various ways. In MacIntyre's later work, he moves toward a more Christian and theological conception of the good life by drawing on Thomas Aquinas's assertion that the human *telos* is "that state of perfect happiness which is the contemplation of God in the beatific vision."[32] In an earlier discussion, I drew on the Westminster Catechism's

---

28. John Rawls, *Political Liberalism* (New York: Columbia University Press, 1993), 3:4.

29. MacIntyre himself later acknowledges the "tradition" of liberalism and subjects it to critique in *Whose Justice? Which Rationality?*, chap. 17.

30. For the purposes of this essay, my account will be suggestive. I develop my suggestions more substantively in Jonathan R. Wilson, *Theology as Cultural Critique: The Achievement of Julian Hartt* (Macon, GA: Mercer University Press, 1996); and Wilson, *Gospel Virtues: Practicing Faith, Hope, and Love in Uncertain Times* (Downers Grove, IL: InterVarsity, 1998).

31. MacIntyre, *After Virtue*, 220.

32. MacIntyre, *Whose Justice? Which Rationality?*, 192.

teaching that the true end of humanity is "to glorify God and enjoy him forever." We may add to this Paul's assertion that the purpose of God's work is that "all of us come to the unity of the faith and of the knowledge of the Son of God, to maturity, to the measure of the full stature of Christ" (Eph. 4:13). Although these statements use different language and images, they give compatible descriptions of the human *telos* revealed in the gospel of Jesus Christ.[33]

The lesson for the church to learn from MacIntyre is that we must revitalize our ability to give an account of the good life for humans that is revealed in the gospel. This revitalization will not end conflict; indeed, it may heighten conflict. But at the same time, on MacIntyre's account, it will enable us to locate those conflicts properly. In so doing, it will also enable us to live more faithfully by the gospel rather than the Enlightenment Project.

The most important lesson to learn from MacIntyre about our attempts to give a Christian account of the good life is that we must learn to live and to think teleologically. That is, Christians must seek continually to give an account of our lives that coheres with our *telos*. In so doing, we can resist, and even overcome, the moral fragmentation of our lives by continually seeking to order our lives toward our conception of the human *telos*. In other words, we must learn to give an account not just of *what* Christians do, but also of why we do it in relation to the conception of the human *telos* revealed in the gospel.

This kind of living and thinking examines our practices to see if they are coherent with our understanding of God's purposes for humanity. Take, for example, the Church Growth Movement. Can we give an account of how practicing the "homogeneous unit principle" coheres with Paul's call to unity in Christ, which occurs in the same letter in which he describes the crumbling of the wall between Jew and Gentile (Eph. 2)? Or consider our practices of forgiveness. Are they ordered toward therapeutic happiness, managerial control, or reconciliation in Christ? At all points in our lives, we must ask whether our lives are directed toward maturity in Christ or toward some other competing, and often unrecognized, *telos*.

MacIntyre, then, teaches us to think teleologically, to identify the human *telos* and order our lives toward it. Such ordering cannot be sustained alone; it requires the other elements of MacIntyre's proposal. Because, as noted above, the quest to identify the human *telos* may intensify rather than reduce conflict, we turn now to MacIntyre's account of this kind of conflict.

### The Living Tradition

According to MacIntyre, a living tradition "is an historically extended, socially embodied argument, and an argument precisely in part about the goods which

---

33. In our section below on "living tradition," we will consider further the arguments within the church over different accounts of the human *telos*.

constitute that tradition."[34] In this description, MacIntyre acknowledges that teleological thinking brings conflict—precisely over the *telos* toward which our thinking should be ordered. But he also places that conflict within the large context of a "living tradition." It is the nature of the conflict and what counts as important in that conflict that constitutes a living tradition.

If we recover this understanding of living tradition for living faithfully in a fragmented world, we will begin to discern ways in which the church has been corrupted in Western culture. We will begin to recover arguments, like the ones noted above, over whether this or that practice of the church is oriented toward the proper end. We will also begin to argue about what constitutes that proper end.

In these arguments, we must learn from MacIntyre how to understand the "rationality" of tradition. First, we must learn what it means to participate in a *living* tradition. In MacIntyre's account, a living tradition may be conservative, but it is not static. Over time, tensions and contradictions may arise internally and externally. A living tradition responds to these tensions and contradictions in various ways. Some traditions decay over time and lose their potency; they "die." Others emerge from such challenges stronger than ever.

In Acts 15, we have a wonderful example of the church's participation in a living tradition. There the early church confronts an apparent contradiction: faith in Christ and the presence of the Holy Spirit have been given to uncircumcised Gentiles. These events are a profound challenge to the tradition of the church. Yet, as John Howard Yoder shows, they respond to this challenge from within the tradition and emerge faithful and strong.[35] The conflict does not end, but it now takes place as a "socially embodied argument" about the goods—in particular, one good, circumcision—that constitute the tradition.

The second lesson we must learn from MacIntyre's account of a living tradition is the rationality of tradition over against other forms of rationality. In the work that follows *After Virtue*, MacIntyre devotes much energy to this topic.[36] This topic is too complex to give a full account here. Suffice it to say that in the gospel the church has not only a living tradition but an ever-present reality. That is, the gospel is not merely something from the past that continues to live on in the memory of the church; it is also, and more significantly, the redeeming work of God in Jesus Christ present in the past and present today. The church's calling is to discern that present reality and live faithfully in it. Thus the life of the church embodies the rationality of the gospel.

In a church marked by the moral fragmentation of the Enlightenment Project, such an outcome cannot occur. But in a church that is seeking to be faithful to a living tradition under the guidance of the Holy Spirit, such an outcome is promised. However, the existence of such a church depends upon further elements in MacIntyre's proposal.

34. MacIntyre, *After Virtue*, 222.

35. John Howard Yoder, *The Priestly Kingdom: Social Ethics as Gospel* (Notre Dame, IN: University of Notre Dame Press, 1984).

36. MacIntyre, *Whose Justice? Which Rationality?*, chap. 18; and MacIntyre, *Three Rival Versions*.

## Practices

In MacIntyre's proposal, "practice" takes on a very specific meaning. In a lengthy and complex description, MacIntyre defines a practice as

> any coherent and complex form of socially established cooperative human activity through which goods internal to that form of activity are realized in the course of trying to achieve those standards of excellence which are appropriate to, and partially definitive of, that form of activity, with the result that human powers to achieve excellence, and human conception of the goods involved, are systematically extended.[37]

From the many things that we may learn from this definition for living faithfully, I will draw out three.[38]

First, we must simply learn to think of the church's activities as practices in MacIntyre's sense. Many, if not most, of the church's activities today lack this understanding of practice. We do many things as a church, but we would find it difficult to give an account of how those activities reflect our conception of the human good and how those activities constitute the church as a community.

For example, the form and style of worship is a source of conflict in many churches today. It is often difficult to see this conflict as anything other than an expression of personal preference. If we formulated the conflict in terms of MacIntyre's practice, then we would better be able to locate the conflict appropriately in relation to the goods of the church and the enhancement of our ability to conceive and extend those goods. In this understanding of our conflicts over worship, "excellence" in worship would be defined in ways "appropriate to, and partially definitive of" the practice of worship, not of, say, group therapy, entertainment, or a motivational rally.

Second, we must learn from MacIntyre's notion of practice the importance of "internal goods." In a morally fragmented culture we often orient our activities toward goods or ends that are external to that activity. In MacIntyre's account of practice, he exposes that mistake. Of course, a practice may lead to goods external to the practice, but the integrity of the practice as practice depends upon the achievement of goods internal to the practice.

Someone may play basketball to achieve goods internal to basketball, such as physical exercise or camaraderie. Or one may play basketball for goods external to

---

37. MacIntyre, *After Virtue*, 187.

38. For further reflection on Christian practices that draw on MacIntyre, see Terrence W. Tilley, "In Favor of a 'Practical Theory of Religion': Montaigne and Pascal," in *Theology without Foundations: Religious Practice and the Future of Theological Truth*, ed. Stanley Hauerwas et al. (Nashville: Abingdon, 1994), 49–74; L. Gregory Jones, *Transformed Judgment*; Jones, *Embodying Forgiveness: A Theological Analysis* (Grand Rapids: Eerdmans, 1995); Stanley Hauerwas, *After Christendom: How the Church Is to Behave If Freedom, Justice, and a Christian Nation Are Bad Ideas* (Nashville: Abingdon, 1990); McClendon, *Ethics*; and McClendon, *Doctrine*.

basketball, such as winning a college scholarship or achieving fame and fortune. In the first instance, basketball is a practice; in the second instance, it is not. Likewise, in the church we may engage in activities as practices, or we may transform our activities into something else. We may, for example, engage in evangelistic activities as a practice to achieve goods internal to that practice: attaining the unity of faith, full knowledge of Christ, and maturity as believers. Or we may transform those activities into something else by seeking to increase our "giving base," having the largest church in town, or increasing our reputation and influence in the denomination. If we learn from MacIntyre to think of the activities of the church as practices, then we will be better equipped to live faithfully in a fragmented world.

Third, we must learn from MacIntyre's conception of practice the need to extend our conception of the good and our powers to achieve that good. In other words, practice takes time and discipline. One of the mistakes of the Enlightenment is to think that moral action and moral community are simply the product of a decision to act morally. That is, in spite of my previous history of acting immorally, I can, in the moment, decide to act morally and actually do so. To be sure, the gospel teaches us that we who are sinners can, by God's grace, be made righteous. But there is also great emphasis on transformation, on growing toward maturity. In theological terms, we are sanctified by the work of the Holy Spirit.

MacIntyre's description of practice gives us an understanding of this process of growth in sanctification that illumines our circumstances so that we may live faithfully with our history as the church in Western culture. Faithful living is not achieved in a moment or through mastering technique. Rather, faithful living is a lifelong process of "practicing church," as we embody and extend the human *telos* revealed in the gospel and our powers to participate in that *telos*.[39]

## Virtues

The virtues, according to MacIntyre, are

> to be understood as those dispositions which will not only sustain practices and enable us to achieve the goods internal to practices, but will also sustain us in the relevant kind of quest for the good, by enabling us to overcome the harms, dangers, temptations, and distractions which we will encounter, and which will furnish us with increasing self-knowledge and knowledge of the good.[40]

MacIntyre's retrieval of "virtue ethics" has received considerable scrutiny from Christian theologians and ethicists. Because the language of virtue is almost

---

39. I recognize that my account of practice here is somewhat cryptic and abstract. That is necessarily so within the confines of this essay. However, no matter how extensive an account one might give of Christian practice, such practice must ultimately take place in actual communities of believers.

40. MacIntyre, *After Virtue*, 219.

entirely missing from the New Testament, and because virtue often, though not necessarily, tends to place undue emphasis on human ability to achieve the good apart from God's grace, the language of virtue needs to be transfigured for the church's use.[41]

Perhaps the most helpful way for the church to use MacIntyre's proposal is to use the language of character, habituations, and disposition. This language emphasizes that our practices are best thought of not as momentary exercises of the will but as activities that *pattern* our life in discipleship to Jesus Christ.[42] This patterning of our lives on the life of Jesus Christ creates in believers the character and the habits that are ordered toward our true *telos*.[43]

This language helps us attend to our history as we seek to live faithfully. In contrast to an account of Christian living that focuses on momentary obedience, patterning our lives in Christ teaches us to live teleologically with a view to where we are headed. As Paul argues in Colossians 3, if our destiny is hidden in Christ, then our lives here and now should be ordered toward that future. At the same time, this emphasis on character also teaches us to attend to our past. When we come to Christ, we come as people formed by many different goods. Those habits that we have acquired through the years undergo transformation through our discipleship to Christ. We acquire new habits as we engage in the practices of the church. If we do not recognize the force of our prior history and habits, we can easily become discouraged by our initial attempts at discipleship. In a culture that prizes the "mastery of technique," we must learn from MacIntyre to prize Christian discipleship as the lifelong practice and acquisition of the character that transforms our lives in Christlikeness.

## Community

In many ways the book in which this chapter originally appeared is an argument, drawn from MacIntyre, about the nature of the church as a "community" in the context of a morally fragmented society. Therefore, for the church to be a community, we must learn to live with our history, in a morally fragmented culture, amid the failure of the Enlightenment Project. In order to do this, we must reclaim our understanding of the human *telos* revealed in the gospel, participate in the living tradition of the Christian faith, and embody that *telos* and that tradition in our practices and virtues (character). From these assertions, we may draw out three characteristics of the church as community.

---

41. Stanley Hauerwas, *Character and the Christian Life: A Study in Theological Ethics* (San Antonio: Trinity University Press, 1975); Hauerwas and Pinches, *Christians among the Virtues*; McClendon, *Ethics*; and Jones, *Transformed Judgment*.

42. Jones, *Transformed Judgment*, 110–12.

43. As with my account of practice, I am aware here that my account of virtue or character remains somewhat cryptic and abstract. I remedy this in *Gospel Virtues*, where I give an extensive account of the central Christian virtues of faith, hope, and love, and the practices that sustain those virtues.

First, the church must be a community that stands over against the world for the sake of the world. Because the church lives by a *telos* different from the various *teloi* of the world, if the church is living faithfully it simply will stand over against the world. However, because the church's *telos* is to witness to God's love for the world in Jesus Christ, the church's life is also for the sake of the world. In the many debates about the relationship between the church and the world, the import of this teleology is often missing. If the church is to be faithful to the gospel, it cannot do other than stand over against the world. Of course, even the faithful church will often look like the world. Our dress, our language, our architecture, our organization, and other elements will be drawn from our culture. But if we have a strong conception of the human good that is rooted in the gospel, then our use of these cultural elements will be significantly transformed. Moreover, to live faithfully the church must be explicit about its transformation of these elements for its own life and for its witness to the gospel.

Second, the church as a community must stand over against the world for the sake of the world. Because the church's conception of the human *telos* is a *telos* for all humanity, the church's faithfulness in living out that *telos* is the means by which the "world" may discover its true end and enter into the grace of God. In this way, then, the life of the church is given up for the salvation of the world just as Jesus Christ gave up his life for our salvation. In this way, the church preaches the gospel through a life lived over against the world.

Third, the church as a community lives by the grace of God. It is called into existence by the work of God the Holy Spirit. Once we were "not a people," but now we are "God's people" (1 Pet. 2:10). As God's people, we are called to point beyond ourselves. Our *telos* is not the survival and success of the church; rather, our *telos* lies beyond even the church:

> But the church cannot and will not preach this word unless it is ready, with true, yea, and fiery, evangelical zeal, to point beyond itself to the kingdom of God. . . . We can say, and we must say, that to join a church may provoke a hunger for a higher righteousness. It may create an awareness of the demand for a world-transcending loyalty, and it may open the eyes for the first time upon the possibilities of communion with God in Christ. We go about seeking those who for these ultimate reasons will identify themselves with those who love Christ and love in him all the sons and daughters of God.[44]

These words of Julian Hartt anticipate in theological rhetoric the argument and the proposal made by MacIntyre in philosophical terms. By the grace of God given through faithful thinking and living, we may once again recover this passion for the gospel that is the very reason for our lives and for the church. In his retrieval of the Aristotelian tradition, MacIntyre gives the church some

---

44. Julian N. Hartt, *Toward a Theology of Evangelism* (Nashville: Abingdon, 1955), 66.

directions for living faithfully in a fragmented world. That tradition needs considerable rethinking in the light of the gospel. This chapter has sought to begin that process, but it can ultimately be achieved only through the lives of faithful disciples who seek the human *telos*, the living tradition, the practices and virtues of the church, and the community that lives out Hartt's call to evangelical faithfulness.

# 9

. . . . . . . . . . . . . . . . .

# Resistance to
# the Demands of Love

*On Sloth*

. . . . . . . . . . . . . . . . . . . .

Rebecca DeYoung

> The secret is that God loves us *exactly* the way we are . . . *and* that he loves us too much to let us stay like this.
>
> —Anne Lamott, *Traveling Mercies*

> Grace is costly because it compels a person to submit to the yoke of Christ and follow him; it is grace because Jesus says: "My yoke is easy and my burden is light."
>
> —Dietrich Bonhoeffer, *The Cost of Discipleship*

## Laziness and Diligence

Picture a hairy, long-toed sloth hanging from a branch, with headphones on, listening to "sloth motivational tapes": "Relax, take your time, what's the hurry? Life goes on whether you're asleep or not." So one of my favorite cartoons of sloth depicts this supposed vice.[1] "Supposed," because on first glance hardly anyone would think of sloth as a serious, much less deadly, sin!

Why is this? It's mostly because, like the cartoonist, we typically think of sloth as laziness. Does laziness really rank with sins like envy and lust in its evil and destructive power? Since when was sitting on the couch watching reruns of *The Office* and munching on a bag of chips a moral and spiritual failure of the first order?

Our first reaction might be to say that sloth *doesn't* belong on the list of the great seven vices. If putting it on the list in the first place wasn't an outright mistake, keeping it there now is certainly outmoded. One author describes the contemporary view of sloth this way:

> ["Sloth"] is a mildly facetious variant of "indolence," and indolence, surely, so far from being a deadly sin, is one of the world's most amiable of weaknesses. Most of the world's troubles seem to come from people who are too busy. If only politicians and scientists were lazier, how much happier we should all be. The lazy [person] is preserved from the commission of almost all the nastier crimes.[2]

Likewise, Wendy Wasserstein's recent book on sloth uses a conception of sloth as laziness and sheer inertia to construct a delightful parody of self-help literature. From the book's jacket:

> With tongue in cheek, *Sloth* guides readers step-by-step toward a life of non-committal inertia. "You have the right to be lazy," writes Wasserstein. "You can choose not to respond. You can choose not to move." Readers will find out the importance of Lethargiosis—the process of eliminating energy and drive, the vital first step in becoming a sloth. To help you attain the perfect state of indolent bliss, the book offers a wealth of self-help aids. Readers will find the sloth songbook, sloth breakfast bars (packed with sugar, additives, and a delicious touch of Ambien), sloth documentaries (such as the author's 12-hour epic on Thomas Aquinas), and the sloth network, channel 823, programming designed not to stimulate or challenge in any way.[3]

In *Harpers* 1987 spoof of the deadly sins, the caption of the ad for sloth read, "If sloth had been the original sin, we'd all still be in paradise." From scholarly to popular accounts of the vice, then, contemporary culture seems often to equate sloth with laziness, inactivity, and inertia.

On the other hand, we *could* accept the same description of sloth and conclude that it *does* deserve to be called a sin—even a serious one. There is both a sacred and a secular version of this answer.

The sacred version goes like this. Sloth is opposed to the great Christian virtue of diligence—that powerful sense of responsibility, dedication to hard work, and

---

1. Leigh Rubin, "Rubes" (Creators Syndicate, 2003).
2. Evelyn Waugh, *London Sunday Times* (Pleasantville, NY: Akadine, 2002), 57.
3. Wendy Wasserstein, *Sloth*, The Seven Deadly Sins (New York: Oxford University Press, 2005).

conscientious completion of one's duties. And what is hard work and dedication at its best, after all, but an expression of love and devotion? The telltale root of our word *diligence* is the Latin *diligere*, which means "to love." Sloth, on this view, is apathy—comfortable indifference to duty and neglect of other human beings' needs. If you won't work hard, you don't care enough. Sloth becomes a sin not merely because it makes us lazy, but because of the lack of love that lies behind that laziness.

Communities that value diligence in this way point to proverbial warnings to "go to the ant, you lazybones" (Prov. 6:6) and the apostle Paul's admonition to do useful work with one's hands (1 Thess. 4:11–12), echoed a few centuries later by John Cassian's call to manual labor in the monastery as a remedy for sloth (or *acedia*, as Cassian and other early Christians called it).[4] Especially if our work is a divinely appointed vocation, as Reformed theology likes to emphasize, sitting around isn't just useless; it's thumbing our noses at God's call. Hence the (in) famous Protestant work ethic. Notably, those who hold this view are not nearly as concerned about the dangers of workaholism, often excusing or praising it under the euphemism "sacrificing for the sake of the kingdom." Even outside religious circles, however, the virtue of diligence is glorified, and slothful "slacking off" is frowned upon. In the stirring words of Henry Ford, "Work is our sanity, our self-respect, our salvation. Through work and work alone may health, wealth, and happiness be secured."[5] Likewise, the *Chronicle of Higher Education* put "discipline"—that is, how diligently we work—at the top of their list of the five top virtues necessary for success in graduate school.[6] "In popular thought the 'capital sin' of sloth revolves around the proverb 'An idle mind is the Devil's workshop,'" writes Josef Pieper.

> According to this concept, sloth is the opposite of diligence and industry; it is almost regarded as a synonym for laziness and idleness. Consequently, *acedia* has become, to all practical purposes, a concept of the middle class work ethic. The fact that it is numbered among the seven "capital sins" seems, as it were, to confer the sanction and approval of religion on the absence of leisure in the capitalistic industrial order.[7]

Since the modern, industrial era, diligence or "industriousness" has become a pragmatic virtue aimed at profitability and professional success. When careers replace religion as a source of meaning, worth, and identity, laziness still carries significant weight. Our society measures personal worth in terms of productivity, efficiency, and the maximization of our potential. So we'd better get busy, or we'll be good for nothing.

4. See *Institutes* 10.8–13, inter alia.

5. Quoted in Robert J. McCracken, *What Is Sin? What Is Virtue?* (New York: Harper and Row, 1966), 29.

6. Thomas H. Benton, "The 5 Virtues of Successful Graduate Students," *Chronicle of Higher Education*, September 5, 2003, http:chronicle.com/article/The-5-Virtues-of-Successful/5060.

7. Josef Pieper, *On Hope*, trans. Mary Frances McCarthy, SND (San Francisco: Ignatius, 1986), 54–55.

## Love and the "Long Course of a Lifetime"

I should confess that when I started studying sloth, I was fairly confident that this would be the *one* vice about which I would never have to worry. If anything, I reasoned, I'm too busy, hardworking to the point of a fault, and something of a perfectionist besides. Carelessness, apathy, laziness, and lack of effort would definitely *not* be my problem! My fragile bubble of self-righteousness quickly burst, however, when I read a little book that argued that busyness and workaholism were not virtuous, but rather sloth's classic symptoms. According to its author, "Not only can *acedia* and ordinary diligence exist very well together; it is even true that the senselessly exaggerated workaholism of our age is directly traceable to *acedia*."[8] It turned out that the apathetic inertia of the lazy person *and* the perpetual motion of the busy person could both reveal a heart afflicted by this vice, according to the traditional conception. How could this be?

If sloth were simply laziness—a vice opposed to the virtue of diligence—that question would be impossible to answer. The full explanation requires turning back to the original definition of sloth found among the desert fathers of the fourth century AD and developed by the Christian medieval theologians who followed in their footsteps. Looking back through sloth's long history in the Christian tradition of spiritual and moral formation, it is striking how far the contemporary conception departs from sloth's original spiritual roots. Retrieving the traditional definition of sloth will help us see how we now tend to mistake sloth's symptoms for ostensible virtues, and how sloth has more to do with being lazy about love than lazy about our work.

For these early Christians, sloth commanded much attention in the spiritual life. Sloth was always categorized as a spiritual vice, as opposed to one with a "carnal" object, like lustful physical pleasures. Sloth could drive one to abandon one's religious commitments altogether.[9] Hence, Evagrius of Pontus's colorful fourth-century description of the vice:

> The demon of acedia, also called the noonday demon (cf. Ps. 90:6), is the most oppressive of all the demons. He attacks the monk about the fourth hour [viz. 10 a.m.] and besieges his soul until the eighth hour [2 p.m.]. First of all, he makes it appear that the sun moves slowly or not at all, and that the day seems to be fifty hours long. Then he compels the monk to look constantly towards the windows, to jump out of the cell, to watch the sun to see how far it is from the ninth hour [3 p.m.], to look this way and that. . . . And further, he instills in him a dislike for the place and for his state of life itself, for manual labour, and also the idea that love has disappeared from among the brothers and there is no one to console him. And

8. Ibid., 55.

9. Morton W. Bloomfield, *The Seven Deadly Sins* (Lansing: Michigan State University Press, 1967), 75; Siegfried Wenzel, *The Sin of Sloth: Acedia in Medieval Thought and Literature* (Chapel Hill: University of North Carolina Press, 1967), 10; Robert E. Sinkewicz, ed. and trans., *Evagrius of Pontus: The Greek Ascetic Corpus* (London: Oxford University Press, 2006), 72.

should there be someone during those days who has offended the monk, this too the demon uses to add further to his dislike (of the place). He leads him on to a desire for other places where he can easily find the wherewithal to meet his needs and pursue a trade that is easier and more productive; he adds that pleasing the Lord is not a question of being in a particular place: for scripture says that the divinity can be worshipped everywhere (cf. John 4:21–24). He joins to these suggestions the memory of his close relations and of his former life; he depicts for him the long course of his lifetime, while bringing the burdens of asceticism before his eyes; and, as the saying has it, he deploys every device in order to have the monk leave his cell and flee the stadium. No other demon follows immediately after this one: a state of peace and ineffable joy ensues in the soul after this struggle.[10]

What the desert fathers meant by *acedia* does imply a failure of effort, a failure linked to a lack of love—the Greek word they use (*a-kedeia*) literally means "lack of care." For them, this vice was primarily a grave spiritual malady, expressed in dejection or a feeling of oppressiveness or even disgust. A lack of physical effort was, if anything, a symptom of a deeper problem.

Throughout Evagrius's account (only briefly represented here), two things are evident: first, sloth is an extremely powerful and serious vice; and second, it is a vice that threatens one's fundamental commitment to one's religious identity and vocation. It is a serious vice because the entire commitment of one's life to God is at stake. It is a spiritual vice, for Evagrius, because it involves inner resistance and coldness toward one's spiritual calling or identity and its attendant practices. He describes it as distaste, disgust, sorrow, oppressiveness, and restlessness, because the slothful feel that it is an intolerable burden to stay true to one's commitment to God with all its daily drudgery and discipline—they would much prefer to escape and run away and be free of their wearisome vocation. This is why, in Evagrius's and Cassian's work, sloth was on the spiritual end of the chain of vices.

In the writings of Evagrius's disciple, John Cassian, we see a shift in emphasis toward the external manifestation of the inner resistance characteristic of sloth. Cassian transplanted desert asceticism into the Latin West, establishing communal forms of monasticism more familiar to us today. Each monk was expected to contribute to the spiritual and physical well-being of the community. Although the desert fathers also emphasized the spiritual importance of manual labor, they did not associate it primarily with sloth, as Cassian did. Cassian explicitly and extensively discusses the importance of manual labor as a remedy for this vice. Early on in its history, then, sloth picked up its association with physical inactivity and shirking manual labor. Cassian uses language like "laziness," "sluggishness," "sleepiness," "inertia," and "lack of effort" in his descriptions of *acedia*, such as this one:

10. *Praktikos* 6.12. Note: Evagrius references Ps. 90:6, which is Ps. 91:6 in our version of Scripture. Quotations from Evagrius follow *Evagrius of Pontus: The Greek Ascetic Corpus*, ed. and trans. Robert E. Sinkewicz (Oxford: Oxford University Press, 2003).

[Monks] overcome by slumbering idleness and acedia . . . [have] chosen to be clothed not by the effort of [their] own toil but in the rags of laziness . . . [and] have grown remiss as a result of sluggishness and . . . are unwilling to support themselves by manual labor.[11]

Even for Cassian, however, idleness is clearly intended to be symptomatic of the inner condition of one besieged by sloth. In this he echoes Evagrius's description of the vice:

Once [*acedia*] has seized possession of a wretched mind, it makes a person horrified at where he is, disgusted with his cell. . . . Likewise it renders him slothful and immobile in the face of all the work to be done within the walls of his dwelling.[12]

On Cassian's account, physical inactivity or lack of effort is *an effect or expression* of one's inner condition. "The work to be done within the walls of his dwelling" includes both spiritual practices and physical duties done on behalf of the religious community. Shirking this "work" in any form signals a distancing of oneself from one's identity and investment as a member of a spiritual community bound by its love for God. Mere (physical) laziness is not necessarily slothful. Rather, shirking one's spiritual duty—whether this involves devotional practices or manual labor on behalf of one's brothers in the monastery—is slothful only if it is linked to inner discontent and resistance to the monk's religious identity as a member of the monastic community.

Both inner and outer manifestations of sloth are thus linked to one's religious commitment and one's attitude toward the demands of the spiritual life. Like Evagrius, Cassian thinks sloth is a serious vice because it threatens to undermine one's fundamental identity as one devoted to developing a lifelong relationship with God and it erodes one's commitment to the religious community formed by that identity.[13] Psalm 119 highlights the contrast between devotedness and *acedia*. In verse 28, the psalmist—defined as one devoted to God's Word—finds

11. *Institutes* 10.21. See also *Conference* 5.

12. Ibid.

13. Originally, *acedia* and the vice of sorrow were distinguished from each other but linked in the concatenation of vices (Cassian especially subscribed to the view that falling prey to one vice made one susceptible to the next one in the chain). Cassian and Evagrius describe sorrow's cause as excessive attachment to (or insufficient detachment from) worldly desires, pleasures, and possessions. One's religious commitment makes one unable to satisfy or attain these desires, and one feels disappointed as a result. This is the vice of sorrow. (Thus, Cassian makes much of total renunciation: the monk cannot keep even a penny of his former fortune when he joins the monastery; this in contrast to the desert fathers, who were allowed a subpoverty level of personal possessions to maintain their livelihood—e.g., basket-weaving materials.) This sorrow in turn produces resentment of one's religious vocation, which now presents itself as the major obstacle to the fulfillment of worldly desires. As such, the vocation and its demands are resented and resisted. This is the vice of sloth. Gregory will later combine sorrow and sloth under the title *tristitia*, and many in the tradition (including Aquinas) will describe sloth itself as an oppressive sorrow on the basis of this relationship between the two vices. My account of sloth, based on Aquinas's

himself overcome with weariness and feels this oppression interfering with his ordinary daily meditation on God's law, which is an expression of his love and devotion to God.

## The Now and the Not Yet

The medieval theologian Thomas Aquinas gives an account of sloth that stands at the crossroads between this ancient ascetic tradition and modern conceptions of sloth as laziness. Aquinas explains why sloth makes the traditional list of great vices. He also explains how sloth reflects a lack of love that can be expressed both as laziness and as restless busyness. His definition needs some unpacking, though. He begins with the cryptic statement that sloth is "aversion to the divine good in us." Huh?

An analogy will help us get a handle on what Aquinas is talking about. Imagine a typical husband and wife. In general, they have a relationship of genuine love and friendship. One evening, they quarrel at dinnertime and head off to opposite corners of the house for the rest of the night. They find it much easier to maintain that miserable distance and alienation from each other than to do the work of apologizing, forgiving, and reconciling. Learning to live together and love each other well after a rift requires giving up their anger, their desire to have their own way, their insistence on seeing the world only from his or her own perspective. Saying "I'm sorry" takes effort, but it is not *simply* the physical work of walking across the house and saying the words that each resists. It might be that this is another wearying version of the same fight they've been fighting for years, and it doesn't feel like they are getting any nearer to resolving it. What's the point of going through the motions of apologizing one more time?

Do they want the relationship? Yes, they do—neither would renege on their commitment to each other. But do they want to do what it takes to be in that relationship—do they want to honor its claims on them? Do they want to learn genuine unselfishness in the ordinary daily task of living together? Well, maybe tomorrow. For now, at least, each spouse wants the night off to wallow in his or her own selfish loneliness. This is true especially when love takes effort, or feels like a formality or an empty ritual.

Why do marriages and friendships make good pictures of what goes wrong in the vice of sloth? For all its joys, any intense friendship or marriage has aspects that can seem burdensome. There is not only an investment of time, but an investment of self that is required for a relationship to exist and grow and flourish. Even more difficult than the physical accommodations are the accommodations of identity: from the perspective of individual "freedom," to be in a relationship of love will change us and cost us. It will require us to restructure our priorities. It

---

texts, also maintains the link Evagrius and Cassian first described, with excessive attachment to the "old self" making commitment to and joy in the "new self" difficult and distasteful.

may compromise our plans. It will demand sacrifice. It will alter the pattern of our thoughts and desires and may transform our vision of the world. It's not just "your life" or "my life" anymore—it's "ours." Seen in this light, it can seem that staying at arm's length and not engaging or investing would be easier and safer—even if ultimately unhappier—than risking openness to love's transforming power and answering its claims on us.

Sometimes marriage or other friendships feel euphoric and energizing; other times, they are tedious, empty, wearying routines, or just plain work. The point is that being committed to any love relationship takes daily nurturing, daily effort, and daily practices that build it up. Neglecting these will slowly break the relationship down. Nurturing grudges or selfish claims instead will erode it and make us resentful of a relationship that now feels like a suffocating trap. Kathleen Norris once said that married love is "eternal, but it's also daily, about as daily and unromantic as housekeeping."[14] It is through daily practices and disciplines, whether we feel like doing them or not, that the decision to love is renewed and refreshed and the commitment of love is kept alive. The slothful person, in this sense, is one who resists the effort of doing day after day after day whatever it takes to keep the bonds of love strong and living and healthy, whether he or she feels particularly inspired about doing it or not.

If we think of our relationship to God like that, we'll be well on our way toward grasping Aquinas's definition of sloth. We know there must be something awry if sloth shrinks back and recoils from something good and divine, instead of taking delight in it. What that good is, however, requires a little more explanation.

"The divine good in us" is just Aquinas's medieval-ish way of talking about the indwelling of the Holy Spirit in our hearts—God's life in us. Paul puts it this way: "I have been crucified with Christ; and it is no longer I who live, but it is Christ who lives in me" (Gal. 2:19–20). When God lives in us, our whole being is transformed: the old has gone, the new has come. By the power of the Spirit, we are to "clothe [our]selves with the new self, created according to the likeness of God in true righteousness and holiness" (Eph. 4:24; see also Col. 3:10). Aquinas calls this grace "a beginning of glory in us."[15] The gift of the Holy Spirit and our new identity in Christ—this is the target of sloth's resistance.

For Christians, God is present in our hearts by his Holy Spirit, empowering us to become new people. The key, however, is that our new identity in Christ is both "now" and "not yet," a promise and a present reality. For now, that presence is a promise and a beginning, a new self born but not yet perfected. Why not yet? Because the Holy Spirit doesn't jump in and create a new self in us overnight or wave a magic wand to conjure up perfection. The project of growing into our new identity takes a lifetime, and a lifetime of cooperation on our part. It's called

14. Kathleen Norris, *The Quotidian Mysteries: On Laundry, Liturgy, and Women's Work* (Mahwah, NJ: Paulist Press, 1998), 53. See also her most recent book, *Acedia & Me: Marriage, Monks, and a Writer's Life* (New York: Riverhead, 2008).

15. *Summa Theologiae* II-II.24.3.

sanctification. In one sense, we *are* Christians, and in another sense, we are still *becoming* Christians. God is both "already" and "not yet fully" present in us. Our love for him has the character both of longing *and* of the restfulness of delight. Thus, it makes sense for Paul to encourage Christians to grow in faith and become more and more like Christ. We can't just say, "I'm saved! Praise the Lord!" and then sit back and assume God is done with us.

It's important to remember that the process of sanctification is the fruit of grace. Becoming Christlike isn't about us working like crazy to improve ourselves and merit a place in God's favor. Sanctification is about effort—but not earning. Second Peter 1:3–7 clears up any misunderstanding here:

> [*God's*] divine power has given us everything needed for life and godliness, *through the knowledge of him who called us by his own glory* and goodness. Thus he has given us, through these things, his precious and very great promises, so that through them you may escape from the corruption that is in the world because of lust, and may become participants of the divine nature. For this very reason, *you must make every effort* to support your faith with goodness, and goodness with knowledge, and knowledge with self-control, and self-control with endurance, and endurance with godliness, and godliness with mutual affection, and mutual affection with love. (emphasis added)

According to this picture of the Christian life, being a Christian is like being married: both involve accepting a new identity that needs to be lived out, day by day, for the rest of your life. A man and a woman take their vows on their wedding day, and from that moment on they *are* married. Yet *being* married, living out those vows and making them a living reality, will take all of their efforts for a lifetime. Their love and identity have a now and not-yet character. It is both a gift and a life-transforming task. It is this transformation of our identity by God's love that the slothful person resists.

That transformation takes time. This is why the tradition consistently opposes sloth to perseverance and commitment. Aquinas once argued that the demons can't have sloth. On the "sloth-as-laziness" interpretation, we might think it's because the demons are spiritual creatures who can't be physically weary or sick of making physical effort. It's rather because their wills were wholly conformed either to love of or rejection of God in a single choice in a single moment, while the human will is sanctified through many choices and actions over a lifetime. Our love for God, our choice to be like him, must be lived out over and over, day after day. The need to persevere in one's commitment over time is what yields an opportunity for sloth.

In a nutshell, to be slothful is to be opposed to the joy we should have over being united with God and committed to him in love. Instead of rejoicing at God's presence in us, the slothful chafe at it and resent the claims that God's love makes on them. Rather than being willing to dedicate themselves to developing and deepening the relationship, they resist its demands. Although sloth can appear symptomatically similar to chronic depression, it is not a matter of brain chemistry, but rather a habit of the heart. Sloth is not primarily a feeling; it is well-entrenched and willful resistance, even as love is fundamentally a choice.

Aquinas's take on sloth explains why it is a really serious vice. In sloth, we resist our identity in Christ and his presence in our hearts. We balk at God's invitation to "be imitators of God" (Eph. 5:1) and to be transformed by him over the rest of our lives. If that's not a description of a significant vice, it's hard to see what else might count.

## The War Within

At the same time, this very explanation raises a hard question. How could we possibly feel put out by God's presence in our heart? What could make us *un*happy about the gift of love that is the secret to our own happiness? God's love and grace is the greatest gift that we could ever possess! Why would anyone who received it want to keep it at arm's length?

Aquinas answers with the apostle Paul's words in Galatians 5:17: Sloth is caused by the opposition of the spirit to the flesh.[16] Initially, this may seem confusing. Does his answer mean that sloth makes us prefer to be a lump of flesh on the couch rather than to pursue our spiritual duties? It sounds like he is saying that sloth strikes when spirituality takes a backseat to bodily comfort. Is sloth laziness after all?

Aquinas and Paul both say no. In the early as well as the later Christian tradition, sloth is always a spiritual vice. That means it is *not* primarily focused on bodily goods like comfort and ease and pleasure, as lust and gluttony are. Instead, when Paul makes the "spirit-flesh" distinction, as Aquinas notes, he is contrasting the old sinful nature with our new redeemed nature in Christ. The battle here is not between body and soul, between the physical and the spiritual. Rather, sloth is the old sinful self resisting transformation into the new self in Christ.

Spiritual battles take place on many fronts. Sometimes bodily pleasures or bodily weariness do make us more susceptible to sin. But in the case of this vice, the battle is first and foremost waged within our hearts. In sloth, we are literally divided against ourselves. We were made for relationship with God. If we are slothful, we have chosen to reject that relationship as the way to find fulfillment and chosen to try to make something else do its work instead.[17] We are trying to make ourselves content with being less than we really are.

---

16. Aquinas, *On Evil* 11.2; *Summa Theologiae* II-II.35.3.

17. Søren Kierkegaard in *The Sickness unto Death*, trans. Howard V. Hong and Edna Hong (Princeton: Princeton University Press, 1985), 67–74, describes this self as one who refuses, in defiance, not to be itself, because to be oneself would involve a relational identity—one binding the self to God. If the refusal is less conscious, *acedia* is more akin to Kierkegaard's despair of weakness (see esp. 55–56). Many modern existentialist thinkers offer good descriptions of a slothlike condition, but Kierkegaard ties his description explicitly to one's identity and relationship to God.

Think back to the marriage example with which we began—the way loving another person requires a thousand little deaths of our old individual selfish nature. *This* is the "work" the slothful one resists. This work may or may not include bodily effort (on some occasions our resistance to it may be prompted by the physical effort required), but the two should not simply be equated. In fact, sloth *cannot* be defined as laziness, since slothful people often pour great physical effort and emotional energy into the difficult task of distracting themselves from the unhappiness of their real condition. As we will see in the next section, slothful people can be very busy. On the other hand, we should also not automatically equate overwhelming physical weariness with sloth: think of parents caring for a newborn infant. Their weariness results from their love and devotedness. The need or desire for rest is not itself a vice.

## Lazy about Love

In the film *Groundhog Day*, weatherman Phil Connors gives us an example—at least by analogy—of sloth's resistance to the daily transformation required by real love.[18] Through an inexplicable turn of events, Phil finds himself waking up each morning, day after day, on February 2—Groundhog Day—having to relive the same day over and over again in Punxsutawney, Pennsylvania. A shallow and self-centered Phil first amuses himself with various hedonistic pleasures, since what he does each day apparently has no consequences. "Don't you worry about cholesterol?" his coworker asks as he scarfs down a tableful of doughnuts. "I don't worry about anything anymore," replies Phil with a smug chuckle. Soon, however, he settles on the project of getting his producer, Rita, into bed with him. He now spends a long succession of days making a great effort to seduce her. While he finds her attractive, he does not really love her—at least, not yet. Rather than change himself, he painstakingly figures out by trial and error what she likes and finds appealing. Then he puts up a false front designed to get her to fall for him—he memorizes lines of French poetry and pretends to share her interests in world peace and her taste in ice cream. His elaborate scheme is meant to manipulate her into giving him what he wants. Although she is initially taken in, Rita eventually sees through his strategy and rejects his advances. "I can't believe I fell for this!" she cries at him in anger. "You don't love me! I could never love someone like you, Phil, because you could never love anyone but yourself!" Phil falls into despair. He sits on the couch all day, eating popcorn and drinking whiskey, apathetically watching the same episode of *Jeopardy!* for the hundredth time. He can't get what he wants the way he is, but he also refuses to change. And so he is at an impasse.

After a few unsuccessful suicide attempts, Phil finally tries a new tactic. He begins, little by little, to genuinely *become* the sort of person who could win Rita's

---

18. *Groundhog Day*, directed by Harold Ramis (Sony Pictures, 2002). This case involves love in a human-human relationship, not a God-human relationship.

love. Like his earlier seduction project, this takes regular and consistent effort on his part—day after day, he studies for a medical degree, he takes piano lessons, he reads French poetry, he extends a helping hand to the young and old. But these efforts, in contrast to his previous stratagems, change his heart. Unlike the old Phil, he is no longer bored and restless, filling time with self-centered diversions and empty pleasures. For he no longer pretends to be but really becomes—through consistent habit and daily discipline—not just a poet, pianist, and philanthropist, but a person capable of unselfish love. Phil is no longer solely motivated by the desire to produce sexual results in his relationship with Rita. Instead, his help for others shows that he has learned to genuinely care about what is right and good—for its own sake. In the end, his changed character attracts the affection not only of all the townspeople but also the love of Rita herself.

What Phil's example shows is that the slothful person can be either a couch potato or a person who is very busy and active—very busy, that is, trying to get what *he* wants *without* having to change or give of himself. Love transforms us. The real work Phil resists, then, is not the physical effort itself (of seducing Rita or of helping the townspeople), but the commitment to love that effort represents.

In a sense, then, it's true that slothful people want the easy life. They find detachment from the old selfish nature too difficult, painful, and burdensome, so they neglect to perform the actions that would maintain and deepen relationships of love. They harden their hearts toward any change that requires sacrifice or surrender on their part. Wanting love to come easily and comfortably is like preferring the sentiment of pop songs and Hollywood romances. It feels wonderful for a little while, but these feelings and momentary "highs" cannot sustain a relationship. They come cheap but don't last. The talk about "forever" has to be sustained by commitments that require daily decisions to keep on loving, even when it's hard or unexciting or doesn't yield a big emotional payoff. Likewise, sloth is the vice of those who want the security of having God's love without the real sacrifice and ongoing struggle to be made anew.

So sloth or *acedia* has turned out to be a spiritual vice after all, a vice marked by resistance to the transforming demands of God's love.[19] Why does the slothful one resist love? Because a love relationship marks an identity change and a corresponding commitment to daily transformation. Novelist Anne Lamott recounts the words of a wise old woman at her church who once told her that "the secret is that God loves us *exactly* the way we are . . . *and* that he loves us too much to let us stay like this."[20] Those with sloth object to not being able to stay

19. The marriage-and-friendship metaphor is especially apt, because for Aquinas the virtue of love that flows out of our participation in God's life (called *caritas*) is defined as *friendship* in which the lover and beloved enjoy the fullest sense of communion and fellowship possible between persons short of the love between the members of the Trinity. Aquinas thinks we can have this friendship with God and each other.

20. Anne Lamott, *Operating Instructions* (New York: Ballantine Books, 1994), 96.

the way they are.[21] Something must die for the new self to be born, and, as in Phil Connor's case, it might be an old self to which we are very attached.

Here we can finally sort out our initial thoughts on sloth. We are right to think of sloth as resistance to effort—but not only, or even primarily, in the sense of being physically lazy or lazy about our work. Rather, it is resistance to the discipline and transformation demanded by our new identity as God's beloved children, created and redeemed to be like him. The slothful like the comforting thought of being saved by love, of being God's own, but balk at facing the discomfort of transformation—the slow putting to death of the old sinful nature—and the discipline it takes to sustain that transforming relationship of love over the long haul.

Slothful people are like the couple in our earlier analogy, who want the dream of being unconditionally loved without having to condition their own selfish desires in return, or who want a perpetual honeymoon, not fifty years of married faithfulness. The slothful are like Evagrius's monk, wanting to live for God in desert contemplation, but finding their zeal flagging in the heat of the day and pining instead for the comfort and worldly happiness of the life they left behind. Traditionally, Lot's wife was taken to be a picture of sloth, because even while being rescued, she is unwilling to fully turn her back on the only home and life and friends she had ever known (Gen. 19). How many of us have felt like we need two angels to drag us out of Sodom, while we look back over our shoulders, wistfully wishing for what we must leave behind? Are we like the people of Israel, poised to enter their homeland and promised rest in Canaan after years of restless wandering, who would rather retreat to the drearily familiar desert than have to fight giants (Num. 13–14; Deut. 1)? Pieper writes that the slothful person "will not [fully] accept supernatural goods because they are, by their very nature, linked to a claim on [the one] who receives them."[22] As one U2 song put it, "Love is not an easy thing; the only baggage you can bring . . . is all that you can't leave behind."[23] Their advice in the song is just what the desert fathers would have recommended and what Lot's wife and the nation of Israel should have done: "You've got to leave it behind. *Walk on.*"

Because it's ultimately about love—accepting God's love for us and the cost of loving him back—sloth earns its place among the top seven vices. Human beings are made for love. To resist it is to deny who we are. In her reluctance to die to her old self, the person with sloth chooses slow spiritual suffocation over the birth pains of new life and spiritual growth. She can't fully accept the only thing that would ultimately bring her joy. She refuses the thing she most desires, and she turns away in revulsion or bored distaste from the only thing that can bring her life. In the perversity of her sin, she prefers sorrow to joy, emptiness to fullness, restlessness to rest.

---

21. This is perhaps why Evagrius describes *acedia* as one of the most oppressive of the vices.
22. Pieper, *On Hope*, 56.
23. U2, "Walk On," *All That You Can't Leave Behind* (PolyGram, 2000).

When describing sloth, it can be difficult to find the right balance between grace and discipline. Christian living should not become another long, legalistic list of demands that we have to meet on pain of not really counting as committed children of God. There is no litmus test of required work here. Love relationships have their fallow seasons, their drier times. On the other hand, we also shouldn't carelessly assume that God will happily leave us where we are and never make any demands on our time or effort, or never need to wean us painfully away from old attachments and desires. Love will require us to learn submission to God's will. Sometimes love is work—difficult, daily work. The key difference between sheer meaningless drudgery, on the one hand, and perseverance through times when our energy and fervor are low, on the other, is that in the latter case we are still fueling a relationship of love and investing ourselves for the long haul in something that ultimately brings rest and joy.

### Restlessness and False Rest

Sloth sabotages sanctification—the transforming power of God's love in us. By sapping our willingness to lay down our old loves for the sake of love of God, it saps our energy for good altogether, since God is the source of that strength. As a result, sloth has a twofold effect. First, it makes us want to avoid activities and people that bring us face-to-face with our identity in Christ—most obviously, things like prayer, worship, Scripture, and the sacraments. Second, however, this vice builds a cold wall between us and the demands of love for others. This explains sloth's association with indifference and apathy—what Aquinas calls "sluggishness" when it comes to heeding the demands of justice. Love for neighbor flows from accepting God's love.[24] The commandment tells us to love our neighbors *as ourselves*. In refusing to accept God's love for himself, with the commitments that brings, the slothful one also forfeits love for his neighbors and his commitment to them. When Rita accusingly says, "You could never love anyone but yourself!" Phil replies honestly, "That's not true: I don't even like myself."

Rooted in resistance to love's demands, slothful apathy and avoidance typically manifest themselves, according to the tradition, in despairing resignation (apathy) or desperate escapism (avoidance). Cassian mentions both effects: "And so the true athlete of Christ, who wishes to engage lawfully in the struggle for perfection, must . . . contend on both sides against this most wicked spirit of acedia in such a way as neither to be *cut down by the sword of sleep and collapse* nor to be driven out from the bulwark of the monastery and *depart in flight*, even for a seemingly pious reason."[25]

24. For Aquinas, we love God for his own sake and love our neighbors as ourselves. Although these two loves cannot be pulled apart, *acedia* strikes primarily at the source love—our love of God—and only secondarily branches out to indifference to what love demands of us on account of our neighbors.

25. *Institutes* 10.5, emphasis added.

Despairing resignation is the form sloth takes if we can't get escape, either in reality or in fantasy, from the thing that makes us sad. When we acknowledge this predicament, we tend to sink under oppressive hopelessness and despair. Phil's drinking and suicide attempts after Rita's rejection show him in this state. Phil realizes that his selfish nature cannot give him what he really needs, but he can't stand the thought of facing life without it, either. There is no way out of his predicament, even through death. Hence, the inner tension and "trapped" feeling that often characterize this vice. We can't escape the truth about who we are called to be, and yet we refuse to face it. Reality is oppressive, unbearable, and distasteful. The slothful person tends to cope by mentally and emotionally "checking out." This sort of resignation is "not to be confused with laziness," according to Frederick Buechner.

> Lazy people, people who sit around and watch the grass grow, may be people at peace. Their sun-drenched, bumblebee dreaming may be the prelude to action or itself an act well worth the acting. . . . Like somebody with a bad head cold, [slothful people] have mostly lost their sense of taste and smell. They know something's wrong with them, but not wrong enough to want to do something about it. Other people come and go, but through glazed eyes they hardly notice them. They are letting things run their course. They are getting through their lives.[26]

The slothful are inwardly unwilling to be moved; they are stuck between a self they cannot bear and a self they can't bear to become. Their outward behavior—sluggishness and inertia—reflects the state of their heart.

On the other hand, if we think we *can* escape from sorrow, we will pour all our energy into any form of flight that shows promise, no matter how desperate. Phil's life of shallow pleasure-seeking and seduction early in the film is his attempt to escape love's demands. Life becomes one long project of distracting ourselves from the truth about our predicament. Augustine famously said that we would be "restless" until we find our "rest in [God]."[27] Blaise Pascal agreed; he predicted that the best way to make people truly miserable would be to take away all their diversions, whether at work or through recreation: "Without [diversions] we should be in a state of weariness, and this weariness would spur us to seek a more solid means of escaping from it. But diversion amuses us, and leads us unconsciously to death."[28] Victor Frankl paints a similar portrait of the workaholic's "Sunday neurosis"—the vacuum of meaning she feels on the day when her work does not fulfill its distracting function every waking

---

26. Frederick Buechner, *Wishful Thinking: A Theological ABC* (New York: HarperCollins, 1993), 109–10.

27. *Confessions* 1.1.

28. "Misery.—The only thing which consoles us for our miseries is diversion, and yet this is the greatest of our miseries. For it is this which principally hinders us from reflecting upon ourselves, and which makes us insensibly ruin ourselves." The quotation in the text concludes this passage. *Pensees* II, trans. W. F. Trotter (New York: E. P. Dutton, 1958), 171.

hour.[29] Sadly, this escapist strategy can take even ostensibly pious forms: we can spend our whole lives avoiding the demands of true discipleship, love, commitment, and change, even if we constantly and busily engage in lots of religious activities. Like the aptly named Sebastian "Flyte" in *Brideshead Revisited*, the restlessness that characterizes our escapist strategies betrays a heart not at peace with who we really are and makes us flee whatever a commitment to love would require of us. This is why the vice of sloth was traditionally opposed to the commandment to rest on the Sabbath, which Aquinas says requires that "the soul take rest in God alone."[30]

Sloth can thus show itself in the total inertia of the couch potato or the restless distractions of endless activity. Somewhere in between these two symptoms of vice is a holy Sabbath rest for the heart that has given itself utterly to God, a heart overjoyed, not oppressed, by the thought that "love so amazing, so divine, demands my soul, my life, my all."[31]

The slothful person ultimately insists on his own way, his own will, his own self-made pseudo-rest. His lack of commitment speaks of an unwillingness to surrender himself to God. It is this resistance that roots the vice of sloth in pride. Unlike other forms of sorrow, grief, or even depression, all of which can be mistaken for sloth, this capital vice results from a choice not to commit oneself, a refusal to give oneself wholly to God and then stay the course. It is the antithesis of Mary's "yes" at the annunciation, a "yes" that finds her faithful to the end, standing at the foot of the cross. The slothful person tries to find happiness while evading the daily demands of self-giving love. He prefers his own diligent efforts to make himself happy with shortcuts and quick fixes. He chooses to avoid the onerousness of love's demands by putting them off and trying to find fulfillment some easier way. By doing so, however, he cuts himself off from the possibility of fulfillment and happiness. And so, says Gregory, sloth eventually brings one to despair.

It is not to those who take up their crosses and find them an unbearable weight, but those who resist the demands of love—those who suffer from the self-imposed burden of *acedia*—that Jesus gives the invitation, "Come to me, all you that are weary and carrying heavy burdens, and I will give you rest. Take my yoke upon you, and learn from me; for I am gentle and humble in heart, and you will find rest for your souls. For my yoke is easy, and my burden is light" (Matt. 11:28–30).

---

29. Victor Frankl, *Man's Search for Meaning* (New York: Pocket Books, 1959), 129. As I explain in "The Vice of Sloth: Some Historical Reflections on Laziness, Effort, and Resistance to the Demands of Love," *The Other Journal* (November 15, 2007), http://theotherjournal.com/2007/11/15/the-vice-of-sloth-some-historical-reflections-on-laziness-effort-and-resistance-to-the-demands-of-love, and Lauren Winner suggests in her essay "Sleep Therapy" (*Books & Culture*, January/February 2006, 7), perhaps our current understanding of sloth as mere laziness occasions misdiagnosis of the vice's real symptoms.

30. *Summa Theologiae* II-II.36.3.

31. Isaac Watts, "When I Survey the Wondrous Cross," in *The Psalter Hymnal* (Grand Rapids: CRC Resources, 1987), no. 384.

## Stabilitas Loci

Sloth is a vice for which it is difficult to find a remedy. Like envy, it has a self-perpetuating dynamic, refusing the very thing required to cure it. The ancient strategy against sloth therefore seems counterintuitive: rather than seeking some new way to infuse life and breath into one's relationship with God, the desert fathers recommended *stabilitas loci*—stability of place. Evagrius writes,

> You must not abandon the cell in the time of temptations, fashioning excuses seemingly reasonable. Rather, you must remain seated inside, exercise perseverance.
> . . . Fleeing and circumventing such struggles teaches the mind to be unskilled, cowardly, and evasive.[32]

In this discipline, the soul should mirror the body: "The spirit of acedia drives the monk out of his cell, but the monk who possesses perseverance will ever cultivate stillness."[33]

In a nutshell, this discipline is about not running away from what you're called to be and do—whether through busyness at work or through imaginative diversions—but rather accepting and staying committed to your true spiritual vocation and identity and whatever it requires. The monk's commitment to the religious life was embodied in his willingness to stay in his cell, rather than flee to the city. To leave the cell was equivalent to abandoning his spiritual purpose and vocation. To stay put physically was also to stay put spiritually, even when one was not spiritually engaged or enthusiastic—in cases of *acedia*, quite the opposite.

Why did Evagrius and Cassian describe the relevant remedial virtues as courageous endurance, long-suffering, and perseverance? How is staying the course supposed to help? The idea is that enthusiasm and energy will wax and wane, and periods of felt alienation from God or spiritual burnout will threaten. Given the human condition and our sinful nature (both our physical frailty and fickleness of will), what we need most against the daily weariness of *acedia* is steady commitment and daily discipline, even when we don't feel like it. A friend once described worship as like a military drill.[34] It is not meant first of all to be personally uplifting in each and every instance, but rather to discipline us and equip us so we can respond immediately and appropriately in battle or a crisis. Our daily training carries us through those times. Analogously, marriage counselors often recommend continuing to act like we love our spouse in times of emotional dryness (for example, kissing him or her every time we leave and return home whether we feel like it or not), because merely persevering in the patterns of loving action is enough to keep us on track and to prepare our hearts for the appropriate feelings to return.

---

32. *Praktikos* 6.28.
33. *On the Eight Thoughts* 6.5.
34. Debra Rienstra, *Great with Child: On Becoming a Mother* (New York: Tarcher/Putnam, 2002), 186–87.

Perhaps in our age we are more prone than ever to expect too much of love as a feeling, and too little of love as an ongoing choice and commitment. In our worship services and our marriages, we expect emotional highs that will carry us through life's difficult times, when we would better expect engagement in daily disciplines to sustain us in our commitments. *Acedia's* greatest temptations are escapism and despair—when we don't feel like being godly or loving anymore, to abandon ship and give up, to drift away inwardly or outwardly toward something more comfortable or immediately comforting. "A light breeze bends a feeble plant; a fantasy about a trip away drags off a person overcome with acedia," write the desert fathers.[35] Thus, its greatest remedy is to resist the urge to get out or give up, and instead to stay the course, stick to one's commitments, and persevere.

---

35. *On the Eight Thoughts* 6.5.

# 10

## Cultivating Gratitude

### *Pray without Ceasing*

PAUL GRIFFITHS

In his First Letter to the Thessalonians, the apostle Paul exhorts his hearers, among whom you and I are included, in these words: "See that none of you repays evil for evil, but always seek to do good to one another and to all. Rejoice always, pray without ceasing, give thanks in all circumstances; for this is the will of God in Christ Jesus for you" (1 Thess. 5:15–18). It is not merely that he encourages us to act in certain ways—to do good, to rejoice, to pray, to give thanks—no, he wants more; he wants us to do these things "always," "without ceasing," "in all circumstances."

What can this mean? Should you rejoice when the person you love dies horribly before your eyes? Should you pray when you are studying, when you are making love, when you are eating, when you are sleeping? Should you give thanks when you get the news that you have contracted a fatal disease that will kill you painfully within six months?[1] It does not sound immediately sensible to say so, and there

---

Originally published as Paul Griffiths, "Pray without Ceasing," *Christian Reflection* 32 (2009): 11–17. Published by the Center for Christian Ethics at Baylor University. Used by permission.

1. Though it should be noted that, in a passage which makes difficult and painful reading, Therese of Lisieux (1873–1897), a saint and doctor of the church, welcomes with delight the expectoration of blood that marks the presence of the tuberculosis that would kill her at the age of twenty-four. See *Story of a Soul: The Autobiography of Therese of Lisieux*, 3rd ed., trans. John Clarke (Washington, DC: ICS Publications, 1996), 210–11.

is much else in Scripture that recommends what sounds like something rather different, such as weeping when faced with the death of a friend, as Jesus himself did.[2] So what does Paul mean?

Let's focus the question by asking specifically about prayer. Paul says that we should do this without ceasing, and he is not alone in saying so. Luke's introduction to the parable of the unjust judge—or, if you prefer, the persistent widow—says much the same thing: "Then Jesus told them a parable about their need to pray always and not to lose heart" (Luke 18:1). At the end of the parable, the unjust judge promises to grant justice to the importunate widow, not because he has become just or reconsidered her case, but "so that she may not wear me out by continually coming" (Luke 18:5). We, it seems—we Christians—are meant to be "continually coming" before God, importuning him in prayer at every moment.

The presence in Scripture of the idea that we should pray without stopping has led many of the church's theologians and preachers to reflect a good deal on what it means to do this. Some of their formulations are striking and elegant. Augustine, for example, in his expository homilies on the Psalter, writes: "Not only do we not sin when we are adoring [God], but when we are not adoring [God] we sin."[3] Adoration (*adoratio/adorare*) is not quite prayer (*oratio/orare*), but they are closely connected: both are intentional actions that bring us before God, turn us toward God's face. And Augustine's formulation makes the very strong claim that adoration—and prayer, if that extension is legitimate—not only suffices to exclude sin, but is necessary for that exclusion. This means, if it is right, that whenever you are not praying (adoring), you are, ipso facto, sinning. This is an intensification of Paul's and Luke's claims, and it makes them, if anything, even more puzzling. If, for example, I am watching a baseball game, delighted by the beauty of the double play I just saw, am I thereby sinning because I am not praying? Just what can Augustine mean?

The reason why it is so difficult for us, Christians though we be, to understand these hard sayings about prayer and adoration—sayings that seem to imply that prayer and life are coextensive, and that all non-prayerful action is deeply damaged to the point of being sinful—is that we have in mind a series of separations that Paul, Luke, and Augustine would prefer us not to have. We separate life into compartments. There is the work compartment, the personal life compartment, and the religion compartment, to name just three, and the walls that separate them are thickly impervious. If you are an office worker, for instance, you probably find it hard to think of the parties you go to, the shoe stores you shop in, and the hobbies you pursue as having all that much to do with the projects you manage, the clients you assist, and the skills you develop on the job; and, very likely, although you may try to see and make real to yourself the connections between your life

---

2. Jesus weeps at the death of Lazarus (John 11:35).

3. "Non solum non peccemus adorando, sed peccemus non adorando," Augustine, *Enarrationes in Psalmos* 98.9, commenting on Psalm 98(99):5. Latin quoted from http://www.augustinus.it/latino /esposizioni_salmi/esposizione_salmo_119_testo.htm.

of prayer and your work and play, this will likely seem difficult, a matter of effort aimed at connecting two very different things. We have to work hard, conceptually speaking, if we are to see what Paul, Luke, and Augustine might have meant by requiring us to make every aspect of our lives a prayer, and that is because, for us, prayer is defined as an occasional activity, like eating and sleeping: these are things we must do sometimes, but that by definition we cannot do all the time.

Let's make this point very specific indeed. The claim is, or seems to be, that if you cannot treat the most boring class you have, or your most painful moments at the dentist, or your most negative emotional moments, as themselves prayers, active adorations of the Triune Lord, then you are, to just the extent that you fail at doing this, sinning. It is not a matter of praying about these things, of bringing them to Jesus in prayer: they are or ought to be themselves prayers. Only if we think of them in this way can it make sense to say what Paul, Luke, and Augustine seem to say. But if this is right, then clearly a different idea about the nature of prayer is in play here than the one we ordinarily have.

For us, prayer is occasional. We speak intentionally to Jesus or Mary or the Holy Spirit or the Father or our favorite saints sometimes, not all the time. We kneel before the Blessed Sacrament—another form of speaking to Jesus—sometimes, not all the time. We get on our knees before bed or offer a blessing at table at the appropriate times of the day, and we think of these as moments of prayer and are certainly not doing them all the time. But for the Christian tradition, for the most part, this is an impoverished understanding of prayer. It is not wrong, it is just inadequate.

Suppose we think, instead, of prayer as most fundamentally and centrally the acknowledgment of gift. To acknowledge something as a gift is to know that it came to you, the recipient, from somewhere else, someone other than you: you did not make it, and you do not deserve it, for if you deserve it, it's not really a gift but rather a payment of debt. To treat what you have been given as a gift—to acknowledge it as such and not to pretend that it was really yours all along, or that you made it yourself, or that it is your due—you have to be grateful, to say thank you (that, incidentally, is what the word Eucharist most essentially means), and to keep on being grateful. Each time you look at or use the gift, if you are alive and awake and self-aware, you remember with gratitude who gave it to you. That is not so difficult with most gifts: the book on your shelf that your grandmother gave you may easily enough conjure in you gratitude for the occasion of its giving whenever you hold it in your hands. But when the gift is life, your very self, all that you have and all that you are—"What do you have that you did not receive?" asks Paul (1 Cor. 4:7), expecting the answer "nothing whatever"—things are more difficult. The challenge then is to be constantly grateful, habitually aware that whatever good things there are in us or in the world around us are not ours, and, therefore, active in the way that grateful people are active: enthusiastically, attentively, lovingly, and, above all, not as though we have done anything to deserve the good things that surround us. And that is what it means to pray: to behave as someone gifted, not as we now use that word, to mean someone to be admired for what they can do—"She's so gifted musically," we say proudly, meaning, usually, that she, rather than God, should be complimented for what she does—but instead to mean someone who in all she does expresses gratitude to the God who made it possible for her to do anything and for there to be a world in which she can do it.

Prayer is gratitude because gratitude is the primary form of adoration and adoration is, in the end, the only thing that counts because it is the form of human love most appropriate to God. All other loves serve this final love, which is prayer at its highest intensity.

But there are still some puzzles here. Are we to be grateful for suffering, death, sin, agony, and hatred? No. Those are not gifts. They are antigifts, loss and lack rather than abundance overspilling. Those we lament. Paul does not mean, as he explains with his characteristic intensity and complexity in the Letter to the Romans, that the damages the world and we ourselves have undergone are subjects for rejoicing or gratitude or love.[4] No, they are the dark side of giftedness, the damage done to the gift by treating it as something else, as a possession to be wholly owned. Lament, then, is the prayerful response to the gift's damage as gratitude is to its wholeness. Both are required in a damaged world, and both belong to prayer.

We have now the lineaments of an answer to the question of what it means to pray always: it is to cultivate the habit of gratitude for gift in such a way that being grateful becomes, for us, an attitude that informs all we do. Such an attitude makes a difference, in fact many differences.

First, you do not use a precious gift from your beloved—her picture, taken and framed for you; a lock of her hair, cut and given to you; a letter written to you in her own hand—in the same way that you use the T-shirt handed to you as an unwanted come-on by the credit-card company hoping for your patronage. The former's particulars are important, and you attend to them as if they were. The latter's are not, and it will scarcely matter to you what they are. This difference in attentiveness has mostly to do with gratitude: it is because what your beloved gives you is gift in the full sense that you attend to it with passion. And for Christians, everything we have—recall, again, Paul's dictum that we have nothing we have not been given—is gift in this sense, given by God who is *interior intimo tuo*, within what is most intimate to yourself, as well as being *superior summo tuo*, above what is highest in you.[5] Cultivating gratitude, the fundamental attitude of prayer, fosters loving attentiveness to the particulars of your own giftedness, and those of the world in which that giftedness is exercised.

Second, the cultivation of gratitude, whether self-consciously or by habit, makes a difference to our receptiveness to God, which is to say to the condition of our

4. I have in mind here especially Paul's discussion, in Rom. 8:18–25, of the groaning that accompanies gratitude in a fallen world—groaning that belongs to hope in such a world and can therefore be understood as a constitutive element of both prayer and adoration.

5. Quoting and paraphrasing Augustine, *Confessions* 3.6.11, in J. J. O'Donnell, ed., *Augustine: Confessions*, vol. 1 (New York: Oxford University Press, 1992), 27.

hearts. Augustine, again, is helpful here. In a letter written to Proba, a wealthy and well-educated Roman widow who had left Rome for North Africa (where Augustine also lived) following the invasion of Rome by Alaric and his Goths in the year 410, he responds to questions about prayer. In response to a difficulty about why the Lord commands us to petition him for particulars when he already knows what we need, he writes:

> He [the Lord] knows what we need before we ask him. Why then he does this [that is, requires us to petition him for particulars] can be troubling to the mind unless we understand that the Lord our God does not want our will, of which he cannot be ignorant, to become known to him; rather, he wants our desire to be exercised in our prayers, so that we become able to receive what he is prepared to give.[6]

Roll those concluding phrases around in your mind. Prayer (*oratio*) exercises desire (*desiderium*). It is, we might say, a regime of discipline for desire, a diet for love.[7] What does prayer do? It makes us capable of something we would not otherwise be capable of, which is reception of the gift, the gift which the Lord is always actively giving us. Without prayer, our hearts are trammeled in the direction of ungrateful possessiveness: we grasp what we have as if it were ours, and in doing so try to make of it something it is not and cannot be. The result is that we lose what we think we have, and also ourselves as aspiring owners of it. Recall that we have nothing ungiven, and so the only way to have what we have been given is to receive it as given, as gift. But with prayer, whether the petitions for particulars of which Augustine here writes, or the habitual cultivation of gratitude of which I have been writing, our hearts are opened, increasingly and gradually, to the possibility of receiving the gift, which is, in the end, sanctification.

Finally, the cultivation of gratitude attenuates fear and brings peace. The risen Lord, after Easter Sunday, constantly reiterates to his disciples when he appears to them that they should not fear and that he brings them peace. The church's liturgy reenacts this day-by-day and week-by-week. Our desires, sculpted into gratitude's shape by ceaseless prayer, become attuned to the fact that the happy or blessed life, the *beata vita*, is in fact being constantly offered to us by the Lord, and that the only thing asked of us is its reception for what it is: prevenient gift. Gratitude of this sort removes deep anxiety. It does not do this immediately, of course, but over time this is the direction in which it tends. If you not only assent to the claim that the Lord wants desperately to give you the blessing of a happy life, but also, by the cultivation of desire-disciplining gratitude, become the kind of person who acts as if that were true—who responds to the world as if its sufferings and

6. Translating from the Latin of Augustine's *Epistola* 130.8.17 (to Proba), as given at http://www .augustinus.it/latino/lettere/lettera_131_testo.htm.

7. I have in mind here John Donne's poem, "Love's Diet." He writes about disciplining, or dieting, the appetite of a lover for his mistress, but the conceit can apply as well, and certainly did apply in Donne's mind, to the disciplining of desires for God.

injustices and agonies, though real, are not the last word—then you will also find fear removed and anxiety assuaged. These are not gifts given all in a moment, but they are delights that become increasingly apparent as the life of prayer deepens and extends itself over the course of a life.

To pray as you work, to make your work a kind of prayer, is to take it seriously as an exercise in loving gratitude. You don't, if you are a Christian, think of the work you do merely as a means to gather resources to do something else. No, you begin to think of the assignment you have been given to do and the colleagues you have been given to help you do it, as gifts that permit you to show gratitude—not principally gratitude to them, though that should be present, but to God, who has made it possible for them to work alongside you. The particular tasks you do, the particular clients you help, the particular skills you learn—all these, if you pay close attention to them rather than treating them with the bored indifference of those who wish to get through them as quickly and effortlessly as possible in order to get on with real life, will become, increasingly, windows into God's creation and occasions for joy. Your work is in this sense an opportunity for prayer, and also an opportunity for training in sanctity: for while you might be baptized in the name of Jesus Christ, which is to say justified by being washed in his blood, you are not yet sanctified, and your work, whatever it is and however you have been given it, will be among the principal means by which you might become more holy than you are now, a more perfect image of the God who made you, and, therefore, someone who is increasingly transparent to the light of God, increasingly equipped for the eternal praise-shout of gratitude which is, I hope but do not know, your and my final destiny.

I have tried to make sense of the scriptural advocacy of prayer without ceasing by depicting prayer as an attitude of gratitude. That attitude can be cultivated, and by then eventually inhabited, like a second skin. Understanding prayer in this way does make it possible to say that prayer can be unceasing. Explicit verbal address to the Lord, then, whether as petition or ejaculation of gratitude, should be understood as an instance of this attitude. Such verbal address has a special importance for Christians, not least because it was prescribed for us by Jesus; but we ought not to understand prayer to be identical with it. Explicit address to the Lord, whether in private or in corporate worship, is a moment of filigreed ornament in a deeper and more quotidian process which is identical with the Christian life as a whole.

# 11

## Why Christian Character Matters

### N. T. WRIGHT

**One**

"Character" is the human equivalent of the writing that runs right through a stick of Brighton Rock. Famously, with that kind of seaside candy, the identifying word ("Brighton," or whatever) isn't simply printed on the top, so that after you'd sucked or bitten at the first half-inch you wouldn't be able to see it anymore. No: the word goes all the way through. Wherever you cut the stick, or bite into it, the letters will always be there.

When we use the word "character" in the sense that I'm giving it here—the sense which it often is assigned in the New Testament, too—we mean something similar. Human "character," in this sense, is the pattern of thinking and acting which runs right through someone, so that wherever you cut into them (as it were), you see the same person through and through. Its opposite would be superficiality: we all know people who present themselves at first glance as honest, cheerful, patient, or whatever, but when you get to know them better you come to realize that they're only "putting it on," and that when faced with a crisis, or simply when their guard is down, they're as dishonest, grouchy, and impatient as the next person.

Originally published as "The Transformation of Character," in N. T. Wright, *After You Believe* (New York: HarperOne, 2010), 27–71. Copyright © 2010 by Nicholas Thomas Wright. Reprinted by permission of HarperCollins Publishers (for the US) and N. T. Wright (for the UK and EEC). Scripture quotations in this chapter are the author's translations.

The point is this: I don't actually know how Brighton Rock and similar candy treats are manufactured, but an ordinary stick of candy doesn't automatically have writing that goes all the way through. Someone has to put it there. Likewise, the qualities of character which Jesus and his first followers insist on as the vital signs of healthy Christian life don't come about automatically. You have to develop them. You have to work at them. You have to think about it, to make conscious choices to allow the Holy Spirit to form your character in ways that, to begin with, seem awkward and "unnatural." Only in that way can you become the sort of "character" who will react instantly to sudden challenges with wisdom and good judgment.

You can tell when this has happened—and when it hasn't. A familiar story makes the point. A famous preacher had a friend who was well known for his short temper. One day, at a party, he asked this friend to help him serve some drinks. The preacher himself poured the drinks, deliberately filling several of the glasses a bit too full. He then passed the tray to his friend. As they walked into the room to distribute the drinks, he accidentally-on-purpose bumped into the friend, causing the tray to jiggle and some of the drinks to slosh over the brim and spill. "There you are, you see," said the preacher. "When you're jolted, what spills out is whatever is filling you." When you're suddenly put to the test and don't have time to think about how you're coming across, your real nature will come out. That's why character needs to go all the way through: whatever fills you will spill out. And it's up to you to do something about it.

Another famous story makes a similar point from a different angle. This time the story is a Jewish one. There was once a rabbi who had a phenomenal reputation for thinking logically and clearly in any and all circumstances. To put him to the test, his students took him out one evening and sent him to sleep by plying him with strong drink. Then they carried him to a graveyard and laid him out neatly in front of a tombstone. They kept watch to see what he would say on waking. When the great man came to, his logic didn't falter for a moment. "Point one," he said: "If I am alive, why am I lying in a graveyard? Point two: If I am dead, why do I want to go to the bathroom?" Even in these bizarre circumstances, his head was as clear as ever.

"Character" in this sense is a general human phenomenon, with "Christian character" as a particular variation on it. We talk about "bad characters," people who, wherever you prod, will reveal unpleasant or destructive characteristics that run right through their life, thought, and actions. Similarly, we talk about people being of "good character." Though different people will mean different specific things by that phrase, most of us know what we have in mind. Such a person will be honest, trustworthy, even-tempered, faithful (including within marriage), kind, generous, and so on.

Within Western culture, much of the expectation of what "good character" includes has been shaped, over many centuries, by certain elements of Christian teaching. Even though the general culture has for a long time shown strong signs of trying to abandon its Christian roots, there is still considerable overlap between the formation of "good character" in widely recognized senses and the formation of "Christian character." Though we shall be concerned with Christian character in particular in these pages, it is part of the Christian claim that being Christian involves becoming more genuinely human. When we explore what it means to develop Christian character, this will therefore overlap considerably with wider questions about the "character" that our whole society urgently needs to rediscover and develop.

So how then is "character" transformed? What sort of a process is it?

## Two

Character is transformed by three things. First, you have to aim at the right goal. Second, you have to figure out the steps you need to take to get to that goal. Third, those steps have to become habitual, a matter of second nature.

That sounds fine, put simply, but of course it's easier said than done. And since many people have approached the question of Christian behavior from quite different angles, we'd better have a brief look at those alternative routes first before we go any further.

For some, the whole idea of character, and of it being transformed in the way I'm describing, is simply foreign territory. Now that he has come to faith, people in his church expect him to behave in a particular way (and *not* to behave in other particular ways), but this is seen, not in terms of character, but in terms of straightforward obligation. In other words, Christians are *expected* to live by the rules. When they fail, as they will, they are simply to repent and try to do better next time. You either live a Christian life or you don't. Any suggestion of some kind of moral transformation—a long, slow change of deep, heart-level habits—would be suspect. It would look like "justification by works"—that is, trying to *earn* one's way to salvation. Keeping the rules doesn't contribute to your justification or salvation. It's just what you're expected to do. If there is any change of character involved, it happened already at conversion, through the action of the Holy Spirit. If the Holy Spirit really has come to live in someone's heart and life, that person automatically wants to live in accordance with God's will. It shouldn't be a matter of moral effort and struggle. After you believe, keeping the rules ought to come easily. (And if it doesn't, runs the unspoken subtext, you ought to pretend that it does.)

For others, what matters is "authenticity." Being true to yourself is what counts. God has accepted you as you are; now you must live out of gratitude for that acceptance. Any attempt to force yourself to keep particular moral rules and standards which seem alien to you is a denial both of God's free acceptance of you and of your own authentic existence. After you believe, you should discover who you really are and live in accordance with that, doing spontaneously whatever your heart, at its deepest level, instructs you to do.

I want here to hold out a vision of Christian living which has superficial similarities with both of these perspectives, but also radical differences. It is a vision
which stands in the tradition of ancient reflection about "virtue," but which has
allowed itself to be transformed by the remarkable moral challenge of Jesus himself
and of the New Testament. I shall spell all this out in more detail presently. For
the moment, let me also sketch, in a fuller but still preliminary way, what I mean
by the formation of "character" within a Christian context, and, within that, what
we might mean by "virtue."

What is the aim, or final goal, of the whole Christian life? Though many Christians in the Western world have imagined that the aim or goal of being a Christian
is simply "to go to heaven when you die," the New Testament holds out something
much richer and more interesting. Yes, those who belong to Jesus in this life go to
be with him once they die—that's a promise made in various places in the New
Testament. But that's only the start of it. In the end—after most of us have had a
time of rest and refreshment in the presence of Jesus himself—God has promised
to give the entire world, the whole created order, a complete makeover. It will
be renewed from top to bottom, so that it is filled at last with the presence and
glory of God "as the waters cover the sea" (Isa. 11:9). And what will happen to
us then? We will be given new bodies in which to live with delight and power in
God's new world. That, as I fully appreciate, is a much bigger and fuller picture
of the ultimate future hope than many Christians have cherished, but it's the one
the New Testament promises us.

Notice what happens if you contemplate this vision of the ultimate goal of
the Christian life and ask yourself, What are the steps which lead to *this* goal, as
opposed to some other?

The answer—given again and again, as we shall see, in the New Testament—is
that the transformation we are promised at the end of time *has already begun in
Jesus*. When God raised him from the dead, he launched his entire project of new
creation, and called people of all sorts to be part of that project, already, here and
now. And that means that the steps we take toward the ultimate goal—the things
which make sense of Christian living in what might otherwise be a long interval
between initial faith and final salvation—already partake of that same character
of transformation.

How this happens we shall consider later. But the result is that there are steps
we can take which lead to this goal, to the resurrection life within the new creation, and which we can take here and now. And these steps are, quite literally,
character transforming. The aim of the Christian life in the present time—the
goal you are meant to be aiming at once you have come to faith, the goal which
is within reach even in the present life, anticipating the final life to come—is the
life of fully formed, fully flourishing Christian character.

The test will be, as with an airline pilot facing a sudden life-or-death challenge,
whether your character is so formed that when the challenge comes you can meet
it with a second-nature Christian virtue, or whether you will flail around, panic,

wonder what on earth you should be doing—and quite possibly fail to act in the way you should have done.

But sudden moral challenges are not, in themselves, the staple diet of Christian living, of the transformed character, any more than hitting a flock of geese is the staple diet of the airline pilot. They are the emergencies, when the character quietly formed over many years rings true, comes into its own. But the character that can face such moments and do the right thing under sudden pressure is the character that has been formed by a much more sustained and positive purpose.

We must begin by putting on the table a few issues which are in a sense in the background but which, as often with great paintings, affect the foreground more than one might think at first glance. First, where does all this belong on the famous map of moral thinking, not least thinking about virtue, in the Western world as a whole? Second, how does this talk of character transformation sit with recent studies in the development of the brain and with the question of how we learn other things, such as languages? The answers to both of these questions will come as a surprise to some, and perhaps an encouragement as well.

## Three

What I have proposed is basically a Christian answer—Jesus's own answer, in fact—to the tradition of moral thinking that goes back to Aristotle. This tradition was well developed in the ancient world, and serious first-century readers who came upon the teaching of Paul and other early followers of Jesus would have had it in mind as they pondered what was being said.

It was Aristotle, about 350 years before the time of Jesus, who developed the threefold pattern of character transformation. There is first the "goal," the *telos*, the ultimate thing we're aiming at; there are then the steps you take toward that goal, the "strengths" of character which will enable you to arrive at that goal; and there is the process of moral training by which these "strengths" turn into habits, become second nature.

For Aristotle, the goal was the ideal of a fully flourishing human being. Think of someone who has lived up to his or her full potential, displaying a complete, rounded, wise, and thoroughly formed character. This particular goal, for which Aristotle used the word *eudaimonia*, is sometimes called "happiness," but Aristotle meant it in a technical sense that is actually closer to our idea of "flourishing."

The steps toward that goal, for Aristotle and his followers, were the strengths of character which, when developed, contributed toward the gradual making of a flourishing human being. The way to attain *eudaimonia*, Aristotle thought, was by practicing these strengths, just as a soccer player undergoes training for all the different muscles of the body and practices all the various ball skills that will be needed. Working on one or two of them isn't enough; there's no point having super-fit legs while the rest of the body is flabby, for example, or being able to kick a soccer ball long distances but not to dribble past an opponent. In the same way, a complete and flourishing human being needs all the basic strengths of character, which we shall look at presently. Aristotle's word for such a strength was *aretē*; later Latin writers used the word *virtus*, from which of course we get "virtue." The "virtues" are the different strengths of character which together contribute to someone becoming a fully flourishing human being.

For Aristotle—and for the tradition which developed after him and formed the world of moral discourse at the time when early Christianity was growing, spreading, and teaching a new way of life—there were four principal virtues: courage, justice, prudence, and temperance. These, Aristotle proposed, were the "hinges" upon which the great door to human fulfillment and flourishing would swing open. That is why those four are often called the "cardinal virtues": *cardo* in Latin means "hinge." (The "cardinals" in the Roman Catholic Church are the "hinge men," the ones on whose ministry the rest "hinges." The birds called "cardinals" have nothing to do with hinges, however, but are simply named for their color, which resembles the scarlet robe of the hinge-men cardinals. The same is true of the sports teams called the "Cardinals"—football in Arizona, baseball in St. Louis.)

The "cardinal virtues" are not the only virtues. But, Aristotle proposed, they are the central ones, and all the others depend on them. Practice these, he said, and you will become a complete, "happy," flourishing human being. That is the goal, the destination of our journey. The virtues are the road which will get you there. Look at people who are suddenly hailed as "heroes," and whose actions are described as "miraculous," and the chances are you'll see people whose characters have been formed in this way. Even in sports this is often true: the player who, in a great sporting crisis, manages to pull off the apparently impossible shot is most likely the player who has practiced that shot over and over in private until it became second nature. I recall the South African golfer Gary Player responding to a critic who described him as "lucky." Yes, he said—and I've noticed that the harder I practice, the luckier I get.

Indeed, I suspect that calling events such as the safe landing of Flight 1549 a "miracle" may be a way in which our culture chooses to ignore the real challenge, the real moral message, of that remarkable sort of event. The virtues *matter*. They matter deeply. When the great door of human nature swings open to reveal its truest secrets, these are the hinges on which it turns.

But these character strengths don't happen all in a rush. You have to work at them. Character is a slowly forming thing. You can no more force character on someone than you can force a tree to produce fruit when it isn't ready to do so. The person has to choose, again and again, to develop the moral muscles and skills which will shape and form the fully flourishing character. And so, just as a long, steady program of physical training will enable you to do all kinds of things—run in a marathon, walk thirty miles in a day, lift heavy objects—which you would previously never have thought possible, so the long, steady program of working on the character strengths, the virtues, will enable you to live in a way you would never have thought possible, avoiding moral traps and pitfalls and exhibiting a genuine, flourishing human life.

Part of the point of all this is that you will then do certain things *automatically* which before you would have struggled to do at all. Certain things will then be second nature. Which is just as well, because if you'd had to stop and think what to do in some particular crisis, the moment would have passed and disaster might have struck.

What the New Testament writers are urging, following Jesus himself, is therefore quite like Aristotle's argument in some ways, but in a significantly different mode. The comparison is somewhat like that between a three-dimensional model sitting beside a two-dimensional one—a cube beside a square, say, or a sphere beside a circle: Jesus and his followers are offering the three-dimensional model toward which Aristotle's two-dimensional one points. When you get the sphere, you get the circle thrown in, as it were, but it now means something rather different.

Reflect for a moment on the three stages we have already noted. The point, each time, is the transformation, and how it happens.

1. Aristotle glimpsed a goal of human flourishing; so did Jesus, Paul, and the rest. But Jesus's vision of that goal was larger and richer, taking in the whole world, and putting humans not as lonely individuals developing their own moral status but as glad citizens of God's coming kingdom.

2. Aristotle saw that to get to the goal of a genuinely human life one should develop the moral strengths he called virtues. Jesus and his first followers, not least Paul, said something similar. But their vision of the moral strengths, corresponding to their different vision of the goal, highlighted qualities Aristotle didn't rate highly (love, kindness, forgiveness, and so on) and included at least one—humility—for which the ancient pagan world (and for that matter the modern pagan world) had no use at all.

3. Aristotle saw that the ultimate aim was to become the kind of character who would be able to act in the right way automatically, by the force of long training of habit. Jesus and Paul agreed, but they proposed a very different way by which the relevant habits were to be learned and practiced.

There is, of course, far more that could be said about the interesting interplay between the framework of moral thought offered by Aristotle and that offered by Jesus and the early Christians. That isn't the main subject of the book, so I will content myself at the moment with this reflection. I think if we'd asked St. Paul what he thought about Aristotle and his scheme of the virtues, he would have said about it roughly what he said about the Jewish Law: it is fine up to a point and as far as it goes, but it can't actually give what it promises. It's like a signpost pointing in more or less the right direction (though it will need some adjustment), but without a road that actually goes there.

**Four**

We move from ancient philosophy to contemporary brain science. When people consistently make choices about their patterns of behavior, physical changes take place within the brain itself. Some might regard this as common sense, but for many it will come as a fascinating and perhaps frightening reality. There is a great deal of work still to be done in this field. Neuroscience is still in comparative infancy. But already the clear indications are that significant events in your life, including significant choices you make about how you behave, create new information pathways and patterns within your brain. Neuroscientists often use the metaphor of the "wiring" of the brain, which is not inappropriate since, though of course there are no wires as such involved, information is indeed passed here and there within the brain by what are basically electric currents.

It isn't just that new patterns of wiring are being put down all the time, corresponding to the choices we make and the behaviors we adopt—though behavior is of course massively habit-forming. Parts of the brain actually become physically enlarged when an individual's behavior regularly exercises them. For example, violin players develop not only their left hand (I once knew a boy at school whose left hand was several glove sizes larger than his right due to playing the violin incessantly for years), but also the section of the brain that controls the left hand. "These regions [of the brain]," writes John Medina in his fascinating book *Brain Rules*, "are enlarged, swollen and crisscrossed with complex associations." As Medina stresses, "The brain acts like a muscle. The more activity you do, the larger and more complex it can become." What's more, he says, "our brains are so sensitive to external inputs that their physical wiring depends upon the culture in which they find themselves." As a result, "learning results in physical changes in the brain, and these changes are unique to each individual."[1] In other words, as we learn to connect various things in new ways, our brain records those connections. The result is rather like a gardener's discovery that a patch which has been dug over before is much easier to dig a second time. A particular set of associations in the brain, especially if it is connected with intense emotions or physical reactions, whether pleasurable or painful, will make it much easier for those associations to be triggered a second time. Contemporary neuroscience is thus actually able to study and map the way in which lifelong habits come to be formed.

One of the most famous instances of this phenomenon concerns the brain structure of London taxi-drivers. The work of E. A. Maguire and others has revealed some remarkable evidence.[2] London is not only one of the largest cities on the planet; it is also one of the most complex, with more one-way streets, twisting back alleys, curving rivers, and other traffic hazards than it's easy to imagine. Before a

1. John Medina, *Brain Rules* (Seattle: Pear, 2008), 58, 61, 62.
2. See Eleanor A. Maguire et al., "Navigation-Related Structural Change in the Hippocampi of Taxi Drivers," *Proceedings of the National Academy of Sciences* 97, no. 8 (April 11, 2000), 4398–403, http://www.pnas.org/content/97/8/4398.abstract.

cabbie is allowed to start work, he or she has to pass a rigorous examination testing mastery of what's called "The Knowledge," a process that involves memorizing thousands of street names and ways to get to those streets at the different times of day or night as the traffic conditions change. The result is not just that they are the most effective taxi-drivers in the world, hardly ever having to consult a map, but also that *their brains have actually changed.* The part of the brain called the hippocampus, which is where we do spatial reasoning (among a wide variety of other things), is typically much larger in cabbies than in the average person. Like bodybuilders who develop muscles the rest of us don't know we've got, cabbies develop mental muscles most of us seldom have to exercise.

This kind of research, so far as I know, is not normally undertaken with a view to religious or moral issues, but the implications in those areas are enormous. We are all aware that we have strong memories of particular events. Some of us may have reflected on the way in which our imaginations and emotional reactions have been conditioned by particular moments of joy or shock, delight or horror, intense pleasure or intense pain. But the thought that not only these special events but millions of "ordinary" ones as well leave traces in the physical structure and "electrical wiring" of our brains comes as startling and striking news to most of us.

Most people in today's Western world, I suspect, think of their minds as more or less neutral machines that can be turned this way and that. When I drive down the road to London, and then when I drive up the road to Edinburgh, nothing changes in the structure of the car. But supposing the car had a kind of internal memory, recording the journeys I'd made, so that when I set off in the general direction of London—a trip I make often—the car might click into "we're going to London" mode and nudge me to take the London-bound road, even if in fact I had been intending *this* time to go to Birmingham? I would then have to make a more conscious choice to refuse the pathway the car had chosen and to compel it to do things it hadn't expected.

In the same way, supposing a decision to cheat on my tax return leaves an electronic pathway in the brain which makes it easier to cheat on other things—or people—as well? Or supposing the decision to restrain my irritation with a boring neighbor on the train, and to cultivate instead a calm patience, leaves a pathway which makes it easier to be patient when someone subsequently behaves in a truly offensive manner? As I say, the research is nowhere near as fully developed as we might like. But it seems as though the idea of developing "moral muscles," by analogy with people going to the gym to develop physical ones, may be closer than we had imagined.

The process of acquiring habits in any sphere can be illustrated in many ways. Learning a musical instrument is an obvious one (think of those violinists with their left-hand neurons working overtime). Learning a second language (music being, of course, a kind of language) is another.

Many people in the world can speak only their mother tongue. It's the only language they've ever learned, and they learned it without reflecting on how they did it. Even *that* makes the point, because as we learn our mother tongue, whatever it is, we are building up a massive and highly complex network of habits, both mental and physical, which interrelate in multiple ways with different life situations.

A great deal of first-language learning, to begin with at least, is simply copycat behavior. The child hears parents and siblings saying things and tries to do the same. But even from an early age, surprising originality can creep in, as the child not only masters habits and patterns of speech but begins to create new ones by subtle variations. And at this stage an enormous amount of what the language specialists call grammar—involving *accidence* (the way words happen to be formed) and *syntax* (the way words fit together within sentences)—and of course vocabulary itself, in both directions ("What's the word for that thing, there?" and "What does this word mean?"), is being assimilated, swallowed whole, all the time. Whether a child is severely dyslexic or a poetic prodigy—and the two might actually sometimes coincide—habits are being formed, patterns laid down in the brain, which means that the language eventually becomes second nature. In most conversations, most of the time, you aren't discussing language, grammar, and vocabulary. Those matters come up only if someone uses a word or a phrase in a way you don't understand. Normally, you aren't even thinking about vocabulary, much less grammar. You're thinking about the subject matter of the conversation.

Learning your mother tongue, then, is a good illustration as far as it goes. But learning a new language, especially as an adult, is better, for two reasons. First, it's a far more conscious activity. Even in an ultramodern language laboratory, where you are imitating the "natural" conditions in which you learned your mother tongue, you still have to *think* about why this word is formed that way and not some other, why these awkward irregular verbs behave in this way when they should really have done the opposite, and so on. You have to master the nuances and metaphors and emphases that make a living language the lovely but difficult thing it is. You will often get it wrong, but it's worth persisting for the goal, the *telos*, of what lies ahead. If you're an English speaker learning German, you must continually remind yourself that the verb comes at the end of the sentence. And, even in a language quite like your own (think of an Italian learning Spanish), there will be a large amount of vocabulary which just has to be memorized. This requires mental effort, the conscious, acted-out intention to imprint these patterns, with their physical outworkings (the contortions of tongue, teeth, lips, and vocal cords), upon the brain, aiming at the point when they will happen without effort and indeed without conscious thought. It is exactly this kind of complex effort, as we shall see, which the early Christians described when they were urging one another to develop the character which anticipated God's new world.

C. S. Lewis describes the transition to understanding a new language in a memorable passage, referring to the time when he was learning ancient Greek:

> Those in whom the Greek word lives only while they are hunting for it in the lexicon, and who then substitute the English word for it, are not reading the Greek at all;

they are only solving a puzzle. The very formula, "*Naus* means a ship," is wrong. *Naus* and *ship* both mean a thing, they do not mean one another. Behind *Naus*, as behind *navis* or *naca*, we want to have a picture of a dark, slender mass with sail or oars, climbing the ridges, with no officious English word intruding.[3]

That is the point at which a second language gives us the clue to how virtue functions: it becomes second nature. Eventually, all being well, you pass beyond the stilted, forced stage to an entirely new sort of "naturalness."

One warning note comes in here. It is possible to learn a new language and then forget it. I learned several languages when I was young. One of them, Syriac, gave me special pleasure, with its liquid sounds and wonderful ancient poetry. But I didn't keep it up through my thirties and forties; and when, in my early fifties, I went back to a Syriac Bible to check something, I found to my sorrow that I couldn't even remember how the alphabet worked. Virtue can be like that, too. Someone who genuinely learns generosity as a child can easily find that the habits of adult life squeeze it out. It then has to be learned, with much more difficulty, all over again. There are, sadly, many times when those who have begun to practice the Christian life encounter the same problem. Stop practicing—allow yourself to forget the goal—and you may lose the language altogether.

Another reason why learning a second language is a good illustration of virtue is that often the reason for doing it is that you want to be able to be at home in the place where that language is spoken, or at least in reading and appreciating the literature of that country (or, in the case of ancient languages, that time). Learning the language thus has a goal in view: that of acquiring those habits of brain and body which will enable you to function already, here and now, as a linguistically competent citizen of that country, with an easy familiarity. The greatest compliment you can pay someone who has learned a second language is to mistake him or her for a native. That, again, is the "reward" for the work—not an arbitrary reward, like a child being given a bicycle because she has passed her exam, but a reward which is the true *telos*, the proper goal, of the original activity.

That's how virtue worked for Aristotle, and that's how it works—once we grasp the important differences between Aristotle and Jesus!—within Christian living. Aristotle's goal, as we saw, was *eudaimonia*, human flourishing. The virtues—the four "cardinal" virtues and the other virtues that hang on those "hinges"—were quite simply the grammar and vocabulary of the language of "flourishing" humanness. Nobody really knows that language as their mother tongue. But we can glimpse that country from time to time and pick up hints about how its language works, what patterns of brain and body are needed to enable us to function as linguistically competent citizens. And the more we practice speaking the language—in other words, the more we learn what it means to act with courage, temperance, prudence, and justice—the more we shall be developing an easy

---

3. C. S. Lewis, *Surprised by Joy: The Shape of My Early Life* (1955; London: Fontana, 1959), 115.

familiarity with how the truly flourishing people live. Who knows, one day we might be mistaken for a native.

If learning virtue is like learning a language, it is also like acquiring a taste, or practicing a musical instrument. None of these "comes naturally" to begin with. When you work at them, though, they begin to feel more and more "natural," until that aspect of your "character" is formed so that, at last, you attain the hard-won freedom of fluency in the language, happy familiarity with the taste, competence on the instrument.

If this is what "character" and "virtue" are all about, how does such exploration of the moral landscape sit alongside the two major moral frameworks which most people in the Western world now assume?

## Five

Come back to the debate—or the attempted debate—between Christians who assume that the question is about discovering the correct rules and applying them and Christians who assume that what matters is discovering "who you really are" and being true to it, in line with Jesus's radical welcome to all comers. These two positions represent, more or less, the two frameworks of moral thought between which most people today find themselves choosing, at least by implication. It's easy for both sides to caricature one another, and at a time of moral nervousness on many fronts we should respect the anxieties that many have. However, we should also look more closely at these frameworks themselves. If, as I believe, the development of character, and the habituation of virtue, offers a better perspective from which to understand our moral dilemmas, we need to see what the alternatives are actually all about.

Take the world of rules, for a start. Many people of my age grew up being taught that there are such things as right and wrong, that these are more or less universal and constant, and that you can know them and do them. Indeed, we had all this drilled into us. (Interesting phrase, that. Do you think, when you hear it, of someone drilling a hole in a piece of wood, or rather of a squad of soldiers doing "drill" so that they learn to obey orders instinctively?) Sometimes these rules are simple but profound in their implications, such as "Do as you would be done by" and "People matter more than things."

In many cultures these rules include, at quite a basic level, prohibitions on murder, theft, and adultery—or (to put it positively) a respect for life, property, and marriage. Most societies most of the time have lived by simple rules of this kind, which then get variously codified into law. The Ten Commandments are one classic example, but there are many others. Many of us were taught not only the Ten Commandments but also various derivatives, so that (confusingly for a child) the prohibitions on stealing, killing, lying, and so on seemed to merge into the equally strong commandments about appropriate table manners, writing thank-you letters, being polite to aged aunts, the "proper" pronunciation of words, not wearing muddy shoes inside the house, and so on. But the point is that many of us grew up in a world of rules, a structured and ordered society where the rules were given and, though there might be disputes about particular ones, if you got them mostly right you were all right, and if you didn't, you weren't. Everyone had a duty to keep the rules, whether or not it suited them. And, tellingly, people often suggested, or even simply assumed, that one of the main things Jesus came to do was to tell us more clearly what the rules were and to give us a wonderful example of how to keep them . . .

. . . Which then runs into difficulties, because people quickly discover that they *can't* keep them, and so a different mode breaks in: Jesus came to bring forgiveness for our rule-breaking, but once we've grasped that, we have to go back to rule-*keeping* again. That is the broad framework within which many people in today's Western world have come to think of the gospel of Jesus Christ.

Actually, the framework comes not from Jesus or the Gospels but from a particular kind of philosophy. Specialists will recognize it as having quite a lot to do, in the modern world, with the eighteenth-century German writer Immanuel Kant. To a people who knew the rules but knew they broke them, the good news was that God would forgive you—but then you had to keep the rules again, because that's what good Christians did. People then got into puzzles about how you could say both of these things together: how you could talk about rules without undermining God's generosity and forgiving grace, and so on. But, in general, people assumed that part of the point of being a Christian was to know what the rules were and to do your best to keep them.

And of course there's a sense in which that is at least part of the truth. Almost nobody supposes that Christian behavior, or for that matter human behavior in general, is entirely a matter of individual choice, with no guidelines whatever. Ironically, those who pour scorn on some of the older rules, not least about sexual behavior, are often those who insist most loudly on some of the newer rules, for instance about caring for the planet and its ecology. And a huge amount of life depends on common recognition of basic rules—about which side of the road to drive the car, for instance. We cannot simply play off "virtue" or "character" against "rules." When Captain Sullenberger made his snap decision about landing the plane on the Hudson River, the point was that he was instinctively doing what the rulebook would have said, had he had time to go and look it up.

The problem comes, I think, not with rules themselves (though there are problems there too), but with a rule-based mentality: not so much "what to do" but "how to do it." There was a massive reaction against "duty" in the middle and later years of the twentieth century in western Europe and North America. This was partly, we may suspect, as a reaction to two generations having been told it was their "duty" to go and die in major wars. The result has been that many people forget the universal importance of rules as providing a framework, a set of solid guidelines, for millions of aspects of daily life, and have come to see rules themselves simply as a problem, cramping one's style, arbitrarily imposing a framework of behavior on people for whom it might well be inappropriate. This is of course unfair to the fundamental idea of "rule," but it is, I think, a reflection of where a fair amount of our world, not least the Western Christian world, now is. It simply won't do merely to assert that the rules exist and that they must be forced on people whether they like it or not. We must search for the larger framework within which appropriate rules may play their proper, though ultimately subordinate, part. And we must recognize that as we do so we are, in terms of Western culture as a whole, playing the game facing straight into a strong gale.

We meet similar problems if we speak, as many do today, in larger terms about "principles" or "values." The two are not actually the same. A principle is a general statement of how things should be, from which specific rules might be derived; a value is some aspect of human life which is prized in itself, and from which principles and thereby rules might be generated. You *uphold* a value—say, of the sanctity of life. You *act from* a principle—say, that one should always ("in principle," as we say) preserve life and not destroy it. You *obey* a rule—"Do not commit murder." But of course in ordinary life people often use these words in a much more fluid, almost interchangeable, fashion. And I suspect that some people speak of "values" and "principles" partly at least because the word "rules" sounds, to many, so negative, restrictive, intrusive, and even arbitrary. People know they want to retrieve some kind of "standards." But "rules" will be unpopular, so they turn to "principles" or "values" instead.

Might it help, then, to think in terms of *Christian* "principles" or "values"? It isn't difficult to highlight various general themes from the moral vision of the New Testament and the early Christians: peace, justice, freedom, love, and several others come readily to mind. But what exactly do these big, abstract words mean? Who says? How do you apply them to particular questions and cases? Is it ever possible, having abstracted such themes from their scriptural and historical settings, to play them off against other aspects of the same Scriptures? If so, on what grounds? If not, what was the point of abstracting them in the first place? Principles and values may have their place, but that place cannot be central. They are, basically, Big Rules, subject to the same problem as the ordinary little rules. When politicians bang on, as they do, about the need to restore values in our society, this is usually distressingly vague. Whose values? Who says? How are you going to restore them without tackling the underlying causes of why, if they're so important, most people seem to ignore them? Some people will even talk about "Christian values" or "Judeo-Christian values," though those are usually just as difficult to articulate, let alone to impose. And if one of your principles turns out to be "the greatest happiness of the greatest number"—the principle known as utilitarianism, which has been extremely popular for nearly two hundred years now—you run into all sorts of interesting problems, about what happiness really is, what you do when people have a wrong idea of it, how you calculate what will bring about the effect of happiness, and how you cope with the minority who are not going to be happy with a proposed action designed to bring happiness. Utilitarianism really deserves a whole discussion to itself, but this must suffice here.

However, the real difficulty with rules is not only that we don't keep them very well, though that's true. Nor that there always seem to be troubling exceptions: when we've been taught always to tell the truth, what do we say to the would-be murderer who asks where his intended victim is hiding? Nor, yet, is the real problem that systems of rules differ markedly from one another: in some cultures you are under a solemn obligation to kill the person who rapes your daughter, and in others you are under a solemn obligation *not* to do so. These are indeed problems. But the biggest problem lies elsewhere.

The real problem is that rules always appear to be, and are indeed designed to be, restrictive. But we know, deep down, that some of the key things that make us human are being creative, celebrating life and beauty and love and laughter. You can't get those by legislation. Rules matter, but they aren't the center of it all. You can tell people that they must obey the rule always to be generous. But if someone gives you a present merely because he is obeying a rule or doing his duty, the glory of gift-giving has slipped through your fingers. If rules are taken as the main thing, then the *truly* main thing seems to be missing. What happened to *character*?

A striking example of this problem occurred as I was rewriting this chapter. A senior government civil servant was discovered to be sending scurrilous emails to a colleague proposing a "dirty tricks" smear campaign against leading members of the opposition. The prime minister's response was to say that new rules would be brought in to prevent this happening—though in fact there is already a strict code about such things, which the civil servant had flagrantly breached. The leader of the opposition suggested, by contrast, that what was needed was a change of culture. But how that might come about he did not say.

Another example from further back. I still meet, from time to time, the man who was headmaster of my school when I was a teenager. He once told me that early on in his time as head, in the mid-1950s, one of the school administrators came to him with a challenge. The previous headmaster, he said, had written a new school rule in the rulebook every day. Why wasn't the new headmaster keeping up this tradition? Didn't he care how people behaved? His response, in order to shelve the question for the moment, was to think quickly and invent a new rule: "No boy may, at any time . . . " But that was the last time he did it. Of course there were rules, and they mattered. But what mattered even more was developing the character of pupils so that they would behave with good sense and judgment in the thousands of areas which *weren't* covered by official rules.

The question of morals or ethics is in fact part of the much larger question of what humans are here *for*. Framing an answer in terms of rules, *any* rules, always implies that human life is a bit like a continual preparation for an examination, with a big assessment coming up and grades to be awarded which might get you into a good job, or a graduate program, or wherever else you hope to end up next. But is human life really a kind of continuous-assessment education program? Is it just a matter of "getting through" by keeping the (mostly negative) rules? Or are the rules there as signposts, pointing to a larger purpose and warning us that there are ways of missing that larger purpose? But if that's the case, what is that larger purpose, and how do we find it? And what about the question which looms up continually within Christian discussion, about how human behavior as a whole relates to the overwhelming grace of God?

This is the point at which the story of the rich young man, and the other scenes in Mark 10, seem to be saying, No: what matters isn't simply keeping a bunch of rules; what matters is character. Not just any old sort of character, either, but a particular sort: the sort Jesus was urging and modeling—the character of patience, humility, and above all generous, self-giving love. And the message of Mark at this point seems to be that you don't get that character just by trying. You get it by following Jesus.

### Six

Rules matter, it seems, but character matters more, and provides a framework within which rules, where appropriate, can have their proper effect. But this is by no means how people have understood Jesus and the Christian message in the last two centuries.

If you asked the average Western person, including the average Western Christian, what Jesus stood for in terms of human behavior, they probably wouldn't tell you about the subtle balance of character and rules. Yes, they would say, Jesus opposed self-righteous legalists who tried to impose their morality on others. But when people say this they don't tend to think ". . . so he urged them to develop character instead," but rather that Jesus offered a kind of radical freedom. This is what many Western Christians think today: Jesus accepted people as they were and urged them to discover their real identity and to be true to that essence. He encouraged people to throw the old rules into the trash can and take up the challenge of living spontaneously, authentically, in the freedom of the spirit rather than the slavery of the letter. This viewpoint is so deeply ingrained in many parts of the Western world in general, and the Western church in particular, that you only have to hint at it and you invoke a whole way of looking at the world which many people instinctively feel is right without further argument.

This point of view is so important that we must go into it in a little more detail. If, as I believe, the New Testament offers us the way of virtue, we need to see more clearly what, for many today, is its principal rival. Like many rivals, it is actually a parody, a caricature, of the real thing.

Three of the greatest opinion-forming movements in the last two centuries of Western thought and culture have led people to set aside the desirability or possibility of virtue altogether. Most people are probably not aware of these movements as historical or cultural forces, but simply imbibe from our present culture—the

culture these movements created—a general sense which Jesus and his first followers would in fact have challenged head-on.

What were these three movements? A brief and broad-brush summary will
suffice. The importance for us is the effect on today's popular imagination rather
than details about where they came from.

1. The romantic movement in the nineteenth century reacted against what it
   saw as cold, rational formalism (here are the rules; keep them; that's your
   duty; don't ask for more). The romantics stressed the importance of inner
   feeling and of actions that flowed from that. As one recent writer put it, they
   advocated "the spontaneous, the unfettered, the subjective, the imaginative
   and emotional, and the inspirational and heroic" rather than having things
   imposed on them by someone else, or by a system of philosophy or politics.[4]
   Don't give us systems; give us life and love and warmth in the soul!

2. The existentialist movement in the early twentieth century highlighted the
   notion of "authenticity." To live "authentically," said the existentialists, is to
   take the dangerous and difficult decision to reject structures and systems
   that constrict and impair our human freedom, and to live in accordance with
   our true inner being. That is the way to a kind of completeness, of human
   fulfillment.

3. As a kind of junior but powerful version of romanticism and existentialism combined, the emotivist movement insisted that all moral discourse
   could be reduced in any case to statements of likes and dislikes. "Murder
   is wrong" simply means "I don't like murder." "Giving to charity is good"
   means "I like people giving to charity." From this point of view, following
   moral rules and following your own inclinations both boil down to pretty
   much the same thing. Often today people who are discussing moral choices
   will say that this person "prefers" Option A or that that person "applauds"
   Option B, as though moral choices were a matter of personal preference or
   taste. Sometimes they speak of "moral attitudes" as though what a particular
   person believed about the rights and wrongs of certain actions were simply an
   "attitude," an innate prejudice which they hadn't bothered to think through.

Whichever of the three you embrace—and in popular culture romanticism,
existentialism, and emotivism tend to swirl together in a confused world of impressions and rhetoric—they arrive at the same general position, which many
today assume, without more ado, is roughly what Jesus himself taught, and what
Christian living ought to be all about. Be yourself; don't let anyone else dictate
to you; don't let other people's systems or phobias cramp your style; be honest
about what you're really feeling and desiring. Get in touch with the bits of yourself

4. Simon Blackburn, *Oxford Dictionary of Philosophy*, 2nd rev. ed. (1994; Oxford: Oxford University
Press, 2008), 319.

you've been screening out; make friends with them and be true to them. Anything else will result in a diminishing of your true, unique, wonderful self.

This whole way of thinking has become entrenched in many parts of our world, not least in many parts of many churches. Some people mistake it for the gospel itself, supposing that the romantic and existentialist rejection of rules is the same thing as Paul's doctrine of "justification by faith apart from works of the law," or the same thing as what Jesus was advocating when he confronted the law-bound Pharisees.

Shakespeare put all this in a classic phrase, set in the mouth of Polonius, a man he is teaching us to see as a bit shallow and pompous (to be precise, "a foolish prating knave"):

> This above all—to thine own self be true,
> And it must follow, as the night the day,
> Thou canst not then be false to any man.
> (*Hamlet*, act 1, scene 3, lines 78–80)

Hmmm. Actually, if you are genuinely true to yourself, you will no doubt be aware of many hidden motives within yourself that other people would ignore, and so may be able to make better choices, both moral and otherwise. But supposing the "self" to which you are true is the self that wants to cheat everyone you meet, including friends and family, out of as much money as possible? In the monetary scandals that came to light in the recent financial crash, several of those who were exposed as serial fraudsters had been utterly true to themselves and utterly false to everyone else.

"Well," you might say, "the fraudulent bankers weren't *really* being true to themselves, because they must have known all along that they were doing wrong." To that I reply that it is exactly part of the problem with our late-modern or post-modern world that the imperative to maximize your own (or your firm's) bank balance has, for many, become the deepest level of truth they can imagine. Once you abolish or sideline older, less apparently tangible notions of morality, what else are you left with?

I came across a perfect contemporary example of the popular-level true-to-yourself philosophy the day after I had given a lecture in late February 2009. Browsing in a junk shop in Laguna Beach, California, I discovered a jokey little sign which read:

> There are times I think I'm doing things on principle,
> But mostly I just do what feels good.
> But that's a principle, too.

"Doing what feels good": it would be easy to caricature that as a typically Californian attitude, but that would ignore the fact that a vast swath of contemporary Western life has operated on precisely this "principle," and has strongly resisted, in the name of "freedom," any attempt to question or challenge it. To move from Californian popular culture to the sharp analysis of one of the great minds of the twentieth century, listen to this analysis by Arthur M. Schlesinger Jr., writing about the impact that the theologian Reinhold Niebuhr had on him and his generation, and about the way in which Niebuhr's influence waned in the 1960s:

> [Niebuhr's] emphasis on sin startled my generation. We had been brought up to believe in human innocence and virtue. The perfectibility of man was less a liberal illusion than an all-American conviction. . . . But nothing in our system prepared us for Hitler and Stalin, for the death camps and the gulags. . . .
>
> [Niebuhr's] influence waned somewhat in the 1960s. The rebel young of those frenzied years, with their guileless confidence in the unalloyed goodness of spontaneous impulses and in the instant solubility of complex problems, had no feeling for Niebuhr.[5]

"Guileless confidence in the unalloyed goodness of spontaneous impulses": that sums up a good deal of the mood that has gripped, and still grips, many in the Western world. We might note that "virtue," in the second line of that quotation, hardly means what it meant in the classical tradition. The whole point of Schlesinger's sharp analysis was that in the America of his youth, and again in the 1960s, there seemed no need for virtue in the sense of a hard-won *second* nature: "doing what came naturally" was quite good enough. Indeed, the refusal to obey "what came naturally," the "spontaneous impulses" whose "unalloyed goodness" could be confidently assumed, has itself often been deemed to be wrong, dangerous, damaging to one's health and well-being. The idea of a goal, an ultimate aim, calling us to a hard road of self-denial—the idea, in other words, that Jesus of Nazareth meant what he said when he spoke of people taking up their cross to follow him!—has been quietly removed from the record, not only of secular Western life but also, extraordinarily, of a fair amount of Christian discourse.

At a less obvious but perhaps still more insidious level, all this goes with that element in cultures both ancient and modern which is generally called "Gnosis" or "Gnosticism." This, loosely, involves the idea that there is a spark of light hidden deep within us—or at least within some of us. This hidden spark (it is supposed) is often buried deep underneath layers of social and cultural conditioning, and even layers of what we ourselves assume to be "who we really are."

Once this spark has been revealed, however, it takes precedence over everything else, trumping every rule, every happiness calculation, and certainly every virtue, classical or otherwise. Whatever we deeply, most truly find within ourselves must be right. My heart is telling me how it is, and I must go with my heart. That is the "guiding light" at the deep center of my true self. *And this, many people today have been taught and seriously believe, is what Jesus of Nazareth came to model and to*

---

5. From his foreword to the new edition of Charles C. Brown, *Niebuhr and His Age: Reinhold Niebuhr's Prophetic Role and Legacy* (1992; Harrisburg, PA: Trinity Press International, 2002), viii–ix.

*teach.* That is the message not only of *The Da Vinci Code* and a good many other popular page-turners, but also of many more serious writers and scholars. It is, after all, the message that many people very much want to hear.

In its corporate version, this kind of philosophy has dominated a good deal of our world. Not for nothing did the great intellectual and cultural revolution of the second half of the eighteenth century call itself "the Enlightenment." Western Europe and North America had "discovered who they really were." They were a race set apart, possessing new knowledge, skills, and techniques which not only could be expressed in terms of conquest of those less "enlightened" but positively *demanded* to be so exploited.

That is a subject for another occasion (though, interestingly, it is what Arthur Schlesinger goes on to speak about immediately after the passage I quoted above). But in its individual version, the Gnosticism of the last two centuries has embedded deep within our imaginations the assumption—I was going to say "the thought," but I suspect that most people don't *think* this, they merely *assume* it—that "being true to oneself" is the central human command, the central (even) "religious" imperative, the central goal and task of every human being, the Holy Grail of personal development. That is simply how millions of people today see themselves and the world.

Examples abound to back this up. The poet John Betjeman had the misfortune to have a father who was running a successful family business and expected his son to follow him into it. Or perhaps we should say that old Mr. Betjeman had the misfortune to have a son who knew in his bones that he was not cut out to be a businessman and who really did want to write poetry. Fortunately, the younger man was eventually "true to himself," in this respect at least. Sadly, however, as his candid self-reflections indicate, when it came to his private life, the "self" to which he tried to be true was deeply confused. He followed its various whims, and thereby created a fair amount of moral and human havoc. There is the problem of romanticism, existentialism, emotivism, and neo-Gnosticism in a nutshell.

Since human beings are deeply mysterious creatures, none of this should surprise us. The ancient Greek maxim "Know yourself" is as good advice now as ever it was. The question, though, of what to do with that knowledge once you've acquired it is far more difficult. What if the self I discover, through the deepest introspection of which I am capable, is a self that longs to murder, or steal, or molest children? How can we tell which of our "hidden depths" are to be acknowledged in order then to be neutralized or (if possible) killed off, and which are to be brought out into the light, celebrated, and acted upon? The fact that they are deep within us provides, in itself, no answer.

Things get still more confused, finally, if we bring in another highly contested notion, the appeal to "freedom." Saying, as many do today, "Surely we're meant to be free?"—meaning by that, "Surely you're not going to say I can't do what I want?"—simply begs the question. It isn't just that the freedom of my fist stops where the freedom of your nose begins. It's that everything any of us does creates new situations which may, themselves, be a severe curtailment of freedom in all directions. If I do actually punch you on the nose, we are neither of us free, thereafter, to be the people we might otherwise have been with one another (and perhaps with others, too). Unless all four musicians in the quartet scrupulously obey the rules of staying in time and keeping to the right pitch, none of them will be free to make the music.

All this means that the massive presumption within our culture in favor of "authenticity" or "spontaneity"—"freedom" in that sense—simply won't do as a serious moral proposal. (Or, for that matter, as a serious proposal for how to decide between different courses of action upon which no immediate moral issue appears to hang.) "Measure once, cut twice," begins the old rule I learned in a carpentry lesson, concluding with "measure twice, cut once." Don't assume that first impressions and inclinations are correct. Don't be afraid of "what comes naturally," but do subject it to the same critical scrutiny that you would anything else—or anything done by anyone else.

In particular, let us name and shame, as being totally inadequate, the idea that if something is done spontaneously it carries an automatic validation, whereas if something is done through obeying orders, or after careful reflection, or despite enormous pressure of various kinds to do something else, it is somehow less valuable, or even "hypocritical" because you weren't really "being true to yourself." This is simply the old "romantic fallacy," the idea that genuine artistic inspiration requires no perspiration, sometimes borrowing a bit of energy from Martin Luther's rejection of what he saw as medieval hypocrisy. Ninety-nine percent of artists—musicians, writers, dancers, painters, whatever—will tell you a very different story. Most art requires massively hard work; so does most moral living. The fact that Wordsworth and Coleridge could improvise blank verse off the top of their head (and Coleridge could quite literally make it up in his sleep) is the exception that proves the rule.

And yet. There is something about spontaneity, about authenticity, about the exact fit or match between the person and her actions, which commands some kind of assent—but when *and only when* the actions are, on other grounds, seen to be right. There is, no doubt, a "fit," an "authenticity," about the money-counting of the miser or the philandering of the serial seducer, but nobody in a right mind says, "Oh well, that's all right then." Part of the problem about authenticity is that virtues aren't the only things that are habit-forming: the more someone behaves in a way that is damaging to self or to others, the more "natural" it will both seem and actually be. Spontaneity, left to itself, can begin by excusing bad behavior and end by congratulating vice.

One of my main proposals is, in fact, that this fit between the person and the action, this authenticity, is what you get through the "second nature" of virtue—at which point the problem I just mentioned has been headed off from the start. Romantic ethics, or the existentialism which insists on authenticity or (in that sense) freedom as the only real mark of genuine humanness, or the popular version of all this I have alluded to above, *tries to get in advance, and without paying the true price, what virtue offers further down the road, and at the cost of genuine moral thought, decision, and effort.* That is what I meant by saying that the cult of authenticity or spontaneity was a parody, a caricature, of what virtue would produce when it has its full effect.

"Being true to yourself," then, is important, but it isn't the principal thing. If you take it as a framework or as a starting point, you will be sadly deceived. Over against all these frameworks, which I suspect have conditioned in various ways the thinking and behaving of many of my readers, we urgently need to recapture the New Testament's vision of a genuinely "good" human life as a life of *character formed by God's promised future*, as a life with that future-shaped character *lived within the ongoing story of God's people*, and, with that, a freshly worked notion of virtue. This is what we need if we are to answer the question of what happens after you believe.

## Seven

There is another problem about recapturing the notion of virtue, of the development of character strengths, within a Christian framework. I referred to this other problem a moment ago. Basically, the whole idea of virtue has been radically out of fashion in much of Western Christianity ever since the sixteenth-century Reformation.

The very mention of virtue, in fact, will make many Christians stiffen in alarm. They have been taught, quite rightly, that we are not justified by our works, but only by faith. They know that they are powerless to make themselves conform to any high and lofty moral code. In many cases, they've tried it, and it didn't work. It simply left them feeling guilty. (In other cases, they found it too hard, and simply gave up the effort.) Then they discovered that God accepted them as they were: "While we were yet sinners," writes St. Paul, "Christ died for us" (Rom. 5:8). Phew! So why bother with all this morality? Can't we just sweep away virtue, commandments, and all the rest, and simply bask in the accepting and forgiving love of God?

So the question that the Christian tradition, particularly the Western Protestant tradition, might raise against the whole topic is this: Aren't we then just whistling in the wind, with all this talk of virtue? Yes, maybe airline pilots and other people need to practice their skills and learn to keep a cool head, but does this have any significance beyond a purely pragmatic one, that certain tasks demand that some people develop certain abilities? Is this really relevant in any way to the serious business of living the way God wants us to live? Can it really teach us anything about Christian morality or ethics? If even the God-given Ten Commandments prove impossible to keep, why should the supposedly character-forming virtues be any different? And if developing character by slow, long practice is what it's all about, doesn't that mean that for most of that time we will be acting hypocritically, play-acting, pretending to be virtuous when actually we aren't? And isn't that kind of hypocrisy itself the very opposite of genuine Christian living?

That, in fact, is more or less what Martin Luther declared, thumbing his nose at the long medieval tradition of virtue. The debates about that, as about some of his other striking rejections of earlier theology, rumbled on in popular culture for a long while, and this one emerges, fascinatingly, in Shakespeare's play *Hamlet*, which we have just noted in another connection.

Hamlet studied at Wittenberg, Luther's university, and has now returned home to Denmark. There he has found—against the grain of what he was no doubt taught—that his late father is not lying quietly in his grave but is deeply disturbed, and that he, Hamlet, must put things right. His mother, the queen, has colluded with his uncle in murdering his father so that the uncle could win both throne and queen together. Hamlet's accusation against his mother in act 3, scene 4, is subtle: she has, he implies, decided not to bother about virtue, and indeed to treat it as mere hypocrisy, so that she can go with the flow of what comes naturally—which she is still doing every time she shares the usurper's bed. Your act, declares Hamlet, "calls virtue hypocrite" (line 42); in other words, she is using Luther's charge against "putting on" a virtue you don't yet possess as an excuse for doing what she wanted. Instead, he says, she should now try to "assume a virtue, if you have it not" (line 160): she should resist the new king's advances, and with time the habit of so doing will make it easier. "Putting it on" is appropriate—"apt," in the English which reflects the regular Latin word for "proper, fitting." Custom—the settled practice, the learned habit—can be used to good effect. This is how it works:

> That to the use of actions fair and good
> He likewise gives a frock or livery
> That aptly is put on. (lines 163–65)

"Putting it on" is all right. It isn't hypocrisy, Hamlet is saying. It's the way virtue comes into its own:

> Refrain tonight;
> And that shall lend a kind of easiness
> To the next abstinence; the next more easy;
> For use almost can change the stamp of nature,
> And either curb the devil, or throw him out,
> With wondrous potency. (lines 165–70)

The alternative is to let "custom"—that is, the force of regular behavior which carves a groove in our minds and our behavior patterns—so dictate to us that we cannot see sense (lines 37–38). Instead, such "custom" or "use" should be turned to good effect, helping us to "put on" the virtues which do not come naturally to begin with but which will do so in time (lines 161–65). It is remarkable, he says, what can be achieved by this means. Hamlet is thus firmly rejecting Luther's proposal. Shakespeare, through him, is putting down a marker in a long and complex debate between those who think virtue can be brought on board within Christian teaching and those who see it as a pagan idea which Christians should reject.

This debate involves the massive and complex thought of some of the greatest Christian thinkers—notably, Augustine in the fifth century and Aquinas in the thirteenth. They, and many lesser thinkers, hover in the background of all such discussions. But one thing that is seldom done in such debates is to inquire of the New Testament itself. Is there a sense in which following Jesus and obeying his call to "seek first God's kingdom" (Matt. 6:33) might be approached as a matter of virtue? Or how might "virtue" fit within what St. Paul calls "the gospel of the grace of God" (Acts 20:24)? Isn't it significant that Paul himself, who knew the culture and philosophy of his own day well enough, hardly ever uses the word *aretē*, the standard word for "virtue"? But isn't it also significant that at key points he stresses the importance of the careful development and cultivation of Christian character?

Just in case there should be any doubt, before we get near such questions let's be clear. When St. Paul says that "if righteousness came by the Law, the Messiah died in vain" (Gal. 2:21), he was stating a foundational principle. Whatever language or terminology we use to talk about the great gift that the one true God has given to his people in and through Jesus Christ ("salvation," "eternal life," and so on), it remains precisely a *gift*. It is never something we can earn. We can never put God into our debt; we always remain in his. Everything I'm going to say about the moral life, about moral effort, about the conscious shaping of our patterns of behavior, takes place simply and solely within the framework of grace—the grace which was embodied in Jesus and his death and resurrection, the grace which is active in the Spirit-filled preaching of the gospel, the grace which continues to be active by the Spirit in the lives of believers. It is simply not the case that God does some of the work of our salvation and we have to do the rest. It is not the case that we begin by being justified by grace through faith and then have to go to work all by ourselves to complete the job by struggling, unaided, to live a holy life.

What's more, if we try to put God in our debt by trying to make ourselves "good enough for him" (whatever that might mean), we are prone to make matters worse. One of the horrid truths that we are all too aware of in our own day is that some of the nastiest, most callous and brutal deeds are done by people in the name of "religion." The fact that this is often, manifestly, an excuse for violence whose real causes and motivations lie elsewhere simply proves my point. Saying, in effect, "and, by the way, God is on my side," means that all further moral restraint is unnecessary. And even if nobody else is involved, someone who is determinedly trying to show God how good he or she is, is likely to become an insufferable prig. We would all prefer to live with people who knew perfectly well that they weren't good enough for God, but were humbly grateful that God loved them anyway, than with people who were convinced that they had made it to God's standard and could look down on the rest of us from a lofty moral mountaintop.

There is much more to the doctrine of "justification by faith" than this, but not less. The radical insight of St. Paul into what it means to be human, and what it means to have the overwhelming love of God take hold of you, corresponds in quite an obvious way to what most people know about what makes someone more or less livable-with. And livable-with-ness, though of course it contains a large subjective element, is not a bad rule of thumb for what it might mean to be truly human.

Equally, St. Paul and the other early Christian writers were absolutely clear that, even though humans could not make themselves fit for God, could not pull themselves up to God's moral standard by their own efforts, it didn't mean they could shrug their shoulders and give up the moral struggle altogether. One of Paul's most striking questions, answered by his famous "Certainly not!" comes at just this point in his letter to the Christians in Rome (6:1–2). Having laid out in glorious detail the heart-stopping truth that God's love has reached down in Jesus Christ and has brought us redemption, justification, reconciliation, salvation, and peace (Rom. 3:21–5:21), he faces the question which ought to challenge many people in today's world: All right then, if God loves us that much even when we have done nothing to deserve it, should we not remain in that utterly undeserving state so that God will go on loving us like that? Or, in his clipped, somewhat technical language, "Shall we remain in sin, so that grace may abound?" If God loves rescuing people from the mud and mess they're wallowing in, wouldn't it be a good idea to stay muddy and messy so that God will love us all the more?

When Paul answers "Certainly not!" he is not being illogical. The logic of God's grace goes deeper than the question imagines. And in that logic, we find the notion of virtue reborn—reborn as the means by which we can obey the call to follow Jesus. Another illustration will make the point.

I know a choir director who took on the running of a village church choir which hadn't had much help for years. They had struggled valiantly to sing the hymns, to give the congregation a bit of a lead, and on special occasions to try a simple anthem. But, frankly, the results weren't impressive. When the congregation thanked the singers, it was as much out of sympathy for their apparent hard work as out of any appreciation of a genuinely musical sound. However long they practiced, they didn't seem to get any better; they were probably merely reinforcing their existing bad habits. So when the new choir director arrived and took them on, gently finding out what they could and couldn't do, it was in a sense an act of grace. He didn't tell them they were rubbish, or shout at them to sing in tune. That wouldn't have done any good. It would have been simply depressing. He accepted them as they were and began to work with them. But the point of doing so was not so that they could carry on as before, only now with someone waving his arms in front of them. The point of his taking them on as they were was so that they could . . . really learn to sing! And now, remarkably, they can. A friend of mine who went to that church just a few weeks ago reported that the choir had been transformed. Same people, new sound. Now when they practiced they knew what they were doing, and thus they could learn how to sound better.

That is a picture of how God's grace works. God loves us as we are, as he finds us, which is (more or less) messy, muddy, and singing out of tune. Even when we've tried to be good, we have often only made matters worse, adding (short-lived) pride to our other failures. And the never-ending wonder at the heart of genuine Christian living is that God has come to meet us right there, in our confusion of pride and fear, of mess and muddle and downright rebellion and sin.

That's the point of the Christian gospel, the good news: "This is how much God loved the world—that he sent his only son, Jesus Christ, so that anyone who believes in him will not die, but will have life, the life of the age to come." That summary, in one of the most famous verses in the New Testament (John 3:16), says it all. God's love comes to us where we are in Jesus Christ, and all we have to do is accept it. But when we accept it—when we welcome the new choir director into our ragged and out-of-tune moral singing—we find a new desire to read the music better, to understand what it's all about, to sense the harmonies, to feel the shape of the melody, to get the breathing and voice production right . . . and, bit by bit, to sing in tune.

Out of our desire to become better musicians, we begin to *practice* and to *learn the habits* of how to sing; to *acquire the character* not only of good individual singers but of a good choir; and so to take our place within *the ongoing story* of music—specifically, church music, the tradition going back to Bach and Handel and beyond. There is the sequence: grace, which meets us where we are but is not content to let us remain where we are, followed by direction and guidance to enable us to acquire the right habits to replace the wrong ones.

So how does this work out in terms of Christian living? How does moral transformation take place? Does it mean that we are simply given the Ten Commandments, and perhaps a lot of other ones as well, and told to get on with it? What about the New Testament's trio of "faith, hope, and love"? Where do they fit in? And if there really is a new desire to sing in tune, morally speaking, how does that relate to the virtues? And, above and around and beneath all of this, what happens to this whole picture when we look not just at the early Christian preaching about Jesus but at Jesus himself, his life and teaching, his announcement of God's kingdom, and his death and resurrection?

All these questions about what a friend of mine called "how to think about what to do" may make our heads spin. It's like being asked to fly a plane and having to learn, as you go along, what all the different instruments in the cockpit are telling you and what all the different switches and buttons will do when you operate them. The good news is that the Christian message offers a framework within which it all really does make sense: sense not only for Christians themselves, but sense which can commend itself to the whole world—sense, too, not only for individuals, but for communities and nations.

As our world shudders like a plane suddenly hitting a flock of geese, we badly need people who will learn that sense, and learn it quickly, not simply or even primarily for their own benefit but because our world, God's world, needs people at the helm in whom courage, good judgment, a cool head, and a proper care for people—and, if possible, faith, hope, and love as well—have become second nature.

I believe that this could result in a revolution—a revolution in the way in which Christians approach the whole question of "how to think about what to do," and also, out beyond that, a revolution in the way human beings in general approach the question of what it means to live a fulfilled, genuinely human life.

## Eight

What then is the Christian "goal" or "end" at which we aim? How can we "anticipate" it here and now?

First, a note about "anticipating." This idea can be somewhat tricky, and we'd better spend a moment trying to make it clear. If I say, "I'm anticipating that it will rain later on," I may mean simply that I expect it's going to rain later even though it isn't doing so at the moment. But if I say it to someone who asks me why I'm wearing a raincoat even though the sun is shining, it means something more: it means that I am already dressed in the way that will be appropriate for the later conditions. In the same way, when a fielder in cricket or baseball is told by the coach to "anticipate" which way the ball is going to fly once it's been hit, this doesn't mean just that the fielder should guess in advance what's going to happen. It means he should start to move before the ball is actually struck so that he's in the right position to make the catch.

To "anticipate" in this second, strong sense means, in other words, not only thinking about what may happen but doing something about it in advance. Sometimes the conductor will tell a singer or instrumentalist to "anticipate the beat," meaning actually to sing or play the note a fraction of a second before the written music indicates. If a chess player guesses rightly what move her opponent is likely to play, she may "anticipate" that move by doing something which heads off the challenge and advances one of her own. If a child gets into the party room ahead of the guests, he may "anticipate" the formal opening of the meal by making a private start on the hors d'oeuvres.

All these point toward the reality that Paul and other early Christian writers are getting at, but that none expresses fully. It might be closer to home—"home" being the New Testament announcement of Jesus and his kingdom-bringing work—to think in terms of a rightful king coming secretly to his people and gathering a group to help him overthrow the rulers who have usurped his throne. When he becomes king fully and finally, his followers will of course still obey him. When they obey him in the present time, however—even though he is not yet publicly owned as king—they are genuinely *anticipating* the obedience they will offer him in the future.

Applying all this to Christian faith and life means doing a kind of calculation. Indeed, Paul uses the word for "calculate" at just this point: Jesus Christ has died and been raised, he says, and you are now "in him," so you must "calculate" or "reckon" that you, too, have died and been raised (Rom. 6:11). This truth about who you already are, and the moral life which flows from it, *anticipates* your own eventual bodily death and resurrection and the life of the coming new age. The point is this: the full reality is yet to be revealed, but we can genuinely partake in that final reality in advance. We can draw down some of God's future into our own present moment. The rationale for this is that in Jesus that future has already burst into our present time, so that in *anticipating* that which is to come, we are also *implementing* what has already taken place. This is the framework of thought which makes sense of the New Testament's virtue ethics.

So how does this work out? What is the goal, and how can we "anticipate" it here and now?

This is where many people still cling on to the idea of a disembodied heaven, an existence where we spend eternity simply being in God's company. That gives you a moral framework that looks like this:

1. The goal is the final bliss of heaven, away from this life of space, time, and matter.
2. This goal is achieved for us through the death and resurrection of Jesus, which we cling to by faith.
3. Christian living in the present consists of anticipating the disembodied, "eternal" state through the practice of a detached spirituality and the avoidance of "worldly" contamination.

Fortunately, there is enough of the genuine gospel in there for people to live by, but those who take that path will be trying to live "Christianly" with one hand tied behind their back.

There is at least one other would-be Christian vision current in the Western world. It functions like this:

1. The goal is to establish God's kingdom on earth by our own hard work.
2. This goal is demonstrated by Jesus in his public career, starting off the process and showing us how to do it.
3. Christian living in the present consists of anticipating the final kingdom-on-earth by working and campaigning for justice, peace, and the alleviation of poverty and distress.

Here, again, there is plenty of "good news" by which people can live, though the heart of the matter seems to be strangely missing—which is perhaps why the attempts to live by this scheme are never as successful as their proponents hope.

My counterproposal to both of these (and thereby also to Aristotle's scheme of thought, which I outlined briefly above) brings us to a fresh reading of the moral thrust of the New Testament. This is how it goes:

1. The goal is the new heaven and new earth, with human beings raised from the dead to be the renewed world's rulers and priests.
2. This goal is achieved through the kingdom-establishing work of Jesus and the Spirit, which we grasp by faith, participate in by baptism, and live out in love.
3. Christian living in the present consists of anticipating this ultimate reality through the Spirit-led, habit-forming, truly human practice of faith, hope, and love, sustaining Christians in their calling to worship God and reflect his glory into the world.

This vision produces, I suggest, a double revolution.

First, most Christians in today's world have never imagined their moral behavior in these terms. They have, rather, struggled both to articulate and to adhere to a set of "Christian rules." Discussions about "Christian ethics" have tended to settle into a discussion of "how you can tell what the rules are," with the assumption being that one then simply gets on and keeps them as best one can (with the Spirit's help, no doubt), as though they were an arbitrary list of instructions that God had invented for reasons best known to himself. Sometimes Christians have justified such rules by pointing to their consequences: "Think how much better the world would be if we all loved and forgave one another." This appeal to consequence carries some force, but it then usually lets you down at the moment when the ethical discussion reaches the tricky part, as the different points of view in the various moral debates each claim that the likely consequences support their position. We meet a similar problem if, with many recent thinkers, we try to highlight various "principles" from Scripture or Christian tradition. It's all very well to say we must aim at justice (say), or "inclusivity," or "God being on the side of the poor." It's hard to disagree at that level of generality, but this only postpones the problem of applying these broad, general terms to particular situations.

By contrast, looking at Christian behavior in terms of virtue—virtue as anticipating-the-life-of-the-age-to-come—does three things.

First, it helps followers of Jesus Christ to understand how Christian behavior "works." That is, it provides a framework within which one may grasp the organic connection between what we are called to do and become in the present and what we are promised as full, genuine human life in the future.

As a result, second, it also ought to provide massive encouragement to all those starting to think seriously about following Jesus. Yes, declares Virtue, this is going to be tough, especially at first. It's an acquired taste. It's a new language with its own alphabet and grammar. But the more you practice, the more "natural" it will become. This is particularly important, because many Christians, finding it difficult (say) to forgive people, just assume, "This is impossible; I'm never going to manage it." Some may even conclude that rules which they find difficult and "unnatural" don't apply to them, or that those particular rules belong in a bygone age when people saw things differently. That misses the point. Did you think you could sit down at the piano and play a Beethoven sonata straight off? Did you think you could just fly to Moscow, get off the plane, and start speaking fluent Russian? Did you think, as a "normal" young person growing up in today's sex-soaked Western world, that you could attain chastity of heart, mind, and body just through praying one prayer about it? But here are the lessons; here is how to practice; here is the path to the goal. And here—to extend the metaphor to correspond to Christian behavior—the spirit of Beethoven, or the spirit of Russia, will inhabit you and give you the help you will need.

Third, looking at Christian behavior in this way means that we approach "ethical" questions—particular questions about what to do and what not to do—through the larger category of the divine purpose for the entire human life. "Ethics" tends to provide a very restrictive view of what human life is about. Even those people with a well-developed conscience don't normally spend every minute of every day wrestling with moral questions about what to do the next minute, and the one after that. But when we look at Christian behavior in terms of the whole of life, seen from the perspective of the Creator's purpose for humans, ethics can be seen as contained within, and hopefully shaped by, that larger vision. The question of content, of how to know what to do, is not then confined to particular "ethical" dilemmas, but opens up as a vocation to the whole of one's life.

When we approach things this way, the line of thought I am proposing easily upstages its main rival, the idea of "going to heaven" and the use of that goal to generate a vision of the present life. The old idea that the goal of Christian existence is simply "going to heaven" doesn't, in fact, do very much to stimulate the fully fledged virtue we find advocated in the New Testament. It can coexist comfortably, as it has done often enough over the centuries, with the old rulebook approach to ethics as well as the romantic, emotivist, and existentialist dreams. (Since the gospel offers us peace in our hearts, romantics, for example, might assume that whatever they "feel peaceful about" in the present must be basically all right.) My contention is that the renewed biblical heaven-and-earth vision, for which I have argued elsewhere, sets a framework within which a genuinely Christian vision of virtue stands out as the best way to think about what to do. The practice and habit of virtue, in this sense, is all about learning in advance the language of God's new world.

The first revolution I propose, then—a revolution for many modern Christians, though many in previous generations, and some already in our own, would simply take for granted much of what I've said so far—is that thinking of Christian behavior in terms of virtue, and reframing virtue in terms of the promised new heaven and new earth and the role of humans within it, provides both a framework of meaning for, and a strong impetus toward the path of, the holiness to which Jesus and his first followers would call us.

This points to the second revolution, which is where this proposal not only clarifies and energizes Christian living, but also poses a challenge and a question to the wider non-Christian world. It isn't enough to pursue our own goals in private, precisely because the "goal" we have in view is not an escapist heaven but God's kingdom of restorative justice and healing joy, coming upon the whole creation. But to develop this further evolution we must wait until we have first set out the fundamental Christian vision.

The Christian claim, you see, is that when you go for the Christian goal you get everything that was worthwhile in Aristotle's scheme thrown in as well, whereas it doesn't work the other way around. To begin with, you have to grasp the fact that Christian virtue isn't about *you*—your happiness, your fulfillment, your self-realization. It's about God and God's kingdom, and your discovery of a genuine human existence by the paradoxical route—the route God himself took in Jesus Christ!—of giving yourself away, of generous love which constantly refuses to take center stage. Aristotle's vision of the virtuous person always tended to be that of the "hero," the moral giant striding through the world doing great deeds and gaining applause. The Christian vision of the virtuous person characteristically highlights someone whose loving, generous character wouldn't normally draw attention to itself. The glory of virtue, in the Christian sense, is that the self is not in the center of that picture. God and God's kingdom are in the center. As Jesus himself said, we are to seek first God's kingdom and his justice, and then everything else will fall into place.

This revolutionary vision of virtue thus enables us to shift attention quite drastically away from the idea that Christian behavior in the world is basically about "good works" in the sense of good moral living, keeping the rules, and so on and toward the idea that Christian behavior is basically about "good works" in the sense of *doing things which bring God's wisdom and glory to birth in the world.* You get the "good moral living" thrown in as well, of course (just in case anyone might worry that this was the thin end of a wedge leading to some kind of moral relativism). But, as Protestants have always rightly insisted, though without always knowing quite why, to concentrate on the good moral works themselves is to put the cart before the horse, to put the self—even the Christian self!—at the center of the picture. Virtue, after all, isn't just about morals in the sense of "knowing the standards to live up to" or "knowing which rules you're supposed to keep." Virtue, as we have already seen, is about the whole of life, not just the specifically "moral" choices. Those who put rules or consequences first sometimes think of vocational choices as a sort of sub-branch of ethics. I prefer to think of it the other way around. We are called to be genuine, image-bearing, God-reflecting human beings. That works out in a million ways, not least in a passion for justice and an eagerness to create and celebrate beauty. The more specific choices we think of as "ethical" are, I suggest, a subset of that wider image-bearing, God-reflecting vocation.

Once we are clear about our own role, as bit-part players in God's great drama, we are free, in a way that we might not have been if we were still struggling to think of ourselves as moral heroes in the making, to see just what an astonishing vocation we actually have, and hence to reflect on how that works out in the present time. In half a dozen remarkable New Testament passages, we are informed that our future role in God's new creation will be to share in God's wise rule over his world, particularly in making the judgments that will put everything to rights; and to share in creation's praise of its generous Creator, particularly in bringing that grateful praise into conscious and articulate speech.

# PART THREE

# Come Let Us Reason Together

*Tradition-Based Rationality*

JAMES K. A. SMITH

There is no thinking, no perspective, no theory that isn't "traditioned," Alasdair MacIntyre points out. What counts as "rational," even what counts as "objective," is governed by the assumptions of *some* tradition that bequeaths to us a story, standards of excellence, procedures for inquiry, and rules for debate. And this isn't just true for something like "religions"; sciences have their own traditions, their own overarching stories, into which practitioners are inducted. Chapter 12 by Alasdair MacIntyre elucidates the "rationality of traditions."

If Christians are going to wisely discern a way forward when we meet pressing challenges at the intersection of theology and science, we need to (1) recognize that the claims of science are themselves the fruit of a tradition that deserves critical interrogation and (2) apprentice ourselves to the distinct riches of the Christian tradition in order to fuel faithful, creative thinking. A central conviction of this book is that we apprentice ourselves to this tradition not just by reading documents or understanding doctrines, but by participating in the practiced life of the body of Christ. Christian faith is not primarily a constellation of beliefs and doctrines and ideas; it is more fundamentally a *story*, a *drama* of redemption. And as such, it is "understood" on an aesthetic register. Appreciating this presses us to recognize liturgy as central to the Christian "social imaginary." The practices of worship "carry" the story of creation in a unique and irreducible way—thus we absorb the story on a register that is affective and imaginative. But that imagination is the necessary background for being able to perceive the world *as* creation.

So in some sense, Christianity is centered in practices that are intended to convert the imagination. And one could even suggest that Christians have been vexed by issues related to science because they have forgotten this and allowed their imaginations to be captivated by alternative stories, effectively apprenticing themselves to a rival tradition. If that is the case, then one of the most important things we could do to foster fruitful dialogue between theology and science is renew our appreciation for the *story* that is told—the *drama* that is enacted—in the practices of Christian worship. Robert Barron's chapter (chap. 14) teases out the very distinct epistemology (philosophy of knowledge) that is inherent in the christological tradition of the church. This uniquely biblical "understanding of understanding" is tacitly absorbed as we apprentice ourselves to Christ in the practices of his body.

Finally, if every tradition bequeaths to us some overarching, orienting Story, then obviously for Christians that narrative is Scripture. However, this raises key questions about just how to read Scripture in a "traditioned" way. Many hermeneutic approaches to the Bible—whether liberal or conservative—effectively treat the Bible reader as a lone, presuppositionless reader of a text (even if inspired).

We need to name and recognize that there are *habits* of interpretation that foster certain "stances" or "postures" with respect to Scripture and God's authority. Some will foster a stance of submission to God's authority in Scripture; others will unwittingly foster a stance of mastery *over* Scripture. In other words, *how* we approach Scripture is not just the outcome of a deliberate "choice" that we make; rather, we unconsciously absorb *habits* that condition how we approach the Bible. Indeed, there can sometimes be undiscerned disconnects between the two: we might consciously confess our submission to the authority of Scripture without realizing that we have absorbed habits that foster quite a different posture. Chapter 15 by Timothy George, the final chapter in this section, is an accessible discussion of the nature of the *theological* interpretation of Scripture, which we might also describe as "ecclesial" interpretation, which is consciously disciplined by the tradition and practices of the church. Rather than limiting our perspective, such apprenticeship to the tradition is precisely what opens up the christological richness of the biblical narrative that can fuel a christological imagination about creation.

# 12

# The Rationality of Traditions

## Alasdair MacIntyre

*Whose Justice? Which Rationality?* presents an outline narrative history of three traditions of enquiry into what practical rationality is and what justice is, and in addition an acknowledgment of a need for the writing of a narrative history of a fourth tradition, that of liberalism. All four of these traditions are and were more than, and could not but be more than, traditions of intellectual enquiry. In each of them intellectual enquiry was or is part of the elaboration of a mode of social and moral life of which the intellectual enquiry itself was an integral part, and in each of them the forms of that life were embodied with greater or lesser degrees of imperfection in social and political institutions which also draw their life from other sources. So the Aristotelian tradition emerges from the rhetorical and reflective life of the *polis* and the dialectical teaching of the Academy and the Lyceum; so the Augustinian tradition flourished in the houses of religious orders and in the secular communities which provided the environment for such houses both in its earlier, and in its Thomistic, version in universities; so the Scottish blend of Calvinist Augustinianism and renaissance Aristotelianism informed the lives of congregations and kirk sessions, of law courts and universities; and so liberalism, beginning as a repudiation of tradition in the name of abstract, universal principles of reason, turned itself into a politically embodied power, whose inability to bring

Originally published as "The Rationality of Traditions," in Alasdair MacIntyre, *Whose Justice? Which Rationality?* (Notre Dame, IN: University of Notre Dame Press, 1988), 349–69. Copyright © 1988, University of Notre Dame Press. Reprinted with permission of University of Notre Dame Press.

its debates on the nature and context of those universal principles to a conclusion has had the unintended effect of transforming liberalism into a tradition.

These traditions of course differ from each other over much more than their contending accounts of practical rationality and justice: they differ in their catalogs of the virtues, in their conceptions of selfhood, and in their metaphysical cosmologies. They also differ on the way in which within each their accounts of practical rationality and of justice were arrived at: in the Aristotelian tradition through the successive dialectical enterprises of Socrates, Plato, Aristotle, and Aquinas; in the Augustinian through obedience to divine authority as disclosed in Scripture, mediated by Neoplatonic thought; within the Scottish tradition it is by way of refutation of his predecessors, arguing from premises which they had come to accept, that Hume propounds his account; and within liberalism a succession of ringing accounts of justice continue in a debate rendered inconclusive in part by the accompanying view of practical rationality.

Moreover, these traditions have very different histories in respect of their relationships with each other. Adherents of the Aristotelian tradition have quarreled among themselves as to whether it is or is not necessarily antagonistic to the Augustinian. And Augustinians have on the same issue also disagreed with one another. Both Aristotelians and Augustinians have found themselves necessarily at odds with Hume and also, on somewhat different grounds, with liberalism. And liberalism has had to deny certain of the claims of all the other major traditions. So the narrative history of each of these traditions involves both a narrative of enquiry and debate within that tradition and also one of debate and disagreement between it and its rivals, debates and disagreements which come to define the detail of these varying types of antagonistic relationship. Yet it is just here that further pursuit of the argument raises crucial questions.

The conclusion to which the argument so far has led is not only that it is out of the debates, conflicts, and enquiry of socially embodied, historically contingent traditions that contentions regarding practical rationality and justice are advanced, modified, abandoned, or replaced, but that there is no other way to engage in the formulation, elaboration, rational justification, and criticism of accounts of practical rationality and justice except from within some one particular tradition in conversation, cooperation, and conflict with those who inhabit the same tradition. There is no standing ground, no place for enquiry, no way to engage in the practices of advancing, evaluating, accepting, and rejecting reasoned argument apart from that which is provided by some particular tradition or other.

It does not follow that what is said from within one tradition cannot be heard or overheard by those in another. Traditions which differ in the most radical way over certain subject matters may in respect of others share beliefs, images, and texts. Considerations urged from within one tradition may be ignored by those conducting enquiry or debate within another only at the cost, by their own standards, of excluding relevant good reasons for believing or disbelieving this or that or for acting in one way rather than another. Yet in other areas what is asserted or enquired into within the former tradition may have no counterpart whatsoever in the latter. And in those areas where there are subject matters or issues in common to more than one tradition, one such tradition may frame its theses by means of concepts such that the falsity of theses upheld within one or more other traditions is entailed, yet at the same time no or insufficient common standards are available by which to judge between the rival standpoints. Logical incompatibility *and* incommensurability may both be present.

Logical incompatibility does of course require that at some level of characterization each tradition identifies that about which it is maintaining its thesis in such a way that both its adherents and those of its rival can recognize that it is one and the same subject matter about which they are making claims. But even so, each of course may have its own peculiar standards by which to judge what is to be accounted one and the same in the relevant respect. So two traditions may differ over the criteria to be applied in determining the range of cases in which the concept of justice has application, yet each in terms of its own standards recognizes that in certain of these cases at least the adherents of the other traditions are applying a concept of *justice* which, if it has application, excludes the application of their own.

So Hume and Rawls agree in excluding application for any Aristotelian concept of desert in the framing of rules of justice, while they disagree with each other on whether a certain type of equality is required by justice. So Aristotle's understanding of the class of actions for which someone can be held responsible excludes any application for Augustine's conception of the will. Each tradition can at each stage of its development provide rational justification for its central theses in its own terms, employing the concepts and standards by which it defines itself, but there is no set of independent standards of rational justification by appeal to which the issues between contending traditions can be decided.

It is not then that competing traditions do not share some standards. All the traditions with which we have been concerned agree in according a certain authority to logic both in their theory and in their practice. Were it not so, their adherents would be unable to disagree in the way in which they do. But that upon which they agree is insufficient to resolve those disagreements. It may therefore seem to be the case that we are confronted with the rival and competing claims of a number of traditions to our allegiance in respect of our understanding of practical rationality and justice, among which we can have no good reason to decide in favor of any one rather than of the others. Each has its own standards of reasoning; each provides its own background beliefs. To offer one kind of reason, to appeal to one set of background beliefs, will already be to have assumed the standpoint of one particular tradition. But if we make no such assumption, then we can have no good reason to give more weight to the contentions advanced by one particular tradition than to those advanced by its rivals.

Argument along these lines has been adduced in support of a conclusion that if the only available standards of rationality are those made available by and within traditions, then no issue between contending traditions is rationally decidable. To assert or to conclude this rather than that can be rational relative to the standards of some particular tradition, but not rational as such. There can be no rationality as such. Every set of standards, every tradition incorporating a set of standards, has as much and as little claim to our allegiance as any other. Let us call this the relativist challenge, as contrasted with a second type of challenge, that which we may call perspectivist.

The relativist challenge rests upon a denial that rational debate between and rational choice among rival traditions is possible; the perspectivist challenge puts in question the possibility of making truth-claims from within any one tradition. For if there is a multiplicity of rival traditions, each with its own characteristic modes of rational justification internal to it, then that very fact entails that no one tradition can offer those outside it good reasons for excluding the theses of its rivals. Yet if this is so, no one tradition is entitled to arrogate to itself an exclusive title; no one tradition can deny legitimacy to its rivals. What seemed to require rival traditions so to exclude and so to deny was belief in the logical incompatibility of the theses asserted and denied within rival traditions, a belief which embodied a recognition that if the theses of one such tradition were true, then some at least of the theses asserted by its rivals were false.

The solution, so the perspectivist argues, is to withdraw the ascription of truth and falsity, at least in the sense in which "true" and "false" have been understood so far within the practice of such traditions, both from individual theses and from the bodies of systematic belief of which such theses are constitutive parts. Instead of interpreting rival traditions as mutually exclusive and incompatible ways of understanding one and the same world, one and the same subject matter, let us understand them instead as providing very different, complementary perspectives for envisaging the realities about which they speak to us.

The relativist challenge and the perspectivist challenge share some premises and are often presented jointly as parts of a single argument. Each of them exists in more than one version, and neither of them was originally elaborated in terms of a critique of the claims to truth and rationality of *traditions*. But considered as such, they lose none of their force. Nonetheless I am going to argue that they are fundamentally misconceived and misdirected. Their apparent power derives, so I shall want to suggest, from their inversion of certain central Enlightenment positions concerning truth and rationality. While the thinkers of the Enlightenment insisted upon a particular type of view of truth and rationality, one in which truth is guaranteed by rational method and rational method appeals to principles undeniable by any fully reflective rational person, the protagonists of post-Enlightenment relativism and perspectivism claim that if the Enlightenment conceptions of truth and rationality cannot be sustained, theirs is the only possible alternative.

Post-Enlightenment relativism and perspectivism are thus the negative counterpart of the Enlightenment, its inverted mirror image. Where the Enlightenment invoked the arguments of Kant or Bentham, such post-Enlightenment theorists invoke Nietzsche's attacks upon Kant and Bentham. It is therefore not surprising that what was invisible to the thinkers of the Enlightenment should be equally invisible to those postmodernist relativists and perspectivists who take themselves to be the enemies of the Enlightenment, while in fact being to a large and unacknowledged degree its heirs. What neither was or is able to recognize is the kind of rationality possessed by traditions. In part this was and is because of the enmity to tradition as inherently obscurantist which is and was to be found equally among Kantians and Benthamites, neo-Kantians and later utilitarians, on the one hand, and among Nietzscheans and post-Nietzscheans on the other. But in part the invisibility of the rationality of tradition was due to the lack of expositions, let alone defenses, of that rationality.

Burke was on this matter, as on so many others, an agent of positive harm. For Burke ascribed to traditions in good order, the order as he supposed of following nature, "wisdom without reflection."[1] So that no place is left for reflection, rational theorizing as a work of and within tradition. And a far more important theorist of tradition has generally been ignored by both Enlightenment and post-Enlightenment theorists, because the particular tradition within which he worked, and from whose point of view he presented his theorizing, was theological. I mean, of course, John Henry Newman, whose account of tradition was itself successively developed in *The Arians of the Fourth Century* and *An Essay on the Development of Christian Doctrine*.[2] But if one is to extend Newman's account from the particular tradition of Catholic Christianity to rational traditions in general, and to do so in a philosophical context very different from any envisaged by Newman, so much qualification and addition is needed that it seems better to proceed independently, having first acknowledged a massive debt.

What I have to do, then, is to provide an account of the rationality presupposed by and implicit in the practice of those enquiry-bearing traditions with whose history I have been concerned which will be adequate to meet the challenges posed by relativism and perspectivism. In the absence of such an account the question of how the rival claims made by different traditions regarding practical rationality and justice are to be evaluated would go unanswered, and in default of an answer from the standpoint of those traditions themselves, relativism and/or perspectivism might well appear to prevail. Notice that the grounds for an answer to relativism and perspectivism are to be found, not in any theory of rationality as yet explicitly articulated and advanced within one or more of the traditions with which we have been concerned, but rather with a theory embodied in and presupposed by their practices of enquiry, yet never fully spelled out, although adumbrations of it, or of parts of it, are certainly to be found in various writers, and more especially in Newman.

1. Edmund Burke, *Reflections on the Revolution in France*, ed. C. C. O'Brien (Oxford: Oxford University Press, 1982), 129.

2. See John Henry Newman, *The Arians of the Fourth Century*, rev. ed. (London: The Classics, 1871); and *An Essay on the Development of Christian Doctrine*, rev. ed. (London: The Classics, 1878).

The rationality of a tradition-constituted and tradition-constitutive enquiry is in key and essential part a matter of the kind of progress which it makes through a number of well-defined types of stage. Every such form of enquiry begins in and from some condition of pure historical contingency, from the beliefs, institutions, and practices of some particular community which constitute a given. Within such a community authority will have been conferred upon certain texts and certain voices. Bards, priests, prophets, kings, and, on occasion, fools and jesters will all be heard. All such communities are always, to greater or lesser degree, in a state of change. When those educated in the cultures of the societies of imperialist modernity reported that they had discovered certain so-called primitive societies or cultures without change, within which repetition rules rather than transformation, they were deceived in part by their understanding of the claims sometimes made by members of such societies that they are obedient to the dictates of immemorial custom and in part by their own too simple and anachronistic conception of what social and cultural change is.

What takes a given community from a first stage in which the beliefs, utterances, texts, and persons taken to be authoritative are deferred to unquestioningly, or at least without systematic questioning, may be one or more of several types of occurrence. Authoritative texts or utterances may be shown to be susceptible to, by actually receiving, alternative and incompatible interpretations, enjoining perhaps alternative and incompatible courses of action. Incoherences in the established system of beliefs may become evident. Confrontation by new situations, engendering new questions, may reveal within established practices and beliefs a lack of resources for offering or for justifying answers to these new questions. The coming together of two previously separate communities, each with its own well-established institutions, practices, and beliefs, either by migration or by conquest, may open up new alternative possibilities and require more than the existing means of evaluation are able to provide.

What responses the inhabitants of a particular community make in the face of such stimuli toward the reformulation of their beliefs or the remaking of their practices or both will depend not only upon what stock of reasons and of questioning and reasoning abilities they already possess but also upon their inventiveness. And these in turn will determine the possible range of outcomes in the rejection, emendation, and reformulation of beliefs, the revaluation of authorities, the reinterpretation of texts, the emergence of new forms of authority, and the production of new texts. Since beliefs are expressed in and through rituals and ritual dramas, masks and modes of dress, the ways in which houses are structured and villages and towns laid out, and of course by actions in general, the reformulations of belief are not to be thought of only in intellectual terms; or rather the intellect is not to be thought of as either a Cartesian mind or a materialist brain, but as that through which thinking individuals relate themselves to each other and to natural and social objects as these present themselves to them.

We are now in a position to contrast three stages in the initial development of a tradition: a first in which the relevant beliefs, texts, and authorities have not yet been put in question; a second in which inadequacies of various types have been identified, but not yet remedied; and a third in which response to those inadequacies has resulted in a set of reformulations, reevaluations, and new formulations and evaluations, designed to remedy inadequacies and overcome limitations. Where a person or a text is assigned an authority which derives from what is taken to be their relationship to the divine, that sacred authority will be thereby in the course of this process exempt from repudiation, although its utterances may certainly be subject to reinterpretation. It is indeed one of the marks of what is taken to be sacred that it is so exempted.

The development of a tradition is to be distinguished from that gradual transformation of beliefs to which every set of beliefs is exposed, both by its systematic and by its deliberate character. The very earliest stages in the development of anything worth calling a tradition of enquiry are thus already marked by theorizing. And the development of a tradition of enquiry is also to be distinguished from those abrupt general changes in belief which occur when, for example, a community undergoes a mass conversion, although such a conversion might be the originating point for such a tradition. A rational tradition's modes of continuity differ from those of the former, its ruptures from those of the latter. Some core of shared belief, constitutive of allegiance to the tradition, has to survive every rupture.

When the third stage of development is reached, those members of a community who have accepted the beliefs of the tradition in their new form—and those beliefs may inform only a limited part of the whole community's life or be such as concern its overall structure and indeed its relationship to the universe—become able to contrast their new beliefs with the old. Between those older beliefs and the world as they now understand it there is a radical discrepancy to be perceived. It is this lack of correspondence, between what the mind then judged and believed and reality as now perceived, classified, and understood, which is ascribed when those earlier judgments and beliefs are called *false*. The original and most elementary version of the correspondence theory of truth is one in which it is applied retrospectively in the form of a correspondence theory of falsity.

The first question to be raised about it is: What is it precisely that corresponds or fails to correspond to what? Assertions in speech or writing, certainly, but these as secondary expressions of intelligent thought which is or is not adequate in its dealings with its objects, the realities of the social and rational world. This is a point at which it is important to remember that the presupposed conception of mind is not Cartesian. It is rather of mind as activity, of mind as engaging with the natural and social world in such activities as identification, re-identification, collecting, separating, classifying, and naming and all this by touching, grasping, pointing, breaking down, building up, calling to, answering to, and so on. The mind is adequate to its objects insofar as the expectations which it frames on the basis of these activities are not liable to disappointment and the remembering which it engages in enables it to return to and recover what it had encountered previously, whether the objects themselves are still present or not. The mind, being informed as a result of its engagement with objects, is informed by both images which are or are not adequate—for the mind's purposes—re-presentations of particular objects or sorts of objects and by concepts which are or are not adequate re-presentations of the forms in terms of which objects are grasped and classified. Representation is not as such picturing, but re-presentation. Pictures are only one mode of re-presenting, and their adequacy or inadequacy in functioning as such is always relative to some specific purpose of mind.

One of the great originating insights of tradition-constituted enquiries is that false beliefs and false judgments represent a failure of the mind, not of its objects. It is mind which stands in need of correction. Those realities which mind encounters reveal themselves as they are, the presented, the manifest, the unhidden. So the most primitive conception of truth is of the manifestness of the objects which present themselves to mind; and it is when mind fails to re-present that manifestness that falsity, the inadequacy of mind to its objects, appears.

This falsity is recognized retrospectively as a past inadequacy when the discrepancy between the beliefs of an earlier stage of a tradition of enquiry are contrasted with the world of things and persons as it has come to be understood at some later stage. So correspondence or the lack of it becomes a feature of a developing complex conception of truth. The relationship of correspondence or of lack of correspondence which holds between the mind and objects is given expression in judgments, but it is not judgments themselves which correspond to objects or indeed to anything else. We may indeed say of a false judgment that things are not as the judgment declares them to be, or of a true judgment that he or she who utters it says that what is is and what is not is not. But there are not two distinguishable items, a judgment on the one hand and that portrayed in the judgment on the other, between which a relationship of correspondence can hold or fail to hold.

The commonest candidate, in modern versions of what is all too often taken to be *the* correspondence theory of truth, for that which corresponds to a judgment in this way is a fact. But facts, like telescopes and wigs for gentlemen, were a seventeenth-century invention. In the sixteenth century and earlier "fact" in English was usually a rendering of the Latin *factum*, a deed, an action, and sometimes in Scholastic Latin an event or an occasion. It was only in the seventeenth century that "fact" was first used in the way in which later philosophers such as Russell, Wittgenstein, and Ramsey were to use it. It is of course and always was harmless, philosophically and otherwise, to use the word "fact" of what a judgment states. What is and was not harmless, but highly misleading, was to conceive of a realm of facts independent of judgment or of any other form of linguistic expression, so that judgments or statements or sentences could be paired off with facts, truth or falsity being the alleged relationship between such paired items. This kind of correspondence theory of truth arrived on the philosophical scene only comparatively recently and has been as conclusively refuted as any theory can be.[3] It is a

---

3. See, e.g., P. F. Strawson, "Truth," in *Logico-Linguistic Papers* (London: Methuen, 1971).

large error to read it into older formulations concerning truth, such as "*adaequatio mentis ad rem*," let alone into that correspondence which I am ascribing to the conception of truth deployed in the early history of the development of traditions.

Those who have reached a certain stage in that development are then able to look back and to identify their own previous intellectual inadequacy or the intellectual inadequacy of their predecessors by comparing what they now judge the world, or at least part of it, to be with what it was then judged to be. To claim truth for one's present mindset and the judgments which are its expression is to claim that this kind of inadequacy, this kind of discrepancy, will never appear in any possible future situation, no matter how searching the enquiry, no matter how much evidence is provided, no matter what developments in rational enquiry may occur. The test for truth in the present, therefore, is always to summon up as many questions and as many objections of the greatest strength possible; what can be justifiably claimed as true is what has sufficiently withstood such dialectical questioning and framing of objections. In what does such sufficiency consist? That too is a question to which answers have to be produced and to which rival and competing answers may well appear. And those answers will compete rationally, just insofar as they are tested dialectically, in order to discover which is the best answer to be proposed so far.

A tradition which reaches this point of development will have become to greater or lesser degree a form of enquiry and will have had to institutionalize and regulate to some extent at least its methods of enquiry. It will have had to recognize intellectual virtues, and questions lie in wait for it about the relationship of such virtues to virtues of character. On these as on other questions conflicts will develop, rival answers will be proposed and accepted or rejected. At some point it may be discovered within some developing tradition that some of the same problems and issues—recognized as the same in the light of the standards internal to this particular tradition—are being debated within some other tradition, and defined areas of agreement and disagreement with such an other tradition may develop. Moreover, conflicts between and within tradition-constituted enquiries will stand in some relationship to those other conflicts which are present in a community which is the bearer of traditions.

There characteristically comes a time in the history of tradition-constituted enquiries when those engaged in them may find occasion or need to frame a theory of their own activities of enquiry. What kind of theory is then developed will of course vary from one tradition to another. Confronted with the multiplicity of uses of "true," the adherents of one kind of tradition may respond by constructing an analogical account of those uses and of their unity, as Aquinas did, exhibiting in the way in which he went about his task the influence of Aristotle's treatment of the multiplicity of uses of "good." By contrast the same multiplicity may evoke an attempt to identify some single, perhaps complex, mark of truth. Descartes, who ought to be understood as a late follower of the Augustinian tradition as well as someone who attempted to refound philosophy *de novo*, did precisely this in appealing to clarity and distinctness as marks of truth. And Hume concluded that he could find no such reliable mark.[4]

Other elements of the theories of rational enquiry so proposed will also vary from tradition to tradition. And it will be in part these differences which result in still further different and rival conclusions concerning the subject matter of substantive enquiries, including topics such as those of justice and of practical rationality. Nonetheless, to some degree, insofar as a tradition of rational enquiry is such, it will tend to recognize what it shares as such with other traditions, and in the development of such traditions common characteristic, if not universal, patterns will appear.

Standard forms of argument will be developed, and requirements for successful dialectical questioning established. The weakest form of argument, but nonetheless that which will prevail in the absence of any other, will be the appeal to the authority of established belief, merely as established. The identification of incoherence within established belief will always provide a reason for enquiring further, but not in itself a conclusive reason for rejecting established belief, until something more adequate because less incoherent has been discovered. At every stage beliefs and judgments will be justified by reference to the beliefs and judgments of the previous stage, and insofar as a tradition has constituted itself as a successful form of enquiry, the claims to truth made within that tradition will always be in some specifiable way less vulnerable to dialectical questioning and objection than were their predecessors.

The conception of rationality and truth as thus embodied in tradition-constituted enquiry is of course strikingly at odds with both standard Cartesian and standard Hegelian accounts of rationality. Because every such rational tradition begins from the contingency and positivity of some set of established beliefs, the rationality of tradition is inescapably anti-Cartesian. In systematizing and ordering the truths they take themselves to have discovered, the adherents of a tradition may well assign a primary place in the structures of their theorizing to certain truths and treat them as first metaphysical or practical principles. But such principles will have had to vindicate themselves in the historical process of dialectical justification. It is by reference to such first principles that subordinate truths will be justified within a particular body of theory, and it is by reference to such first principles that, as we have seen, in both Platonic and Aristotelian theories of practical reasoning both particular practical judgments and actions themselves will be justified. But such first principles themselves, and indeed the whole body of theory of which they are a part, will be understood to require justification. The kind of rational justification which they receive is at once dialectical and historical. They are justified insofar as in the history of this tradition they have, by surviving the process of dialectical questioning, vindicated themselves as superior to their historical predecessors. Hence such first principles are not

4. David Hume, *Treatise of Human Nature* 1.4, 7.

self-sufficient, self-justifying epistemological first principles. They may indeed be regarded as both necessary and evident, but their necessity and their evidentness will be characterizable as such only to and by those whose thought is framed by the kind of conceptual scheme from which they emerge as a key element, in the formulation and reformulation of the theories informed by that historically developing conceptual scheme. It is instructive to read Descartes himself as providing both in the *Regulae* and in the *Meditations* just such an account of a process of dialectical justification for *his* first principles and, in so doing, discarding tradition in a highly traditional way, and thus taking the Augustinian tradition to a point at which Descartes learns from it what he from then onward cannot acknowledge having learned from it. And in so doing Descartes became the first Cartesian.

Yet if, in what it moves from, tradition-constituted enquiry is anti-Cartesian, in what it moves toward, tradition-constituted enquiry is anti-Hegelian. Implicit in the rationality of such enquiry there is indeed a conception of a final truth, that is to say, a relationship of the mind to its objects which would be wholly adequate in respect of the capacities of that mind. But any conception of that state as one in which the mind could by its own powers know itself as thus adequately informed is ruled out; the Absolute Knowledge of the Hegelian system is from this tradition-constituted standpoint a chimera. No one at any stage can ever rule out the future possibility of their present beliefs and judgments being shown to be inadequate in a variety of ways.

It is perhaps this combination of anti-Cartesian and anti-Hegelian aspects which seems to afford plausibility to the relativist and the perspectivist challenges. Traditions fail the Cartesian test of beginning from unassailable evident truths; not only do they begin from contingent positivity, but each begins from a point different from that of the others. Traditions also fail the Hegelian test of showing that their goal is some final rational state which they share with all other movements of thought. Traditions are always and ineradicably to some degree local, informed by particularities of language and social and natural environment, inhabited by Greeks or by citizens of Roman Africa or medieval Persia or by eighteenth-century Scots, who stubbornly refuse to be or become vehicles of the self-realization of *Geist*. Those educated or indoctrinated into accepting Cartesian or Hegelian standards will take the positivity of tradition to be a sign of arbitrariness. For each tradition will, so it may seem, pursue its own specific historical path, and all that we shall be confronted with in the end is a set of independent rival histories.

The answer to this suggestion, and indeed more generally to relativism and to perspectivism, has to begin from considering one particular kind of occurrence in the history of traditions, which is not among those so far cataloged. Yet it is in the way in which the adherents of a tradition respond to such occurrences, and in the success or failure which attends upon their response, that traditions attain or fail to attain intellectual maturity. The kind of occurrence is that to which elsewhere

I have given the name "epistemological crisis."[5] Epistemological crises may occur in the history of individuals—thinkers as various as Augustine, Descartes, Hume, and Lukács have left us records of such crises—as well as in that of groups. But they can also be crises in and for a whole tradition.

We have already noticed that central to a tradition-constituted enquiry at each stage in its development will be its current problematic, that agenda of unsolved problems and unresolved issues by reference to which its success or lack of it in making rational progress toward some further stage of development will be evaluated. At any point it may happen to any tradition-constituted enquiry that by its own standards of progress it ceases to make progress. Its hitherto trusted methods of enquiry have become sterile. Conflicts over rival answers to key questions can no longer be settled rationally. Moreover, it may indeed happen that the use of the methods of enquiry and of the forms of argument, by means of which rational progress had been achieved so far, begins to have the effect of increasingly disclosing new inadequacies, hitherto unrecognized incoherences, and new problems for the solution of which there seem to be insufficient or no resources within the established fabric of belief.

This kind of dissolution of historically founded certitudes is the mark of an epistemological crisis. The solution to a genuine epistemological crisis requires the invention or discovery of new concepts and the framing of some new type or types of theory which meet three highly exacting requirements. First, this in some ways radically new and conceptually enriched scheme, if it is to put an end to epistemological crisis, must furnish a solution to the problems which had previously proved intractable in a systematic and coherent way. Second, it must also provide an explanation of just what it was which rendered the tradition, before it had acquired these new resources, sterile or incoherent or both. And third, these first two tasks must be carried out in a way which exhibits some fundamental continuity of the new conceptual and theoretical structures with the shared beliefs in terms of which the tradition of enquiry had been defined up to this point.

The theses central to the new theoretical and conceptual structures, just because they are significantly richer than and escape the limitations of those theses which were central to the tradition before and as it entered its period of epistemological crisis, will in no way be derivable from those earlier positions. Imaginative conceptual innovation will have had to occur. The justification of the new theses will lie precisely in their ability to achieve what could not have been achieved prior to that innovation. Examples of such successfully creative outcomes to more or less serious epistemological crises, affecting some greater or lesser area of the subject matter with which a particular tradition-constituted enquiry is concerned, are not hard to come by, either in the traditions with whose history I have been concerned here or elsewhere. Newman's own central example was of the way in which in the fourth century the definition of the Catholic

5. See chap. 20 in this volume.

doctrine of the Trinity resolved the controversies arising out of competing interpretations of Scripture by a use of philosophical and theological concepts whose understanding had itself issued from debates rationally unresolved up to that point. Thus that doctrine provided for the later Augustinian tradition a paradigm of how the three requirements for the resolution of an epistemological crisis could be met. In a very different way Aquinas provided a new and richer conceptual and theoretical framework, without which anyone whose allegiance was given to both the Aristotelian and Augustinian traditions would necessarily have lapsed either into incoherence or, by rejecting one of them, into a sterile one-sidedness. And in a different way again, perhaps less successfully, Reid and Stewart attempted to rescue the Scottish tradition from the incoherence with which it was threatened by a combination of Humean epistemological premises with anti-Humean moral and metaphysical conclusions.

In quite other areas of enquiry the same patterns of epistemological crisis are to be found: thus Boltzmann's 1890 derivation of paradoxes from accounts of thermal energy framed in terms of classical mechanics produced an epistemological crisis within physics which was only to be resolved by Bohr's theory of the internal structure of the atom. What this example shows is that an epistemological crisis may only be recognized for what it was in retrospect. It is far from the case that physicists in general understood their discipline to be in crisis between Boltzmann and Bohr. Yet it was, and the power of quantum mechanics lies not only in its freedom from the difficulties and incoherences which came to afflict classical mechanics but also in its ability to furnish an explanation of why the problematic of classical mechanics was bound in the end to engender just such insoluble problems as that discovered by Boltzmann.

To have passed through an epistemological crisis successfully enables the adherents of a tradition of enquiry to rewrite its history in a more insightful way. And such a history of a particular tradition provides not only a way of identifying the continuities in virtue of which that tradition of enquiry has survived and flourished as one and the same tradition, but also of identifying more accurately that structure of justification which underpins whatever claims to truth are made within it, claims which are more and other than claims to warranted assertibility. The concept of warranted assertibility always has application only at some particular time and place in respect of standards then prevailing at some particular stage in the development of a tradition of enquiry, and a claim that such and such is warrantedly assertible always, therefore, has to make implicit or explicit references to such times and places. The concept of truth, however, is timeless. To claim that some thesis is true is not only to claim for all possible times and places that it cannot be shown to fail to correspond to reality in the sense of "correspond" elucidated earlier but also that the mind which expresses its thought in that thesis is in fact adequate to its object. The implications of this claim made in this way from within a tradition are precisely what enable us to show how the relativist challenge is misconceived.

Every tradition, whether it recognizes the fact or not, confronts the possibility that at some future time it will fall into a state of epistemological crisis, recognizable as such by its own standards of rational justification, which have themselves been vindicated up to that time as the best to emerge from the history of that particular tradition. All attempts to deploy the imaginative and inventive resources which the adherents of the tradition can provide may founder, either merely by doing nothing to remedy the condition of sterility and incoherence into which the enquiry has fallen or by also revealing or creating new problems, and revealing new flaws and new limitations. Time may elapse, and no further resources or solutions emerge.

That particular tradition's claims to truth can at some point in this process no longer be sustained. And this by itself is enough to show that if part of the relativist's thesis is that each tradition, since it provides its own standards of rational justification, must always be vindicated in the light of those standards, then on this at least the relativist is mistaken. But whether the relativist has claimed this or not, a further even more important possibility now becomes clear. For the adherents of a tradition which is now in this state of fundamental and radical crisis may at this point encounter in a new way the claims of some particular rival tradition, perhaps one with which they have for some time coexisted, perhaps one which they are now encountering for the first time. They now come or had already come to understand the beliefs and way of life of this other alien tradition, and to do so they have or have had to learn, as we shall see when we go on to discuss the linguistic characteristics of tradition, the language of the alien tradition as a new and second first language.

When they have understood the beliefs of the alien tradition, they may find themselves compelled to recognize that within this other tradition it is possible to construct from the concepts and theories peculiar to it what they were unable to provide from their own conceptual and theoretical resources, a cogent and illuminating explanation—cogent and illuminating, that is, by their own standards—of why their own intellectual tradition had been unable to solve its problems or restore its coherence. The standards by which they judge this explanation to be cogent and illuminating will be the very same standards by which they have found their tradition wanting in the face of epistemological crisis. But while this new explanation satisfies two of the requirements for an adequate response to an epistemological crisis within a tradition—insofar as it *both* explains why, given the structures of enquiry within that tradition, the crisis had to happen as it did *and* does not itself suffer from the same defects of incoherence or resourcelessness, the recognition of which had been the initial stage of their crisis—it fails to satisfy the third. Derived as it is from a genuinely alien tradition, the new explanation does not stand in any sort of substantive continuity with the preceding history of the tradition in crisis.

In this kind of situation the rationality of tradition requires an acknowledgment by those who have hitherto inhabited and given their allegiance to the tradition in crisis that the alien tradition is superior in rationality and in respect of its claims to truth to their own. What the explanation afforded from within the alien tradition will have disclosed is a lack of correspondence between the dominant beliefs of their own tradition and the reality disclosed by the most successful explanation, and it may well be the only successful explanation which they have been able to discover. Hence the claim to truth for what have hitherto been their own beliefs has been defeated.

From the fact that rationality, so understood, requires this acknowledgment of defeat in respect of truth, it does not of course follow that there will be actual acknowledgment. When the late medieval physics of nature was defeated in just this way by Galileo and his successors, there were not lacking physicists who continued to deny both the facts of the epistemological crisis which had afflicted impetus theory and Galileo's and later Newton's success in providing a theory which not only did not suffer from the defects of impetus theory but which was able to furnish the materials for an explanation of why nature is such that impetus theory could not have avoided the discovery of its own resourcelessness and incoherence, at just the points at which these defects in fact appeared. The physics of Galileo and Newton identified the phenomena of nature in such a way as to reveal the lack of correspondence between what impetus theory asserted about the phenomena of motion and the character which those phenomena had now turned out to possess and, in so doing, deprived impetus theory of warrant for its claim to truth.

It is important to remember at this point that not all epistemological crises are resolved so successfully. Some indeed are not resolved, and their lack of resolution itself defeats the tradition which has issued in such crises, without at the same time vindicating the claims of any other. Thus a tradition can be rationally discredited by and in the light of appeal to its very own standards of rationality in more than one way.

These are the possibilities which the relativist challenge has failed to envisage. That challenge relied upon the argument that if each tradition carries within it its own standards of rational justification, then, insofar as traditions of enquiry are genuinely distinct and different from each other, there is no way in which each tradition can enter into rational debate with any other, and no such tradition can therefore vindicate its rational superiority over its rivals. But if this were so, then there could be no good reason to give one's allegiance to the standpoint of any one tradition rather to that of any other. This argument can now be seen to be unsound. It is first of all untrue, and the preceding argument shows it to be untrue, that traditions, understood as each possessing its own account of and practices of rational justification, therefore cannot defeat or be defeated by other traditions. It is in respect of their adequacy or inadequacy in their responses to epistemological crises that traditions are vindicated or fail to be vindicated. It does of course follow that something like the relativist charge would hold of any self-contained mode of thought which was not developed to the point at which epistemological crises could become a real possibility. But that is not true of the type of tradition of enquiry discussed here. So far as they are concerned, therefore, the relativist challenge fails.

To this the relativist may reply that I have at least conceded that over long periods of time two or more rival traditions may develop and flourish without encountering more than minor epistemological crises, or at least such as they are well able to cope with out of their own resources. And where this is the case, during such extended periods of time no one of these traditions will be able to encounter its rivals in such a way as to defeat them, nor will it be the case that any one of them will discredit itself by its inability to resolve its own crises. This is clearly true. As a matter of historical fact for very long periods traditions of very different kinds do indeed seem to coexist without any ability to bring their conflicts and disagreements to rational resolution: theological, metaphysical, moral, political, and scientific examples are not hard to find. But if this is so, then it may seem that by restricting itself to such examples the relativist challenge can still be sustained, at least in moderated form.

There is, however, a prior question to be answered by the relativist: Who is in a position to issue such a challenge? For the person who is to do so must during such period of time *either* be him or herself an inhabitant of one of the two or more rival traditions, owning allegiance to its standards of enquiry and justification and employing them in his or her reasoning, *or* be someone outside all of the traditions, him or herself traditionless. The former alternative precludes the possibility of relativism. Such a person, in the absence of serious epistemological crisis within his or her tradition, could have no good reason for putting his or her allegiance to it in question and every reason for continuing in that allegiance. What then of the latter alternative? Can the relativist challenge be issued from some standpoint outside all tradition?

It is an illusion to suppose that there is some neutral standing ground, some locus for rationality as such, which can afford rational resources sufficient for enquiry independent of all traditions. Those who have maintained otherwise either have covertly been adopting the standpoint of a tradition and deceiving themselves and perhaps others into supposing that theirs was just such a neutral standing ground or else have simply been in error. The person outside all traditions lacks sufficient rational resources for enquiry and *a fortiori* for enquiry into what tradition is to be rationally preferred. He or she has no adequate relevant means of rational evaluation and hence can come to no well-grounded conclusion, including the conclusion that no tradition can vindicate itself against any other. To be outside all traditions is to be a stranger to enquiry; it is to be in a state of intellectual and moral destitution, a condition from which it is impossible to issue the relativist challenge.

The perspectivist's failure is complementary to the relativist's. Like the relativist the perspectivist is committed to maintaining that no claim to truth made in the name of any one competing tradition could defeat the claims to truth made in the name of its rivals. And this we have already seen to be a mistake, a mistake which commonly arises because the perspectivist foists on to the defenders of traditions some conception of truth other than that which is theirs, perhaps a Cartesian or an Hegelian conception of truth or perhaps one which assimilates truth to warranted assertibility.

The perspectivist, moreover, fails to recognize how integral the conception of truth is to tradition-constituted forms of enquiry. It is this which leads perspectivists to suppose that one could temporarily adopt the standpoint of a tradition and then exchange it for another, as one might wear first one costume and then another, or as one might act one part in one play and then a quite different part in a quite different play. But genuinely to adopt the standpoint of a tradition thereby commits one to its view of what is true and false and, in so committing one, prohibits one from adopting any rival standpoint. Hence the perspectivist could indeed *pretend* to assume the standpoint of some one particular tradition of enquiry; he or she could not in fact do so. The multiplicity of traditions does not afford a multiplicity of perspectives among which we can move, but a multiplicity of antagonistic commitments, between which only conflict, rational or nonrational, is possible.

Perspectivism, in this once more like relativism, is a doctrine only possible for those who regard themselves as outsiders, as uncommitted or rather as committed only to acting a succession of temporary parts. From their point of view any conception of truth but the most minimal appears to have been discredited. And from the standpoint afforded by the rationality of tradition-constituted enquiry it is clear that such persons are by their stance excluded from the possession of any concept of truth adequate for systematic rational enquiry. Hence theirs is not so much a conclusion about truth as an exclusion from it and thereby from rational debate.

Nietzsche came to understand this very well. The perspectivist must not engage in dialectical argument with Socrates, for that way would lie what from our point of view would be involvement in a tradition of rational enquiry, and from Nietzsche's point of view subjection to the tyranny of reason. Socrates is not to be argued with; he is to be mocked for his ugliness and his bad manners. Such mockery in response to dialectic is enjoined in the aphoristic paragraphs of *Götzen-Dämmerung*. And the use of aphorism is itself instructive. An aphorism is not an argument. Gilles Deleuze has called it "a play of forces," something by means of which energy is transmitted rather than conclusions reached.[6]

Nietzsche is of course not the only intellectual ancestor of modern perspectivism and perhaps not at all of modern relativism. Durkheim, however, provided a clue to the ancestry of both when he described in the late nineteenth century how the breakdown of traditional forms of social relationship increased the incidence of *anomie*, of normlessness. *Anomie*, as Durkheim characterized it, was a form of

6. Gilles Deleuze, "Pensée Nomade," in *Nietzsche aujourd'hui?*, vol. 1, *Intensités*, ed. Maurice de Gandillac and Bernard Pautrat (Paris: Union Générale d'Éditions, 1973).

deprivation, of a loss of membership in those social institutions and modes in which norms, including the norms of tradition-constituted rationality, are embodied. What Durkheim did not foresee was a time when the same condition of *anomie* would be assigned the status of an achievement by and a reward for a self, which had, by separating itself from the social relationships of traditions, succeeded, so it believed, in emancipating itself. This self-defined success becomes in different versions the freedom from bad faith of the Sartrian individual who rejects determinate social roles, the homelessness of Deleuze's nomadic thinker, and the presupposition of Derrida's choice between remaining "within," although a stranger to, the already constructed social and intellectual edifice, but only in order to deconstruct it from within, or brutally placing oneself outside in a condition of rupture and discontinuity. What Durkheim saw as social pathology is now presented wearing the masks of philosophical pretension.

The most obtrusive feature of this kind of philosophy is its temporariness; dwelling too long in any one place will always threaten to confer upon such philosophy the continuity of enquiry, so that it becomes embodied as one more rational tradition. It turns out to be forms of tradition which present a threat to perspectivism rather than vice versa.

So we are still confronted by the claims to our rational allegiance of the rival traditions whose histories I have narrated, and indeed, depending upon where and how we raise the questions about justice and practical rationality, by a number of other such traditions. We have learned that we cannot ask and answer those questions from a standpoint external to all tradition, that the resources of adequate rationality are made available to us only in and through traditions. How then are we to confront those questions? To what account of practical rationality and of justice do we owe our assent? How we do in fact answer these latter questions, we now have to notice, will depend in key part upon what the language is which we share with those together with whom we ask them questions and to what point the history of our own linguistic community has brought us.

# 13

## Aquinas and the
## Rationality of Tradition

### Alasdair MacIntyre

Two different characterizations of Aquinas as a philosopher might be presented: the first as someone who understood philosophical activity as that of a craft and indeed of the chief of crafts, the second as someone who carried forward two hitherto independent traditions of thought, merging them into one in such a way as to provide a direction for still further development of a new unified tradition. But if we are to understand the relevance of these two characterizations to Aquinas's conception of moral enquiry, it is first necessary to show how they relate to each other.

To become adept in a craft one has to learn how to apply two kinds of distinction, that between what as activity or product merely seems to me good and what really is good, a distinction always applied retrospectively as part of learning from one's earlier mistakes and surpassing one's earlier limitations, and that between what is good and best for me to do here and now given the limitations of my present state of education into the craft and what is good and best as such, unqualifiedly. But the way in which these distinctions are to be applied within some particular craft is rarely fixed once and for all. Every craft has a history and characteristically

Originally published as "Aquinas and the Rationality of Tradition," in Alasdair MacIntyre, *Three Rival Versions of Moral Enquiry* (Notre Dame, IN: University of Notre Dame Press, 1990), 127–48. Copyright © 1990, University of Notre Dame Press. Reprinted with permission of University of Notre Dame Press.

a history not yet completed. And during that history differences in the materials to which that craft gives form, differences in the means by which form is imposed upon matter, and differences in the conceptions of the forms to be achieved not only require new ways of applying these distinctions but themselves sometimes are the outcome of new ways in which these distinctions are applied. So learning how to make these distinctions adequately involves learning how to go on learning how to apply them. One has to acquire a certain kind of knowing how which enables one to move from the achievements of the past, which depended upon the making of these distinctions in one way, to the possibility of new achievements, which will depend upon making them in what may be some very different way. It is the possession and transmission of this kind of ability to recognize in the past what is and what is not a guide to the future which is at the core of any adequately embodied tradition. A craft in good order has to be embodied in a tradition in good order. And to be adequately initiated into a craft is to be adequately initiated into a tradition.

Secondly, because this is so, someone who has been initiated into a craft and has acquired in some measure this kind of knowing how will have made him- or herself part of the history of that craft, and it is in terms of that history that their actions *qua* craftsperson will be intelligible or otherwise. But no one who engages in a craft is only a craftsperson; we come to the practice of a craft with a history *qua* family member, *qua* member of this or that local community, and so on. So the actions of someone who engages in a craft arc at the point of intersection of two or more histories, two or more enacted dramatic narratives. The importance of this latter point is evident when we consider that the lives which are thus lived out are themselves the subject matter of the craft of moral philosophy, that is, of philosophical enquiry insofar as it addresses moral questions.

The philosophical theorist has to enquire: What is the good specific to human beings? Each individual has to enquire: What is *my* good as a human being? And while no true answer can be given by the philosophical theorist which is not somehow or other translatable into true answers that can be given to their practical questions by ordinary human individuals, no true answers can be given to their questions by such individuals which do not presuppose some particular type of answer to the philosopher's question. There is then no form of philosophical enquiry—at least as envisaged from an Aristotelian, Augustinian, or Thomistic point of view—which is not practical in its implications, just as there is no practical enquiry which is not philosophical in its presuppositions.

There is, of course, according to Aquinas a form of moral knowledge which is not itself theoretical. The practice of the virtues and the experience of having one's will directed by the virtues yields knowledge by way of what Aquinas calls "connaturality";[1] and a great many ordinary agents, educated into that practice within households or local communities, learn to be and are virtuous without ever

1. Aquinas, *Summa Theologiae* II-II.45.2.

explicitly raising philosophical questions. But when established moral traditions encounter situations of change in which old virtues have to be embodied in new ways and rules extended to cover new contingencies—and as the two key craft distinctions find new applications—the moral life from time to time inescapably raises theoretical questions. It does so because in such situations we are forced back to a reconsideration of first principles and how they apply to particulars: "The practical intellect . . . has its *principium* in a universal consideration and in this respect is the same in subject as the theoretical intellect, but its consideration reaches its terminus in a particular thing which can be done."[2]

So theoretical and practical enquiry are intertwined and the enquiries of the philosopher, framed in universal concepts, are always at least in the background— and sometimes in the foreground—when questions of the particularities of their lives and the goods to be pursued in them are raised by ordinary persons. The history of the moral life and the history of moral enquiry are aspects of a single, albeit complex, history. And to be initiated into the moral life is to be initiated into the tradition whose history is that complex history. How is that initiation to be achieved?

For most persons, at least so long as they inhabit a tolerably well-ordered form of social life, it will be in the course of their practical education at the hands of some teacher. But Aquinas held that all education is in an important way self-education: "A teacher leads someone else to the knowledge of what was unknown in the same way that someone leads him or herself to the knowledge of what was unknown in the course of discovery."[3] It follows that the order of good teaching is ideally the same as the order of effective learning, and a book which is well designed to teach, perhaps especially a book designed to teach teachers as the *Summa Theologiae* was, will follow the order of exploratory learning, through which the pupil relives the history of enquiry up to the highest point of achievement which it has reached so far, by rescrutinizing those arguments which have sustained the best supported conclusions so far. Hence the *Summa* sets out in its ordering of universal concepts the framework for a type of narrative of moral enquiry to be enacted by individuals who do and will exhibit their rationality by participating in the forms of rationality established by and through a particular tradition and indeed, insofar as moral enquiry is integral to the moral life itself, a framework for a set of narratives of particular lives. The intended reader of the *Summa*, like those who originally heard the lectures and participated in the disputations which went to its making, is in his or her reading engaged in conceptualizing and reconceptualizing his or her own activities in such a way as to answer the fundamental questions of moral enquiry. But here an already familiar type of difficulty reemerges.

To understand why both the virtues and obedience to divine law are required if we are to achieve our good, we have to learn what the *Summa* has to teach on

2. Aquinas, *Commentary on the Ethics* 6.2.
3. Aquinas, *Quaestiones Disputatae, De Veritate* 11.2.

these topics, whether it be from the *Summa* itself or from elsewhere. But we can only learn this, so it turns out, and we can only know how to read the *Summa* rightly if we already to some degree at least and in some way possess certain virtues, intellectual virtues certainly in the first place, but among those intellectual virtues is *prudentia, phronēsis*, that virtue of practical intelligence and judgment which itself cannot be possessed unless the moral virtues are possessed. So we are once again involved in an apparent circularity akin to that of the *Meno*. The key to the resolution of this form of the difficulty is, as in other cases, in the "To some degree . . . and in some way." We have to begin by acquiring enough of the virtues to order our passions aright, so that we are neither distracted nor misled by the multiplicity of the goods which they seem to propose to us and so that we acquire the initial experiences of rule following and action guiding from which we can begin to learn both how to understand our precepts and maxims better and how to extend the application of those precepts and maxims to an increasing range of particular situations. It is in so doing that we acquire the kind of knowing how to apply those key craft distinctions of which I spoke earlier, a knowing how which is both a knowing how to act and a knowing how to learn how to act, putting our nascent virtues themselves to the work of acquiring those same virtues in more adequate form. And it is because we have to learn in this way in this sequence that formal systematic moral enquiry, including the reading of the *Summa Theologiae*, has the place that it has in the overall order of intellectual development and training.

The subjects with which to begin, according to Aquinas, are those through which we learn inference and abstraction, logic and mathematics. Next we are to learn how to apply the principles of inference and abstraction to experience. By this time we should have reached the stage in which we have had sufficient practical experience of pursuing and reformulating goals, of following rules and of disciplining the passions to provide a basis for entering upon systematic moral enquiry. And achievement in this will satisfy one more prerequisite, that for entering upon those metaphysical and theological studies which complete all enquiry, in part by making explicit what is presupposed by the intelligibility discovered in all enquiry.[4]

The *Summa Theologiae* was not misnamed; it is itself a work of instruction at this highest stage, comprehending and integrating into itself however that in the other disciplines which theology needs, and providing also the framework within which the other disciplines have to be understood. The autonomy of subordinate disciplines is real but limited, and Aquinas's understanding of both that autonomy and those limitations was at odds with the dominant Augustinian curriculum. What was at issue here can be most easily understood by considering once more the curricular dilemma which the substantial restoration of the Aristotelian corpus presented for the thirteenth-century university, a dilemma stemming from some of the unresolved difficulties in the Augustinian account of knowledge.

4. Aquinas, *Commentary on the Ethics* 6.1.

On the view which had been constructed from Augustine's Platonism all understanding involved a reference to the universal exemplars in the divine mind. So a theological account of the relationship of God to his creation was required by every enquiry which aimed at understanding: the dependence of all other disciplines upon theology seemed thereby to be secured. But just because the nature of the relationship between the particulars studied in those other disciplines, the universal concepts through which those particulars are apprehended by those engaged in those other disciplines, and the exemplars in the divine mind, themselves not directly accessible to finite minds, remained unexplained and obscure, in practice the links between theology and the other disciplines were minimal. So there was an increasing tendency for those disciplines to proceed with a de facto autonomy in respect of their relationships both to theology and to each other, so that the curriculum lost any real unity. It was in response to just this tendency in its earlier forms that Hugh of St. Victor has written the *Didascalion* in order to restore genuine sovereignty to scriptural theology within a reunified curriculum. But the *Didascalion* did not and could not have provided a remedy for the situation in which the reception of the Aristotelian corpus presented its problems.

At the level of university organization the question was: in which faculty should the works of Aristotle be studied and taught? If the physical and metaphysical works were assigned to the Faculty of Arts, then teachers in that faculty would be entitled to pronounce independently on matters on which theology had been sovereign and, when the original ban on the teaching of those works by the Faculty of Arts came to be disregarded by the late 1240s, earlier Augustinian fears were confirmed by the growth of Averroist teaching in support of heterodox conclusions concerning the mortality of the soul and the eternity of the world. But were Aristotle's physical and metaphysical works instead to be assigned to the Faculty of Theology, theology itself would have to become philosophical in a quite new and, as it was to turn out, generally unacceptable way. It had at first been among the theologians that the new philosophical themes, theses, arguments, and methods had had the most willing and constructive reception: William of Auxerre (d. 1231) had sought to reconcile the Augustinian and Aristotelian theories of knowledge, and William of Auvergne (d. 1269) had identified what was centrally at issue between Platonic and Aristotelian theories of knowledge. Yet it was only after Albertus Magnus had set new standards in the presentation of Aristotle's own views that the extent to which theology itself might have to become a philosophical discipline became clear. And this would have involved a break with the conventional Augustinian understanding of theology.

When Aquinas wrote the *Summa*, he prepared himself for the task of writing the parts concerned with detailed moral enquiry in the IIa-IIae by writing a commentary on the *Nicomachean Ethics* at the same time as he was also continuing his exposition of St. Paul's epistles. It was the systematic character of Aquinas's insistence upon giving, within the same extended structures of argument, their due both to Pauline doctrine and to Aristotelian theory which resulted in his

producing a work whose genre separated it both from the conventional ortho-
doxies of the thirteenth-century curriculum and from the Averroist program. As
metaphysics stands to the other disciplines within the Aristotelian scheme, so a
theology which has integrated metaphysical commentary into itself is now to stand,
but this theology has to argue with and cannot merely dictate to the subordinate
disciplines in a form of active dialectical encounter, which both the Averroist
insistence on the autonomy of philosophy and the conventional Augustinian
theology found no room for.

The *Summa* therefore constituted an affront to the thirteenth-century Parisian
version of those institutional academic boundaries by which both agreements
and conflicts are conventionally defined. And once we have perceived this, the
question of what the *Summa* is, a text the quite unusual lucidity of whose Latin
is apt to conceal the originality of the author's intentions, forces us back upon
the question of what kind of persons we will have to be or become, either in the
thirteenth century or now, in order to read it aright. The concept of having to be
a certain sort of person, morally or theologically, in order to read a book aright—
with the implication that perhaps, if one is not that sort of person, then the book
should be withheld from one—is alien to the assumption of liberal modernity
that every rational adult should be free to and is able to read every book. Yet this
liberal assumption consorts uneasily with the idiom of recent literary interpretation. Consider, for example, the role played in Paul de Man's writings by such words
as "blindness," "insight," "asceticism," "irony," and "bad faith," words that signal
to us moral relationships between author and text and between text and reader
which can have the power to disrupt and undermine academic *explications de texte*.

The *Summa* has just this power. Consider in this respect two very different
ways of reading questions 90 to 97 of the Ia-IIae, those which concern law, divine,
natural, and human. One way is to focus on those questions in relative isolation
from other writings of Aquinas, with only the necessary minimum of citation
from elsewhere. The effect is to produce a reading whose assumption is that with
sufficient scholarly understanding of the particular words of this particular text
we could elucidate Aquinas's doctrine on law. Yet those whose reading of Aquinas
has tended to approximate to this end of the spectrum of readings have notably
disagreed among themselves and have, sometimes at least, done so because they
have imported into their interpretation philosophical principles alien to Aquinas.
Aquinas, for example, asserts that the *principium* of the natural law is: "Good is to
be done and evil is to be avoided" (94.2) and that all other precepts of the natural
law are based upon this. But how? Eric D'Arcy gives an account of the *principium*
as analytic, a tautology, using a post-Kantian conception of analyticity. Germaine
Grisez interprets the *principium* in the light of a post-Humean fact-value distinction. Neither refers us to the Platonic and Aristotelian understanding of "good,"
and it is perhaps because of this that Grisez can say in the course of distinguishing
his account from Maritain's that "Aquinas does not present the natural law as if it
were an object known or to be known; rather, he considers the precepts of practical

reason themselves to be natural law," the perhaps unintended implication of which is that the precepts of practical reason cannot themselves be objects of knowledge.[5]

What these disputes make clear is that questions 90 to 97 are not self-interpreting and that, even if it is a mistake to import alien philosophical concepts, nonetheless Aquinas's discussion has to be understood in terms of some principles or structure beyond what is said in answer to these particular questions. What is insisted upon by an alternative mode of reading is that questions 90 to 97 could only be asked and answered in the way that Aquinas asks and answers them after questions 1 to 89 have been asked and answered. What the discussion of good in question 1 had initially made clear was that when someone identifies a good as being the true good, that is, the end to which by virtue of his or her essential nature moves, he or she, unless hindered or directed in some way, moves toward it. So "such and such is the good of all human beings by nature" is always a factual judgment, which when recognized as true by someone moves that person toward that good. Evaluative judgments are a species of factual judgment concerning the final and formal causes of activity of members of a particular species.

The concept of good, then, has application only for beings insofar as they are members of some species or kind; Aquinas in question 96 speaks of our good *qua* being, shared with all other beings, our good *qua* animal being, shared with all other animals, and our good *qua* rational being, the common good of rational beings. Our understanding of those goods changes over time and in the course of changing is subject to error, and in the passage from question 1 to questions 90 to 97 we are guided through the arguments which might have entangled us in error, so that when we arrive at questions 90 to 97 we are able to characterize our earliest and most primitive, albeit genuine, understandings of the natural law from the standpoint of the mature understanding which we have now acquired. And in all of this the conclusions of part I are presupposed. What this view of the reading of Aquinas points us toward is the conclusion that the *Summa* can only be read as a whole and can only be evaluated as a whole. The parts clearly each have their own import, but they have their import in their character as parts of that whole. It is thus on this view a good deal more difficult to encounter, let alone to evaluate, Aquinas's thought than either Thomists or their opponents have some-times supposed. For the abstraction of particular theses and the matching of these against particular theses similarly abstracted from Kant or Hume or whomever deforms the reading of Aquinas's theses. Yet such deformation is inherent in a great many of our contemporary curricular and publishing habits: questions 90 to 97, for example, are most often published separately as the *Treatise on Law*, and students often enough are invited to consider this fictitious treatise alongside the *Grundlegung* or the *Rechtsphilosophie*, as though each of them offered rival answers to one and the same set of questions about the nature of law, questions which can

---

5. Germain Grisez, "The First Principle of Practical Reason," in *Aquinas: A Collection of Critical Essays*, ed. Anthony Kenny (Garden City, NY: Doubleday, 1969), 347.

be formulated, so it is assumed, without already having committed oneself by the presuppositions of their formulation to speak either from outside or from within that universe of discourse which is the *Summa* taken as a whole.

What then this type of holistic reading of the *Summa* puts in question, in a way that nineteenth- and early twentieth-century Thomism often did not, is how one can be a critic of the *Summa* without first having been a genuine participant in its processes of dialectical enquiry and discovery, through which the themes of the debates so far, and more especially of the debate between Augustinians and Averroists, were and are reformulated and carried forward. Yet if our dominant curricular and interpretive habits make it difficult to come to terms with the *Summa* thus understood, so in their own way, as we have already seen, did the curricular and interpretive habits of the thirteenth century. The *Summa* has proved easy enough to domesticate academically in terms other than its own, but to read it in its own terms from within the tradition which Aquinas reconstituted in the course of writing it is the only way to reckon with it in other than mock and distorting encounter.

To this it may be said, indeed should be said, that Aquinas in the passages to which I have been alluding is speaking of a knowledge of the natural law which human beings have by nature and that, since we are all human beings after all, we can surely all judge equally of what he says, plain persons and philosophers or theologians alike. Consider then Aquinas's portrait of the plain person in relation to the precepts of the natural law. The plain person initially, as plain child, exhibits his or her knowledge of the *principium* of the natural law, which is the *principium* of practical reasoning, in the same way that he or she exhibits his or her knowledge of the principle of noncontradiction, that is to say, not in any ability to formulate the principle explicitly, but by showing a potentiality to do just that, in the way in which the truth of the principle is presupposed in a multiplicity of particular practical judgments. What will be there presupposed will, however, not only be the *principium* of the natural law understood as a single precept, but that *principium* in its application to the various aspects of human nature in terms of which it has to be spelled out. For the *principium* enjoins the pursuit of our good, and the good of human beings has various aspects or parts. So an apprehension of those goods and ends will be implicit in the plain person's particular practical judgments.

Disagreements about how the *principium* is to be formulated and understood at the level of philosophical enquiry are then going to be as apt to occur as similar disagreements about the principle of noncontradiction. And just as such disagreements are only to be resolved or even adequately formulated in the context of an account of a complex of related concepts, so the explicit articulation of the concepts involved in the *principium* also must involve a web of concepts, concepts which can only be spelled out in terms of their range of uses and applications. So that in moving from the earliest and most primitive apprehensions of our good to a mature understanding of it we have to explore the meaning and use of such concepts as those of end (*telos*), happiness, action, passion, and virtue. What is constant in this movement is the core of our initial apprehension, that if we are to achieve an understanding of good in relation to ourselves as being, as animal, and as rational we shall have to engage with other members of the community in which our learning has to go on in such a way as to be teachable learners. And thus we accomplish the first realization of our good by in the most elementary way respecting the good of those others in encounter with whom we have to learn. What we grasp initially in understanding the binding force of the precepts of the natural law are the conditions for entering a community in which we may discover what further specifications our good has to be given.

The movement toward that further specification may take place at a number of very different levels, but it is in important ways one and the same movement, whether articulated in fully adequate philosophical and theological terms as in the *Summa* or in the relatively inarticulate apprehensions of those who learn *per inclinatione*, through the directedness of their lives in living out the virtues. Where does this movement begin? It may begin either from being taught by parents within the household or, if that is unfortunately lacking, within the wider community, learning from that in its laws which exemplifies the natural law. What that teaching points toward is a discrimination of the ends which one may pursue in the light of that ultimate end or good, which is the true good of one's kind. What is that good?

In the first five questions of the Ia-IIae, Aquinas recapitulates those arguments in book 1 of the *Nicomachean Ethics* by which Aristotle had shown that wealth, honor, pleasure, and even the virtues, the peculiar excellences of the human soul, cannot be that good. To this list he adds, in a way that Aristotle would certainly not have objected to, power and the goods of the body. But then in a way quite unexpected by any devoted reader of Aristotle up to this point—a reader who had been using, for example, Aquinas's own commentary on book 1—Aquinas turns the criteria for an ultimate good to which Aristotle had appealed against Aristotle and uses them to show, first, that the ultimate good must lie in the relationship of the soul to something outside itself and, secondly, that in no state available in this created world can the type of good in question be found. There are indeed a variety of imperfect happinesses to be found in this world, but neither separately nor in conjunction can they constitute the human end.

So Aristotle was invoked against Aristotle in the interests of Scripture and of Augustine, not because Aquinas was rejecting Aristotelianism, but because he was trying to be a better Aristotelian than Aristotle. But the Aristotelianism which results has something of a tragic character to it. Without some rationally warranted belief in, some genuine knowledge of, that perfect goodness in relationship to which alone the soul finds ultimate good—that divine goodness by reference to which alone, in Augustine's Platonic terms, the unity underlying and ordering the range of uses and applications of the concept of good can be discovered—the soul would find itself directed beyond all finite goods, unsatisfiable by those goods, and yet able to find nothing beyond them to satisfy it. Permanent dissatisfaction would be its lot. What would such a soul become, a soul perhaps which, having first embraced a materialist version of Averroism, then went on to discover from Aquinas's arguments the radical imperfection of the only happiness to be envisaged from within philosophy thus understood? It would surely become a Hobbesian soul, concluding both that "there is no such *Finis ultimus* (utmost ayme) nor *Summum Bonum* (greatest good) as is spoken of in the Books of the old Morall Philosophers" and that desire could only issue in the successive pursuit of always unsatisfying objects, "a perpetuall and restless desire of Power after power, that ceaseth only in Death." So a Hobbesian shadow is cast by Aquinas's revision of Aristotle, itself a foreshadowing of much else to come.

I remarked earlier that for an Aristotelian, whether Thomist or otherwise, what is good or best for anyone or anything is so in virtue of its being of a certain kind, with its own essential nature and that which peculiarly belongs to the flourishing of beings of that kind. Particularities of circumstance are of course highly relevant to the determination of what is good and best for one here now. But what one brings to each particular situation, if practically well-educated, are dispositions to judge concerning those particularities in the light of truths about the good of one's species. And to be practically well-educated is to have learned to take plea-sure in doing and judging rightly in respect of goods and to have learned to be pained by defect and error in the same respect. So the pleasure and pain which are mine *qua* me supervene upon that doing or being or achieving good which is mine *qua* rational animal. Take away the notion of essential nature, take away the corresponding notion of what is good and best for members of a specific kind who share such a nature, and the Aristotelian scheme of the self which is to achieve good, of good, and of pleasure necessarily collapses. There remains only the individual self with its pleasures and pains. So metaphysical nominalism sets constraints upon how the moral life can be conceived. And, conversely, certain types of conceptions of the moral life exclude such nominalism.

Thus inescapably from the Aristotelian point of view an understanding of one-self as having an essential nature and the discovery of what in one belongs to that nature and what is merely *per accident* enters into the progress of the self, includ-ing the self of the plain person, even though that understanding and discovery may take place in a way that presupposes rather than explicitly formulates the philosophical theses and arguments involved. What, more precisely, is it that has to be understood and discovered, and why? What has to be discovered is how to order the passions so that they may serve and not distract reason in its pursuit of the specific end, the good. What has to be understood are the different relationships in which the passions may stand to reason and to the will and to the different dispositions to judge and to act which exhibit a right ordering of the passions. So an antinominalist philosophical psychology provides the basis for an account of those dispositions which, perfectly possessed, are the distinctively human perfections, the virtues.

Rules and virtues are interrelated. To possess the virtue of justice, for example, involves both a will to give to each person what is due to him or her and a knowledge of how to apply the rules which prevent violations of that order in which each receives his or her due. To understand the application of rules as part of the exercise of the virtues is to understand the point of rule following, just because one cannot understand the exercise of the virtues except in terms of their role in constituting the type of life in which alone the human *telos* is to be achieved. The rules which are the negative precepts of the natural law thus do no more than set limits to that type of life and in so doing only partially define the kind of goodness to be aimed at. Detach them from their place in defining and constituting a whole way of life and they become nothing but a set of arbitrary prohibitions, as they too often became in later periods. To progress in both moral enquiry and the moral life is then to progress in understanding *all* the various aspects of that life. Rules, precepts, virtues, passions, actions as parts of a single whole. Central to that progress is the exercise of the virtue of *prudentia*, the virtue of being able in particular situations to bring to bear the relevant universal and to act so that the universal is embodied in the particular. That virtue is acquired through experience, the experience of judging in respect of how and in what ways the universal has been or is to be embodied in the particular and of learning how to learn from these experiences. But there comes a point at which no degree of prudence, or of the other virtues which are required if one is to have and to exercise prudence, will avail to further one's progress toward one's ultimate good.

What one discovers in oneself and in all other human beings is something surd and unaccountable in terms of the rational understanding of human nature: a rooted tendency to disobedience in the will and distraction by passion, which causes obscuring of the reason and on occasion systematic cultural deformation. This type of disruption of the moral life is very different from that which results from a Hobbesian denial of there being any ultimate end. For in this latter type of case the ultimate end is already at least partly in view. What the discovery of willful evil disrupts, or apparently disrupts, is the intelligible scheme through which the individual is able to understand him- or herself as both directed toward and explicable in terms of that end. And just as an Averroist denial of any achievable state beyond those of this present life pointed forward toward a Hobbesian reduction of good and evil to pleasure and pain, so the discovery of human inability and resourcelessness to live by the natural law and to achieve the excellences of the virtues, the discovery of sin, points forward to a kind of existential despair which was completely unknown in the ancient world but which has been a recurrent malady of modernity. Yet for Aquinas, by contrast, it is in fact this discovery of willful evil which makes the achievement of the human end possible. How so? The acknowledgment by oneself of radical defect is a necessary condition for one's reception of the virtues of faith, hope, and charity.

It is only the kind of knowledge which faith provides, the kind of expectation which hope provides, and the capacity for friendship with other human beings and with God which is the outcome of charity which can provide the other virtues with what they need to become genuine excellences, informing a way of life in and through which the good and the best can be achieved. The self-revelation of God in the events of the scriptural history and the gratuitous grace through which that revelation is appropriated, so that an individual can come to recognize his or her place within that same history, enable such individuals to recognize also that prudence, justice, temperateness, and courage are genuine virtues, that the apprehension of the natural law was not illusory, and that the moral life up to this point requires to be corrected in order to be completed but not displaced. So a Pauline and Augustinian account retrospectively vindicates that in Aristotle which had provided a first understanding of the core of the moral life.

Take away or reject the Aristotelianism in the Thomist account, but leave the despair of moral achievement and the gratuitousness of grace, and what is fore-shadowed is Luther. What an adequately corrected Aristotelianism provides for Aquinas, which is notably absent in Luther and in his ideological heirs, is an opportunity for showing how the understanding of prudence, justice, temperateness, and courage in the light afforded by charity, hope, and faith, and more especially charity, which is the form of all the virtues, furnishes a richly detailed account of the moral life. So, in the best accounts of the virtues to be given so far, inadequacies are remedied by using the Bible and Augustine to transcend the limitations not only of Aristotle but also of Plato (for in his account of the cardinal virtues Aquinas is quite as indebted to Plato as to Aristotle) and by using Aristotle as well as Augustine to articulate some of the detail of the moral life in a way that goes beyond anything furnished by Augustine.

Two features of that detailed treatment are of crucial importance. Modern Catholic protagonists of theories of natural law have sometimes claimed that we can fully understand and obey the natural law without any knowledge of God. But according to Aquinas all the moral precepts of the Old Law, the Mosaic Law summed up in the Ten Commandments, belong to the natural law, including those which command us as to how we are to regard God and comport ourselves in relation to him. A knowledge of God is, on Aquinas's view, available to us from the outset of our moral enquiry and plays a crucial part in our progress in that enquiry. And it would be very surprising if this were not so: the unifying framework within which our understanding of ourselves, of each other, and of our shared environment progresses is one in which that understanding, by tracing the sequences of final, formal, efficient, and material causality, always refers us back to a unified first cause from which flows all that is good and all that is true in what we encounter. So in articulating the natural law itself we understand the peculiar character of our own directedness, and in understanding the natural law better we move initially from what is evident to any plain person's unclouded moral apprehension to what is evident only or at least much more clearly to the *sapientes*, those whom Aquinas saw as masters of the master craft (I-II.100.1), and to what supernatural revelation discloses. But in so doing we progress or fail to progress, both as members of a community with a particular sacred history, the history of Israel and the church, and as members of communities with secular political histories.

So a second crucial feature of Aquinas's detailed treatment of the moral life is its political dimension. And in part because the histories of sacred and secular communities intersect at key points, in part because of the internal structures of both types of community, the conflicts of the moral life are on occasion bound up with the conflicts of competing jurisdictions: so it was in Aquinas's own time both within the University of Paris and between the university authorities, the episcopal authority, and the royal authority; so it was also between imperial and papal power and in the kingdom of Naples. It was thus through and in a variety of conflicts that the universal truths of, for example, Aquinas's account of what justice is in all its parts and aspects had to find their highly particularized embodiments. And it was and is in so doing that the craft skills of philosophy were and are exercised in elaborating the key distinctions of the moral life, itself always, as we have seen, at some level a life of moral enquiry.

In all these respects the individual moral life continues and extends that tradition which provided it with its initial context for reappropriating and extending teachings out of a variety of pasts. So the enquiries of the individual moral life are continuous with those of past tradition, and the rationality of that life is the rationality both embodied in and transmitted through tradition. What the *Summa* achieves is a definitive statement at the level of theory of the point reached by its moral and theological tradition so far. What its sequences portray are a set of possibilities awaiting further embodiment in particular persons, circumstances, times, and places.

What then would it be for the sequences of the *Summa*—in which there is a progression from what must be first presupposed about God and human nature in the first part, through the sequences of moral enquiry of the first and second parts of the second part, to the recognition in the third part of the revealed truths which define for us the kingdom of God—to be mirrored in the enacted dramatic narratives of particular human lives lived out in particular communities? Aquinas himself does not supply an answer to this question, but Dante does. Yet to understand the import of Dante's answers we need first to notice one further aspect of Aquinas's position. The individual human being is a unity in whom the directedness of the different aspects of his spiritual and social existence have to be ordered hierarchically into a unified mode of life. Yet those different aspects each have their own importance: it is the individual *qua* biological unit, the individual *qua* family member, the individual *qua* citizen of this commune or subject of this monarch, the individual *qua* Dominican friar or Benedictine monk who discharges what is due in justice and charity to him- or herself and others in these roles. Hence arises a variety of tensions, and the practical problems of the integrity of the self are the counterpart to the practical problems of competing jurisdictions. The virtues which conjointly inform the actions of an integrated self are also the virtues of a well-integrated political community.

Aquinas himself seems to have negotiated these problems with a rare singleness of purpose, with that purity of heart, which, as Kierkegaard said, is to will one thing. He had when very young been a student at the University of Naples, the first lay medieval university, founded by the apostate emperor Frederick II; he was a member of a family deeply involved in the Italian conflicts between the papacy and Frederick II, and he moved between teaching at both Paris and Naples and at the papal court at a time when the interests of the French monarchy in the kingdom of Naples added a further dimension to the political complexities in which he could have become entangled. It was therefore notable that he always rejected any political role, refusing earlier the abbacy at Monte Cassino and later the archbishopric of Naples. And this single-minded insistence on the intellectual character of his vocation underlay the quality for which Dante most admired Aquinas, his *discrezione*, his ability to make the right moral and intellectual distinctions.

Some nineteenth-century Thomists paid Dante what they took to be the compliment of reading him as a Thomist. But it is in part because he was not, because he constructed poetically and philosophically from the Augustinian and Aristotelian traditions a synthesis that was genuinely his own, that his agreements with Aquinas are so impressive. So in the imagined universe of the *Commedia* the vices of those who inhabit the *Inferno*, the virtues of those in the *Paradiso*, and the virtues and vices of those engaged in the transformations of the *Purgatorio* do indeed together particularize the accounts of the virtues and vices in the Ia-IIae and IIa-IIae of the *Summa* and need to be read as its partial counterpart. What that particularization reinforces is both Aquinas's thesis that the badness and failure of any one part of a self entails the badness of the whole and his thesis that there is no badness of any part which is not the redeemable corruption or distortion of some good. The modern reader of the *Commedia* is, however, apt to find just these features in Dante, which exhibit his agreement with Aquinas, problematic.

How can Dante, for example, so obviously admire his own teacher, Brunetto Latini—yet another author of an encyclopedia—and nonetheless place him in Hell? If Brunetto Latini was so admirable in so many ways, as indeed he was, how can he suffer that unqualified condemnation for the sin of sodomy which places him in the *Inferno*? The answer is clearly given by Aquinas: the doing of many good deeds is perfectly compatible with the perverse choosing of something in oneself which is defect and error and affirming it as what one intends unalterably to be. And it is this choice which is one's own choice of exclusion from the community of the perfected. So hell is persistence in defection from the integrity both of a self and of its communities.

Among those thus assigned to the *Inferno* was Emperor Frederick II, whom Nietzsche was to call "that great free spirit" and to place among "the finest examples" of "marvellously incomprehensible and inexplicable beings, those enigmatical men, predestined for conquering and circumventing others" (other examples were Alcibiades, Caesar, and Leonardo da Vinci). What Nietzsche praised in each of them was what he perceived as a ruthless affirmation of the self and its powers; what Dante saw as Frederick's self-condemnation was, so it seems, the very same affirmation. And conversely what Dante and Aquinas saw as achievement of the good, Nietzsche saw as emasculation and impoverishment. What is at issue here is in part the answer to the questions: In what larger story or stories, if any, is the story of each individual embedded? And in what still larger story is that story in turn embedded? And is there then a single history of the world within which all other stories find their place and from which the significance of each subordinate story derives? Dante's affirmative answer embodies a challenge to his future readers: tell me your story and I will show you that it only becomes intelligible within the framework provided by the *Commedia*, or rather within some framework provided by that scriptural vision which the *Commedia* allegorizes. For Nietzsche all such stories, so understood, are misuses and abuses of the historical imagination, a misunderstood reification of masks.

Yet Nietzsche greatly admired Dante, while viewing with contempt the ecclesiastical antagonists of Frederick II. For he saw in Dante's writing, as did that oddly neglected Nietzschean, Stefan George, the very same creative, assertive strength which he also saw in Frederick II and in Leonardo. So that a Nietzschean reader's retort to Dante—and indirectly to Aquinas—would be: admit that in telling your stories about Frederick II and Brunetto Latini what you were in fact affirming was your self as an expression of the will to power, just as much as Frederick II and Brunetto Latini did, something for which you placed *them* in hell. So on a Nietzschean reading Dante's text takes on a different antagonistic set of meanings, one at odds with Dante's avowed moral intentions. And, as it is with Dante, so it would also *mutatis mutandis* be with Aquinas. But what resources, if any, can Aquinas then provide for a response to this Nietzschean reading? To answer this question, we need further to recognize that from a Thomistic standpoint, as I have characterized it, questions of rational justification may arise at four different levels.

There is first of all that of the genuinely uninstructed plain person, posing the question "What is my good?" in a number of particularized ways, whose teacher has to assist him or her in the actualization of those potentialities which will carry such persons from their initial bare moral apprehensions to a discovery of the place of those apprehensions in a larger scheme. There is secondly the person who shares that larger scheme and is already able to articulate it in the Aristotelian terms which are its most adequate expression, so that demands for rational justification are framed in terms of a shared understanding of natural enquiry and a shared conception of first principles, even if what is at issue is on occasion their precise formulation. It was from within this kind of agreement that Aquinas conducted his debate with some rival Islamic, Jewish, and Latin Averroist positions. Such debate is necessarily very different from that between antagonists each of whom systematically rejects to some significant degree the other's first principles and conception of rational enquiry.

In this third type of debate, characterized by some large degree of incommensurability, the type of claim which has to be made and then established or refuted is precisely that which Aquinas advanced to Augustinians in respect of his amended and enlarged Augustinianism and to Averroists in respect of his amended and enlarged [Aristotelianism]. It is, as we noticed earlier, the claim to provide a standpoint which suffers from less incoherence, is more comprehensive and more resourceful, but especially resourceful in one particular way. For among those resources, so it is claimed, is an ability not only to identify as limitations, defects, and errors of the opposing view what are or ought to be taken to be limitations, defects, and errors in the light of the standards of the opposing view itself, but also to explain in precise and detailed terms what it is about the opposing view which engenders just these particular limitations, defects, and errors and also what it is about that view which must deprive it of the resources required for understanding, overcoming, and correcting them. And at the same time it will be claimed that what is cogent, insightful, and true in that opposing view can be incorporated within one's own view, providing on occasion needed corrections of that view.

This then is the kind of claim in terms of which the rational superiority of Aquinas's philosophical and theological synthesis of traditions to previous versions of Augustinianism and Aristotelianism can be retrospectively exhibited. And it is also the kind of claim in terms of which the superiority of Thomism to later challenges, to Cartesian, Humean, Kantian, or Nietzschean critiques would have to be shown. A mistake of much nineteenth- and early twentieth-century Thomism was to suppose that the task of rational justification against their Cartesian, Humean, or Kantian adversaries was of the second, rather than of this third, type. That is, they believed that they shared with their philosophical opponents more in the way of first principles and of a conception of rational enquiry than was in fact the case. Yet against Nietzschean opponents it would not be enough to recognize this error. For it may well be the case, and it is in large part to Nietzsche himself that we are indebted for our understanding of this, that a philosophical or theological position may be so organized, both in its intellectual structures and in its institutionalized modes of presentation and enquiry that conversation with an opposing position may reveal that its adherents are systematically unable to recognize in it even those errors, defects, and limitations which ought to be recognized as such in the light of their own and its standards.

When such a situation is encountered, either in the form of a blindness imputed to one's opponents or in the form of a blindness imputed to one by one's opponents, where such blindness is alleged to arise systematically from the way in which either or both points of view are intellectually and socially organized and not merely from the psychological characteristics of particular individuals, then yet another task of a fourth kind is added to the work of rational justification. What has to be supplied is a cogent theoretical explanation of ideological blindness, the kind of theory to which notable contributions have been made by Gramsci in respect of Croce, by Mannheim in respect of different types of Utopianism, and most of all by Nietzsche. What did Aquinas have to say at this fourth level? Can a Thomist hope to construct a genealogy for Nietzsche's genealogizing?

There is one Thomist book on Nietzsche.[6] Copleston was understandably and rightly preoccupied in 1942 with the question of how European culture was to be defended from the Nazis, and his presentation of Nietzsche was of a philosopher deeply opposed to everything that National Socialism stood for, but whose enquiries issued in positions which could not sustain an intellectually or morally effective alternative. It echoes in a curious way Stefan George's final verdict on Nietzsche as a hero who failed. But while Copleston pointed us toward a genealogy for genealogy, he did not actually provide it. Where then would such a genealogy have to begin? The answer is: with what Aquinas says about the roots of intellectual blindness in moral error, with the misdirection of the intellect by the will and with the corruption of the will by the sin of pride, both that pride which is an inordinate desire to be superior and that pride which is an inclination to contempt for God. Where Nietzsche saw the individual will as a fiction, as part of a mistaken psychology which conceals from view the impersonal will to power, the Thomist can elaborate out of materials provided in the *Summa* an account of the will to power as an intellectual fiction disguising the corruption of the will. The activity of unmasking is itself to be understood from the Thomistic standpoint as a mask for pride.

What I have articulated so far is not at all the substance of those arguments by means of which Aquinas or Dante or their Thomistic successors would have to vindicate the positions of the *Summa* and of the *Commedia*. What I have perhaps achieved at least in the barest outline is a statement of what is at issue and what *kinds* of argument would have to be deployed. And in so doing it has become plain that the intellectual issues which divide Nietzschean genealogy from Thomistic tradition and both from the academic stance of the encyclopedist cannot be dissociated from answers to questions about the moral errors and ideological distortions which enter into moral enquiry.

6. Frederick Copleston, *Friedrich Nietzsche: Philosopher of Culture* (London: Burns, Oates, and Washbourne, 1942).

# 14

## The Epistemic Priority of Jesus Christ

### Robert Barron

### The Scriptural Warrant

One of the characteristic marks of the modern style of philosophizing is the predilection for commencing the intellectual project with epistemology. Most moderns hold that the limits and capacity of knowledge must be firmly established before one can fruitfully endeavor to explore issues in politics, ethics, or metaphysics. I have purposely resisted this modernism by commencing my project with an investigation of the narrative icons concerning Jesus Christ. It is my conviction that we don't read Jesus through the lens of a predetermined epistemology, but rather that we understand the nature of knowledge in general through those narratives.

But is this coherent? Do Christians know in a distinctive way? Are both the object of their intellectual investigation and their manner of rational procedure unique? Do Christians become aware of the centrality of Jesus Christ after a long and epistemologically neutral inquiry, or does that awareness condition all modes of their intellection from the beginning? The questions fix us on the horns of a dilemma. To answer them affirmatively seems to place Christians in an irresponsibly fideistic and sectarian position, compromising their capacity to enter into conversation with those outside their community of discourse; but to answer

Originally published as "The Scriptural Warrant" and "The Nature of the Christ-Mind," in Robert Barron, *The Priority of Christ: Toward a Postliberal Catholicism* (Grand Rapids: Brazos, 2007), 133–35, 153–88. Copyright © 2007. Used by permission.

them negatively seems to force Christians to abandon their claim that Christ has primacy in all things, including, presumably, what and how we know.

This tension is, of course, not new. It is a defining problematic in the roiled history of Christian theology, having given rise to the numerous battles between "Athens" and "Jerusalem" played out in the writings of Tertullian, Origen, Aquinas, Bonaventure, Jacques-Bénigne Bossuet, Newman, Barth, Rahner, and many others. What I shall endeavor to do here is to address this problem, not so much in the hope of "solving" it as in the desire to show a way forward. I am convinced that one form of the liberal-conservative dispute is a function of an awkward handling of this old and knotty tension and that a consistently and generously christological approach opens a more promising path. I will try to show that a mind radically conditioned by the narratives concerning Jesus Christ—gatherer, warrior, and Lord—actually grasps reality most richly and thus, paradoxically enough, makes possible the most creative conversation with the non-Christian culture.

## Scripture's Claims for Christ

It is difficult to read the New Testament and not be struck by the maximalist claims constantly being made about Jesus Christ. He is "Lord" (Matt. 21:3), "Son of God" (Heb. 1:2), "Son of Man" (Matt. 12:8), "Messiah" (Mark 8:29), "Son of David" (Luke 18:39), "the Alpha and the Omega" (Rev. 1:8), "Author of life" (Acts 3:15), and, in the ecstatic words of Thomas the former doubter, "My Lord and my God" (John 20:28). But there is no more extraordinary and far-reaching description of Jesus's significance than the one found in the first chapter of the letter to the Colossians. There we read that Jesus is "the image [*eikōn*] of the invisible God, the firstborn of all creation," the one in whom "the fullness of God was pleased to dwell" (Col. 1:15, 19). Lest we miss the power of these statements, their implications are clearly spelled out: "In him all things in heaven and on earth were created, things visible and invisible, whether thrones or dominions or rulers or powers" (v. 16). In this Jesus, all things have come to be; he is the prototype of all finite existence, even of those great powers that transcend the world and govern human affairs. If we are tempted to understand his influence as only a thing of the past, we are corrected: "In him all things hold together" (v. 17). Jesus is not only the one in whom things were created but also the one in whom they presently exist and through whom they inhere in one another. And if we are inclined to view the future as a dimension of creation untouched by Christ, we are set straight: "Through him God was pleased to reconcile to himself all things, whether on earth or in heaven, by making peace through the blood of his cross" (v. 20). Individuals, societies, cultures, animals, plants, planets, and the stars—all will be drawn into an eschatological harmony through him. Mind you, Jesus is not merely the symbol of an intelligibility, coherence, and reconciliation that can exist apart from him; rather, he is the active and indispensable means by which these realities come to be. This Jesus, in short, is the all-embracing, all-including, all-reconciling Lord of whatever is to be found in the dimensions of time and space.

A text that parallels the first chapter of Colossians in the intensity and range of its claims is, of course, the prologue to the Gospel of John. If in Colossians the particular figure Jesus of Nazareth is identified with the creative power of God, in the Johannine text the process is reversed: now the transcendent Logos of God is appreciated as the one who became concretely available in this Jesus: "The Word became flesh." But the assertion of Christ's absolute ontological priority remains the same: this Jesus is the Word that was with God from the beginning and through whom all things that exist came to be and continue in being.

Now what follows from these breathtaking descriptions is a centrally important epistemic claim: that Jesus cannot be measured by a criterion outside of himself or viewed from a perspective higher than himself. He cannot be understood as one object among many or surveyed blandly by a disinterested observer. If such perspectives were possible, then he would not be the all-grounding Word or the criterion than which no more final can be thought. If we sought to know him in this way, we would not only come to incorrect conclusions but also involve ourselves in a sort of operational contradiction. To be consistent with these accounts, we must say that Jesus determines not only what there is to be known (since he is the organizing principle of finite being) but also how we are to know what is to be known (since the mind itself is a creature, made and determined through him).

A Christ-illumined mind in search of Christ-determined forms seems to be the epistemology implicit in Colossians and the Johannine prologue. Further, as Bruce Marshall has argued, this primacy implies that the narratives concerning Jesus must, for Christians, be an epistemic trump, that is to say, an articulation of reality that must hold sway over and against all rival articulations, be they scientific, psychological, sociological, philosophical, or religious.[1] To hold to Colossians and the prologue to John is to have a clear negative criterion concerning all claims to ultimate truth: whatever runs contrary to the basic claims entailed in the narratives concerning Jesus must certainly be false.

## The Nature of the Christ-Mind

Having considered two possible challenges to my central assertion, we are now in a position to look more carefully at the epistemic claim implied in Colossians and the Johannine prologue. What precisely is the Christ-mind, and what does it mean to say that we approach all of our knowing through this mind? What is at stake in having, as Paul put it in Philippians, "the same mind . . . in you that was in Christ Jesus" (2:5)? It means, to state it in most basic form, that what we know and how

1. Bruce Marshall, *Trinity and Truth* (Cambridge: Cambridge University Press, 2000), 44–47.

we know is conditioned by what was revealed in Jesus Christ. It is my conviction that the Christ-consciousness displays itself in terms of seven dimensions.

## The Intelligibility of Coinherence

Colossians tells us that in Jesus all things have come to be and that all things hold together and find their fulfillment in him. He is before, during, and after all finite existence, creating, surrounding, and pulling it to completion. Further, the John prologue informs us that this Jesus is the incarnation of the Word by which the Father has made all that is, without exception. Therefore to acknowledge the epistemic primacy of Jesus Christ is, first, to assume the intelligibility of all that is.[2] Since all has been made through, and will be ordered by, a divine rationality, there must be form in all finite being as a whole and in each particular thing that exists; what comes to be through Logos is, necessarily, logical. This implies, of course, that there is an unavoidable correspondence between the activity of the mind and the structure of being: intelligence will find its fulfillment in this universal and inescapable intelligibility.

Many have pointed out that it is no accident that the physical sciences—astronomy, physics, chemistry, biology—developed and flourished in the Christian West.[3] People formed in the biblical conviction that finite reality is intelligible, made through the divine Logos, will rather naturally move out to meet the physical world with confident rationality, and their investigations will proceed without hesitation to the farthest reaches of the macrocosmic and the microcosmic realms. Without this intuition, which can only be called mystical, none of the sciences would get under way. Of course, this correspondence can be turned in the opposite direction and used as a *manuductio* for scientific seekers after God. One could argue that the universality of objective intelligibility (assumed by any honest scientist) can be explained only through recourse to a transcendent subjective intelligence that has thought the world into being, so that every act of knowing a worldly object or event is, literally, a re-cognition, a thinking again of what has already been thought by a primordial divine knower. Hence, every scientific act is, ipso facto, an affirmation of God's existence. This kind of argument, obviously, is shaped by the same insight that we found in Thomas's Johannine commentary: natural reason is a participation in the pure intelligibility of the Logos and thus is necessarily congruent with the deepest perceptions of theology.

We find a similar intuition in the curiously equivalent claims of Jacques Derrida and George Steiner that to know anything at all is, implicitly, to know that God exists, for it is to accept the reign of the Logos or transcendent intelligibility. To be sure, Derrida denies just this type of logocentrism, and his denial is a function of his assertion of the permanently open-ended and undecidable nature of

2. See Joseph Ratzinger, *Introduction to Christianity* (San Francisco: Ignatius, 1990), 106.

3. John Polkinghorne, *Faith, Science, and Understanding* (New Haven: Yale University Press, 2000), 18–19.

human knowing. Steiner accepts it, precisely because he affirms the possibility of real speech and knowledge. For our purposes, what is most interesting is the logical connection that both see, from different sides and with opposite intentions, between knowledge and what can only be called "faith."[4]

But there is more to it than this. In the language of the John prologue, the ground of the world's intelligibility is a Word spoken by a speaker. Further, it is an utterance that bears the full power of the one who utters it: "The Word was with God, and the Word was God" (John 1:1). This Word cannot be identical to the one who speaks it, for then there would be no real speech. At the same time, there must be an unsurpassable closeness between the two, even to the point of oneness of essence, since the communication is so complete. This implies that the primordial intelligibility is a being-with-the-other, or better, a being-in-the-other, a coinherence. Now it is through this Word that the entire world is made, and hence it is by this Word that all things are intelligibly marked. Therefore relationality, being-for-the-other, must be the form that, at the deepest level, conditions whatever is *and* the truth that satisfies the hunger of the mind. It is not simply reasonability that characterizes the real, but this type of reasonability.

This principle becomes even clearer when we follow the narrative of the prologue to the point of the enfleshment of this Word. The primordial divine conversation partner becomes a creature in order to draw creation into the embrace of the divine life, to be a light in the darkness. In dialogue with Nicodemus, the Logos personally delineates the nature of this mission: "God so loved the world that he gave his only Son, so that everyone who believes in him may not perish but may have eternal life" (John 3:16). Through the incarnation, the coinherence of the Father and the Logos seeks to provoke a coinherence of creation with God and of creatures with one another. In light of the entire Gospel, we know that the momentum of this enfleshment is toward the total self-gift of the cross: "When I am lifted up from the earth, [I] will draw all people to myself" (John 12:32). In the Colossians hymn, we find that the final unification of all things will take place through Jesus, but the description is made precise: "through the blood of his cross" (Col. 1:20). Consistently therefore, Christian revelation insists that the most radical sort of being-for-the-other—self-donation—is the nature of the Logos that has marked all created reality. Invoking Marshall's negative formulation of the epistemic priority of Christ, we must say then that any philosophy, science, or worldview that does not see relationality, being-for-the-other, as ontologically fundamental must be false. To state it more positively, we can assert that what the mind correctly seeks as it goes out to meet the intelligibility of the real is always a form of coinherence.

In the thirteenth century, Bonaventure maintained that all of the nontheological arts and sciences taught in the university find their proper center in theology, the

---

4. See George Steiner, *After Babel: Aspects of Language and Translation* (Oxford: Oxford University Press, 1998), 110.

science that speaks directly of Christ the Logos.[5] As the rationality of God the Creator, Christ is the physical, mathematical, and metaphysical center of the universe and hence the point of orientation for all of the sciences dealing with those dimensions.

In the nineteenth century, at the high-water mark of modern foundationalism, John Henry Newman felt compelled to call for the reinsertion of theology in the circle of university disciplines. Following the inner logic of Christian revelation, Newman, like Bonaventure, saw that theology not only should be around the table but must be the centering element in the conversation, precisely because it alone speaks of the Creator God who is metaphysically implicit in all finite existence.[6] Thus the sciences become hypermaterialist and reductive when they are severed from their theological ground, and the arts, when celebrated for their own sake, apart from a theological purpose, become morbid, sentimental, or bizarre; even abstract mathematics devolves into a fussy and self-preoccupied rationalism when its link to sacred geometry is lost. And Newman saw that, once theology is displaced, some other discipline necessarily takes its position at the center and thereby disturbs the proper harmony among the sciences, for no other discipline has the range or inclusiveness properly to hold the center.

I stand in this tradition as I call for the epistemic primacy of Christ, and I see the same implication for the other intellectual disciplines. Though theology obviously does not determine the particular methods, strategies, and techniques of the individual sciences, it does legitimately name their fundamental orientation as a quest for the intelligibility of coinherent relationality.

## A Praxis of Epistemic Participation

If relationality is the basic form of the real, then it follows that the optimal mode of knowing is through relation with the thing or event to be known. If mutual participation is the fundamental form of intelligibility, then the subject's participation in the object, and the object's sharing in the subject, is the most correct epistemic method. This insight corresponds to the ancient dictum that like is known by like. How odd all of this sounds to one shaped by the concern for sheer objectivity in knowing. On such a reading, a thing is properly known in the measure that the distorting perspective and prejudice of the subject are eliminated. But such an epistemology assumes just the conflictual and atomistic metaphysics rendered otiose by the claim that mutuality is the ultimately real.

A tour of a few aspects of Thomas Aquinas's deeply Christian account of knowledge helps to illustrate the principle I have invoked. In the light of the New Testament, Thomas, as we have seen, held that all things are intelligible because they are thought into being by the Creator God. God doesn't know things because

5. Bonaventure, "Unus est magister noster Christus," in *Le Christ Maitre*, ed. Goulven Madec (Paris: J. Vrin, 1990).

6. John Henry Newman, *The Idea of a University* (Notre Dame, IN: University of Notre Dame Press, 1986).

they exist (as we do); rather, they exist because he knows them. There is, there-fore, a correspondence at the deepest level between knower and known in the very constitution of finite reality: being known by another, namely God, is the ontological perfection of a created thing. This correlation, this mutuality, is played out, *mutatis mutandis*, at the level of purely finite knowing. For Thomas, the intel-ligibility of an object calls out to a potential knower, and the knower seeks out the intelligibility of the object, each one finding its perfection in the other. The intelligible thing is lit up and brought to fulfillment in the act of being known, and the knower's desire is fulfilled in the same act. It is decidedly not the case for Thomas that the knower imposes an intelligibility on the object that it otherwise wouldn't have (as in more typically modern construals), but at the same time, the knower is not distanced from the object in the act of knowing—just the contrary. A sort of harmony or consonance is established between knower and known in any act of real intellection. Fergus Kerr comments that Aquinas's epistemology is not of the "subjective-observer" type but of the "objective-participant" variety.[7]

All of this is caught in the wonderfully understated scholastic adage *Intellectus in actu est intelligibile in actu*: the intellect actualized by the object *is* the actualization of the intelligibility of that object. This is neither the imposition of meaning on the object by the subject nor the total bracketing of the subject in favor of brute objectivity; rather, it is the mutual illumination of both subject and object in the coinherent act of knowing. The mystical dimension of ordinary knowing becomes clear when we recall that the mutuality between finite knower and finite known is a participation in that elemental mutuality between divine knower and creature that constitutes the very being of the creature. That is, the intellectual coinherence of God and creature—the relationality that the creature *is*—is mimicked in a real though imperfect way in the coinherence between the ordinary act of intelligence and ordinary intelligibility.

In the eighteenth century, Goethe voiced a critique of the regnant Newtonian form of reason, which is to say, a rationality fiercely analytical, experimental, and invasive.[8] The Newtonian scientist rather aggressively drew the object into the world of the subject, compelling it to respond to the subject's concerns and ques-tions. Goethe proposed in its place a more contemplative form of rationality, one that respected the otherness of the object, carefully following its rhythms and structure, refusing to impose itself. Hence the Goethean knower would not rip the plant from the ground in order to dissect it but would instead sit with the plant in its own environment, draw it, document its movements, and so on, allowing it to ask and answer its own questions.

Thomas's account, with its roots in the New Testament and not in modernity, goes beyond the split between Newton and Goethe. It is not a matter of privileging

---

7. Fergus Kerr, *After Aquinas: Versions of Thomism* (Oxford: Blackwell, 2002), 27.

8. See Hans Urs von Balthasar, *The Glory of the Lord: A Theological Aesthetics*, vol. 5, *The Realm of Metaphysics in the Modern Age* (San Francisco: Ignatius, 1990), 362–63.

either subject or object but rather of seeing the essential link between them, born of the unbreakable bond between knower and known, which itself is grounded in the even more basic connection between divine knower and creaturely existence. That mind, object, and Creator coinhere is assumed by Aquinas. When that coinherence is questioned, as it was in the modern period, we face the finally unresolvable dilemma between Newtonian and Goethean epistemology, between the demands of the subject and the integrity of the object. What Thomas proposes is an active mutuality of knower and known that can be properly described as a type of love. It is not as though the subject utterly effaces itself in the presence of the object or that the object surrenders utterly to the demands of the subject. On the contrary, each, in a way proper to itself, gives itself to the other and finds its own perfection in that coinherence.

It is against this background that we should understand Aquinas's definition of the truth as *adequatio rei et intellectus*, the correlation of thing and intellect. This has been taken as a classical expression of the correspondence theory of truth frequently and gleefully attacked by its critics from William James to Richard Rorty.[9] The difficulty, of course, is that the critics read the Aquinas definition through the lens of the modern demarcation of subject and object and thereby misinterpret it. They assume that Aquinas imagined a self-contained subject trying to effect a correspondence with the objective world through a mental picture or proposition, as in the early Wittgenstein. In fact, the *adequatio rei et intellectus* that Aquinas speaks of is the mutually enhancing coinherence of objective intelligibility and the subjective act of intelligence. *Res* is not a "thing" dumbly out there but an actuality oriented to real and possible knowers, and *intellectus* is not so much a mental space that is to be filled with adequate representations of objects as an operation of the mind called into actuality through participation in the intelligibility of the objective realm.

Lonergan comments that there are two types of emptiness: that of the box and that of the stomach. The box is dumbly empty, whereas the stomach is, if you will, intelligently empty, since it knows what it wants. The mind, prior to experience, is empty (hence a *tabula rasa*), but empty like a stomach, since by its nature it seeks participation with being. And as the word itself suggests, existence is a standing out from itself (*ex-istere*). To exist is to emerge into the light of intelligibility, to show up, to become available to a possible knower. The truth as *adequatio* that Thomas insists upon is the meeting of these two other-oriented, "extraverted" dynamics of knower and known.

Here we might actually effect a link between this Christian idea of epistemic participation and William James's account of knowing. Basic to James's epistemology is the conviction that the categories of subject and object have to be transcended in favor of a unified notion of experience.[10] The knower, for him, is not a detached

9. See Richard Rorty, *Philosophy and the Mirror of Nature* (Princeton: Princeton University Press, 1979), esp. 44–45.

10. William James, *The Principles of Psychology* (Cambridge, MA: Harvard University Press, 1981), 262–75.

observer, hovering outside of the world of objects and seeking an adequate account of them; on the contrary, the knower is a swimmer in the never-ending and always unfolding current of life, plunging, coasting, floating, diving into the stream, sometimes navigating it with relative success, often carried away by it. Or to shift the metaphor, the knower is like a bird that flies along the air currents of existence, now perching, now looking, now being carried aloft against its will. So tight in fact is the connection between knower and known that the usual distinctions we make between them break down and they become aspects of one totality. For James, the seer is affected by what he sees, and what he sees is changed in the act of being seen, each one conditioned by the moves of the other. "Experience" is the name that James gives to this irreducible unity that can be examined, for the sake of argument and according to one's purposes, under the aegis of either subjectivity or objectivity. It is on the basis of this radical *Ineinander* of subject and object that James objects to the classical "correspondence" theory of truth, but what is his own account but a particularly dramatic assertion of knowing through epistemic participation?

A real advance in epistemology effected by James, but one in continuity with the participation view I have been proposing, is his claim that emotion is as involved in the act of knowing as is intellection. James was concerned that a one-sided valorization of the rational effectively cuts one off from enormously important dimensions of experience that can be accessed only in nonrational ways. This principle, of course, guides much of his work in the philosophy of religion, but it can and should be applied more generally to all forms of knowing. Indeed, most of the great advances in the sciences have taken place not through plodding rational analysis but through intuitive insights, hunches, feelings, emotionally charged gropings in the direction of things only vaguely seen.

James has been echoed recently by Martha Nussbaum, who insists that feelings such as jealousy, sadness, loss, and longing have a cognitive value in the measure that they amount to an assessment of the importance of a given object. In the involving account of her mother's death, Nussbaum shows that her intense feelings of anxiety and grief in the wake of her mother's passing indicated, far more clearly than did her thinking, just who her mother was and what she meant to her.[11] The emotions are, in a sense, the body's way of knowing the truth.

None of this, it seems to me, is the least bit incompatible with the Christian doctrine of knowing through coinherent participation. What it adds is the clear sense of emotion and body as vehicles of a more intense participation in the object to be known.

## Intersubjectivity

One of the principal illusions of Descartes was the conviction that he could find epistemic *terra firma* by retreating into the privacy of his own subjectivity. Turning

---

11. Martha Nussbaum, *Upheavals of Thought: The Intelligence of Emotions* (Cambridge: Cambridge University Press, 2001), esp. 19–49.

away from the world (which he took to be a realm of incertitude) and from his fellow seekers (who did nothing but disagree with each other), Descartes turned toward the *cogito*, the stubbornly private "I think." But this, as we saw, is operationally self-defeating. Descartes couldn't even make the moves that he did without the intensely intersubjective facts of language and culture, and his very willingness to write down what he experienced witnesses to his clear interest in other minds as a test of truth. Lonergan gave voice to much of postmodernity's dissatisfaction with this side of the Cartesian project when he implied that the *cogitamus* matters much more than the *cogito*. Whenever a mathematician cogitates, she is assuming a whole range of truths—from the multiplication tables to the value of pi—that she has never verified for herself. Rather, she is relying on the work of others in the tradition, work furthermore that has been independently verified by the theorizing and practical applications of thousands upon thousands of researchers, teachers, builders, and so on, across the centuries. Were she intent upon Cartesian certitude, grounded in her own verification of truth, she would never get a serious project off the ground. The same can be said, of course, of any scientist. Every astronomer, physicist, chemist, or biologist assumes unquestioningly in his own work a staggering number of observations, calculations, and measurements that have been made by others. Every act of knowledge that the mathematician or scientist achieves is, inescapably, intersubjective, a *cogitamus* much more than a *cogito*.

But the one who assumes the epistemic priority of Jesus Christ should be perfectly at home with this assertion of the dimension of intersubjectivity in knowing. We have already seen that for the Christian the form of objective intelligibility is coherence and that the method of accessing the truth is radical and mutual participation of knower and known. For the Christian, authentic knowledge comes not through isolation or objectification but rather through something like love. Therefore it should not be surprising that the fullness of knowing would occur through an intersubjective process, with knowers, as it were, participating in one another as each participates in the thing to be known. If, as the Johannine prologue implies, the ground of being is a conversation between two divine speakers, it seems only reasonable that the search for intelligibility here below takes place in the context of a steady and loving conversation.

In a lyrical and compelling section of *Truth and Method*, Hans-Georg Gadamer reminds us that a healthy conversation is something like a game.[12] As two players surrender to the movement and rules of the game of tennis, they are carried away beyond themselves in such a way that the game is playing them much more than they are playing it. In a very similar way, when two or more interlocutors enter into the rhythm of an intellectual exchange, respectful of its rules and of one another, they are quite often carried beyond their individual concerns and questions and taken somewhere they had not anticipated, the conversation having played

12. Hans-Georg Gadamer, *Truth and Method* (New York: Continuum, 1990), 101–34.

them. The fundamental requirement for this sort of shared self-transcendence is a moral one: each conversationalist has to surrender her need to dominate the play for her purposes; each must efface herself, not only before the others but, more importantly, before the transcendent goal that they all seek. To have a conversation is humbly to accept the possibility that one's take on things might be challenged or corrected, that the other's perspective might be more relatively right than one's own.

David Burrell has argued in a very similar vein that friendship must provide the matrix for any productive intellectual exchange. This means more than mere mutual respect, as indispensable as that is. Drawing on Aristotle, Burrell states that a friendship will endure only in the measure that the two friends have given themselves to a transcendent third, to the good, or the true, or the beautiful that surpasses both of them and that both seek together. As long as their love is centered on one another, it will dissipate; when it is directed beyond them, it will, paradoxically, thrive. So the truth is best sought by friends, because friends, by definition, will efface themselves before it. Obviously two or more people locked in antagonism, each trying to refute the other and defend his own claims, will rarely move toward the truth, since concern for the truth has become subordinate to their animosity and egotism. By the same token, two or more people infatuated with one another will rarely discover the truth since it has similarly been subordinated to their interest in one another.

In his remarkable studies of ancient philosophy, Pierre Hadot has shown that the philosophical schools of antiquity were not so much academies where a doctrine was learned as training grounds where a form of life was inculcated. "Philosophy" was a way of being in the world, and the ancient masters—Pythagoras, Socrates, Plato, Aristotle, Epicurus—were the personal embodiments of that way.[13] Students came to them not so much to learn their objective teaching as to apprentice to them learning the lifestyle that would conduce to wisdom and ethical excellence. Thus, the Platonic dialogues should not be read primarily as repositories of Plato's key philosophical ideas but as instruction manuals for how to engage in a constructive philosophical conversation. In the *Republic*, for example, we apprentice to the master Socrates in his calm detachment, his concentration on the issue at hand, his use of apt metaphors—and most important, his subtle and respectful manner of engaging his interlocutors. And we take as a negative model Thrasymachus in his anger, rashness of judgment, arrogance, and lack of respect for a truth that transcends his self-interest. The clear implication is that one is invited not so much to think like Socrates as to be like him.

One senses much the same thing in the writings of Thomas Aquinas. His first responsibility as a master of theology was the preaching of the Word; this obligation led to Scripture commentary and the holding of disputed questions

13. Pierre Hadot, *Philosophy as a Way of Life: Spiritual Exercises from Socrates to Foucault* (Oxford: Blackwell, 1995), 81–108.

on controversial issues. These *quaestiones disputatae* were public debates, lively exchanges between master and students, the latter posing objections of all varieties and the former compelled to respond respectfully and with persuasive counterarguments. The dynamism and style of these public dialogues were mimicked (to greater or lesser degree of fidelity) in the literary form adopted by Aquinas in practically all his writings. A question is posed (even one as basic as *utrum Deus sit*), objections are brought forward in a logically coherent way, a citation from a scriptural or patristic authority is given, a definitive answer is laid out, and finally the objections are carefully reconsidered in light of the answer. Hardly ever does Aquinas brush an objection aside as simpleminded or irrelevant; in point of fact, usually the response shows the validity of some element of the objection.[14] Chesterton said that a love for the tradition is a willingness to embrace "the democracy of the dead," giving those long gone a voice in the living conversation.[15] This valorization of the tradition is everywhere apparent in Aquinas's method: he quotes biblical authorities, fathers of the church, pagan philosophers, Muslim commentators, and Jewish rabbis always with reverence. Aristotle is "the Philosopher," Averroes is "the Commentator," and Maimonides is always "rabbi Moyses." Thomas's page is thus characterized not by authoritarian diktats but by a vivid back-and-forth movement of question and answer, a disciplined and respectful give-and-take of objection and response. We might press the matter and say that Thomas's method encourages the virtue of friendship necessary for a productive pursuit of the truth. Now just as Platonists transformed the dialogues into doctrine, Thomists distilled Thomas's conversations into clear and distinct ideas. Yet one senses that for Aquinas the ultimate purpose was not indoctrination but the inculcation of method, a radically intersubjective way of thinking.

This picture would remain crucially incomplete if we did not clarify further the limits and rules of a productive intellectual conversation. As we have seen, humility, openness to the other, a willingness to be corrected, and inclusion of challenging perspectives are all necessary for dialogue, but conversation devolves into shrill chattering unless certain restrictions are in place. Obviously, Gadamer respects the table of conversation, but he doesn't invite absolutely everyone to the table. Were there too many conversants, no one could cogently hear an argument. Were there people incapable of fluent and coherent speech, the discussion would never get under way. And most important, were there people around the table who did not share the moral convictions of the community of conversation, a sort of verbal violence would hold sway. Similarly, Aquinas attends to an impressive array of perspectives, and he listens to an extraordinarily diverse community of scholars, but he doesn't entertain every objection, and he doesn't listen to every voice. Some arguments are just silly, which is to say, they don't participate, even

14. Robert Barron, *Thomas Aquinas: Spiritual Master* (New York: Crossroad, 1996), 32, 60.
15. G. K. Chesterton, *Orthodoxy*, in *Collected Works* (San Francisco: Ignatius, 1986), 1:251.

in an elementary way, in the truth of the Logos; and some arguers are stupid or disrespectful, which is to say, they don't allow themselves to be conformed, even marginally, to the moral demands of the Logos. Thus, it is an intellectually and ethically disciplined intersubjectivity that honors the Christ-mind.

We find something similar in the writings of John Henry Newman, a thinker who in many ways inherited the virtues of both the ancient philosophical and the classical Christian traditions. In his *Essay on the Development of Christian Doctrine*, which he wrote during the time of his transition from Anglicanism to Roman Catholicism, Newman pulls the neat trick of using the fact of doctrinal development to validate a more ancient and "conservative" version of Christianity. Protestantism, he argues, solves the problem of development in teaching and practice by essentially ignoring it, radically valorizing the form of Christian life discernible in the scriptural witness.[16] Whatever deviates from that norm is a corruption; whatever imitates it is a valid expression of Christianity. But Newman was profoundly uneasy with this proposal, since it required the believer to bracket practically the whole of church history from the earliest patristic period until modern times. Councils, lives of the saints, speculations of theologians, innumerable practical developments would all have to be seen, ipso facto, as corruptions. Anglicanism employed a more subtle method with roots in the speculation of Vincentius of Lerins. Vincent had said famously that legitimate Christian teaching is that which has been held *semper, ubique, et ab omnibus* (always, everywhere, and by everybody). Deviations are, of course, many, but the truths of the faith enjoy a discernible universality across time and space.[17] But here again, Newman balked. For if this Vincentian principle were consistently applied, one would have to say that doctrines of the Trinity and the divinity of Christ are not valid Christian teaching, since they have certainly not been believed everywhere and by all: think only of the lengthy period during which Arianism held sway.

What Newman proposed, in line with the *Lebensphilosophie* of his time, was the notion of the development of doctrine. Any idea, he said, is a living thing, since it exists only in a lively mind. The mind is not what Hume thought it was, an empty theater in which ideas dumbly appear; rather, the mind is a restless, curious instrument that constantly turns ideas over and around, sifting, weighing, assessing them, wondering about them and comparing them to other ideas. An idea is like a multifaceted diamond, and the fullness of it is "the sum total of its possible aspects."[18] In accord with his deep anti-Cartesianism, Newman holds that this manifestation of the totality of an idea is not possible simply through the efforts of one mind, however subtle and vigorous. On the contrary, it is only when an idea has been brought to the far richer and more powerful sifting process of an entire community of minds that it begins fully to show itself.

16. John Henry Newman, *An Essay on the Development of Christian Doctrine* (Westminster, MD: Christian Classics, 1968), 8.

17. Ibid., 10.

18. Ibid., 34.

Now if this is true with regard to ideas in general—even relatively simple—how much truer when one of the master ideas of Christian faith is under consideration. The incarnation, for instance, is so inexhaustibly rich a concept that its aspects, implications, dimensions, and applications can only appear gradually and through an especially concentrated play of lively minds. No one thinker, no one community of discourse, no one school, no one time could possibly exhaust such an idea. This is, of course, precisely why the idea of the incarnation has had a rich history, stretching from the biblical period, through the roiled debates of the early councils, to the speculations of Augustine and Aquinas, to the ruminations of the mystics, and finally to the work of the political and liberation theologians of our time. Without this process of intersubjective weighing, turning, and assessing, the notion of the incarnation couldn't even have begun to present itself with relative adequacy. Rahner suggested this evolutionary quality of the idea of the incarnation in his programmatic essay "Chalcedon: Beginning or End." Obviously, the Chalcedonian formula ended the christological debate in a significant sense by precluding certain interpretive possibilities. In Newman's language, it closed off certain corrupt readings. At the same time, in the very laconicism of its expression, it called forth further development, amplification, and explanation.

Newman was uneasy with both modernity and Protestantism in regard to this living quality of ideas. In its Cartesian and Newtonian forms, modernity seemed to suggest that the private knower, through an immediate intuition or a disciplined empirical analysis, can unambiguously grasp the truth of nature, and Lutheran Protestantism held that the individual believer, reading the Bible without the interpretive aid of the church, can understand the deepest truths of salvation. Both assumed a certain stasis at the level of ideas and a subjectivism at the level of epistemology. For Newman, knowing is more like a disciplined game involving a ball perpetually in motion and a team of lively players, in accord with definite rules, alternately tossing, holding, passing, and kicking it.

## A Mind in Love

The first words out of the mouth of Jesus in Mark's Gospel are these: "The time is fulfilled, and the kingdom of God has come near; repent, and believe in the good news" (Mark 1:15). The term translated by the moralizing "repent" is *metanoeite*, derived from two words, *meta* (beyond) and *nous* (mind). Jesus is urging his hearers not primarily to change their behavior but to go beyond the mind that they have, to see things in a new way, to adopt a different attitude.[19] Essential to this epistemic conversion is faith (*pistis*), for he implies that the *metanoia* will make possible the trusting acceptance of the good news: *pisteuete ton euangelion*. This is not so much acceptance of new data as willingness to enter into the world opened up by the novelty of Jesus himself, to believe what has become a possibility in

19. Robert Barron, *And Now I See: A Theology of Transformation* (New York: Crossroad, 1998), 4.

him. As becomes clear in the course of the Gospels, the kingdom of God is not primarily social reform, ethical renewal, or political transformation (though it gives rise to all of these); the kingdom, first, is Jesus himself, the coming together of divinity and humanity, the Word made flesh.

What is the opposite of this trust? What is the quality of mind that must be transformed in the course of *metanoia*? At the close of the narrative of the calming of the storm at sea, as the disciples, half-afraid, half-fascinated, look up at Jesus, the Master says to them, "Why are you afraid? Have you still no faith?" (Mark 4:40). The implication is that the opposite of trust is fear, a turning in on oneself, a refusal to move into the power of Jesus's way of being. To have the Christ-mind is to know the world not through the distorting lens of one's self-absorption and fear but through the clarifying lens of the kingdom, which is to say, the coming together of divinity and humanity. To enter trustingly into that surprising coinherence of Creator and creature is to adopt the right way of seeing all that can be seen.

At the very beginning of the *Summa Theologiae*, Thomas Aquinas, as we have seen, holds that theology is a discipline that goes beyond the range of the philosophical sciences. Revelation-based *sacra doctrina* orients us to the properly supernatural end that, in a curious paradox, is naturally ours. And if we turn to the beginning of the third part of the *Summa*, we find that the culmination of revelation is the event of the incarnation. Theological vision is, accordingly, an ecstatic form of seeing, conditioned by the novelty of the enfleshment of God, and the theologian, by definition, is someone who is willing to be drawn up beyond herself in an attitude of trust in the power of that miracle. In terms of Mark's Gospel, the theological knower is one who has undergone *metanoia*, a radical transformation of vision through the incarnation. But if, as I have been arguing, the theological mind is the paradigmatic mind, then all forms of human knowing are, at their best, marked by this same trust, this same capacity for ecstasy, this same willingness to see the world in terms of an incarnational teleology.

In one of his sharply worded attacks on Aristotelian scholasticism, Martin Luther said that the fatal flaw in Aristotle's metaphysics and epistemology is their focus on being, which is to say, the present constitution of a thing. Though he remained interested in past and future (efficient and final causality), Aristotle held that the proper object of philosophical investigation is substance (*ousia*). But this, says Luther, from the biblical perspective, is distorted, for God is far more interested in the future, the ultimate destiny, of things. This appears most plainly in the renaming of key figures throughout the biblical narrative: Abram becomes Abraham, Jacob becomes Israel, Simon becomes Peter, Saul becomes Paul. Through this shifting of names, God signals that he reads each of these figures from the perspective of the future. He is interested in them in the measure that they serve the divine purpose of bringing about the transformation of the world through grace. Furthermore, when the philosopher makes the present the focus of his intellectual concern, he labors under the illusion that he is in control of the object to be known, when in point of fact it is only the Lord of the future who truly knows. Therefore, a trusting decentering of the ego is an essential element in a Christian epistemology. Luther's criticism can be seen as an extremely prescient anticipation of a modern science that would almost completely bracket questions of teleology and divine intentionality, rendering a scientistic, immanentist view of the universe. The mind that has undergone *metanoia* reads all things through the lens of the incarnation, which is to say, from the perspective of the absolute future that God holds out to his world.

We see something related if we consult the much-commented-upon hymn text that Paul integrates into his Letter to the Philippians. The author urges his readers to "let the same mind be in you that was in Christ Jesus" and then proceeds to spell out the nature of this attitude: "Though he was in the form of God, [Jesus] did not regard equality with God as something to be exploited, but emptied himself, taking the form of a slave, being born in human likeness" (Phil. 2:5–7). Like Jesus in his inaugural address in Mark's Gospel, Paul is inviting his listeners to *metanoia*, a transformation of mind, more precisely, a taking on of the mind that characterizes Christ himself. If in the Markan context this conversion was a matter of moving from fear to trust, here it amounts to the transition from arrogance to humility or autonomy to obedience. Jesus's mind (which remains the absolute criterion for all correct knowledge) is, in a supreme paradox, a mind that obeys, that does not cling to its own prerogatives but rather looks to the direction of another—the Father. And this obedience is total, for he "became obedient to the point of death—even death on a cross" (Phil. 2:8). This is the mind that Paul urges us to adopt, one capable of total other-orientation, complete self-denial, one that looks stubbornly to the purposes of the other who is God.

In line with his Thomist intuitions, Bernard Lonergan appreciated God (the fullness of being) as the lure for the mind, even in its simplest acts of cognition. Whenever the mind seeks truth, it is operating under the impulse and aegis of the Truth itself; whenever it endeavors to see, it is implicitly seeking the fullness of the beatific vision, the act that would be, in Lonergan's famous phrase, "knowing everything about everything."[20] God's intelligence has grounded the intelligibility of the world and hence animated the intelligently seeking human mind. This entails, first, that the dynamisms of the mind must be fundamentally extraverted, oriented to the other. The cognitive act corrupts when it turns inward, thwarting its own natural tendency outward toward the fullness of all that can be known. It implies, second, that any cognitive act is a sort of obedience to God, for God is the Truth that suffuses all that can be known. In light of these basic epistemic assumptions Lonergan formulated his imperatives to any and all knowers: "Be attentive, be intelligent, be reasonable, be responsible."[21] All four of these are calls to overcome self-absorption, to look outward, to conform oneself to the demands

20. Bernard Lonergan, *Understanding and Being*, in *The Collected Works of Bernard Lonergan*, vol. 5 (Toronto: University of Toronto Press, 1990), esp. 146–55.

21. Bernard Lonergan, *Method in Theology* (Toronto: University of Toronto Press, 1990), 18.

of the all-surrounding divine truth. As such, they are directives to habituate the mind toward love and trust in God. They are a summons toward *metanoia*.

To be attentive—to see, hear, taste, smell, and touch what is before us—is much more difficult than it may seem. If the mind were simply a *tabula rasa*, it would but have to rest passively before being and allow itself to be written on. But the mind is alert even in its emptiness. It has consequently to look in a focused and disciplined way, avoiding the lazy tendency to accept the "obvious." It is required to take time before an object or event, seeing its many aspects, watching it unfold across time and space. Above all, it must overcome its tendency toward selective perception, seeing only what it wants to see, only what it might be convenient to see. To be attentive is to take in the novel, the strange, the deeply disconcerting, the dangerous. It is to respect what God has chosen to create in all of its uniqueness and specificity and not presume that one knows the physical world a priori.

To be intelligent, in Lonergan's sense, is to look for formal patterns, to seek out the intelligible structures that run through whatever exists. The summons to intelligence corresponds to the assumption of universal reasonability, the mystical intuition that undergirds the sciences. But this assumption is only the beginning, the condition for the possibility of real intelligence. The actual seeing of the pattern is as difficult and demanding as real attentiveness, involving a perception that is both penetrating and playful.

When a scientist has been sufficiently attentive to the data before her, she begins to formulate a series of hypotheses, likely explanations for their unique arrangement. She senses a number of possible intelligible patterns that undergird the phenomenon under investigation—some simple, others complex, still others quite speculative and unlikely. This arraying of intellectual possibilities—hypotheses to be tested—is what Lonergan means by *intelligence*. It is contained in a series of often interrelated "aha" experiences, insights, graspings of form.

In *A Portrait of the Artist as a Young Man*, James Joyce gives a wonderful description of aesthetic intelligence. In the context of a lively discussion of the nature of beauty, Stephen Daedalus asks his friend Lynch to consider "a basket which a butcher's boy had slung inverted on his head."[22] He then invites him to examine the basket more closely, "passing from point to point, led by its formal lines, apprehending it as balanced part against balanced part, feeling the rhythm of its structure." To see at this level, to participate with the mind in the rhythm of a thing's formal complexity, to sense what Aquinas called its *consonantia*, is to be intelligent. In both the scientific and aesthetic contexts we sense a similar demand and commitment: the seeing of the form calls one outside of himself into a sort of ecstatic participation in the thing or event under investigation. The "rhythm of structure" has a primacy, compelling the mind into imitation.

22. James Joyce, *A Portrait of the Artist as a Young Man*, in *The Portable James Joyce*, ed. Harry Levin (New York: Penguin, 1987), 479.

The third Lonerganian imperative is "be reasonable." This is a summons to the mind to be decisive, to make a judgment among the various hypotheses presented to it, to determine which of many admittedly bright ideas is the right idea. Finally there is only one relatively adequate explanation for a phenomenon, one rational structure that truly informs it. This emerges at the end of a long process of experimentation, reflection, discussion, the marshaling of evidence, and the arrangement of argument and counterargument. At the level of judgment, the determination of this truth is made. As the word itself suggests, decision is always a bloody business, involving a cutting off. It is enticing to contemplate a range of interesting suggestions and ideas, reveling in their possibilities, aspects, and implications; it is painful to opt ultimately for one, since it entails the leaving behind of all the others, intriguing as they are. In judgment, the knower is called to accept the hard truth, to draw the reasonable conclusion even if it goes against his hopes and expectations.

In the Christian vision, the truth of a thing is a reflection of the Truth that made it, a participation in the Logos that informs it. Making a judgment is, accordingly, honoring the will of the Creator God, following his more elemental decision. Lonergan speaks frequently of the properly functioning mind as having the "unrestricted desire to know." To have this desire is to want the truth above all, without cavil or hesitation, and hence it is to love God with one's mind, to seek God even at the greatest cost. Here we see the connection to the Pauline hymn in Philippians. To have the same mind that was in Christ Jesus is to have a desire to follow the will of the Father even to the total emptying out of one's self. Jesus judged that the will of the Father was that he come to the cross. Though every emotion and inclination in him veered away from that fate (as is recounted in the Gethsemane narrative), he perdured in his judgment. The Christian knower is the one who, in a similar way, honors God through her judgment, overcoming the self-absorption that would blind her to the truth.

The final of the Lonerganian imperatives—"be responsible"—is a call to live out the implications of one's judgments. Having seen things in a particular way, having decided, now one must adjust one's body, feelings, and actions to that vision. This could take the form of publishing certain findings, undergoing a moral conversion, resolving to pray, seeking reconciliation with a former friend, going to war, or going to confession. Some people are remarkably attentive, sparklingly intelligent, even decisive, but remain incapable of living out their decisions. But those who lack the courage of their convictions are, despite their intellectual achievements, alienated from a participation in truth, for as the Gospel of John suggests, the truth is finally something that one does. This final imperative draws the knower out of herself into an ecstasy that involves the totality of her existence. To follow it is to participate in the truth with body, will, mind, and heart. If the four imperatives are followed habitually and the mind is thereby allowed to develop in accord with its deepest intentionality, one grows into the state of being "unconditionally in love with God," which is to say, unrestrictedly conformed to the demands of the truth. This is the mind and heart of the saint; this is the Christ-mind in its fullest expression. It is the mind that has undergone *metanoia*.

The central tension of this chapter comes once more to the surface: How is the particularity of the Christ-mind related to the mind as such? Can someone who has surrendered to the Christian form of cognition enter into conversation with a non-Christian? Or to turn the question around: Wouldn't a non-Christian happily admit that the well-functioning mind operates according to something like Lonergan's imperatives? Could there be a Buddhist, a Hindu, an agnostic scientist, an atheist social commentator who would not say that it is a desideratum to be attentive, intelligent, reasonable, and responsible? And if that is true, then how are any of these imperatives distinctively Christian?

Lonergan helps us to see how these are finally only pseudoproblems. Christians maintain that the Logos that became incarnate in Jesus Christ is the Logos by which all things, including the mind, are made. Hence it should not be surprising that what appears explicitly as an epistemic implication of the incarnation is participated in to varying degrees by anyone who exercises his mind in a responsible way. Here we are close to Aquinas's treatment of the relation between theology and the "natural" reason that explores the *preambula fidei*: both are participations in the Logos, the former being far more intense and complete than the latter, but both stemming ultimately from the same source. Lest this sound too bland, too much like a mere distinction in degree and not kind, we must consider that the Christian is called to a love of the truth that mirrors the Truth's love of him or her, and that this love is manifested as a gift of self unto death. The Lonerganian "saint," the one unrestrictedly in love with God, is someone marked by the Christ-pattern, the kenosis of the mind and self in the presence of the truth.

If we combine the two insights that I have been developing in this section, we might say that the mind by which all things came to be, through which they subsist, and by which they will be reconciled, the mind, furthermore, by which a knower properly understands all things, is one of other-orientation, trust, and obedience. It is a mind that looks with uncompromising attention to the present and future intentions of God in the world. The perspective that cannot be contextualized or positioned by any higher perspective—the Christ-mind—is a mind of love and in love.


## The Fallen Mind

It is a commonplace of the Christian tradition that the fall had implications at all levels of a person's being. Original sin affected not only the will but the body, the passions, the imagination, and the mind as well.[23] Because of sin, each of the

---

23. "And if one were to deny . . . that the whole Adam, because of that sinful disobedience, was changed in body and soul for the worse, let him be anathema." *Decree concerning Original Sin*, para. 1, in *Decrees of the Ecumenical Councils*, ed. Norman Tanner (London: Sheed and Ward, 1990), 666.

powers within a person has become corrupt, and, more to the point, they have fallen into disharmony with one another. What God intended to be a smoothly functioning and well-integrated organism has become a diseased body—able to operate but slow, disjointed, awkward, at cross-purposes to itself. Nowhere is this disjointedness more powerfully described than in chapter 7 of Paul's Letter to the Romans: "So I find it to be a law that when I want to do what is good, evil lies close at hand. For I delight in the law of God in my inmost self, but I see in my members another law at war with the law of my mind, making me captive to the law of sin that dwells in my members" (Rom. 7:21–23). To some degree, Paul would have realized this inner disharmony through the Greek philosophical tradition to which he was heir. As we have seen, the philosophical schools of the ancient world were moral training grounds, places where one passed through a strict discipline in order to learn how properly to think. It was a basic assumption among these philosophers that there is something wrong with the way most people naturally act and reason. But Paul knew the depths of the problem from the biblical tradition, which puts the dysfunction of human beings—even heroes such as Moses and David—on constant display.

Paul bequeathed this sense of the fallen self to the subsequent Christian tradition, where it was especially developed by Augustine. The *Confessions* is the story of how a darkened mind comes very gradually and painfully to a glimpse of the light; *The City of God* is the account of how a corrupt and perverted civilization is called to conversion; and *De Trinitate* is an account of how a poorly ordered soul achieves integration through an alignment with the persons of the Trinity. All three works are unintelligible without the undergirding assumption of the fall and its effects.

From Augustine, this notion was transferred to the medieval Christian consciousness. We have already seen how for Thomas the sinful mind is sunk in the *tenebrae*, unable properly to see, appreciate, or evaluate the world. But the theme of the fallen mind is even more clearly emphasized in Thomas's colleague Bonaventure, who, anticipating Luther, remained extremely wary of what he took to be the overconfident and immanentist speculations of the Aristotelians of his own time. What particularly bothered Bonaventure was the blithe assumption that a Christian could uncritically take in the thinking of a philosopher whose mind was fallen and untransformed by grace. Among the thinkers of the Reformation, this theme was taken up but in a somewhat exaggerated way. Luther's perhaps legitimate suspicions of rationalist scholasticism devolved into a complete contempt for "whore reason," and this led in turn to his embrace of the *sola scriptura* principle and his suspicion of all forms of natural theologizing.

Perhaps this very exaggeration of the motif of the fallen mind contributed to the counterreaction of the Enlightenment. All the major Enlightenment figures took for granted that there is something the matter with the mind, but they tended to see the problem as exterior rather than interior. They acknowledged that the European intellect was not functioning at full capacity, but they felt that this was not because of intrinsic weakness but because it had been shackled by uncriticized dogmatisms, clouded by religious obscurantism, and infantilized by political authoritarianism. In the mathematical method of Descartes, the strict geometry of Spinoza's ethics, and the rationalism of Kant's religion, we get some idea of what the *Aufklärers* believed the enlightened mind could produce once these various hindrances were removed. In his programmatic essay "What Is Enlightenment?" Kant calls for European intellectuals to achieve their majority, to dare to know on their own, free from the tutelage of religion and tradition.[24] The basic assumption is that the mind is good and strong but simply underdeveloped. Having witnessed the moral outrages of the twentieth century, postmodern thinkers, as we have seen, are far less impressed by the intrinsic goodness and integrity of the mind and far more willing to reconsider the Christian view of an intellect that is kinky, twisted, at odds with itself.

Once more, Lonergan helps us to grasp the nettle of this issue. As a Jesuit, Lonergan was immersed in the spiritual tradition of Ignatius of Loyola, for whom conversion was an essential lifelong preoccupation. As a philosopher and theologian, Lonergan placed special stress on this dynamic in relation to the functioning of the intellect. Throughout his writings on epistemology he asserts that the mind must be summoned to conversion, precisely because it has a tendency to dysfunction. The term *conversion*, with its religious and moral overtones, is quite apt, for the problem with the mind is not simply technical but rather personal and spiritual. The poorly operating mind is one that has turned in on itself (*curvatus in se*) and in its self-preoccupation lost contact with the objective world. It is a mind, in our terminology, insufficiently in love. Lonergan sums up his position in the wonderfully pithy observation that authentic objectivity (contact with the real) is a function of properly constituted subjectivity (the converted mind).[25] Traditionalists who complained that Lonergan's interest in the dynamics of subjectivity amounted to a surrender to Cartesianism missed the centrality of the theme of the fallen mind. If the mind were uncompromised, one could simply "turn to the things themselves," but it is the weakened intellect that prevents the "things in themselves" from properly appearing.

A return to the four imperatives explored in the last section—"be attentive, be intelligent, be reasonable, be responsible"—will be helpful here. A first mark of the fallen mind is inattentiveness: it does not contact the real because it is not alert enough to see. I mentioned above the tendency toward selective perception— seeing only what one wants or is predisposed to see—but we might also point to simple perceptive laziness. We don't take in the world because perception requires too much effort. Thus a scientist might not collect all the necessary data before launching into a theoretical explanation; a commentator might not

---

24. Immanuel Kant, "What Is Enlightenment?," in *The Foundations of the Metaphysics of Morals*, trans. Lewis White Beck (Indianapolis: Bobbs-Merrill, 1978), 85.

25. Lonergan, *Understanding and Being*, 173–74.

notice all the details of a given political battle before proffering an explication; a golfer might not take in all the vagaries of his situation before choosing a particular club. In each case, a person is willing to assert himself—theoretically or practically—without sufficient attention to the objective. Another reason for this imperative is fear: sometimes we don't or won't see because we have been told not to look. There are, of course, innumerable examples of this kind of censorship and restriction over the centuries. Religions, cultures, political regimes, schools of philosophy, and scientific establishments have all, for various reasons, placed certain areas outside the purview of attentive minds. Here we can appreciate the moral courage that is required of someone who would, in a fallen world, carry out the command to look.

A second quality of the compromised mind is unintelligence, stupidity. To be intelligent is to have insights, which is to say, to penetrate to the level of form, to appreciate the ontological patterns that characterize a given thing or situation. When asked what he took to be the essence of his artistic genius, Pablo Picasso said that it was the capacity to appreciate visual analogies: this bicycle seat is like the head of a bull; the curve of this pear is like the curve on the body of a guitar, which in turn is like the curve of a woman's figure. This sort of seeing of related patterns—Tracy's analogical imagination—is a mark of intelligence. Thus the unintelligent person is someone who is dazzled by surfaces and never seeks to look deeper, who sees light, color, and movement but never attends to texture, structure, and interconnection. To be stupid is not to raise questions such as "Why is this so?" and "What makes these many one?" and "How is this like that?" We have seen that simple attentiveness requires effort, but intelligence calls for an even greater level of engagement and self-transcendence. To seek after patterns is to ask questions relentlessly (think of Aquinas's almost manic piling up of questions in the *Summa*), to follow the evidence where it leads, to participate in endless conversation, to entertain novel perspectives. The fallen mind is marked, in Tillich's phrase, by "self-complacent finitude." Blandly at home with the superficial and the familiar, it rests in itself and thus becomes sluggish, dull-witted, uncurious. It cannot summon the moral or intellectual energy to raise even one good question, much less a series of them. Again, intimidation can play a role here. Many curious minds are cowed into complacency by the threat of punishment or ostracism.

The third mark of the fallen mind is unreasonability, the incapacity to make a judgment. In the course of a lively and curiously intelligent investigation, a thinker will entertain a number of intriguing possibilities and likely hypotheses, but, as we saw, only one can be relatively adequate. To be reasonable is to be able to discriminate from among these many the one that corresponds to the truth. The unreasonable mind stays fixed on the fence of ambivalence, unable to decide. There can be a variety of grounds for this indecision. First, a person might be entertained by the sheer beauty and multiplicity of the intellectual options on display and be unwilling to close off any of them. In that case, the aesthetic improperly triumphs over the noetic. Second, a person might, in her incertitude, be terrified to choose; or she might be concerned that a particular decision will hurt and disappoint those she loves or relies upon. Third, someone might realize that a given decision would involve a major change in her life, a change she is unwilling to make. In these cases, the desire for self-protection would improperly trump the desire for the truth. For these and many other reasons, the fallen mind, even if it has become relatively attentive and intelligent, can settle into self-regarding unreasonableness.

Finally, the mind in the *tenebrae* is irresponsible, unwilling to carry out the practical and ethical implications of a judgment. If something has been determined to be true, then the life of the one who has made the determination must be shaped in accord with that truth. Thus the responsible person makes the objective truth the norm of his subjectivity. When John Paul II calls for a clear correspondence between freedom and truth, he is responding to the fourth of Lonergan's imperatives. It is perhaps in terms of this imperative that we appreciate most readily the tragedy of the fallen mind, for the irresponsible mind is equivalent to the unintegrated self, the riven subject. Hamlet, who knows precisely what he must do but cannot do it, is irresponsible in this sense, as is Pilate, who knows full well the innocence of Jesus even as he sends him to the cross. All of Jesus's own condemnations of the Pharisees and keepers of the law hinge upon the irresponsible disconnection between their stated convictions and their concrete practice.

Therefore the fallen mind, the mind in the shadows, has a tendency toward inattentiveness, stupidity, unreasonability, and irresponsibility; it is *curvatus in se*, self-absorbed, fearful, pusillanimous. The central paradox is this: only those who have been touched by the Christ-mind, the intellect in love, realize the limitation of the minds they have. Only those who have begun to stand in the light recognize the smudges and shadows on what they had taken to be the clear transparent pane of the intellect. Just as the saints—Augustine, Francis, Thérèse of Lisieux—are most aware of their sinfulness, so those illumined by the Christ-mind are most conscious of the fallenness of their intellect. Saints of the mind realize that perfect attention, intelligence, reasonability, and responsibility are only asymptotically approached through grace, and thus they cultivate a becoming epistemic humility.

## The Incarnate Mind

The prologue to John unambiguously celebrates the transcendence and divine majesty of the Logos ("the Word was with God, and the Word was God"), but it just as clearly states the immanence and humility of that same Logos ("the Word became flesh and lived among us"). Colossians certainly stresses the sublimity and transhistoricality of Christ ("he is the image of the invisible God"), but it just as clearly posits his particularity and historicity ("he is the head of the body, the church"). In the first letter of John, we find the same juxtaposition in an even more jarring expression: "We declare to you what was from the beginning, what we have heard, what we have seen with our eyes . . . and touched with our hands, concerning the word of life" (1 John 1:1). The Word of life, existing with God from the beginning, is *touched with human hands.*

This incarnation of the Logos, celebrated in the New Testament and defended throughout the history of the church, gives to Christians a distinctive epistemic style. The Word, which has made all things and which illumines properly functioning minds, is oriented to flesh and, by implication, is at home with all of the messy particularity of time, space, history, language, and culture. This means that Christians don't seek intelligibility, even of the highest sort, apart from matter and history, and that they are consequently uneasy with epistemological dualisms and angelisms of any kind. Because the Word did not despise the flesh, Christians prefer to know, in Wittgenstein's phrase, "on the rough ground."

In a classical context, both Plato and Plotinus advocated a praxis of separation from the body as a condition for the possibility of authentic knowing. Until one manages to escape from the shackles of materiality and particularity, one is destined to remain epistemologically at the level of mere opinion; only upon effective dissociation of mind from matter (achieved through various practices) can an adept access the forms and hence attain authentic knowledge. Insight is possible but at the cost of a severe disciplining of sense and imagination. The solitariness of this process became especially clear in Plotinus. If the body is the problem, then association with other bodies, with all their attendant distortions and prejudices, simply exacerbates the difficulty. Hence, at the highest pitch of Plotinian intellection, one finds himself "alone with the Alone." In the modern framework, we find a similar dualism and subjectivism. For Descartes, since the mind is known through a clear and distinct intuition while the body belongs to the dubious realm of the sensory, there must be a radical demarcation between body and mind. And the latter must be able to function (indeed function better) in separation from the distortions and ambiguities of the former. A similar preference for the pure mind and a concomitant distrust of the physical can be seen in the austere ethics of Spinoza and in both the epistemology and religion of Kant.

An especially interesting locus of modern epistemic angelism is Locke's philosophy of mind. In his empiricism, Locke seems innocent of any charge of Platonism, Cartesianism, or epistemological dualism, but if we attend to his account of the dynamics of assent, we can pick up the strain that I have been exploring. Like most moderns, Locke was deeply concerned with clarifying and policing the process of thought so that the obscurantisms of the past might be avoided. Descartes's cluttered city was the result of sloppy thinking, and it could be rebuilt on the basis of a more careful intellectual procedure. Locke identified the key problem as the often faulty relationship between inference and assent.[26] In a word, too many people give to propositions an assent out of proportion to the quality of

---

26. See John Henry Newman, *An Essay in Aid of a Grammar of Assent* (Notre Dame, IN: University of Notre Dame Press, 1979), 136–37.

inference offered as a foundation for the assent. Thus, though I might have only a somewhat convincing argument, or perhaps even no argument at all, for a given claim, I nevertheless give my full assent to it. Or, to turn it around, though I have a very clear inferential support for a particular assertion, I only give it mild assent or no assent at all. The problem can be effectively addressed only when it is seen as a properly moral one: for Locke, it is *unethical* to give to a proposition an assent that is disproportionate to its inferential support. Thus, if one has a poor argument for a claim, he ought to give it mild assent; if he has a fairly good argument for it, he ought to give it middling assent; if he has a clinching inferential demonstration for it, he ought (in the fully moral sense of "ought") to give it full and unhesitating assent. How is one to know whether he is an authentic seeker of the truth? Locke can think of only one valid test: "There is one unerring mark of it, viz. the not entertaining any proposition with greater assurance than the proofs it is built on will warrant."[27]

John Henry Newman, though he guarded throughout his life a deep respect for Locke, made his disagreement with this Lockean proposal the centerpiece of his epistemological masterpiece *An Essay in Aid of a Grammar of Assent*. His fundamental complaint was that the tight linking of assent to inference made sense only on the assumption of some sort of epistemological angelism, "a view of the human mind . . . which seems theoretical and unreal."[28] In point of fact, says Newman, we fully assent to numerous propositions for which there is, at best, vague inferential support. We know from direct experience, for example, that numerous assents endure even long after their logical substructure has vanished or been forgotten. So many of our most basic convictions and beliefs about the world—what Newman calls "the clothing and furniture of the mind"—are accepted unquestioningly and implicitly though we could only in rare cases articulate the logical arguments upon which they are grounded. On the other hand, sometimes assent gives way even when the inferential arguments used to justify it are still vigorously in place. Though the reasons for a conviction remain unassailed, the conviction itself fails. "Sometimes our mind changes so quickly, so unaccountably, so disproportionately to any tangible arguments . . . as to suggest the suspicion that moral causes, arising out of our condition, age, company, occupations, fortunes, are at the bottom."[29] We no longer accept a proposition because someone we deeply admire does not accept it; we fail to subscribe to a point of view because we are no longer children; we stop believing something because we have suddenly lost our money and good name. In none of these cases does the transition from belief to disbelief have anything to do with shifts in the argumentative base.

Then again, sometimes assent is never given even in the face of well-crafted and persuasive arguments. Newman remarks that at times "we find men loud in their

27. John Locke, *An Essay concerning Human Understanding*, chap. 7, quoted in Newman, *Essay in Aid of a Grammar*, 138.

28. Newman, *Essay in Aid of a Grammar*, 139.

29. Ibid., 142.

admiration of truths which they never profess."[30] Though the mind might grasp the truth of a demonstration immediately, it can take years for the act of assent to develop, or though the intellect might see a necessary connection between proposition A and proposition B, the body, emotions, and heart remain unconvinced. In other cases, pressure and coercion can play a dissuasive role: Newman cites the couplet "A man convinced against his will / Is of the same opinion still." And this applies even in regard to mathematical demonstrations that play themselves out over a series of steps and logical inferences. Though each move be impeccably made, the mathematician is sometimes unable to give her assent to the proof until a number of other nonrational factors come into play.

Now on Locke's reading, these ruptures between inference and assent would be signs of moral and intellectual dysfunction, but for Newman they should not be so construed; instead they should be taken as evidence that the mind in fact does not operate according to the rationalist strictures that Locke has set for it. The mind finds itself inescapably embodied, conditioned by emotion, and situated in a social network, but this context is not a problem to be overcome; rather it is to be appreciated as itself a contributing factor to the intellectual process.

To make his critique of a one-sided rationalism more pointed, Newman examines the advantages and limitations of the classical syllogism. Newman admired Aristotle even more than Locke, but he felt that the logical tool developed by Aristotle contributed only in part to the act of assent. In its standard form, the syllogism displays itself in a tripartite way: if A and B, then C, A taken as a universal, B as an instance of A, and C as the explication of the implied relationship between A and B. What allows the syllogism to work is that symbols are substituted for words, or abstractions for individuals. Symbols and abstractions stand for pure notions, stripped as far as possible of all particularization, and it is this very streamlining that enables them to be manipulated with such compelling logical force. Words, on the other hand, are indicative of individuals in all of their peculiarity, and they accordingly carry with them a whole set of connotations, implications, connatural senses, and poetic overtones. This undisciplined, unfocused, untamable quality of words—which makes them uniquely apt in the description of the particularly real—disqualifies them from use in syllogisms. In his setting aside of words, "the logician for his own purposes . . . turns rivers, full, winding, and beautiful, into navigable canals."[31]

This means that the premises of a syllogism will effectively catch universal qualities and general trends but will tend to miss the individual exceptions to the rule. "All men have their price; Socrates is a man; therefore Socrates has his price" will be a correct calculation precisely in the measure that the unique individual Socrates is like all or most other men. In the measure that he is not, the syllogism will, despite its impressive logical structure, fail to generate the truth. Newman

30. Ibid.
31. Ibid., 215.

concludes that the syllogism is "open at both ends," implying that the nondefinitiveness of the necessarily abstract premises conduces to the nondefinitiveness of the conclusion.[32] Again, this is not to say that such a form of reasoning does not have its uses: it is, in fact, an extremely helpful indicator of the direction in which particular truth lies. But it is to say that syllogistic inference in and of itself is never enough to bring the mind to assent in concrete matters. What we notice here is the correlation between the abstract logical form of the syllogism and a purely disembodied mode of intellection. If we were pure minds (angels), the syllogism would be enough; inasmuch as we are embodied spirits in search of an incarnate truth, more is required.

This "more" Newman refers to as "informal inference." This mode of reasoning includes the formal element of syllogistic ratiocination but supplements it with a range of intuitions, feelings, hunches, and above all, an instinct for the convincing power of convergent probabilities. Newman gives several examples of the actual functioning of this mode of thinking, but the best known is his account of how we come to the unambiguous assent that Great Britain is an island.[33] No sane person doubts the claim that Great Britain is an island or would hesitate even for a moment in making practical judgments on the basis of that claim. Anyone who would seriously maintain the opposite would be considered not only intellectually deficient, but mad. But when we look for the set of clear, logical inferences upon which this assent is based, we are frustrated. We assent to the insularity of Great Britain without hesitation or cavil, even though there is no syllogism that has generated the assent. How then has the mind in forming this judgment actually operated? It has done so through the sifting and assessing of a range of probable arguments, some clearly formulated, most felt and intuited rather than explicitly thought out. That Great Britain is surrounded by water "we have been taught in our childhood, and it is so in all the maps; we have never heard it contradicted or questioned, . . . every book we have read invariably took it for granted, our whole national history, the routine transactions and current events of the country . . . imply it in one way or another."[34] None of these arguments or observations amounts, obviously, to a clinching demonstration; any and all of them could be questioned or doubted by a stubborn skeptic. If Locke were correct in his assumption that assent should be strictly tied to the quality of inference, these numerous probabilities ought to lead to a mitigated or only partial assent: we are nearly or for the most part sure that Great Britain is an island. But in point of fact, our assent to this claim is not mitigated or qualified.

Now what is to prevent this embrace of informal inference from devolving into sheer irrationality? Here Newman introduces the controversial notion of the illative sense, the epistemological innovation for which *The Grammar of Assent* is perhaps best known.[35] We speak rather naturally of an aesthetic sense, that which

32. Ibid., 227.
33. Ibid., 234.
34. Ibid., 234–35.
35. Ibid., 270–99.

makes one capable of good judgments in matters of beauty; we also are well aware of the moral sensibility, that which enables one to determine the right course of action *in concreto*, what Aristotle called *phronēsis* and Aquinas *prudentia*. These are both faculties of discrimination and assessment, and both orient one to the particular case rather than to general principles. Though she carries a wealth of aesthetic convictions and ideas in her mind, the aesthete determines that *this* sculpture is beautiful through her feel for art, born of thousands of experiences, past judgments, and intuitions. And though he is possessed of numerous moral laws and guiding axioms, the good man knows what to do *here and now*, not through a dispassionate appeal to those general norms but through his feel for the situation, his varied experience in making nuanced judgments. Newman asserts that there is a parallel capacity in regard to determinations concerning what is true. This is the illative sense, from the Latin *latus*, implying a carrying or bringing over. The illative sense is that feel for the truth which allows one to sift through, assess, and assemble a number of probable arguments that are converging in the same direction. It is the power to take those hunches and intuitions that fall short of absolute persuasiveness and "carry them over" to assent.

One strand of steel cannot lift a massive load, but if a hundred strands of the same size and density are wrapped one around the other, they will constitute a cord more than powerful enough to lift the weight. One bucket with a hole in it will not efficiently transfer water from one receptacle to another. But that bucket placed within a series of equally defective buckets will be a perfectly adequate bearer of the water. Similarly, one flawed or merely probable argument will not bring the mind to assent, but a conglomeration of probable arguments, each imperfect but conducing to the same conclusion—as in the "Great Britain is an island" case—will move the mind to acquiescence. The illative sense is the intuitive power that presides over this process, reading and directing it. As I have been hinting, this capacity is largely unconscious, a matter of feel more than ratiocination, and it is honed through wide experience. Newman says that a judge should announce her decision clearly and unambiguously but should refrain from giving the reasons for her determination, for the judgment is probably correct, though the reasons consciously given are almost certainly inadequate as an explanation. In a similar way, through the illative sense one can be perfectly right in his epistemological judgment but utterly incapable of telling precisely how or why this is so.

When *The Grammar of Assent* was published in the early 1870s, it was met with fierce resistance on the part of some traditional Catholic philosophers who felt that it advocated, against the regnant neoscholasticism of the day, an irresponsible emotionalism or relativism in matters of knowing. After all, how does one adjudicate a dispute between two highly responsible and intuitive people who, through the exercise of their respective illative senses, have come to precisely opposite conclusions on a key issue? As I hope I have made clear in this presentation, the illative sense is by no means irrational or disconnected from the exigencies of formal inference. Thus one can show through appeal to syllogistic-style reasoning that a given position is inconsistent or incoherent. But what the illative sense adds is the necessary complement to pure reason, the role that the nonrational dimensions of body, emotion, experience, and intuition undoubtedly play in the process of coming to judgment. Here it can be seen as congruent with my earlier reflections on the cognitive quality of emotion. Perhaps it tells us that when seeking to resolve a dispute with an interlocutor, one simply has to be more patient, more careful, more willing to attend to the extrarational but by no means irrational elements that contribute to intellection.

In the terms I have been using, Newman has presented an epistemology that is incarnational and therefore christological in style. The Word—the rational truth in all of its forms—manifests itself in the vagaries and particularities of history and is received according to the capacity and complexity of an embodied mind. Truth is come to neither through escape from the body (Platonism) nor sequestration of the mind from the body (modern Cartesianism and Lockeanism), but through a rough, incarnate interaction of matter and spirit. If classical and modern epistemologies are relatively dualist, Newman's Christian epistemology is one of coinherence, stressing as it does the *Ineinander* of reason and emotion, cognition and intuition, body and soul.

One of the deftest moves that Newman makes is to show that this illative way of knowing—which rationalist critics had seen to be an irrationalism typical of religious thinking—is in fact characteristic of all manners of intellection, from the scientific through the psychological to the philosophical. Anticipating Lonergan, he says that every type of knowledge develops from an array of assumptions, received traditions, creative intuitions, leaps of faith. Like Aquinas, Newman realizes that all forms of intellectuality are participations in the Logos and are, as such, incarnate in their mode and finality.

## The Prophetic Dimension

In the first chapter of the Gospel of Mark, we find the account of Jesus's confrontation with the demoniac in the Capernaum synagogue. While Christ is preaching, the possessed man furiously shouts, "What have you to do with us, Jesus of Nazareth? Have you come to destroy us?" (Mark 1:24). It is most important to note that Jesus's initial encounter with the demonic takes place in a synagogue, a formally sanctioned place of prayer. This foreshadows the long and intense struggle that he will have throughout his public life with the representatives of the official religion of his time: the Pharisees, scribes, rabbis, and elders of the people. This shouldn't surprise us, since Jesus is consistently described as a prophet, and prophets—from Amos to Jeremiah—were antagonists of the religious-political establishment. In the Old Testament tradition, the *nabi* is a truth-teller and religious visionary, someone who speaks the word of God and stubbornly reads the world through the interpretive lens of that word. And this mission implies opposition, confrontation, and critique, since the keepers of worldly order are frequently looking through other lenses and listening to other words.

Now Jesus is not simply a speaker of the divine word; he is the incarnation of that Word, the personal embodiment of the divine purpose. Thus he is prophetic to the depth of his being, and his prophetic vocation will manifest itself in all of his speech, gestures, and actions. This entails that his confrontation with fallen powers and dysfunctional traditions will he highly focused, intense, and disruptive.

An episode recorded in all four Gospels is Jesus's paradigmatically prophetic act of cleansing the temple. Standing at the heart of the holy city of Jerusalem, the temple was the political, economic, cultural, and religious center of the nation. Turning over the tables of the money changers and driving out the merchants, shouting in high dudgeon, upsetting the order of that place was to strike at the most sacred institution of the culture, the unassailable embodiment of the tradition. It was to show oneself as critic in the most radical and surprising sense possible. That this act of Jesus the warrior flowed from the depth of his prophetic identity is witnessed to by the author of John's Gospel: "His disciples remembered that it was written, 'Zeal for your house will consume me'" (John 2:17). Many of the historical critics of the New Testament hold that this event—shocking, unprecedented, perverse—is what finally persuaded the leaders that Jesus merited execution.[36]

The crucifixion itself is presented in the elegantly crafted narratives of the Gospels as the supreme prophetic gesture of Jesus. Christ is put to death not by minor officials but by a coterie of the leading religious and political authorities of the time, both Jewish and Roman. Standing before Pilate in the ludicrous getup that the soldiers have dressed him in, Jesus is a sort of court jester, commenting ironically, in the manner of King Lear's fool, on the corruption of the one passing judgment on the Judge. Over the cross Pilate places the notice, in the major languages of the culture, that this man is the king of the Jews. Meant as jest and mockery, it is in fact an indictment (readable by any and everyone) of the corrupt powers that put to death the author of life. In the Letter to the Colossians, upon which we have been so reliant throughout this chapter, we find Paul's magnificent summation of the prophetic significance of the crucifixion: "He [Christ] disarmed the rulers and authorities and made a public example of them, triumphing over them in it" (Col. 2:15). Like a conquering Roman general dragging his captives through the streets, Jesus publicly displays the powers of the world whom he had defeated through his cross.[37]

Now how does all of this impinge upon questions of epistemology? It does so in the measure that, in this prophetic quality of the incarnate Logos, the central epistemic category of the capacity for self-criticism emerges. What becomes unavoidably clear in the course of the New Testament narratives (I have considered

---

36. See N. T. Wright, *Jesus and the Victory of God* (Minneapolis: Fortress, 1996), 335–36.
37. See William Placher, *Narratives of a Vulnerable God* (Louisville: Westminster John Knox, 1994), 10–20.

just a few obvious cases) is that there is nothing acquiescent, passive, or uncritically accepting in the attitude of Jesus, especially in regard to his own most sacred
traditions. That Jesus reverences the traditions of his people is indisputable, but
that he is willing to turn on them dramatically when they have become corrupt or
self-contradictory is equally incontestable. Even when threatened by the coercive
power of the state, Jesus refuses to back down and maintains his critical integrity.
And as Paul insinuates in Colossians, the risen Jesus, bearing the wounds of his
crucifixion, stands as a permanent criticism of those powers that so marked him.

But it is most important to attend to precisely *how* Jesus questions and criticizes.
He does so not by standing outside the tradition but by appealing to a forgotten
strand or a deeper intuition of the tradition itself. Thus in the cleansing of the
temple, as we saw, he is able to see and excise the rot because he has thoroughly
immersed himself in the monotheistic mysticism of classical Judaism. He can
go to the cross—implicitly critiquing the keepers of the tradition who sent him
there—because he is personally rooted in the will of his Father, that will which
informs the tradition as a whole. In the Sermon on the Mount, Jesus is able blithely
to reinterpret some of the most sacred words of revelation—"You have heard that it
was said, 'You shall love your neighbor and hate your enemy.' But I say to you, Love
your enemies and pray for those who persecute you" (Matt. 5:43–44)—because
he speaks from the deepest and most abiding assumptions of the revelation tradition itself. He does not assume a perspective outside of revelation and then affect
a critique from that abstract space; rather, he moves from place to place within
the whole of revelation, positioning himself now here, now there, and seeing from
those various points of vantage the signs of corruption, the indications that the
tradition is out of line with itself. What he embodies thereby is the paradox of the
fiercest loyalty giving rise to the fiercest self-criticism.

A major emphasis of the *Aufklärers* is the need for hoary traditions to submit
to analysis and critique. This accounts for the pointed, skeptical, edgy quality of
much Enlightenment epistemology, and it explains its often strongly antireligious
bias. One of the most consistent defenders of the Enlightenment tradition today,
especially in its epistemological implications, is Jürgen Habermas. A brief analysis
of his philosophy might help us to assess the relationship between the prophetic
critique characteristic of the Christ-mind and the critique of tradition and institution associated with the Enlightenment. With his roots in the Frankfurt school,
throughout his career Habermas has maintained a deep interest in the dynamics of
dysfunctional societies—more precisely, in the ways that social groups engage in
oppressive and distorting praxis.[38] He has recognized that, like individuals, societies
and cultures can become neurotic and self-destructive through repressions born
of fear. Thus the violent imposition of one political viewpoint leads to silencing,
self-loathing, and antagonism throughout a society—and all of this conduces

38. See especially Jürgen Habermas, *The Theory of Communicative Action*, vol. 1 (Boston: Beacon,
1987); Habermas, *Communication and the Evolution of Society* (Boston: Beacon, 1979).

to a profound distortion of speech. People in oppressive political situations are so afraid to give voice to their convictions that they lose confidence in the very category of truth and in the power of speech to bring clarity and liberation. This is why, in his later writings, Habermas has focused thoroughly on the nature of speech acts, in both their ideal and distorted forms.

Taking seriously J. L. Austin's distinction between the locutionary (declarative) and illocutionary (performative) dimensions of the speech act, Habermas remarks that every declaration made in the course of a conversation has at least a rudimentary illocutionary force.[39] When someone says to a conversation partner even something as banal as "It's a nice day," she is implicitly eliciting her partner's agreement, seeking common ground. In a properly functioning conversational environment, one's interlocutor is free to respond, "Yes, it is," or "Actually no, it's a rather gloomy day." But the illocutionary dimension breaks down, collapses in on itself, if one speaker is holding a gun to the head of the other as she makes her statement. In that case, the "Yes, it is" of the respondent has no real significance, even if it accurately reflects his views.

All of this becomes even more pointed and complex when it is a question not of comments about the weather but of constructing arguments and counterarguments. If I were to formulate an argument in favor of George W. Bush's policy on Iraq while threatening you with dismissal from your job in the case of your disagreement, neither my argument nor your response would have any real illocutionary force. Conditions permitting real conversation would have collapsed because of profound inequality and implied violence among the conversants. Obviously, the means and modes of intimidation in dysfunctional societies are usually much subtler than the brandishing of a gun or the direct threat of unemployment, but the effect remains the same.

In light of these observations, we can begin to sketch the contours of the ideal speech situation as Habermas envisions it. A properly functioning communicative society is one in which the equality of the conversation partners is guaranteed, where there is no threat of coercion or violence, where appeals to special revelation and privilege are disallowed, and where only ordinary or commonly accepted canons of reasonableness may be invoked in the adjudication of disputes. Paramount is the capacity of each conversant to engage in criticism of any institution—religious or secular—that threatens his or her integrity and freedom in self-expression. Only under these strict conditions will speech acts retain their illocutionary power of persuasion and fair exchange.

How can someone who has accepted the epistemic primacy of Jesus Christ assess this Enlightenment-based proposal? A Christian response to Habermas's program might serve (happily enough) as a summary of all that I have developed throughout this section. In their willingness to raise a critical voice against any

---

39. See J. L. Austin, *How to Do Things with Words* (Cambridge, MA: Harvard University Press, 1962), 98–107.

form of corruption, even in the most sacred places, Christianity and the Enlightenment at their best come together. Jesus cleansing the temple and hanging from his cross is a figure infinitely more radical than any of the *lumières*, revolutionaries, and *philosophes* of the Enlightenment, and *ecclesia semper reformanda*—a foundational dictum of the community of Christ—is a call to institutional reform easily as disturbing as any slogan of the *Aufklärung*. More to the point, in their repudiation of all forms of violence, the Christ-mind and Habermas's ideal speech community coincide.

Now, it is painfully obvious that actual Christian communities throughout history have rarely if ever lived up to this ideal of noncoercion, but of course the same could be said of those varied political systems that have emerged from the Enlightenment. As I have presented it, the Christ-mind is one that looks for and relies upon coinherence as it goes about its work. One-in-the-other, a balance of identity and community, is the basic form of Christian intellection, and hence an epistemic praxis of violence would be radically out of step with such a form. Moreover, I have argued that the proper setting for the Christ-mind is a community of dialogue, an intersubjective conversation, since the God who grounds intelligibility is himself a conversation of coinhering persons. Habermas and the committed Christian, then, come together in their suspicion of excessively subjective and privatized views of truth and their embrace of lively exchange as the optimal matrix for truth seeking.

At this point, though, the differences become evident. In the Habermasian ideal speech community, claims to special revelation or privileged insight are precluded. But practitioners of the Christ-mind have accepted the revelation of God in Christ and have, in light of that event, committed themselves to seeking forms of coinherence. They take as their epistemic starting point not a neutral "quest" for truth but the ontological priority of Jesus Christ, crucified and risen from the dead.

Do the two sides here simply fall into antagonism and mutual suspicion? Perhaps one way to avoid that outcome is to show that Habermas's program is not, in point of fact, so different from the Christian program in its acceptance of certain basic and uncriticized assumptions. Without making a case for it, Habermas assumes that "secular" reason—free from the taint of the supernatural—is the sole model of rationality. But why, the Christian might ask, does the bracketing of all claims to revelation or religious insight make a conversation necessarily more reliable? Might such arbitrary exclusion not in fact skew the quest irredeemably in an immanentist direction, guaranteeing a secular conclusion in advance? Thus it is finally a question not of revelation versus reason but rather of two competing claims to revelation, two competing sets of elemental presuppositions.

Another key difference emerges around the issue of egalitarianism. As we saw, in Habermas's ideal speech community the equality of all the conversants is respected, and all claimants to special insight or privileged status are excluded. But those who claim a fundamental revelation can have no truck with this sort of radical leveling. The Christian holds that what is ontologically and epistemically ultimate arrived in a historical revelation witnessed by certain privileged individuals and that these receivers in turn passed on to their successors—official and otherwise—the power of the revelation. Thus Paul says, "I handed on to you as of first importance what I in turn had received: that Christ died for our sins in accordance with the scriptures, and that he was buried, and that he was raised on the third day" (1 Cor. 15:3–4), and the author of the first letter of John claims, "We declare to you what we have seen and heard so that you also may have fellowship with us" (1 John 1:3). What is on display here is not a community of coequal conversants, each on a disinterested quest for the truth, but a hierarchically organized and epistemically disciplined society, in which the passing on of a central conviction is absolutely essential.

From the beginning, Christian communities—with the possible exception of certain groups of the Radical Reformation—have recognized the indispensability of order and authority and have been consequently suspicious of appeals to radical egalitarianism. If everyone has equal access to the truth and equal claim to authority, then the conversation loses its direction and devolves into chatter. And again, the Christian is likely to peek behind the facade of the Habermasian system and spy the various forms of ordering, hierarchy, and exclusion that go on there. She will notice that her distinctively religious voice has been silenced and that her equality as a conversation partner has hardly been acknowledged, and she will also see that the secular discussion itself is necessarily policed and disciplined by authority figures, keepers of the revelation, such as Habermas himself. She will conclude that the Enlightenment critique of religious authoritarianism rings just a tad hollow.

So can the Christ-mind meet the demands of the Enlightenment? In its call for respect among all conversation partners, its insistence upon noncoercion and nonviolence in discussion, and its summons to criticize the corruptions of even the most sacred institutions, the answer is assuredly yes. But in its egalitarianism and antiauthoritarianism, in its rejection of any claim to revelation, in its embrace of a purely immanentist construal of rationality, the answer is just as assuredly no.

## Conclusion

What I hope to have shown in the course of this chapter is the coherence of an unabashedly Christoform epistemology. I have tried to demonstrate that those who assume the epistemic priority of the narratives concerning Jesus Christ are neither insane nor irresponsible, or at the very least, no less sane or responsible than those who assume the purportedly neutral epistemic stance of modernity. Cartesians, Humeans, and Kantians presumed certain principles in order to clarify their thinking; so, I have argued, Christians presume certain principles flowing from Scripture and theological tradition in order to clarify their reflection on the world. The battle, therefore, is not between the prejudiced and the unprejudiced but between two camps, each prejudiced in a distinctive manner. This acknowledgment does not lock us into sectarianism or relativism; rather, it opens the door to an argument far more fruitful than the one that held sway between Christian and secular thinkers throughout most of modernity.

# 15

## Reading Scripture with the Reformers

### Scripture and Tradition

In light of their two-front struggle against the Catholic elevation of the church above the Bible and the radical distancing of Word from Spirit, the mainline reformers were forced to clarify their understanding of the relationship between Scripture and tradition.[1] The principle of *sola scriptura* is found in all of the classic confessions of the Reformation, but nowhere is it more clearly stated than in the solemn Protestation (from which the word "Protestant" derives) set forth on behalf of the evangelical cause at the Diet of Speyer in 1529:

> There is, we affirm, no sure preaching or doctrine but that which abides by the Word of God. According to God's command, no other doctrine should be preached. Each text of the holy and divine Scriptures should be elucidated and explained by other texts. This holy book is in all things necessary for the Christian; it shines clearly in its own light, and is found to enlighten the darkness. We are determined by God's grace and aid to abide in God's Word alone, the holy gospel contained in the biblical

Originally published in "Whose Bible? Which Tradition?," in Timothy George, *Reading Scripture with the Reformers* (Downers Grove, IL: InterVarsity, 2011), 102–36, here pp. 118–34. Copyright © 2011 by Timothy George. Used by permission of InterVarsity Press, PO Box 1400, Downers Grove, IL 60515. www.ivpress.com.

    1. For a fuller discussion of this theme, see Timothy George, "An Evangelical Reflection on Scripture and Tradition," *Pro Ecclesia* 9 (2000): 184–207.

books of the Old and New Testaments. This Word alone should be preached, and nothing that is contrary to it. It is the only Truth. It is the sure rule of all Christian doctrine and conduct. It can never fail us or deceive us. Whosoever builds and abides on this foundation shall stand against all the gates of hell while all merely human additions and vanities set up against it must fall before the presence of God.[2]

With such a robust commitment to the authority of the written Word of God, how could the reformers still claim that they were part of the ongoing Catholic tradition, indeed the legitimate bearers of it? To answer this question, it is necessary to see how the Bible functioned as a critical principle in the thought of the reformers. They almost always used the word "tradition" in the plural to refer to those "human traditions instituted to placate God, to merit grace, and to make satisfaction for sins," as the Augsburg Confession puts it.[3] Zwingli was more radical than Luther in his liturgical prunings, eliminating holy days, incense, the burning of candles, the sprinkling of holy water, church art, and musical instruments—this "whole rubbish heap of ceremonials" and "hodge-podge of human ordinances" that amounted to nothing but "tom foolery."[4] In both cases, however, the majority use of *traditiones* referred to specific practices and acts believed to be departures from, or distortions of, true worship and sound piety. This negative attitude toward tradition echoed the oft-quoted words of Jesus in Mark 7:8 (NIV): "You have let go of the commands of God and are holding on to the traditions of men."

The Protestant criticism of "human traditions" was severe at points, but it did not mean the wholesale rejection of all that came before Luther's hammer blows in Wittenberg on October 31, 1517. Indeed, the Reformation appeal to the Bible implied the intrinsic connection between Scripture and tradition in a genuine evangelical sense. This was seen in numerous ways in the writings of the reformers. Here we shall mention only three: their sense of continuity with the church of the preceding centuries, their embrace of the ecumenical orthodoxy of the early church, and their desire to read the Bible in dialogue with the exegetical tradition of the church.

*Ecclesial continuity.* In their efforts to restore what a noted Puritan of a later age called "the old glorious beautiful face of Christianity," many of the spiritualist and radical reformers denounced the Catholic tradition entirely.[5] Kaspar Schwenckfeld was among the most radical of this lot. He forbade baptism by water, declared a moratorium on the Lord's Supper, and announced that the true

2. On the Diet of Speyer, see E. G. Leonard, *A History of Protestantism* (Indianapolis: Bobbs-Merrill, 1968), 1:122–28.

3. Philip Schaff, *Creeds of Christendom* (repr., Grand Rapids: Baker, 1977), 12.

4. Edward J. Furcha and H. Wayne Pipkin, eds. and trans., *Huldrych Zwingli: Writings*, vol. 1, *The Defense of the Reformed Faith*, and vol. 2, *In Search of True Religion* (Allison Park, PA: Pickwick, 1984), 1:70–71,73; 2:86–90.

5. John Owen, *A Vindication of the Animadversions on Fiat Lux: Wherein the Principles of the Roman Church, as to Moderation, Unity and Truth are Examined and Sundry Important Controversies* (1664; repr., London: Banner of Truth Trust, 1967), 207.

church was no longer to be found on earth but had ascended to heaven in 1530.[6] In writing against the errors of Schwenckfeld and other radicals, Luther declared, "We do not act as fanatically as the sectarian spirits. We do not reject everything that is under the dominion of the pope. For in that event we should also reject the Christian church. . . . Much Christian good, nay, all Christian good, is to be found in the papacy and from there it descended to us."[7] In his 1535 commentary on Galatians, Luther further described the nature of this "descent." Although the church of Rome is horribly deformed, Luther said, it still is holy because it retains baptism, the Eucharist, "the voice and text of the Gospel, the sacred Scriptures, the ministries, the name of Christ, and the name of God. . . . The treasure is still there."[8] Calvin, too, was willing to extend the word "church" to local congregations in Roman obedience so long as the gospel could be discerned in the preaching of the Scriptures and the celebration of the Lord's Supper. Thus the reformers affirmed the tradition of the living word and believed they could discern it, albeit with difficulty, even within the contemporary church of Rome.

*Ecumenical orthodoxy.* The Protestant reformers embraced the trinitarian and christological consensus of the early church, as expressed in the decrees of the first four ecumenical councils (Nicaea, 325; Constantinople I, 381; Ephesus, 431; Chalcedon, 451). They understood these classic statements of Christian doctrine as necessitated by, and congruent with, the teaching of Scripture. Significantly, when Protestants began to publish their own evangelical confessions, they did not, as it were, begin all over again with new statements and original reflections on the person of Christ and the reality of the Trinity. Rather, they accepted the Apostles' Creed, the Nicene Creed, and the Athanasian Creed "as the unanimous, catholic, Christian faith," pledging themselves to uphold the doctrine set forth in these historic standards while rejecting "all heresies and teachings which have been introduced into the church of God contrary to them."[9]

This approach was true not only of Lutherans and Calvinists but also of Congregationalists and Baptists, who belonged to the wider Reformed tradition. Thus, in 1679, long before they had taken up the slogan "No creed but the Bible," Baptists in England published a confession of faith in which they reprinted *en toto* the three historic creeds and commended them as something that "ought early to be received and believed."

> For we believe that they may be proved by most undoubted authority of Holy Scripture and are necessary to be understood of all Christians; and to be instructed

6. See George H. Williams, *The Radical Reformation* (repr., Kirksville, MO: Sixteenth Century Journal Publishers, 1992), 428–33.

7. Heiko A. Oberman, *The Dawn of the Reformation: Essays in Late Medieval and Early Reformation Thought* (Edinburgh: T&T Clark, 1986), 285; Luther, *Weimarer Ausgabe* 26:146–47.

8. *Luther's Works* 26:24.

9. This is from the opening paragraphs of the Formula of Concord. See T. G. Tappert, ed., *The Book of Concord* (Philadelphia: Fortress, 1959), 465.

in the knowledge of them by ministers of Christ, according to the analogy of faith, recorded in sacred Scriptures, upon which these creeds are grounded and catecheti-cally opened and expounded in all Christian families for the edification of young and old which might be a means to prevent heresy and doctrine and practice, these creeds containing all things in a brief manner that are necessary to be known, fun-damentally, in order of our salvation.[10]

As this Baptist statement shows, the early councils and creeds were embraced as witnesses and expositions of the faith, as accurate summaries of Scripture ("an abbreviated word," to use the expression of John Cassian), not as independent authorities alongside of or supplementary to the Bible.[11] While Scripture alone remained the only standard by which all doctrines had to be understood and normed, the early creeds were not mere ad hoc statements that could be used or dispensed with willy-nilly at the whim of an individual theologian or congregation. Rather, they belonged to the unfolding pattern of Christian truth, which could be abandoned only at great peril.[12]

In this sense, tradition served as a kind of guardrail on a dangerous mountain highway keeping the traveler focused on the goal of the journey by preventing precipitous calamities to the right and the left. True enough, the reformers did not consider themselves irrevocably bound to the language and thought forms of the early creeds and councils, as Luther made clear in his writing against Latomus in 1521: "Even if my soul hated this word *homoousios*, still I would not be a heretic, if I hold fast to the fact defined by the council on the basis of Scripture."[13] But when Calvin tried to articulate the doctrine of the Trinity in biblical language alone, his thoughts were misinterpreted in an antitrinitarian way. Thus he was forced, as Athanasius had been in the early church, to use nonbiblical language precisely in order to be faithful to the biblical message.[14]

*Exegetical dialogue.* In their commentaries on the Bible, the reformers of the sixteenth century revealed a close familiarity with the preceding exegetical tradi-tion, and they used it respectfully as well as critically in their expositions of the sacred text. The Bible was seen as the book given to the church gathered and

10. Article 38 of "The Orthodox Creed" in *Baptist Confessions, Covenants and Catechisms*, ed. Timothy George and Denise George (Nashville: Broadman & Holman, 1996), 120–21.

11. John Cassian, *On the Incarnation of Christ* 6.4 (Patrologia Latina 50:149), cited by George Tavard, "Scripture and Tradition," *Journal of Ecumenical Studies* 5 (1968): 315.

12. See the surprisingly strong statement by the Princeton theologian Charles Hodge: "If the Scriptures be a plain book, and the Spirit performs the functions of a teacher to all the children of God, it follows inevitably that they must agree in all essential matters in their interpretation of the Bible. And from that fact it follows that for an individual Christian to dissent from the faith of the universal Church (i.e., the body of true believers), is tantamount to dissenting from the Scriptures themselves." *Systematic Theology* (repr., Grand Rapids: Eerdmans, 1970), 1:184.

13. *Luther's Works* 32:244; *Weimarer Ausgabe* 8:117–18: "Quod si odit anima mea vocem homo-ousion, et nolim ea uti, non ero haereticus. Quis enim me coget uti, modo rem teneam, quae in Concilio per scripturas definita est?"

14. See Calvin, *Institutes* 1.13.5.

guided by the Holy Spirit. In the early church, Vincent of Lerins set forth as a threefold test of catholicity, "What has been believed everywhere, always, and by all." This Vincentian canon, as it came to be called, was restated by Calvin in his definition of the church as

> A society of all the saints, a society which, spread over the whole world, and exist-ing in all ages, and bound together by the doctrine and the one Spirit of Christ, cultivates and observes unity of faith, and brotherly concord. With this church we deny that we have any disagreement. Nay, rather, as we revere her as our mother, so we desire to remain in her bosom.[15]

Defined in this way, the visible church had a real, even if relative and subordi-nate, authority since, as Calvin admitted, "We cannot fly without wings."[16] It was this instrumental authority of the church that Augustine had in mind when he remarked that he would not have believed the Bible unless he had been moved to do so by the church. George Tavard, a modern Catholic scholar, has expressed well the Protestant understanding of the coinherence—though not the coequality—of Scripture and tradition as "a vertical descent of the Third Person upon the members of the church, and a horizontal succession of charismatic transmission by which the Word is handed on."[17]

## Is the Bible Clear?

At the heart of Reformation hermeneutics is the claim that, as the original Prot-estants put it at Speyer in 1529, the Bible "shines clearly in its own light." What could this possibly mean when, on the face of it, the Bible is filled with many puzzling enigmas, mysterious symbols, and dark sayings?

The clarity or perspicuity of Scripture presupposes another, equally counter-intuitive assertion by the early reformers: Scripture is its own interpreter, *sacra scriptura sui ipsius interpres*. This claim first surfaced in 1520 during Luther's early struggles with the papacy.

> Say for once—if you can—according to which judge, according to which criterion, can a point of contention be decided when the opinions of two of the church fa-thers disagree with one another? In such a case, the decision has to be based on the judgment of Scripture, which cannot happen if we do not give Scripture pride of place.... Having said this, the Holy Scripture itself on its own, to the greatest extent

---

15. John C. Olin, ed., *John Calvin and Jacopo Sadoleto: A Reformation Debate* (New York: Harper Torchbooks, 1966), 61–62.

16. Ibid., 77.

17. Tavard, "Scripture and Tradition," 318. On this issue, see also David C. Steinmetz, "Luther and Calvin on Church and Tradition," in *Luther in Context* (Bloomington: Indiana University Press, 1986), 85–97.

possible, is easy to understand, clearly and plainly, being its own interpreter [*sui ipsius interpres*], in that it puts all statements of human beings to the test, judging and enlightening, as is written in Psalm 119[:130]: "The explanation," or according to its actual meaning in the Hebrew: the opening or the gate—"of your words enlightens and gives understanding to youngsters." The Spirit clearly points here to the enlightenment [of Scripture] and teaches that insight is given only by means of the Word of God, as through an open door or (as those [scholastics] say) through a first principle [*principium primum*], from which one must start in order to come to the light and to insight.[18]

At one level, the claim that Scripture interprets itself was nothing new in the sixteenth century. In book 2 of his hermeneutical handbook, *On Christian Doctrine*, Augustine had established the principle that the obscure and doubtful passages in Scripture should be understood in light of the clearer and more certain ones.[19] The idea that in the Bible a clearer place makes known a more difficult one was a staple of both medieval and Reformation exegesis. However, the Protestant reformers used it in a distinctive way: to support their argument for the primacy of Scripture against the claims of what one scholar has called "the ecclesiastical positivism of the Roman church."[20] In the first work of Protestant theology published in French (1529), Guillaume Farel gave a good summary of this approach:

It is necessary to discourse upon and convey the Scripture in fear and reverence of God, of whom it speaks, diligently regarding it not in bits and pieces, but entirely, considering that which goes before and that which follows, and to what end it has been written, and for what purpose it says what Scripture contains, regarding the other places, where that which is said in a passage more clearly and openly, comparing one passage of Scripture with the other. For it is written by one and the same Spirit, who speaks more clearly by one than by the other, how that all that which they have said which Scripture contains "has been spoken by the Holy Spirit" (2 Pet. 1:20–21). And from this it happens that one place makes known the other.[21]

The declaration of Scripture's inherent clarity, however, involves more than the application of sound philological rules to the reading of a text. It is another way of saying that the Bible cannot be "read like any other book." To read the Bible is to encounter a numinous other. The Bible does not lend itself to being

18. *Weimarer Ausgabe* 7:97 (*Assertio omnium articulorum*, 1520), cited in Oswald Bayer, *Martin Luther's Theology: A Contemporary Interpretation* (Grand Rapids: Eerdmans, 2008), 74. The principle that "Scripture interprets itself" is also found in Thomas Aquinas, *Summa Theologiae* I.1.9. See Otto Weber, *Foundations of Dogmatics* (Grand Rapids: Eerdmans, 1981), 1:281.

19. Augustine, *On Christian Doctrine*, trans. D. W. Robertson Jr. (Indianapolis: Bobbs-Merrill, 1958), 101–17.

20. Eric W. Gritsch, "Introduction to Church and Ministry," *Luther's Works* 39:xvi.

21. William Farel, "Summary (1529)," in *Reformed Confessions of the Sixteenth and Seventeenth Centuries*, ed. James T. Dennison Jr. (Grand Rapids: Reformation Heritage Books, 2008), 1:65. A facsimile of the 1534 French edition has been provided by Arthur Piaget, *Sommaire et Briefve Declaration* (Paris: E. Droz, 1935).

analyzed and mastered as a mere literary artifact from antiquity. As Calvin said, the Bible is "something alive, and full of hidden power which leaves nothing in [anyone] untouched."[22] John Rogers, a former disciple of William Tyndale, said something similar to Bishop Stephen Gardiner before being consigned to the flames of Smithfield during the reign of Mary Tudor. You can prove nothing by the Scriptures, Gardner said to Rogers, for the Scripture is dead without a living expositor. To which Rogers retorted, "No, the Scripture is alive!"[23] This is how Luther put it: The Spirit "cannot be contained in any letter, it cannot be written with ink, on stone, or in books as the law can be, but it is written only in the heart, a living writing of the Holy Spirit."[24]

The Bible is its own interpreter in the sense that it does its own interpreting: it interprets its readers. The Bible is alive because through it the Spirit convicts of sin, awakens faith in believers, and conveys its intended meaning to those who approach it with humility and prayer. This is a very different model of Scripture reading from the one dominant in historical-critical methodologies since the Enlightenment. There the Bible is an object of disinterested inquiry, a thing to be mastered and managed rather than a word of address from the living God. Luther had his own struggles with the Aristotelian academic theology of his day, and the way he admonished his fellow Scripture scholars still rings true today: "It behooves us to let the prophets and apostles stand at the professors' lectern, while we, down below at their feet, listen to what they say. It is not they who must hear what we say."[25]

Luther can also speak of the "soundness" and "simplicity" as well as the lucidity of Scripture.[26] Between 1519 and 1521, Luther was engaged in writing a commentary on the Psalms. He had earlier lectured on the Psalms (1513–1516) prior to the *Sturm und Drang* of the Reformation crisis. These new lectures incorporated his maturing insights about the nature of the Bible, the church, and the Christian life. In his second series of lectures on Psalms, Luther's Christ-centered and gospel-centered understanding of justification by faith is clearly on parade. As Luther would later say, Jesus Christ is "the King of Scripture who is the price of my salvation."[27] Jesus Christ is the Alpha and Omega of the Bible; all Scripture

22. John Calvin, *The Epistle of Paul the Apostle to the Hebrews and the First and Second Epistles of St. Peter*, trans. William B. Johnston (Grand Rapids: Eerdmans, 1983), 51.

23. John Foxe, *Acts and Monuments*, ed. T. Pratt (Philadelphia: J. & J. L. Gihon, 1813), 6:596.

24. *Luther's Works* 39:182–83.

25. *Luther's Works* 34:284. See Bayer's comment: "No one who refers to the reformational 'Scripture principle' should fail to take into account the paradox that lies therein. This Word makes sense only when understood as the description of a conflict—the conflict that academic theology presented at the time of Luther, still presents today, and will continue to present in time to come. Whoever speaks of the 'scriptural principle' can do so only in radical criticism of a concept of academic study that assumes there is a timeless, pure a priori" (*Martin Luther's Theology*, 73–74).

26. *Luther's Works* 32:236.

27. *Weimarer Ausgabe* 40/1:458. See Paul Althaus, *The Theology of Martin Luther* (Philadelphia: Fortress, 1966), 80.

must be understood in favor of Christ and not against him. The clear light of Christ radiates through the Old Testament as well as the New, for "all of Scripture has a clear meaning in terms of the Gospel."[28] Luther came to this insight in part through his focus on the single sense of Scripture. This is the sense that "drives home Christ" and manifests the Bible's clear message of salvation to all regardless of social status or academic training. For this reason, Luther can say that "even the humble miller's maid, nay, a child of nine if it has faith," can understand the Bible.[29] The Bible was to be made available to the common people because its basic message was clear and plain for all to see and read.

The debate over the clarity of the Bible was taken to a new level in the exchange between Erasmus and Luther on the bondage of the will. In the opening salvo, Erasmus charged that Luther made too many assertions ignoring the fact that God has left many matters in Scripture veiled in secrecy. There is much obscurity in the Bible, doctrines we should contemplate "in mystic silence" rather than seeking to penetrate with "irreverent inquisitiveness." Which doctrines does Erasmus have in mind? The ones he mentions all have to do with the dogmatic tradition of the church—the divinity and humanity of Christ, the Trinity, the designation of the mother of Jesus as Theotokos, the God-bearer, as well as the controverted doctrine of predestination, the matter at stake in his quarrel with Luther. On all such doctrines, Erasmus insinuates, he would side with the skeptics if he could get away with it, that is, if the church would allow it. However, on other matters, Erasmus concedes, the Scriptures do speak quite plainly. There is no need for controversy when the Bible speaks about behavior and morality, when it sets forth "the precepts for the good life."[30]

Luther responded to Erasmus's tilt toward skepticism by declaring that the Holy Spirit is no skeptic. He also reasserted the need for assertions, "for it is not the mark of a Christian mind to take no delight in assertions; on the contrary, a man must delight in assertions or he will be no Christian. And by assertion . . . I mean a constant adhering, affirming, confessing, maintaining, and an invincible persevering."[31] As to Scripture, Luther admits that it contains many texts that seem obscure and abstruse. But the problem, he claims, is not with the Bible but with us. It is our blindness, indolence, and sin that places a veil over our hearts and minds and prevents us from understanding the clear meaning of the text. Just as a person hidden away in some dark corner of an alley should not blame the sun for shining so clearly in the bright light of day, so those blinded to the truth of

28. Althaus, *Theology of Martin Luther*, 80. See also *Luther's Works* 34:112.

29. *Luther's Works* 31:341. See B. A. Gerrish, *The Old Protestantism and the New* (Chicago: University of Chicago Press, 1982), 57. See also Siegfried Raeder, "The Exegetical and Hermeneutical Work of Martin Luther," in *Hebrew Bible/Old Testament: The History of Its Interpretation*, vol. 2, *From the Renaissance to the Enlightenment*, ed. Magne Saebo (Göttingen: Vandenhoeck & Ruprecht, 2008), 363–406.

30. E. Gordon Rupp and Philip S. Watson, eds., *Luther and Erasmus: Free Will and Salvation* (Philadelphia: Westminster, 1969), 37–40.

31. Ibid., 105.

the Bible should "stop imputing with blasphemous perversity the darkness and obscurity of their own hearts to the wholly clear Scriptures of God."

> For what still more sublime thing can remain hidden in the Scriptures now that the seals have been broken, the stone rolled from the door of the sepulcher (Matt. 27:66; 28:2) and a supreme mystery brought to life, namely, that Christ the Son of God has been made man, that God is three in one, that Christ has suffered for us and is to reign eternally? Are not these things known and sung even in the highways and byways? Take Christ out of the Scriptures and what will you find left in them?[32]

Later in his treatise against Erasmus, Luther makes an important distinction between the outer clarity and the inner clarity of Scripture. The inner clarity is the special gift of the Holy Spirit by which the individual Christian is enlightened. As Susan Schreiner has pointed out, Luther was drawn to "the experiential, affective language of interiority and immediacy" to describe the reality of the Spirit's internal work of verifying the truth of Scripture in the heart of the believer. Thus Luther could speak of a "feeling," "tasting," "sweetening," or "experiencing" that resulted from the work of the Holy Spirit within.[33] In his early commentary on the Magnificat, Luther declared that no one "can correctly understand God or his Word unless he has received such understanding immediately from the Holy Spirit. But no one can receive it from the Holy Spirit without experiencing, proving, and feeling it. In such experience, the Holy Spirit instructs us as in his own school."[34] The emphasis on the internal clarity of Scripture became a major axiom of Reformation exegesis. In Zwingli's sermon "The Clarity and Certainty of the Word of God," originally preached to cloistered Dominican nuns in 1522, the reformer of Zurich spoke about the "concurrent or prevenient clarity" of the Word of God that "shines on the human understanding," and "enlightens it in such a way that it understands and confesses the Word and knows the certainty of it." This is accomplished in "a gentle and attractive way" so as to bring assurance of the Savior's presence.

> And the gospel gives us a sure message, or answer, or assurance. Christ stands before you with open arms, inviting you and saying (Matt. 11:28): "Come unto me, all ye that labor and are heavy laden, and I will give you rest." Oh glad news, which brings with it its own light, so that we know and believe that it is true, as we have

---

32. Ibid., 110.

33. Susan E. Schreiner, "'The Spiritual Man Judges All Things': Calvin and the Exegetical Debates about Certainty in the Reformation," in *Biblical Interpretation in the Era of the Reformation: Essays Presented to David C. Steinmetz in Honor of His Sixtieth Birthday*, ed. Richard A. Muller and John L. Thompson (Grand Rapids: Eerdmans, 1996), 193.

34. *Luther's Works* 21:299; *Weimarer Ausgabe* 7:546: "Denn es mag niemantgot nochgottes wortrecht vorstehen, er hubs denn on mittel von dem heyligen geyst. Niemant kansz aber von dem heiligenn geist habenn, er erfaresz, vorsuchs und empfinds denn, unnd yn der selben erfarung leret der heylig geyst alsz ynn seiner eygenen schule."

fully shown above. For the one who says it is a light of the world. He is the way, the truth, and the light. In his Word, we can never go astray. We can never be deluded or confounded or destroyed in his Word. If you think there can be no assurance or certainty for the soul, listen to the certainty of the Word of God.[35]

Calvin echoes this same theme in his teaching about the internal witness of the Holy Spirit. The same Spirit who inspired the writers of Scripture long ago is present whenever believers today open the sacred text to study and learn. The Spirit is the inviolable nexus between inspiration and illumination.[36]

Beyond the internal clarity of Scripture conveyed to the believer by the Spirit, Luther argued for the Bible's external clarity. This objective, external clarity was related to the public ministry of the Word and was thus a major concern for preachers and teachers of Scripture. No less than the Catholic tradition, the churches of the Reformation emphasized the necessity of a well-ordered ministry and a program of rigorous theological education for its pastors and teachers. Indeed, the Protestant reformers were pioneers in this effort with the founding of new universities and academies devoted to the study of biblical languages and exegesis. (The establishment of Jesuit seminaries following the Council of Trent did much to close this gap by raising the level of preparation for many priests.) While the reformers found strong scriptural support for their doctrine of the Bible's inner clarity in the words of Paul in 1 Corinthians 2:15 (ESV), "The spiritual person judges all things, but is himself to be judged by no one," they found an equally compelling justification for their focus on the external clarity of Scripture in the story of Philip and the Ethiopian eunuch in Acts 8:26–38. "Do you understand what you are reading?" Philip poses to the eunuch the quintessential hermeneutical question. In commenting on this account in Acts, Calvin offers three distinct insights about the right way to read and understand Scripture. First, the Ethiopian scholar had been reading from the book of Isaiah. Calvin surmises that he would surely have been able to grasp many things he was reading in the prophet, his discourse on the goodness and power of God for example. But there were other things hidden from him, obscurities he may have encountered "in every tenth verse or so." Yet the eunuch did not throw away the scroll of Isaiah in frustration or disgust. He kept on reading and pondering even though some of the text's meaning he could not yet fathom. This is a good example for us, Calvin says. "There is no doubt that this is the way we must also read Scripture; we ought to accept eagerly and with a ready mind those things which are clear, and in which God

---

35. Geoffrey W. Bromiley, ed., *Zwingli and Bullinger*, Library of Christian Classics 24 (Philadelphia: Westminster, 1953), 73, 75, 84.

36. *Institutes* 1.7.1–5. According to John Webster, Calvin developed his doctrine of the internal witness of the Holy Spirit as "a pneumatological replacement for the idea of ecclesial approbation." *Holy Scripture: A Dogmatic Sketch* (Cambridge: Cambridge University Press, 2003), 62. The contemporary relevance of the Reformation doctrine of the clarity of Scripture is set forth in James P. Callahan's excellent essay, "*Claritas Scripturae*: The Role of Perspicuity in Protestant Hermeneutics," *Journal of the Evangelical Theological Society* 39, no. 3 (September 1996): 353–72.

reveals his mind; but it is proper to pass by those things which are still obscure to us, until a clearer light shines."

Second, the Ethiopian seeker displays a proper humility and modesty when he recognizes precisely that he is not able on his own fully to comprehend the mysteries of the text before him. In taking this attitude, the eunuch proves himself teachable. *Docilitas*, teachableness, is one of the marks of a true disciple of Christ, and this man has shown himself to be "one of God's pupils by reading the Scripture." This is far from the idea that one can master the Bible by an act of will or sheer academic brilliance. Calvin comments, "There must certainly be very little hope of a person who is swollen-headed with confidence in his own abilities ever proving himself docile."

And, finally, Calvin uses the example of Philip's witness to the eunuch to argue for the importance of interpreters and teachers in the church. We must make use of all the aids that the Lord has given for the understanding of Scripture, including written commentaries and the public preaching of the Word. Yes, Calvin acknowledges, God could have given to the seeker from Ethiopia a direct revelation of the meaning of Isaiah. After all, God chose an angel to direct Philip to his chariot. But, while the sovereign God remains ever free to work in extraordinary ways, we must not disparage the ordinary means he has given to the church through the written Word and the sacraments, baptism in this instance. "It is certainly no ordinary recommendation of outward preaching," Calvin declares, "that the voice of God sounds on the lips of men, while the angels keep silence."[37]

Clarity of Scripture, then, does not obviate the need for careful study and exegesis of the Bible. Nor does it mean that all difficulties are immediately or easily resolved. But this is no reason to withhold the Scriptures from the common people, for in matters related to one's eternal destiny the Bible speaks clearly for all to read and understand. The framers of the Westminster Confession in the seventeenth century set forth this Reformation principle in these classic words:

> All things in Scripture are not alike plain in themselves, nor alike clear unto all; yet those things which are necessary to be known, believed, and observed, for salvation, are so clearly propounded and opened in some place of Scripture or other, that not only the learned but the unlearned, in a due use of the ordinary means, may attain unto a sufficient understanding of them.[38]

---

37. John Calvin, *The Acts of the Apostles 1–13*, trans. John W. Fraser and W. J. G. McDonald (Grand Rapids: Eerdmans, 1965), 243–48.

38. Schaff, *Creeds*, 3:604. See also John Leith, *Assembly at Westminster: Reformed Theology in the Making* (Richmond: John Knox, 1973).

# PART FOUR

# All Things Hold Together in Christ

*Exploring God's World*

James K. A. Smith

Having seen the importance of the practices of the body of Christ for inculcating the intellectual virtues necessary for faithful thinking, we can now finally turn to a consideration of the so-called natural world itself—the focus of the sciences. But here, too, we continue to push back on the dominant paradigms in the science-theology dialogue. Specifically, we are concerned that too many "Christian" engagements with science are functionally deistic. While allegedly focusing on "creation," these habits of mind end up accepting the modern category of "nature" and simply treat nature *as* "creation." The result is a disenchanted understanding of creation and a corresponding view of the Creator that is distant and deistic—a constant temptation for science-theology paradigms. Most significantly, such models functionally invoke a Creator who seems to have little to do with the cross, a Creator divorced from Christ. As a result, the Creator invoked in such discussions seems to bear little resemblance to the God we know in Jesus. Chapter 18, on Charles Taylor, provides a historical account of how this deism emerged in the West and was appropriated by Christian thinking, albeit unwittingly.

In contrast, the sources in this section invite a radical retooling of our theologies of creation in ways that take seriously a trinitarian understanding of God and the world he has created. As Stanley Hauerwas succinctly puts it, "The God we worship and the world God created cannot be truthfully known without the cross, which is why the knowledge of God and ecclesiology—or the politics called the church—are interdependent"[1] Instead of grounding the theology-science encounter first and foremost in the creational narratives of Genesis 1–2, these chapters invite us to consider a christological account of creation that is centered in the prologue to John's Gospel, in which we encounter the Word become flesh and learn that "all things came into being through him, and without him not one thing came into being" (John 1:3). It is in this creative Son that "grace and truth" meet—just what the science-theology conversation needs.

Any integrally *Christian* understanding of the natural world, then, will have to work from a robustly *christological* understanding of creation—will have to take seriously the supremacy of Christ so eloquently hymned in Paul's Letter to the Colossians:

> He is the image of the invisible God, the firstborn of all creation; for in him all things in heaven and on earth were created, things visible and invisible, whether thrones or dominions or rulers or powers—all things have been created through him and for him. He himself is before all things, and in him all things hold together. He is the head of the body, the church; he is the beginning, the firstborn from the dead, so that he might come to have first place in everything. For in him all the fullness of God was pleased to dwell, and through him God was pleased to reconcile to himself all things, whether on earth or in heaven, by making peace through the blood of his cross. (1:15–20)

As Mark Noll argues in chapter 16, Christian scholarship is not rooted in merely "theistic" claims—and should certainly not be rooted in a functional deism. Rather, as he argued in *Jesus Christ and the Life of the Mind* (Grand Rapids: Eerdmans, 2011), the proper place for Christians to begin serious intellectual labor "is the same place where we begin all other serious human enterprises. That place is the heart of our religion, which is the revelation of God in Christ" (p. xii). So distinctly *Christian* thinking about creation and the natural world needs to be disciplined by a christological imagination. This means our thinking about science needs to be accountable not only to scriptural passages about creation but to the christological confessions of the church, since those, too, tell us something about the creation that "holds together" in him. Thus Noll points to the creeds of the church as a kind of "idolatry check" on our thinking: "Understanding more about Christ and his work not only opens a wide doorway to learning, but also checks tendencies toward idolatry that are as potent among scholars as the rest of mankind" (p. ix).

Chapters 19 and 20, by Stanley Hauerwas and Alasdair MacIntyre respectively, provide a model of how such thinking about science and creation would look differently when disciplined by a christological imagination. And Jonathan Wilson closes the volume in chapter 21 by reframing the importance of science in light of the mission of the church.

1. Hauerwas, *With the Grain of the Universe: The Church's Witness and Natural Theology* (Grand Rapids: Brazos, 2001), 21.

# 16

Come and See

*A Christological Invitation for Science*

Mark Noll

We believe in one God the Father all-powerful, Maker of heaven and of earth, and of all things both seen and unseen. And in one Lord Jesus Christ . . . , through whom all things came to be. . . .

We all with one voice teach the confession of one and the same Son, our Lord Jesus Christ: the same perfect in divinity and perfect in humanity, the same truly God and truly man, of a rational soul and a body; consubstantial with the Father as regards his divinity, and the same consubstantial with us as regards his humanity; like us in all respects except for sin; begotten before the ages from the Father as regards his divinity, and in the last days the same for us and for our salvation from Mary, the Virgin God-bearer as regards his humanity; one and the same Christ, Son, Lord, Only-begotten, acknowledged in two natures which undergo no confusion, no change, no division, no separation; at no point was the difference between the natures taken away through the union, but rather the property of both natures is preserved and comes together into a single person and a single subsistent being; he is not parted or divided into two persons, but is one and the same only-begotten Son, God, Word, Lord Jesus Christ.

—The Definition of Faith of the Council of Chalcedon

Originally published as "'Come and See': A Christological Invitation for Science," in Mark Noll, *Jesus Christ and the Life of the Mind* (Grand Rapids: Eerdmans, 2011), 99–124. Copyright © 2011 Wm. B. Eerdmans Publishing Company, Grand Rapids, MI. Reprinted by permission of the publisher; all rights reserved.

The bearing of Christology on science involves historical as well as theological awareness. Historical awareness is required because the relationship between God's "two books," Scripture and nature, has changed significantly over the course of centuries between biblical times and the present. So long as Christian communities thought it was a straightforward task to harmonize what Scripture seemed to communicate about the natural world and what observing nature or reflecting on nature seemed to communicate, the discussion was contained.

This situation, with some exceptions, largely prevailed until the sixteenth century and the beginnings of the modern scientific era. Yet even in the centuries when challenges to a "literal" reading of Scripture were still relatively few, perceptive believers knew that considerable sophistication was necessary to bring together biblical interpretation and interpretations of nature. Thus, early in the fifth century, St. Augustine noted that perceptive non-Christians really did know a great deal about "the earth, the heavens, and the other elements of the world, about the motion and orbit of the stars and even their size and relative positions, about the predictable eclipses of the sun and moon, the cycles of the years and the seasons, about the kinds of animals, shrubs, stones, and so forth." Given such able observers, he held it was "a disgraceful and dangerous thing for an infidel to hear a Christian, presumably giving the meaning of Holy Scripture, talking nonsense on these topics." When this kind of nonsense proliferated, the great danger was that those outside the faith would believe that the Scriptures themselves ("our sacred writers") taught the nonsense and so would be put off from the life-giving message of the Bible. Augustine expressed this danger in this way: "If they find a Christian mistaken in a field which they themselves know well and hear him maintaining his foolish opinions about our books, how are they going to believe those books in matters concerning the resurrection of the dead, the hope of eternal life, and the kingdom of heaven, when they think their pages are full of falsehoods on facts which they themselves have learnt from experience and the light of reason?" His closing injunction was to chastise "reckless and incompetent expounders of Holy Scripture" who "defend their utterly foolish and obviously untrue statements" by calling on "Holy Scripture for proof and even recit[ing] from memory many passages which they think support their position."[1] Yet comparatively speaking, in Augustine's own lifetime and for long thereafter, there were relatively few occasions when efforts at uniting scriptural teaching with knowledge gained from study of nature posed great difficulties.

That situation changed when the results of modern science called into question a growing array of straightforward, or "literal," interpretations of the Bible. From the sixteenth century onward, the number of apparent problems accumulated. Hard-won conclusions in the natural sciences, gained through ever more intense and ever more sophisticated study of nature, seemed to contradict what the Scriptures

---

1. Augustine, *The Literal Meaning of Genesis*, 2 vols., translated and annotated by John Hammond Taylor, SJ (New York: Newman, 1982), 1:42–43.

taught. Thus, the earth was the center of neither the solar system nor the entire universe (as might be concluded from some biblical passages); the earth was billions of years old (not of recent vintage); the universe was unimaginably vast (not sized by human scale); animal "species" designated temporary way stations on continuously changing paths of evolutionary development (not permanently fixed entities); human beings were part of this evolutionary development (not a species distinct in every way from animals).

As these seeming contradictions became urgent in the development of modern science, believers wrestled long and hard to keep what was learned from nature and what was learned from Scripture in sync. While the difficulties for each particular question involving Scripture and nature were important, it is even more important to remember that they mattered only because of the larger framework spelled out by St. Augustine. Since Scripture described the new life offered in Christ, which was the most important thing for all humans in all of history, to cast substantial doubt on Scripture for secondary concerns was to shake confidence in what the Bible revealed concerning the most important matter. Yet once that relationship between Scripture on all things (including nature) and Scripture on the most important thing (reconciliation with God in Christ) is kept in view, progress may be possible on issues involving Scripture and science. The key is that if Christ is the central and unifying theme of Scripture, then Christ should be preeminent in understanding scriptural revelation about everything else, including nature.

To view scientific exploration as a christological concern, it is helpful first to explore historical reasons for the difficulties besetting efforts at bringing scientific knowledge and biblical wisdom together. We will briefly explore some of that history as a prelude to the positive presentation, which begins with a case study from the career of the conservative Presbyterian theologian B. B. Warfield. Warfield, who taught at Princeton Theological Seminary in the late nineteenth and early twentieth centuries, is significant for our purposes because of how he deployed a crucial stance developed in thinking about Jesus when he came to evaluate modern theories of evolutionary development. The chapter ends by suggesting how explicit christological perspectives might guide Christian believers in thinking about the workings of science.

## The Bible and Science Historically Considered

Of the many books that have treated the record of religious-science engagement since the sixteenth century, the best have demonstrated that there has never been a simple conflict between biblical theology and natural science.[2] Rather, that

2. See especially John Hedly Brooke, *Science and Religion: Some Historical Perspectives* (New York: Cambridge University Press, 1991); David C. Lindberg and Ronald L. Numbers, eds., *God and Nature: Historical Essays on the Encounter between Christianity and Science* (Berkeley: University of California Press, 1986); and David C. Lindberg and Ronald L. Numbers, eds., *When Science and Christianity Meet*

history has been marked by a sustained series of negotiations, breakthroughs, well-publicized flashpoints, much conceptual rethinking, lots of ignorant grand-standing, some intellectual overreaching by starry-eyed avatars of a supremely all-competent "Science," some intellectual overreaching by determined "defend-ers" of Scripture, much noncontroversial science carried out by Christians, a huge quantity of scientific advance accepted routinely by believers, and much more.

At the dawn of modern science in the early seventeenth century, the iconic experimenter and polemicist Galileo Galilei recorded exceedingly wise words about how to combine investigations of nature with complete trust in Scripture. Implicit in his comments was an anchorage in christological realities that I hope to make explicit at the end of this chapter. If Galileo's guidelines had been followed, the history of science and religion in the modern West would have been much calmer than what actually unfolded. Galileo's comments are worth quoting in full before exploring why it has been so difficult to follow his proposals for peace between belief in Scripture and reliance on the results of scientific investigation. His standpoint combined a number of basic dispositions:

- trust that sense experience, rigorously controlled and creatively contem-plated, could reveal truths about nature;
- trust that biblical interpretation and scientific interpretation cannot in principle conflict because God is the author of both Scripture and nature;
- realization that much in the Bible is not intended as a scientific description of the world;
- realization that interpretation of Scripture and interpretation of nature often require legitimately different procedures, and confidence that what God allows humans to learn about nature could help discern what God has revealed in Scripture.

Here is what Galileo wrote:

It is most pious to say and most prudent to take for granted that Holy Scripture can never lie, as long as its true meaning has been grasped; but I do not think one can deny that this is frequently recondite and very different from what appears to be the literal meaning of the words.... I think that in disputes about natural phenomena one must begin not with the authority of scriptural passages but with sensory ex-perience and necessary demonstrations. For the Holy Scripture and nature derive equally from the godhead, the former as the dictation of the Holy Spirit and the latter as the most obedient executrix of God's orders; moreover, to accommodate the understanding of the common people it is appropriate for Scripture to say many things that are different (in appearance and in regard to the literal meaning of the words) from the absolute truth; on the other hand, nature is inexorable and

---

(Chicago: University of Chicago Press, 2003). An excellent reference work is Gary B. Femgren, ed., *The History of Science and Religion in the Western Tradition: An Encyclopedia* (New York: Garland, 2000).

immutable, never violates the terms of the laws imposed upon her, and does not care whether or not her recondite reasons and ways of operating are disclosed to human understanding; but not every scriptural assertion is bound to obligations as severe as every natural phenomenon; finally, God reveals Himself to us no less excellently in the effects of nature than in the sacred words of Scripture . . . ; and so it seems that a natural phenomenon which is placed before our eyes by sensory experience or proved by necessary demonstrations should not be called into question, let alone condemned, on account of scriptural passages whose words appear to have a different meaning.

However, by this I do not wish to imply that one should not have the highest regard for passages of Holy Scripture; indeed, after becoming certain of some physical conclusions, we should use these as very appropriate aids to the correct interpretation of Scripture and to the investigation of the truths they must contain, for they are most true and agree with demonstrated truths. . . . I do not think one has to believe that the same God who has given us senses, language, and intellect would want to set aside the use of these and give us by other means the information we can acquire with them, so that we would deny our senses and reason even in the case of those physical conclusions which are placed before our eyes and intellect by our sensory experiences or by necessary demonstrations.[3]

As helpful as what Galileo said in the early seventeenth century may still be four hundred years later, it is obvious that his hopes for smooth sailing on the sea of science-religion interaction have not been realized. The tumults that have arisen, however, are not random or uncaused. Many, in fact, have been propelled by habits of mind established in Western thinking well before the age of scientific revolution or that came to prominence during the era of the Enlightenment. In other words, thinking about science and religion has always been strongly influenced, sometimes absolutely determined, by important assumptions about *how* that thinking should take place.[4]

Because some of these assumptions arose in the Middle Ages, the recondite debates of thirteenth-century Catholic philosophers actually go far in explaining difficulties that continue to this day.[5] One particular dispute that has exerted a great influence on later Western history concerned the relationship of God's being to all other beings. Thomas Aquinas, the Dominican friar who lived from 1225 to 1274, argued that this relationship was *analogical*, that is, while humans and the created world were certainly *like* God in many ways, the essence of God remained ultimately a mystery known only to himself. Aquinas may well have been thinking of the passage in Isaiah 55:9 where the Lord tells the prophet,

3. "Galileo's Letter to the Grand Duchess" (1615), in *The Galileo Affair: A Documentary History*, ed. Maurice A. Finocchiaro (Berkeley: University of California Press, 1989), 92–94.

4. The following paragraphs are taken, with revisions, from Mark A. Noll, "Evangelicals, Creation, and Scripture: An Overview," BioLogos Forum (November, 2009), http://biologos.org/uploads/projects /Noll_scholarly_essay.pdf, 1–3.

5. This section relies on Amos Funkenstein, *Theology and the Scientific Imagination from the Middle Ages to the Seventeenth Century* (Princeton: Princeton University Press, 1986), esp. 25–31.

> As the heavens are higher than the earth,
> so are my ways higher than your ways
> and my thoughts than your thoughts.

The fact that God created the world out of nothing (*creatio ex nihilo*) was a crucial part of Aquinas's argument, because it meant that, while human minds could understand communication from God (i.e., revelation in nature, in Scripture, in Jesus Christ), they could in principle never grasp the essence of God. An interesting by-product of this position, which has taken on surprising relevance in contemporary debates, was Aquinas's understanding of randomness or contingency. Everything in the world, he insisted, happened because of God's direction. But some things happen contingently, or with the appearance of randomness. The logic of their contingency was perfectly clear to God, but because God in his essence is hidden to humans, humans may not be able to grasp how what they perceive as random could be part of God's direction of the universe.

The opposing view was maintained by the Franciscan priest and philosopher Duns Scotus, a younger contemporary of Aquinas who lived from 1266 to 1308. His position argued for the *univocity* of being. The only way to know the essence of anything is through its existence. Although God is much greater and much wiser than humans, his being and the being of all other things share a common essence. God is the creator and redeemer of humans, but his actions toward humans can (at least potentially) be understood reasonably well because the same laws of being apply to God as to everything else; the same way that we explain causation in every other sphere explains how God causes things to act and to be.

Scotus's approach to metaphysics (= the science of being) became, with a few exceptions, the dominant view in later Western history. It was particularly significant when joined to one more principle, this one from the English Franciscan, William of Ockham (1288–1348). Ockham's famous "razor" held that the simplest explanation was always the best explanation ("do not multiply entities unnecessarily"). Applied to science, this principle came to mean that if a natural event is explained adequately by a natural cause, there is no need to think about supernatural causes or even about the transcendent being of God. The combination of these philosophical positions is responsible for an assumption that prevails widely to this day: *once something is explained clearly and completely as a natural occurrence, there is no other realm of being that can allow it to be described in any other way.*

For a very long time, this assumption was not regarded as anti-Christian, since God was considered the creator of nature and the laws of nature as well as the active providential force that kept nature running as he had created it to run. During the Reformation era, Protestants maintained that conviction, but also began to place a new stress on the importance of Scripture for understanding God, themselves, the church, and everything else.[6] That emphasis was one of the important factors accelerating the rise of modern science. In particular, as Protestants set aside symbolic interpretations of Scripture, which had been prominent in the Middle Ages, they stressed straightforward examination of texts in what was often called a literal approach. This approach, in turn, stimulated a similar effort at examining the natural world in such a way that the medieval idea of God communicating to humans through "two books" (nature and Scripture) took on greater force. The assumption that became very important in this process was that *those who believed God created the physical world and revealed himself verbally in Scripture should harmonize in one complete picture what they learned about nature from studying nature and what they learned about nature from studying Scripture.* In both cases, literal knowledge was crucial, along with a belief that sources of literal knowledge could be fitted together harmoniously.

By the late seventeenth century, when science in its early modern form began to expand rapidly, yet a third conviction became important, which was worked out especially in the many efforts that went into constructing *natural theology*.[7] Natural theology was the project of explaining, often in considerable detail, what God's purposes were in creating the various parts of nature. Natural theology became a major enterprise when the earlier assumptions—metaphysical univocity and harmonization of the "two books"—encountered rapidly expanding knowledge about the physical world. Learned believers recognized the potential threat of this expanding knowledge—if scientific investigation could explain how nature worked as a system unto itself, maybe reliance on God and reference to the Scriptures were expendable. In response to this challenge, savants like Cotton Mather in the American colonies (*The Christian Philosopher*, 1721) and William Denham in England (*Physico-Theology*, 1713) offered elaborate explanations for how the structures of the physical and animal worlds revealed God's purposes in creating things as he had made them.

The tradition of natural theology received its most famous exposition in a book by William Paley, an Anglican archdeacon, published in 1802. Its title explained what it was about: *Natural Theology; or, Evidence of the Existence and Attributes of the Deity, Collected from the Appearances of Nature.* Paley's method was to describe features of animal, human, or material life and then to show how these features manifested God's design in and for nature. For example, the fact that animal and human bodies were symmetrical in outward appearance even as their internal organs and functions were asymmetrical provided Paley with "indubitable evidences, not only of design, but of a great deal of attention and accuracy in prosecuting the design."[8] The very important assumption behind the natural theology promoted

6. See in particular Peter Harrison, *The Bible, Protestantism, and the Rise of Natural Science* (New York: Cambridge University Press, 1998).

7. For particularly astute treatment, see Brooke, *Science and Religion*, 192–225.

8. William Paley, *Natural Theology*, ed. Matthew D. Eddy and David Knight (1802; New York: Oxford University Press, 2006), 101.

by Paley was that *not only did God create and providentially order the natural world, but humans could figure out exactly how and why God ordered creation as he did.* This assumption became critically important when later investigators of nature concluded that it was not necessary to think about God's intentions when figuring out how nature worked, and so belief in God was wrongheaded. In turn, those conclusions naturally antagonized the ones who continued to believe in God and therefore insisted either that new discoveries did in fact reveal a providential design or that the new discoveries had to be false.

Perhaps not many today who are engaged with contemporary debates in science and religion pause to think about historical turning points deep in the past. But the assumptions of univocal metaphysics, harmonization, and natural theology created powerful channels in which much subsequent discussion has flowed.

During recent decades, much of the conflict involving religion and science has resulted from polemicists on all sides carrying deeply entrenched convictions, attitudes, and assumptions into the present. Sorting out ancient mental habits from recent novelties is difficult, however, in part because there are so many different factors feeding into the current situation, and in part because evaluating these factors requires delicately balanced judgments. As examples of broader concerns, the awareness that nonbelievers of several types regularly use the supposedly assured result of modern science to attack traditional Christianity is hardly a baseless fantasy. In addition, Christian believers of all sorts can only applaud the devotion to Scripture that has been so prominent in conservative Protestant history, but many believers today—including a growing number of evangelicals—question some of the assumptions about how best to interpret Scripture that evangelicals sometimes treat as interchangeable with trust in Scripture itself.

When considered historically, however, it seems obvious that the modern strength of young-earth Creation Science is almost entirely explainable as the continuation of former predispositions.[9] To be sure, skillful publications like John Whitcomb and Henry Morris's *The Genesis Flood*, which appeared in 1961, have added new elements to the mix. And of course, they have been matched blow for blow by skillful antitheistic works like Richard Dawkins's *The God Delusion* that was published in 2006.

Yet the terms of debate in this modern polemical literature depend almost entirely on assumptions about metaphysical univocity, harmonization, and natural theology—as applied to modern questions and disseminated by democratic appeals to a broader public. In its turn, the Intelligent Design movement, with much more sophistication, still demonstrates a strong commitment to metaphysical univocity, harmonization, and natural theology, along with the use of modern probability theory and a tendency to treat the court of public opinion as a capable judge

9. For the best history, see Ronald L. Numbers, *The Creationists*, expanded ed. (Cambridge, MA: Harvard University Press, 2006); and for a solid general survey, Michael Ruse, *The Evolution-Creation Struggle* (Cambridge, MA: Harvard University Press, 2005).

of controversial issues. Again, critics of Creation Science and Intelligent Design, both believers and unbelievers, also often share some of these attitudes, especially those derived from metaphysical univocity, harmonization, and natural theology.

If what I have sketched here portrays the past with any accuracy, it should be clear that when conservative Bible-believers object to different aspects of modern science, they do so on the basis of assumptions as well as arguments. Often missing in those considerations, however, are direct appeals to the heart of the Christian faith as defined by the person and work of Christ. Coming back to that center offers a better way of discriminating more accurately between assumptions well grounded in solid theology and those that are not.

## A Case Study: B. B. Warfield, *Concursus*, and Evolution

A case study that shows how profitable it can be to approach scientific issues with christological principles is provided by the career of Benjamin B. Warfield. Warfield forcefully affirmed "this conjoint humanity and divinity [of Christ], within the limits of a single personality."[10] It was precisely this regard for the Chalcedonian definition of Christ's person and work that enabled Warfield to handle with relative ease the knotty questions about evolution that arose during his lifetime.

From his position at Princeton Theological Seminary, Warfield wrote steadily from the 1880s until shortly before his death in 1921 about many aspects of his era's developing evolutionary theories.[11] These writings included major essays devoted to Darwin's biography ("Charles Darwin's Religious Life" in 1888 and "Darwin's Arguments against Christianity" the next year); several substantial articles directly on evolution or related scientific issues ("The Present Day Conception of Evolution" in 1895, "Creation versus Evolution" in 1901, "On the Antiquity and Unity of the Human Race" in 1911, and "Calvin's Doctrine of Creation" in 1915); and many reviews of relevant books, some of them mini-essays in their own right.

In these works, Warfield repeatedly insisted on distinguishing among Darwin as a person, Darwinism as a cosmological theory, and evolution as a series of explanations about natural development. Of key importance was his willingness throughout a long career to accept the possibility (or even the probability) of evolution, while also denying Darwinism as a cosmological theory. In his mind, these discriminations were necessary in order properly to evaluate both the results of disciplined observation (science) and large-scale conclusions drawn from that science (theology or cosmology). Crucially, a christological perspective was prominent when he applied these discriminations to evolutionary theory.

10. Benjamin B. Warfield, "The Human Development of Jesus," in *Selected Shorter Writings*, vol. 1, ed. John E. Meeter (Philipsburg, NJ: Presbyterian and Reformed, 1970), 164.

11. Most of these works are reprinted, with editorial introductions, in B. B. Warfield, *Evolution, Science, and Scripture: Selected Writings*, ed. Mark A. Noll and David N. Livingstone (Grand Rapids: Baker, 2000).

For positioning Warfield properly on these subjects, it is also vital to stress a conjunction of his convictions that has been much less common since his day. Besides his openness toward evolution, that is, Warfield was also the ablest modern defender of the theologically conservative belief in the inerrancy of the Bible.

During the late nineteenth century when critical views of Scripture came to prevail in American universities, Warfield was as responsible as any other American for refurbishing the conviction that the Bible communicates revelation from God entirely without error. Warfield's formulation of biblical inerrancy, in fact, has even been a theological mainstay for recent "creationist" convictions about the origin of the earth.[12] Yet while he defended biblical inerrancy, Warfield was also a cautious, discriminating, but entirely candid proponent of the possibility that evolution might offer the best way to understand the natural history of the earth and of human-kind. On this score his views place him with more recent thinkers who maintain ancient trust in the Bible while also affirming the modern scientific enterprise and mainstream scientific conclusions.[13] Warfield did not simply assert these two views randomly, but he sustained them learnedly, as coordinate arguments.

In the course of his career, both Warfield's positions and his vocabulary did shift on the question of evolution. But they shifted only within a fairly narrow range. What remained constant was his adherence to a broad Calvinistic conception of the natural world—of a world that, even in its most physical aspects, reflected the wisdom and glory of God—and his commitment to the goal of harmonizing a sophisticated conservative theology and the most securely verified conclusions of modern science. To state once again his combination of positions, Warfield consistently rejected materialist or ateleological explanations for natural phe-nomena (explanations that he usually associated with "Darwinism"), even as he

12. For the direct use of Warfield on the inerrancy of Scripture, see John C. Whitcomb Jr. and Henry M. Morris, *The Genesis Flood: The Biblical Record and Its Scientific Implications* (Philadelphia: Presbyterian and Reformed, 1961), xx.

13. For example, Bernard Ramm, *The Christian View of Science and Scripture* (Grand Rapids: Eerdmans, 1954); Russell L. Mixter, ed., *Evolution and Christian Thought Today* (Grand Rapids: Eerdmans, 1959); D. C. Spanner, *Creation and Evolution: Some Preliminary Considerations* (London: Falcon Books, 1966); Malcolm A. Jeeves, ed., *The Scientific Enterprise and Christian Faith* (Downers Grove, IL: InterVarsity, 1969); Donald M. MacKay, *The Clockwork Image: A Christian Perspective on Science* (Downers Grove, IL: InterVarsity, 1974); Thomas F. Torrance, *Christian Theology and Scientific Culture* (New York: Oxford University Press, 1981); Davis A. Young, *Christianity and the Age of the Earth* (Grand Rapids: Zonder-van, 1982); Charles E. Hummel, *The Galileo Connection: Resolving Conflicts between Science and the Bible* (Downers Grove, IL: InterVarsity, 1986); J. C. Polkinghorne, *One World: The Interaction of Science and Theology* (Princeton: Princeton University Press, 1986); Howard J. Van Till, *The Fourth Day: What the Bible and the Heavens Are Telling Us about the Creation* (Grand Rapids: Eerdmans, 1986); John Houghton, *Does God Play Dice? A Look at the Story of the Universe* (Leicester, UK: Inter-Varsity, 1988); Philip Duce, *Reading the Mind of God: Interpretation in Science and Theology* (Leicester, UK: Apollos, 1998); Alister McGrath, *The Foundations of Dialogue in Science and Religion* (Oxford: Blackwell, 1998); Francis Collins, *The Language of God: A Scientist Presents Evidence for Belief* (New York: Free Press, 2007); Denis O. Lamoureux, *Evolutionary Creation: A Christian Approach to Evolution* (Eugene, OR: Wipf & Stock, 2008); and Karl W. Giberson, *Saving Darwin: How to Be a Christian and Believe in Evolution* (New York: HarperOne, 2008).

just as consistently entertained the possibility that other kinds of evolutionary explanations, which avoided Darwin's rejection of divine agency, could satisfactorily explain the physical world.

In several of his writings, Warfield carefully distinguished three ways in which God worked in and through the physical world. The most important thing about these three ways is that Warfield felt each of them was compatible with the theology he found in an inerrant Bible, if each was applied properly to natural history and to the history of salvation. "Evolution" meant developments arising out of forces that God had placed inside matter at the original creation of the world-stuff, but that God also directed to predetermined ends by his providential superintendence of the world. At least in writings toward the end of his life, Warfield held that evolution in this sense was fully compatible with biblical understandings of the production of the human body. "Mediate creation" meant the action of God upon matter to bring something new into existence that could not have been produced by forces or energy latent in matter itself. He did not apply the notion of "mediate creation" directly in his last, most mature writings on evolution, but it may be that he expounded the concept as much to deal with miracles or other biblical events as for developments in the natural world.[14] The last means of God's action was "creation ex nihilo," which Warfield consistently maintained was the way that God made the original stuff of the world.

On questions relating to evolution, orthodox Christology became relevant when Warfield invoked the concept of *concursus*. By this term he meant the coexistence of two usually contrary conditions or realities. In speaking of the person of Christ he had used a closely related term, "conjoined." For broader intellectual purposes, the key was to apply the same sense of harmoniously conjoined spheres to other domains.

Warfield held that the biblical authors were completely human as they wrote the Scriptures, even as they enjoyed the full inspiration of the Holy Spirit. This principle, grounded in Christology and exemplified in the Bible, was also his guide for positing an (evolutionary) approach to nature where all living creatures were thought to develop fully (with the exception of the original creation and the human soul) through "natural" means. Warfield's basic stance, expressed first about Christ and then extrapolated for Scripture, was a doctrine of providence that saw God working in and with, instead of as a replacement for, the processes of nature. Late in his career, this same stance also grounded Warfield's opposition to "faith healing." In his eyes, physical healing through medicine and the agency of physicians was as much a result of God's action (if through secondary causes) as the cures claimed as a direct result of divine intervention.[15] *Concursus* was as

14. Warfield deployed a similar vocabulary in a discussion of miracles that he published at about the same time; see "The Question of Miracles," in *The Bible Student* (March–June, 1903), reprinted in *The Shorter Writings of Benjamin B. Warfield*, vol. 2, ed. John E. Meeter (Nutley, NJ: Presbyterian and Reformed, 1973), 167–204.

15. See Warfield, *Counterfeit Miracles* (New York: Scribner, 1918).

important and as fruitful for his views on evolution as it was for his theology as a whole. It was a principle he felt the Scriptures offered to enable humans both to approach the world fearlessly and to do so for the greater glory of God.

Warfield's strongest statement on evolution came in 1915 when he published a lengthy article on John Calvin's view of creation.[16] Although he never stated it in so many words, it is clear that the convictions he ascribed to Calvin were also his own. He summarizes what he read in Calvin: "It should scarcely be passed without remark that Calvin's doctrine of creation is, if we have understood it aright, for all except the souls of men, an evolutionary one." God had called the "indigested mass" into existence *ex nihilo*, with a full "promise and potency" of what was to develop from that mass. Yet, according to Warfield's summary of Calvin, "all that has come into being since—except the souls of men alone—has arisen as a modification of this original world-stuff by means of the interaction of its intrinsic forces." Warfield went on to affirm a robust doctrine of providence, whereby "all the modifications of the world-stuff have taken place under the directly upholding and governing hand of God, and find their account ultimately in His will." Critically, however, he saw these later modifications taking place through "secondary causes." And once "secondary causes" were viewed as the means by which the original creation was modified, we have, according to Warfield, "not only evolutionism but pure evolutionism."

Warfield makes clear that Calvin did not himself explicitly embrace evolutionary theory since Calvin "had no conception" of "the interaction of forces by which the actual production of forms was accomplished." Thus, lacking the information provided by modern students of nature, Calvin did not advocate a "theory" of evolution. But, Warfield insists, he did teach "a doctrine of evolution" that pictures God as producing the material stuff of the world "out of nothing," but then "all that is not immediately produced out of nothing is therefore not created—but evolved." Warfield then translates Calvin's notion of "secondary causes" into what he defines as "intrinsic forces." Warfield's summary repeats a second time: "And this, we say, is a very pure evolutionary scheme."

The point where Christology enters is where Warfield explains the deeper theology at work. In his summary, "Calvin's ontology of second causes was, briefly stated, a very pure and complete doctrine of *concursus*, by virtue of which he ascribed all that comes to pass to God's purpose and directive government." For readers of Warfield in the twenty-first century, it is frustrating that he did not go further in expounding on this theological basis. He does say that the "account" of how "secondary causes" work is "a matter of ontology; how we account for their existence, their persistence, their action—the relation we conceive them to stand in to God, the upholder and director as well as creator of them." But for his

---

16. For Warfield's complete essay, see "Calvin's Doctrine of the Creation," in *The Works of Benjamin B. Warfield*, vol. 5, *Calvin and Calvinism* (New York: Oxford University Press, 1931), 287–349. The quotations that follow are taken from Warfield, *Evolution, Science, and Scripture*, 308–9.

purposes with this essay, Warfield does not explore those ontological issues. The regret now is that, if he had taken up these ontological questions, he might have considered the Western tradition of univocity that had, in effect, dispensed with *concursus* in explaining the physical world.

As it is, we still have a most intriguing contribution to theology, science, and science considered in connection with theology. Warfield's discussion of Calvin on evolution certainly indicated that he thought his very high view of biblical inspiration was fully compatible with comprehensive forms of evolutionary science (as distinct from evolutionary cosmology). Whether Warfield interpreted Calvin correctly or not, whether Warfield understood correctly his era's scientific discoveries (in which he was well read for an amateur), or whether his own efforts at bringing together his era's scientific knowledge and his interpretation of the biblical record were correct—these are all important but secondary issues. The main point lies elsewhere. The Scriptures that Warfield trusted implicitly revealed a God to him who created the world, providentially superintended the world, and gave human beings the capacity to explain the world naturally (in terms of "secondary causes"). The key theological principle that enabled Warfield to draw these conclusions was his belief in the classical Christology of Nicaea and Chalcedon.

Warfield's writings on evolution, the last of which appeared in the year of his death, 1921, cannot, of course, pronounce definitively on theological-scientific questions at the start of the twenty-first century. They can, however, show that sophisticated theology, nuanced argument, and careful sifting of scientific research are able to produce a much more satisfactory working relationship between science and theology than the heated strife that has dominated public debate on this subject since the time of Warfield's passing.


## A Christology for Science

The theologian Robert Barron has nicely clarified much of what lies behind recent conflicts over human origins that feature supposedly biblical truths contending against supposedly scientific conclusions. In his words, "Recent debates concerning evolutionist and 'creationist' accounts of the origins of nature are marked through and through by modern assumptions about a distant, competitive, and occasionally intervening God, whether the existence of such a God is affirmed or denied."[17] Barron's response to these modern debates is a sophisticated exposition of classical Christology aimed at his theological peers. My effort is much simpler and is aimed at academics in general, but it comes from the same christological perspective.

17. Robert Barron, *The Priority of Christ: Toward a Postliberal Catholicism* (Grand Rapids: Brazos, 2007), 221. For convenience, I return several times in the following paragraphs to this book by Robert Barron. But there are other parallel efforts, for example, from the physicist and Anglican theologian John C. Polkinghorne, in books like *Belief in God in an Age of Science* (New Haven: Yale University Press, 1998) and *Science and the Trinity: The Christian Encounter with Reality* (New Haven: Yale University Press, 2004).

## Christ as Creator, Sustainer, Redeemer

Classical Christian orthodoxy as expressed in the creeds that summarize the Scriptures begins at the beginning: nature owes its existence to and is sustained by Jesus Christ. From this starting point several important ramifications follow naturally.

One is the implication that the best way of finding out about nature is to look at nature. This implication comes directly from the christological principle of contingency. As described in the Gospels, individuals who wanted to learn the truth about Jesus had to "come and see." Likewise, to find out what might be true in nature, it is necessary to "come and see."

The process of "coming and seeing" does not lead to infallible truth about the physical world since there is no special inspiration from the Holy Spirit for the Book of Nature as there is for the Book of Scripture. But "coming and seeing" is still the method that belief in Christ as Savior privileges for learning about all other objects, including nature. This privileging means that scientific results coming from thoughtful, organized, and carefully checked investigations of natural phenomena must, for Christ-centered reasons, be taken seriously.

From this perspective, the successes of modern science in recent centuries testify implicitly to the existence of a creating and redeeming God. To once again quote Robert Barron, scientific activity by its very nature "implies . . . an unavoidable correspondence between the activity of the mind and the structure of being: intelligence will find its fulfillment in this universal and inescapable intelligibility." But how can this implication be justified? According to Barron, "The universality of objective intelligibility (assumed by any honest scientist) can be explained only through recourse to a transcendent subjective intelligence that has thought the world into being, so that every act of knowing a worldly object or event is, literally, a recognition, a thinking again of what has already been thought by a primordial divine knower."[18] In lay language, the "transcendent subjective intelligence" and the "primordial divine knower" guarantee the possibility that a researcher's mind can grasp something real about the world beyond the mind. The Scriptures—in John 1, Colossians 1, and Hebrews 1—provide a name for that "intelligence" and that "knower." In these terms, the existence of nature and the possibility of understanding nature presuppose Jesus Christ.

A second implication arising from the centrality of Christ in creation concerns the interpretation of Scripture. Classic biblical texts about the purpose of the Bible reinforce the foundational principle that the believers' confidence in Scripture rests on its message of salvation in Jesus Christ. Thus, in John 20, the Gospel story has been written down so "that you may come to believe that Jesus is the Messiah, the Son of God, and that through believing you may have life in his name" (20:31). In 2 Timothy 3, the inspired or God-breathed "sacred writings" have as their main purpose instruction "for salvation through faith in Christ Jesus" (3:15). And in

---

18. Barron, *Priority of Christ*, 154. See chap. 14 in this volume.

2 Peter 1, "the prophetic message more fully confirmed" as these prophets were "moved by the Holy Spirit" (1:19, 21) deals preeminently with "the power and coming of our Lord Jesus Christ" (1:16).

As these passages suggest, salvation in Christ anchors the believer's confidence that all of Scripture is trustworthy. But because of that supreme fact, the effort to understand *how* Scripture is trustworthy for questions like the ordering of nature should never stray far from consideration of Christ and his work. Yet as we have seen, "Christ and his work" includes, as an object, the material world of creation, and as a method, "come and see." In other words, following the Christ revealed in Scripture as Redeemer means following the Christ who made it possible for humans to understand the physical world and offered a means ("come and see") for gaining that understanding.

Final and ultimate disharmony between what "come and see" demonstrates about Christ and what "come and see" reveals about the world of nature is impossible. This Christ is the same one through whom God has worked "to reconcile to himself all things . . . making peace through the blood of his cross" (Col. 1:20) and in whom "all things . . . were created" and in whom "all things hold together" (1:16–17).

Yet it is indisputable that on some science-theology questions, trust in Christ (and therefore trust in Scripture) has seemed to conflict with trusting in what Christ-authorized procedure ("come and see") reveals about a Christ-created and Christ-sustained world. The parade of difficult questions arising from the effort to bring together standard interpretations of Scripture and standard interpretations of the natural world is a long one. Trying to answer these questions has been a consistent feature of the modern scientific age.

- In the nineteenth century, many earnest believers were wondering, if "coming and seeing" in geology and astronomy led to the conclusion that material existence has a very long history, should the "days" of Genesis 1 be understood as long periods of time or should a new interpretation of Genesis 1:1 be adopted that posits a "gap" between "in the beginning" and "God created"?
- More recent advances in both historical understanding (the ancient Near East) and empirical science (genetics, biology, astronomy) have prompted questions about the creation accounts of early Genesis. Well-trained scientists with strong Christian convictions have followed the Christ-rooted procedure of "coming and seeing" in their study of physical evidence for the origin of the universe and have concluded that much of standard evolutionary theory seems well grounded.[19] Similarly, well-trained biblical scholars with strong Christian convictions have followed the Christ-rooted procedure of "coming and seeing" in their study of ancient Near Eastern cultures and

19. "The BioLogos Forum: Science and Faith in Dialogue" is a portal with much discussion of such research; see http://biologos.org/.

have concluded that the early chapters of Genesis seem to be directly concerned about attacking idol-worship that substituted the sun or the moon for God.[20] Given the combination of these two streams of testimony, should it be thought that early Genesis is not concerned with modern scientific questions but is very much concerned about encouraging worship of the one true God who is the originator and sustainer of all things?

- Even more recently, the rough consensus on evolutionary change assembled from many scientific disciplines makes for even more complex questions: for example, if human evolution seems indicated by a wide range of responsible scientific procedures ("come and see"), how might responsible biblical interpretation understand the New Testament stress on Christ (very definitely in historical time and historical space) as overcoming the sinfulness inherited from Adam and Eve, whom Scripture, at least on a surface level, also represents as individuals in historical time and historical space?

All such questions caused understandable consternation when they were first raised, since they challenged specific interpretations of Scripture that had been tightly interwoven with basic interpretations of the entire Bible. Even after long and hard thought, such questions continue to pose definite challenges.

Answering such questions responsibly requires sophistication in scientific knowledge and sophistication in biblical interpretation—exercised humbly, teachably, and nondefensively. Unfortunately, these traits and capacities have not always predominated when such questions are addressed. But the difficult questions will almost certainly only continue to multiply because of two ongoing realities: the Holy Spirit continues to bestow new life in Christ through the message of the cross found in Scripture, and responsible investigations lead plausibly to further evolutionary conclusions from the relevant scientific disciplines.

## A Chalcedonian Perspective

The multiplication and intensification of such questions are, however, no cause for despair. For those with Christ these questions present instead a golden opportunity for returning to first principles. Almost the very first of those first principles is the Chalcedonian definition of Christ as fully divine and fully human in one integrated person.

20. For example, Derek Kidner, *Genesis: An Introduction and Commentary* (Downers Grove, IL: InterVarsity, 1967); Henri Blocher, *In the Beginning: The Opening Chapters of Genesis* (Downers Grove, IL: InterVarsity, 1984); Meredith G. Kline, "Space and Time in the Genesis Cosmogony," *Perspectives on Science and Christian Faith* 48 (1996): 2–15; Bruce K. Waltke and Cathi J. Fredricks, *Genesis: A Commentary* (Grand Rapids: Zondervan, 2001); and John H. Walton, *The Lost World of Genesis One: Ancient Cosmology and the Origins Debate* (Downers Grove, IL: InterVarsity, 2009).

If the mystery of divinity and humanity fully inhabiting a single being is at the heart of Christian faith, and if this faith offers Christ as the definite answer to the deepest mysteries of existence itself, then there is a way forward. It is not a way forward along the path of late medieval univocity when it was assumed that a natural explanation for any phenomenon was a fully sufficient explanation. It is not a way forward along the path of William Paley's natural theology, where it is assumed that humans may have God-like knowledge about the final purpose of physical phenomena. And it is not a way forward that either trivializes the Scriptures or distrusts modern science for ideological reasons. It is instead a way forward that tries to give both the study of nature its proper due as made possible because of Christ's creating work, and the interpretation of Scripture its proper due as revealing the mercy of redemption in Christ.

On specific questions concerning evolution, promising recent suggestions resting on classical Christology have come from Catholic scientists and theologians who draw on the insights of Thomas Aquinas. In particular, Thomas resisted the push toward univocity as he defended the complexity of the divine-human mystery at the heart of the universe. In his own day, as we have seen, Duns Scotus treated God and humanity as existing on a common metaphysical plane; God was infinitely greater than humans, but in quantity, not quality. No, said Thomas Aquinas, since humans are creatures and the Triune God was the creator, humanity and deity do not share the same metaphysical plane. Hence, there must always be separation between human knowledge about existence and divine knowledge. Robert Barron states Thomas's position carefully: "Aquinas maintained consistently throughout his career that God is inescapably mysterious to the human intellect, since our frame of reference remains the creaturely mode of existence, which bears only an analogical resemblance to the divine mode of being. The 'cash value' of the claim that God exists is that there is a finally mysterious source of the to-be of finite things."[21]

One of the payoffs in the twenty-first century from this thirteenth-century insight is relevant to debates about evolution, where the consensus in several scientific specialties posits a key role for "randomness" in describing physical changes over time. Thomas Aquinas offered what amounts to a prescient response when he described the contingency of much that transpires in the world (his contingency may be taken as roughly our randomness): "The effect of divine providence is not only that things should happen somehow, but that they should happen either by necessity or by contingency. Therefore, whatsoever divine providence ordains to happen infallibly and of necessity happens infallibly and of necessity; and that happens from contingency, which the divine providence conceives to happen from contingency."[22] God, in other words, never works capriciously, even

21. Barron, *Priority of Christ*, 13.
22. *A Summa of the Summa*, ed. Peter Kreeft (San Francisco: Ignatius, 1990), 174 (from Thomas Aquinas, *Summa Theologiae* I.22.4).

though some providentially determined actions may look to humans like pure contingency. The metaphysical difference between God and humanity explains this difference in perspective.

A very recent Catholic statement has applied this type of reasoning to arguments between those who advocate Intelligent Design and those defending a purely un-guided evolutionism. According to its authors, because this debate concerns "whether the available data support inferences of design or chance," the debate "cannot be settled by theology." That is to say, when empirical results are in view, the way to solve the questions is to "come and see." But the statement goes on with sophisti-cated attention to broader contexts: "It is important to note that, according to the Catholic understanding of divine causality, true contingency in the created order is not incompatible with a purposeful divine providence. Divine causality and created causality radically differ in kind and not only in degree. Thus, even the outcome of a truly contingent natural process can nonetheless fall within God's providential plan for creation."[23] Questions of chance and randomness exist on two levels, the empiri-cal and the philosophical/theological. Each level deserves its own serious attention.

Under the assumptions promoted by medieval univocity, early modern theo-ries of harmonizing Scripture and nature, and natural theology in the era of the Enlightenment, it has become customary to think that scientifically demonstrated randomness in nature counts as knockdown evidence against the existence of God. But this is both a logical and an ontological error. As phrased recently by the philosopher Alvin Plantinga, it is a logical error to move from asserting, "We know of no irrefutable objections to its being biologically possible that all of life has come to be by way of unguided Darwinian processes," to concluding: "All of life has come to be by way of unguided Darwinian processes."[24] It is an ontological error for the same reason that it is erroneous to think that if Jesus hungered and thirsted, he could not be the Son of God.

Satisfactory resolution of problems stemming from responsible biblical in-terpretation brought together with responsible interpretations of nature will not come easily. Such resolution requires more sophistication in scientific knowledge, more sophistication in biblical hermeneutics, and more humility of spirit than most of us possess. But it is not wishful thinking to believe that such resolution is possible. It is rather an expectant hope that grows directly from confidence in what has been revealed in Jesus Christ. If, therefore, humbly responsible think-ers, properly equipped scientifically and hermeneutically, conclude that the full picture of human evolution now standard in many scientific disciplines fits with a trustworthy interpretation of Scripture, that conclusion can be regarded as fully compatible with historic Christian orthodoxy as defined by the normative creeds.

23. The Roman Curia: Pontifical Commissions, "Communion and Stewardship: Human Persons Created in the Image of God" (July 23, 2004), published in *La Civilta Cattolica*, 2004, 1:254–86, http://www.vatican.va/roman_curia/congregations/cfaith/cti_documents/rc_con_cfaith_doc_20040723_communion-stewardship_en.html.

24. Alvin Plantinga, "The Dawkins Delusion," *Books & Culture*, March/April 2007, 22.

# 17

## Encountering God's World

### Curiositas *vs.* Caritas

PAUL GRIFFITHS

The book in which this chapter originally appeared is about intellectual appetite. This appetite, Aristotle claimed at the beginning of the *Metaphysics*, is natural to us, a proper constituent of human nature like (he did not say this) the capacity to torture or to laugh. It is, he seems to have thought, an appetite other creatures lack. They seek food or sex or safety or sensual pleasure, and finding these involves seeking and getting knowledge of a sort—the whereabouts of the food or the mate, for instance. But dogs and cats, and even (probably) dolphins and nonhuman primates, are never primarily interested in knowing where the food or the mate is. No, what they want is to eat the food or copulate with the mate, and they seek knowledge as a means to that end. We often seek knowledge in this way, too, as a necessary means for getting something else—power, security, self-congratulation, adulation, money. But sometimes we do something different: we cosset and indulge an appetite for knowledge quite independent of any other end. Sometimes, it seems, we just want to know: how to prove Fermat's Last Theorem, whether there is life on planets in other solar systems, if that

Originally published in "Introduction," "Curiositas," and "World," in Paul Griffiths, *Intellectual Appetite: A Theological Grammar* (Washington, DC: Catholic University Press, 2009), 1–4, 9–28. Copyright © 2009. Permission conveyed through Copyright Clearance Center, Inc.

thing over there is an elm tree, what Dickens's plans were for bringing *Edwin Drood* to a conclusion, how best to explain the slaughter of the innocents and the inevitability of betrayal. And it is this appetite, an appetite for knowledge *simpliciter*, for nothing other, that Aristotle seems to have thought of as properly and uniquely human.

I am not especially interested in whether Aristotle is right about the restriction of this appetite to human beings. Most of us—we human beings, that is—think that some living beings other than ourselves (angels, demons, pretas, djinns, sprites) have intellectual appetite, as well, and therefore judge the Aristotelian restriction wrong. Christians, certainly, think, unless they have misconstrued Christianity, that there are angels and that they have intellectual appetites. But these topics, interesting though they are, are not my concern here. I am interested only in the question of human intellectual appetite: what it is and how it should be catechized, disciplined, and configured.

What I offer is a depiction or display of the grammar of a Christian understanding of what a catechized and disciplined appetite for knowledge ought to look like. Any such display involves depicting not only the lexicon and grammar of a particular account of what it is to want to know, but also, inevitably, some among the assumptions about the way the world is, the way human knowers are, and the point of seeking and finding knowledge, which inform any such account. It is not possible to think about intellectual appetite without also thinking about these difficult and controversial topics, and certainly, Christians make no attempt to avoid them. My display of the grammar of their account of intellectual appetite will therefore include the relevant ontological and teleological lexicon. And not only this. Thinking about intellectual appetite rapidly shows that this appetite always demands and receives formation by culture, and that this formation can be and is varied, sometimes in the direction of deepening damage and sometimes in that of remedying it. Even if you think, as Aristotle did and as most Christians do, that intellectual appetite is natural to us, this does not mean that a human being in a state of nature—without the company of other human beings, for example—would be any more likely to develop a distinctively human form of appetite for knowledge than to become a language-user. And that means not likely at all. An account of intellectual appetite therefore requires attention to catechesis, curriculum, and pedagogy.

The Christian account of intellectual appetite—by calling it "the" Christian account I do not mean to suggest that all Christians would assent to it; I mean only to say, descriptively, that the vast majority of self-described Christians who have thought and written about the topic have given an account in essentials like this one; and, normatively, that this is in fact the account of the matter orthodox Christians should give (though I will not argue for that last claim)—has of course its competitors. This interweaving is meant to serve one of my subsidiary purposes, which is to show that no account of as complex and interesting a matter as the ordering of intellectual appetite can be free of commitment to controversial positions on ontological and anthropological questions, and that, therefore, the extent to which any particular account of this sort seems obviously or uncontroversially true to you is exactly the extent to which you have not thought about it. I will not, however, attempt to depict these competitors to the Christian view of intellectual appetite in anything like their fullness. That is a task for those who find them attractive or convincing. Their presence in my account is as foils to the Christian account, as examples of Egyptian gold, to use an ancient Christian figure for the good things to be learned from the pagans, good things that need always to be transfigured by baptism if they are to serve their proper purposes.

Neither will I be offering systematic arguments in favor of the Christian account and against its competitors. This is because I share with John Henry Newman the conviction, expressed most trenchantly in a sermon on faith and reason delivered in 1839 (while still Anglican), that, "When men understand what each other mean, they see, for the most part, that controversy is either superfluous or hopeless." Carefully descriptive juxtaposition of opposed or otherwise contrasting views, coupled with the making and offering of precise and perspicuous distinctions, is almost always more productive than argument, whether aimed at refutation of an opposed position or defense of one's own.

This lack of interest in argument does not indicate a lack of interest in truth. It seems to me that the understandings of world and person interwoven with the Christian view of intellectual appetite are perspicuously and seductively beautiful, while those belonging to its competitors are, in comparison, impoverished, parched, and opaquely inadequate to their task. If I do my job of display well, it is possible that some readers who do not already inhabit this account of things may be seduced into paying it a visit, and since the account I offer is very hospitable, indeed maximally hospitable (not because I am offering it, but because God has; all I am doing is transmitting it), the visit may turn out to be long, long enough that the visitor effectively takes up permanent residence. But that is a scenario for pagan readers. For Christians, I offer a reminder. The account of intellectual appetite in these pages has been forgotten rather than rejected by Christians, and this is because they are in unreflective thrall to one among its competitors without being aware that there is an alternative.

. . . . . . . . . . . . . . . . . .

My interest in intellectual appetite is prompted and stimulated by premodern Christian thought about it, and most especially by that of late-antique Christians writing and thinking in Latin. Among the terms they used to describe intellectual appetite was *curiositas*, which comes into English, inevitably but misleadingly, as "curiosity." It was a commonplace for all Latin-using Christian intellectuals from Tertullian at the end of the second century through at least to Bossuet in the seventeenth to say that *curiositas* is a vice, and that it needs to be distinguished from virtuous forms of the desire to know, which, beginning in the third century, began to be called *studiositas*. This Latin word, I suppose, has to be rendered "studiousness," though that is, if anything, still more misleading than calquing *curiositas* with "curiosity." This Christian distinction shows at once that there are different ways to construe intellectual appetite descriptively, and to judge it normatively—or at least that Christians thought such distinctions necessary, and put a good deal of effort into making them.

The premodern Christian commonplace that curiosity is a vice is for us surprising and puzzling. This is because, beginning in the fifteenth century, curiosity was transferred rapidly and almost without remainder from the table of the vices to that of the virtues, so that by the eighteenth century David Hume, in *A Treatise of Human* Nature (2.3.10), could treat the topic as though the term unproblematically labeled a disinterested desire to know the truth—and could do so in apparent ignorance that there had been a two-millennia-long enterprise of trying to discriminate acceptable or virtuous forms of the desire to know from unacceptable or vicious forms of that same appetite, and of using "curiosity" to label the latter. For Hume, and, mostly, for us, Christian or not, appetite for knowledge is an undifferentiated good. The result of curiosity's transformation from a darkly destructive vice into a shining virtue for which we pat children on the head and compliment students is that, for us, the idea that there are vicious forms of intellectual appetite sounds at first puzzling and then, usually, obscurantist. For us there are only proverbial remnants of the idea that curiosity is a vice (we recall that it killed the cat). But for the most part, the enterprise of distinguishing good appetites for knowledge from bad ones is mysterious, and the long Christian tradition of attempting to do that largely forgotten, or, when remembered, excoriated.

Why did Christians make such distinctions in the first place? First, there are elements internal to the Christian tradition that suggest appetite for knowledge is not an undifferentiated good. Some among these are scriptural. The story of the fall of the first human beings in the opening chapters of Genesis appears on the surface of the text to have something to do with seeking knowledge that should have been shunned, or perhaps with knowledge wrongly sought. The compressed but suggestive account of the two banquets in the book of Proverbs (9:1–18) suggests a distinction between understanding rightly offered and received, and understanding's simulacrum, deceptively offered and disastrously grasped. St. Paul, in the First Letter to the Corinthians (3:18–23), and in the Letter to the Colossians (2:4–8), inveighs against the wisdom of the world, and against empty, seductive philosophy; and St. John uses a phrase in his first letter, *hē epithymia tōn ophthalmōn* (1 John 2:16), which was early rendered into Latin as *concupiscentia oculorum* (sometimes, in the Old Latin versions, *desiderium oculorum*, but *concupiscentia* eventually became standard) and almost unanimously understood by premodern Christians to refer to a disordered appetite for knowledge. The seventeenth-century translators of Scripture into English appointed by King James rendered John's phrase with decided vigor as "the lust of the eyes," and a high proportion of Christian thinking about the question of intellectual appetite took place by way of gloss and commentary upon this phrase. If the eyes can lust, desire inappropriately to see, then surely they can also seek vision (knowledge) chastely and rightly. But what, exactly, is the difference between these two modes of knowledge seeking, these two kinds of intellectual appetite?

As the canon of Scripture approached closure in the third century, the texts just mentioned, along with many others, became interwoven with other urgent needs facing Christian thinkers to bring into being a fabric of thought and practice that encouraged them to write extensively and with energy about how to distinguish a rightly ordered appetite for knowledge from a wrongly ordered one, and to attempt to institute programs of catechesis that would order the intellectual appetites of Christians in the right way. Among these exigencies was the need for distance from what later came to be called Gnosticism. Gnosticism is a portmanteau term for a variety of movements of thought in the Mediterranean world of late antiquity that agreed on making human flourishing dependent upon possession of a kind of specialized knowledge available only to an elite. Some of these movements were pagan, some Jewish, and some Christian or quasi-Christian; orthodox Christians found it necessary to keep them at a distance. They did this by, first, rejecting the idea that salvation is dependent upon ratiocination, or upon the capacity to benefit from specialized intellectual training; and then, second, by thinking through what it is that all Christians do need to know and be able to do, and what, therefore, are the appropriate means of catechetical training to make it possible for them to know and do these things. All this required Christian thinkers to work at distinguishing their catechesis from that of the Gnostics.

Another circumstance that required Christian attention to formation of the appetite for knowledge was that they found themselves forced into awareness of and engagement with pagan catechetical regimes from the beginning. This was inevitable for a tribe occupying a subordinate place in a pagan world whose pedagogy was well established and unavoidable for all who sought literacy and a rhetorical and literary education that would permit them to interact as equals with the elite among their pagan rivals. Christians therefore had, for many centuries, catechetical regimes that depended upon and assumed those of the pagans: if you wanted to learn how to read and write Latin or to master the pagan classics (Homer, Vergil, Cicero, Seneca), for instance, you could do so only in pagan schools. This resulted in anxiety: how to differentiate the goals of pagan catechesis from those of Christian catechesis? What, in the pagan catechetical regimes, could safely be accepted and used, and what had to be transformed or rejected? As Christians began to occupy a more prominent place in the still largely pagan culture of the late Roman Empire, pagans began to feel a reciprocal anxiety about their own catechetical practices, and to address it by entering the same theoretical territory, sometimes with heavy rhetorical and conceptual artillery. But that was a later development: the peculiar situation of Western Christians in the first five centuries forced them to give sustained theoretical attention to what they wanted the members of the tribe to know and be able to do and, therefore, to the catechetical disciplines likely to be most effective in bringing the desired results about.

In partial response to this theoretical pressure, Christian theorists developed the technical vocabulary I have mentioned, to which the term *studiositas* was central. This was a label used by Christians for their own preferred form of the catechized and disciplined appetite for knowledge, and in contrast to the disciplined form of the same appetite they thought preferred by their elite pagan rivals, for which they preferred the label *curiositas*, For pagans, too, *curiositas* could be a crass, vulgar, and dangerous appetite for knowledge no one should want, knowledge that would damage anyone who might be unfortunate enough to get it. Seneca and Apuleius both use the word in this fashion. But it could also sometimes be an appropriately passionate response to and redress of ignorance. For Christians, however, the word almost always labeled an appetite always potentially vicious and usually actively so; and their discussions of it were polemical, aimed at separating their catechetically formed identity from that of their pagan interlocutors by offering a critique of the disciplinary regimes that produced *curiositas* by contrasting them with those that produced *studiositas*.

Christian thinkers had a balancing act to perform here. On the one hand, it was clear to them that the intellectual appetite could be malformed, and that some bodies of knowledge were of no interest to Christians and might be damaging to them: astrological knowledge and skill in various forms of magical technique were the standard examples. On the other hand, they wanted to affirm that the cosmos and everything in it must of necessity be good because it has been spoken into being by a good God, which suggests that knowledge about the workings of the cosmos and its inhabitants must also be desirable: Why would God give human beings the capacity to seek and find such knowledge if it not to understand more fully the depths of goodness and beauty in the created order? Then there was the pressing question of whether, and to what extent, Christians should study pagan literature and, if they did, what they should expect to get out of it. A gamut of responses is evident among late antique Christians. Tertullian fulminates about Athens as a symbol of pagan learning; Jerome swears that he will stop reading pagan literature and then rapidly breaks his oath; and Augustine, among the most thoroughly imbued with pagan learning of late antique Christians, lays out a careful program of study for Christians, in which literacy, pagan literature, history, and (what we would call) the natural sciences are given a place, but a carefully circumscribed and guarded one.

This gamut of response to the question of how Christians should have their intellectual appetites formed and the extent to which they should study pagan materials has always been evident in Christian thought; versions of it remain with us today. But at every point on this gamut there was (and largely still is) agreement that some methods of disciplining the appetite for knowledge malform it, while some form it as it should be formed. "Curiosity" was the Christian term of art for the former, and "studiousness" for the latter.

Yet some care is necessary here. The pagan catechesis of the intellectual appetite criticized by Western Christians in late antiquity as productive of curiosity was not in every respect dissimilar from the catechesis that produced the studiousness they commended. Both worked on the same appetite with the purpose of giving it form and making it active. Both, too, were concerned to emphasize that not every member of the tribe, pagan or Christian, needed advanced formation of the appetite for knowledge. Most did not, having neither aptitude nor need for such formation. They needed to have their appetite for knowledge formed only to the extent that permitted meeting material needs (usually, then, by training in some craft: farming, butchery, soldiering, building, navigation, and so on) and fulfilling whatever functions the tribe took to be incumbent upon all its members. These latter, for the Roman Empire, were few because the social order was highly stratified, which meant many stratum-specific essentials and few universal ones: the essential skills for slaves and citizens, for example, had little overlap. For the late antique Christian church, less fundamentally and deeply stratified, there were some strongly marked functions—principally liturgical—required for every member of the tribe, and therefore a universal catechesis aimed at providing the knowledge and skill needed for these. But for late antique pagans and Christians both, long and deep exposure to a regime of disciplined catechetical formation of the appetite for knowledge was for the few—as it also is for us in early postmodernity.

This long-lived body of Christian theorizing about what it is to want to know and how that appetite ought to be disciplined is one of the principal theoretical resources for anyone who wants to think about this topic today. But it is not the only one. There is also a body of theoretical thought on the proper formation of the appetite for knowledge that is self-consciously not Christian and sometimes polemically anti-Christian. This tradition began in the fifteenth century (there are earlier anticipations) and had reached its classical form by the seventeenth. It is evident in the work of, among others, Descartes, Bacon, Spinoza, Leibniz, and Locke, for each of whom the provision of rules for directing the understanding— and, thus, the elaboration of a regime of disciplining the intellectual appetite—was a matter of great interest. Its high modern form can be seen in Kant, and then, soon after, in Wilhelm von Humboldt, most especially in their works on the ordering and proper relation of the disciplines taught in the then-new research university. This concern was developed by Max Weber at the beginning of the twentieth century and is most especially evident in his concern to separate fact from value and to limit academic work to the sphere of the former. All this implies a particular understanding—or, more accurately, a family of understandings—of forming and ordering the intellectual appetite.

Yet even in von Humboldt at the beginning of the nineteenth century and much more dramatically in Heidegger's reaction in the 1920s and 1930s to Weber's advocacy of a pure, disinterested *scientia*, there is something else. The Germans call it *Bildung*, often rendered "education," but really implying not only the intellectual formation of those subject to it but also their moral and spiritual formation. The interwar German advocacy of *Bildung* plus *Wissenschaft* as the twin poles around which the university should be ordered was largely discredited by its embroilment with Nazism, or if not explicitly with Nazism then with equally murky pagan views about the nature and meaning of the German spirit and the catechetical methods appropriate to its formation. There is a very approximate analogue to this concern with *Bildung* in American (and to some extent also French) resistance to the Weberian justification of the research university, evident most clearly in emphasis, evident in the literature of the last century or so, upon the importance of offering moral formation at least to undergraduates—and in the occasional clear and strident rejection of any such idea.

Cartesian and Baconian rules for directing the intellect (not identical with one another by any means, but similar in the matters raised here) are in many ways different from a Weberian pedagogy in pure science; in spite of these differences, however, there is a direct genealogical link between the seventeenth-century aspiration toward a *mathesis universalis*—of, that is, mapping all knowledge onto a manipulable grid and providing clear principles of method that would permit the attainment of certainty about any topic—and the late-nineteenth and early twentieth-century hope for institutions of higher education free of commitments to value. Both the link and the differences have been made clear by the explosion of work since the 1960s on the history and meaning of pedagogical practice in the West, prompted in considerable part by Michel Foucault's work in the topic, which is still in many ways definitive of the field.

The complex historical story can, in its American form, be summarized in the following way, at least with regard to elite institutions and their epigones (the story would be much more complex were I to say anything about self-consciously Christian or Jewish institutions of higher education): For a short while, from the late nineteenth century until the 1960s, European and American intellectuals, relying, usually unreflectively, upon this body of early and high modern theory about the proper formation of the intellectual appetite, had confidence in the regimes of intellectual discipline by which they had been formed and in the desirability of forming new generations in accord with them. They shared, in broad outline at least, a vision of what it meant to seek understanding and of how budding intellectuals should be trained to seek it, and this vision was given institutional form in the institutions of higher education we now inhabit. But once the Weberian orthodoxy about the vocation of the academic as an intellectual devoted to value-free analysis of what is found in the empirical sphere had crumbled, which it had by the 1960s in both Europe and North America, it became apparent that there were other possibilities, other ways in which the intellectual appetite could be formed, other regimes of discipline (again, Foucault's language, unavoidable and very useful: it's Christian language *manqué*); and the anxiety this produced led to worried depictions and explanations of the decay of the university, enthusiastic advocacy of committed scholarship in which the scholar is understood principally as an agent of social change, and so on. Most institutions of higher education in North America and Europe are now explicitly, and often publicly, aware that there is no unanimity within their walls about what intellectual appetite is and how it should be formed. They are also aware that the catechetical regimes they have in place are, by and large, not doing a job that makes anyone happy. Hence the flood of worried literature, which shows an anxiety interestingly analogous to that evident in late antique Christian theorizing about catechesis. Both bodies of work show a distinctively academic form of anxiety about what it is to want to know and how that appetite ought best to be catechized, an anxiety produced by the challenging awareness of a multiplicity of competing understandings of and recommendations about these topics.

This study is written out of this context: forgetfulness on the part of Christians of our heritage of serious thought about the proper formation of the desire to know, and confusion and anxiety on the part of pagan thinkers about the same topic.

### Curiositas

> And so, every love that belongs to a studious soul which wants to know what it does not know is not a love of what it does not know but rather of what it does know. It is because of what it does know that it wants to know what it does not know. But someone so curious as to be carried away by nothing other than a love of knowing the unknown, and not because of something already known, should be distinguished from the studious and called curious. But even the curious do not love the unknown. It is more accurate to say that they hate the unknown because they want everything to become known and thus nothing to remain unknown.

Augustine writes here, in the tenth book of his work on the Holy Trinity (10.1.3), that the love which belongs to the studious is prompted always by a love for something already known, not by a love for what is not yet known. He then notes that the curious might be carried away or dragged off by force (all implications to be found in *rapiatur*, a word that lies behind the English verb "to rape") solely by love directed at knowing what they do not yet know, and might in that way be distinguished from the studious. But even the curious, so understood, do not really love what they do not know. It would be better to say that they hate what they do not know, because they would like that set to be null, an ambition to be realized only by coming to know everything. Therefore, they wish to extinguish all unknowns. The studious, by contrast (it is not said in this passage, but implied), have a more limited desire, which is to come to love what they know more fully by seeking knowledge toward which its love (both subjective and objective genitive intended here) points them. The studious are directed, then, by love; the curious, knowledge seekers though they are, by anxious hatred of what they know not.

Premodern Western Christians used the word *studiositas* for what they thought of as well-formed intellectual appetite, and *curiositas* for its deformed kissing cousin. It will be useful to begin with a formal definition of each. The definitions that follow are concordant with those found in the Christian tradition, but are not identical with any of them. I give them not in an exegetical spirit, but rather as a contributor to a tradition of thought whose authority I accept and that I consider it a privilege to speak out of and thereby to extend.

Curiosity is a particular appetite, which is to say a particular ordering of the affections, or, more succinctly, a particular intentional love. Its object, what it wants, is new knowledge, a previously unexperienced reflexive intimacy with some creature. And what it seeks to do with that knowledge is to control, dominate, or make a private possession of it. Curiosity is, then, in brief, *appetite for the ownership of new knowledge*, and its principal method is enclosure by sequestration of particular creatures or ensembles of such. The curious want to know what they do not yet know, and they often want to know it *ardentissimo appetitu*, with supremely ardent appetite. But the appetite for new knowledge that belongs to them ravishes them: they are violated and dragged away, with full consent and eager cooperation, by what is likely to seem to them a noble desire for *nihil aliud quam scire*, nothing other than to know the *incognita*. The appetite of the curious is in that way closed, seeking a sequestered intimacy: the knowledge they seek is wanted as though it were the only thing to be had, and this means that the curious inevitably come to think that the only way in which they can be related to what they seek to know is by sequestration, enclosing a part of the intellectual commons for their own exclusive use, and thus mastering it.

Studiousness, like curiosity, is a particular love, a specific ordering of the affections. And like curiosity it has knowledge as its object, which it seeks. But the studious do not seek to sequester, own, possess, or dominate what they hope to know; they want, instead, to participate lovingly in it, to respond to it knowingly as gift rather than as potential possession, to treat it as icon rather than as spectacle. A preliminary definition of studiousness, then, is: *appetite for closer reflexive intimacy with the gift*. The appetite of the studious may rival that of the curious in ardor; but the former, unlike the latter, treat what they seek to know as iconic gift and thereby as open to and participatory in the giver. Objects of knowledge so understood can be loved and contemplated, but they cannot be dominated by sequestration. The studious therefore seek a peculiar reflexive intimacy with what they want to know, and they seek it with the understanding that they, as knowers, have creaturely participation in the giver in common with what they want to come to know. This understanding carries with it another, which is that this commonality makes cognitive intimacy possible. And the studious are committed to treating the intellectual commons as indeed common, and not as a field of conquest, a set of objects to be sequestered.

Both intellectual appetites seek knowledge: that is what makes them forms of intellectual appetite. But they do so with different purposes: where curiosity wants possession, studiousness seeks participation. They also differ in the kinds of knowledge they seek. Curiosity is concerned with novelty: curious people want to know what they do not yet know, ideally, what no one yet knows. Studious people seek knowledge with the awareness that novelty is not what counts, and is indeed finally impossible because anything that can be known by any one of us is already known to God and has been given to us as unmerited gift. When, therefore, one of us comes to know something we had not known before, something new to us—and of course this is frequent—we do no more than participate in what is given and we delight in that fact. Local novelty—coming to know something new to you or me or new to a particular place and time—may occur for the studious, but it is not of central importance to them and is certainly not the reason for which they seek knowledge. But the deepest contrast between curiosity and studiousness has to do with the kind of world that the seeker for and professor of each inhabits. The curious inhabit a world of objects, which can be sequestered and possessed; the studious inhabit a world of gifts, given things, which can be known by participation, but which, because of their very natures, can never be possessed.

These formal contrasts between two highly catechized forms of intellectual appetite need to be given sense by closer analysis of the constituent terms of the definitions. I begin that analysis with attention to the grammar of the world, first in its universal form, and then in its specifically Christian construal.

## World

> What is called "world" is not only the fabric made by God—heaven and earth, sea, visibles and invisibles; those who live in the world are also called "world," just as the term "house" includes both walls and those who live inside them. And sometimes we praise the house and criticize its inhabitants.

Augustine here (*In Epistolam Ioannis* 2.12) comments on 1 John 2:16, in which (in the Latin version he knew) the possessive desire of the eyes (*concupiscentia oculorum*) is said to belong to the *mundus*, the world, and therefore to be shunned. What, he asks, does this word "world" mean? Isn't it the ordered beauty of the fabric woven by God, things visible and invisible, the heavens and the earth? Why then should saying that something belongs to it imply that it should be shunned? Wouldn't calling something "world" or "worldly" rather suggest that it is to be loved and embraced? He then says, to check this move, that "world" can be used to refer not only to that created fabric, but also to those who live in it, just as "house" can refer not only to the walls but also to those who live within them. "And sometimes," he says rather baldly, "we praise the house and criticize its inhabitants." If, then, "world" means all there is, what it refers to is both dark and light, presence and absence, damage and healing; and what is to be shunned is the darkness, the damage, and the absence.

"World" is an item of central importance to the lexicon of intellectual appetite. Its extension—the range of things it embraces—is all that is, seen and unseen, heard and unheard, touched and untouched, tasted and untasted, smelled and unsmelled, thought and unthought. This covers everything of which knowledge might be sought, which explains its centrality to the grammar of intellectual appetite. Intellectual appetite is appetite for knowledge of something, or some ensemble of things, or some set of relations connecting a thing or things, or (even) for all things and all relations. That is to say, it is a transitive appetite that may also be reflexive (one may seek knowledge of oneself, as well as knowledge of the appetite that one has for knowledge: that latter is what I seek here), and so "world" is a term proper to the universal grammar of intellectual appetite.

This is not to say that the English word "world" belongs to that universal grammar. It is what that word means that so belongs, in both its sense (all that may be known) and its reference (all that is . . .). Even in English, other words are possible: "cosmos," the beautifully ordered whole, has strong credentials, for example; and "world" has come to have other senses (planet, for example). But still, "world" seems best for users of English: short, fully Anglo-Saxon etymologically speaking, and, for most native speakers, easily comprehensible in the meaning given.

Defining the extension of the term "world" as "all that is" is not intended to suggest any commitment as to what it means for any particular or ensemble of particulars to exist, or as to what kinds and particulars there are. There are many incompatible views about these matters, including at least those held and sometimes defended by idealists, solipsists, and materialists (and, as we shall see, Christians); but holders of all such views must, in stating and defending or assuming them, accept and use the sense and reference of the term "world" just given. Differences about the being of the world, of any particular in it, and of what particulars there are in the world belong to particular construals of the world, not to its universal grammar.

The world is given to us without our request or consent. It is a place where we have found ourselves as far as our memories can reach, and which we cannot leave without dying. We have no control over either state of affairs. The world in which we find ourselves gives itself as an array of particulars related one to another. These particulars—this dog, that tree, my mother, the United States of America, the opening notes of the C-Major prelude in Bach's *Wohltemperierte Klavier*, azalea blooms in May, Mary Theotokos, the humidity of a summer's afternoon in the American Midwest, the sudden setting of the sun in the West African tropics—appear at first to us in an unbroken flood. We receive them as particulars only by learning to sort the flood into kinds, and to catalog instances of those kinds as they come before us. Absent that learned capacity, the world's particulars (whatever exactly their kinds) still give themselves, as does the world; but they cannot be accepted as given because they cannot be recognized.

Fortunately, sorting and cataloging are learned early and quickly, if at first crudely. The mother's touch and smell, and especially her breast, are rapidly recognized as importantly different from other touches and smells; the caress of light on the eye is soon distinguished from darkness, and is sought as pleasurable and desirable, as are warmth on the skin and sweetness on the tongue. And then, with an unfortunate inevitability but equal ease and rapidity, pain is recognized for what it is and its occasions avoided whenever possible.

These early sortings, which have mostly to do with the feel of things to the infant, become quickly more complex, exponentially so as language is acquired, for every natural language is a treasure-house of sortals, a thesaurus of terms for kinds and for the ordering of those kinds into hierarchies of value. And these later more complex sortings of the particulars of the world cease to have to do mainly with the feel of things, with the physical and emotional valence of things as they appear in consciousness. They begin now to have to do also with local wisdom, the wisdom of the tribe about the kinds of things there are in the world. This wisdom always uses criteria additional to those deployed by the infant, criteria that often have little to do with the phenomenal feel of things.

Among these criteria are appeals to value: kinds are always ordered hierarchically by their value, whether value directly to those doing the sorting, or value according to some hierarchy more or less distant from the sorter. Although there is much disagreement about the kinds of kind there are, and about the place each bears in a hierarchy, and about the boundaries between, and therefore the individuation of, particulars, there is universal agreement in practice that there are particulars, that they must be sorted into kinds, and that these kinds are not all of the same value. All of us do and must behave as if we thought this, and all who think about such matters at all (a small portion of humanity, fortunately) do and must agree that such hierarchical sorting of apparent particulars is unavoidable.

This is not to say that all agree on the account to be given of what we do when we individuate particulars one from another and sort those individuated particulars into kinds. Some think that in so acting we conform our language and thought to a mind- and language-independent order of things. Others think that we construct useful fictions. And yet others think that we sometimes do the one and sometimes the other. It is another and still more difficult question whether we should have much confidence in the degree to which our particular sortings and individuations conform to a mind- and language-independent order of things, even if we think that there is such an order. Disagreements about these matters belong to construals of the world's universal grammar, not to that grammar itself.

There is universal agreement about much more than the inevitability of sorting particulars into kinds and ordering those kinds hierarchically. There is universal agreement in practice about the claim that the semantic content of anything said or written in one natural language can be rendered with no more than partial semantic loss into something said or written in some other natural language. And this agreement, which requires no agreement about how sentences (or words) mean, or about just what is done when translation occurs, has important implications. Since you are reading these words, you can read English, the language in which I am writing. Even if that is not your first language, and even if as you read it you are translating it mentally into some other, you have some understanding of what I have written. And if it is your first language, an easy habitation for you, then you will have understood me with ease. These facts mean that the sorted, ordered, hierarchically categorized world which has been given to me, that, with more or less ease, I inhabit as natural, overlaps to a very considerable extent with the one that has been given to you. You, unlike me, may not distinguish wasps from bees, working instead with a single undifferentiated sortal such as "yellow-striped flying stinging insects"; you may doubt the existence of some particulars (the parrots that live wild in Chicago—perhaps you think, wrongly, that parrots live wild only in tropical and subtropical regions) which I take to have been presented to me; we may disagree about the properties that some particular has (I think that the Chicago White Sox have the property of being the baseball team that all rational people should support, and you, while perhaps acknowledging the existence of such a team, doubt that it bears any such property); and so on. But these differences do not go deep, as their easy comprehensibility itself shows. We—you and I, that is, and all other humans—assume that we inhabit a world sorted and ordered in very much the same fashion. Our assumption that we can communicate with one another shows this; and that what I have written can be translated into other languages, with, we all think, nothing worse than mild betrayal and moderate loss, and thereby be made understandable to those who inhabit those languages, establishes it. All natural languages, we all assume, are intertranslatable; it is a criterion of languagehood that this be so; languages are engines for sorting, hierarchizing, and cataloging particulars; and so, linguistically particular orderings of the things in the world are intertranslatable. The differences between my sortings and yours are, then, I assume (and so do you), no serious or unremovable bar to my understanding of what yours are, even if there are things about your sortings I neither like nor agree with.

The world becomes habitable as a world when its flood of appearances is sorted and cataloged. Any such sorting and cataloging amounts to a construal of the world, which is to say a specification and precision of its universal grammar. There are many, perhaps infinitely many, possible construals of the world; but only a few are of deep and lasting importance for the history of human thought. Most of those are what we would now (not very usefully) call religious: Buddhist, Christian, Jewish, Islamic, Confucian, and so on. The construals of the world offered by these traditions of thought and practice differ very significantly one from another, but they share some formal features, most notable among which is that they are articulated with an understanding of what human life is for, which is to say of its proper goal. Each of them is thus also committed to an understanding of what constitutes a well-ordered or a disordered life. The religious construals of the world are not alone in that; they share it, for example, with Marxism, and with late capitalist liberalism. But these secular construals, as their name suggests, are the more or less malformed and corrupted bastard offspring of their religious parents.

# 18

## The Religious Path to Exclusive Humanism

*From Deism to Atheism*

JAMES K. A. SMITH

How, in a relatively short period of time, did we go from a world where belief in God was the default assumption to our secular age in which belief in God seems, to many, unbelievable? This brave new world is not just the old world with the God-supplement lopped off; it's not just the world that is left when we subtract the supernatural. A secular world where we have permission, even encouragement, to not believe in God is an accomplishment, not merely a remainder. Our secular age is the product of creative new options, an entire reconfiguration of meaning.

So it's not enough to ask how we got permission to stop believing in God; we need to also inquire about what emerged to replace such belief. Because it's not that our secular age is an age of disbelief; it's an age of believing otherwise. We can't tolerate living in a world without meaning. So if the transcendence that previously gave significance to the world is lost, we need a new account of

Originally published as "The Religious Path to Exclusive Humanism: From Deism to Atheism," in James K. A. Smith, *How (Not) to Be Secular: Reading Charles Taylor* (Grand Rapids: Eerdmans, 2014), 47–59. Copyright © 2014 Wm. B. Eerdmans Publishing Company, Grand Rapids, MI. Reprinted by permission of the publisher; all rights reserved.

meaning—a new "imaginary" that enables us to imagine a meaningful life within this now self-sufficient universe of gas and fire. That "replacement" imaginary is what Charles Taylor calls "exclusive humanism," and his quarry is still to discern just how exclusive humanism became a "live option" in modernity,[1] resisting typical subtraction stories that posit that "once religious and metaphysical beliefs fall away, we are left with ordinary human desires, and these are the basis of our modern humanism."[2] This is an important point, and we won't understand Taylor's critique of subtraction stories without appreciating it: on the subtraction-story account, modern exclusive humanism is just the natural *telos* of human life. We are released to be the exclusive humanists we were meant to be when we escape the traps of superstition and the yoke of transcendence. On such tellings of the story, exclusive humanism is "natural." But Taylor's point in part 2 of *A Secular Age* is to show that we had to *learn* how to be exclusively humanist; it is a second nature, not a first.

So what made that possible?

## Enclosure and Immanentization: Relocating Significance

As we've already seen, often the features of our secular age were generated from religious and theological moves. Taylor sees a *theological* shift in the understanding of providence in early modernity that, in turn, leads to an *anthropological* (or even anthropocentric) shift in four movements. Anticipating how Taylor will describe this later, we might see this as a fourfold process of "immanentization"—a subtle process by which our world, and hence the realm of significance, is enclosed within the material universe and the natural world. Divested of the transcendent, *this* world is invested with ultimacy and meaning in ways that couldn't have been imagined before. Taylor sees this reflected in four "eclipses" that are domino effects of this process.

The first, and most significant, is an eclipse of what he calls a "further purpose" or a good that "transcends human flourishing."[3] In the premodern, enchanted social imaginary, there was an end for humans that transcended "mundane" flourishing "in this world," so to speak. As he puts it elsewhere, "For Christians, God wills human flourishing, but 'thy will be done' doesn't reduce to 'let human beings

---

1. Charles Taylor, *A Secular Age* (Cambridge, MA: Harvard University Press, 2007), 222.

2. Ibid., 253.

3. Though I think Taylor formulates this infelicitously. Because he seems to limit "human flourishing" to "this-worldly" or "mundane" flourishing, he ends up positing a tension between *creaturely* goods and *eternal* goods; that is, he ends up creating a tension between the order of creation and the order of redemption—between nature and grace. I think this is a hangover of a certain type of scholastic Thomism. In the Protestant and Reformed tradition, we would emphasize a fundamental continuity between nature and grace, creation and redemption, even if redemption is also always "more" than creation. So whatever "ascetic" disciplines are required of us "in this life" are not repressions of flourishing but rather constraints *for* our flourishing.

flourish.'"[4] In short, both agents and social institutions lived with a sense of a *telos* that was eternal—a final judgment, the beatific vision, and so on. And on Taylor's accounting, this "higher good" was in some tension with mundane concerns about flourishing. This entailed a sense of obligation "beyond" human flourishing. In other words, this life is *not* "all there is"—and recognizing that means one lives this life differently. It will engender certain ascetic constraints, for example: we can't just eat, drink, and be merry because, while tomorrow we may die, that's not the end. After that comes the judgment. And so our merriment might be curtailed by this "further purpose," as Taylor describes it.

But Taylor sees an important shift in this respect, particularly in the work of Adam Smith and John Locke, among others. Whereas historically the doctrine of providence assured a benign *ultimate* plan for the cosmos, with Locke and Smith we see a new emphasis: providence is primarily about ordering *this* world for mutual benefit, particularly *economic* benefit. Humans are seen as fundamentally engaged in an "exchange of services," so the entire cosmos is seen anthropocentrically as the arena for this economy.[5] What happens in the "new Providence," then, is a "shrinking" of God's purposes, an "economizing" of God's own interests: "God's goals for us shrink to the single end of our encompassing this order of mutual benefit he has designed for us."[6] So even our theism becomes humanized, immanentized, and the *telos* of God's providential concern is circumscribed within immanence. And this becomes true even of "orthodox" folk: "even people who held to orthodox beliefs were influenced by this humanizing trend; frequently the transcendent dimension of their faith became less central."[7] Because eternity is eclipsed, the this-worldly is amplified and threatens to swallow all.

Taylor describes the second aspect of this anthropocentric shift as the "eclipse of grace." Since God's providential concern for order is reduced to an "economic" ordering of creation to our mutual benefit, and since that order and design is discernible by reason, then "by reason and discipline, humans could rise to the challenge and realize it." The result is a kind of intellectual Pelagianism: we can figure this out without assistance. Oh, God still plays a role—as either the watchmaker who got the ball rolling, or the judge who will evaluate how well we did—but in the long middle God plays no discernible role or function, and is uninvolved.[8] This

4. Charles Taylor, "A Catholic Modernity?," in *Believing Scholars: Ten Catholic Intellectuals*, ed. James L. Heft, SM (New York: Fordham University Press, 2005), 17. But as I noted above, I think Taylor is positing something of a false dichotomy here.

5. Taylor, *Secular Age*, 177.

6. Ibid., 221.

7. Ibid., 222. This point seems germane to contemporary evangelicalism, which is increasingly casting off its "otherworldly" piety and becoming newly invested in the flourishing of this world. For a winsome encapsulation of this, see N. T. Wright, *Surprised by Hope: Rethinking Heaven, the Resurrection, and the Mission of the Church* (San Francisco: HarperOne, 2008). Taylor's point is that even orthodox Christians unwittingly absorbed this immanentizing, anthropocentric shift. For articulation of this concern, see Hans Boersma, *Heavenly Participation: The Weaving of a Sacramental Tapestry* (Grand Rapids: Eerdmans, 2010).

8. Taylor, *Secular Age*, 222–23.

is why Taylor describes all these as features of a "providential *deism*"—a deism that opened the door for exclusive humanism.

Since what matters is immanent, and since we can figure it out, it's not surprising that, third, "the sense of mystery fades." God's providence is no longer inscrutable; it's an open book, "perspicuous." "His providence consists simply in his plan for us, which we understand."[9] Mystery can no longer be tolerated.

Finally, and as an outcome, we lose any "idea that God was planning a transformation of human beings which would take them beyond the limitations which inhere in their present condition."[10] We lose a sense that humanity's end transcends its current configurations—and thus lose a sense of "participation" in God's nature (or "deification") as the *telos* for humanity.

But what underlay these shifts? Taylor emphasizes economic-centric *harmony* as the new focus and ideal: "The spreading doctrines of the harmony of interests reflect the shift in the idea of natural order . . . in which the economic dimension takes on greater and greater importance, and 'economic' (that is, ordered, peaceful, productive) activity is more and more the model for human behaviour."[11] Like the roof on Toronto's SkyDome, the heavens are beginning to close. But we barely notice, because our new focus on this plane had already moved the transcendent to our peripheral vision at best. We're so taken with the play on this field that we don't lament the loss of the stars overhead.

## How Apologetics Diminishes Christianity

In this context Taylor offers an analysis of the apologetic strategy that emerges in the midst of these shifts—not only as a response to them, but already as a reflection *of* them. In trying to assess just how the modern social imaginary came to permeate a wider culture, Taylor focuses on Christian responses *to* this emerging humanism and the "eclipses" we've just noted. What he finds is that the responses themselves have already conceded the game; that is, the responses to this diminishment of transcendence already accede to it in important ways (Taylor will later call this "pre-shrunk religion").[12] As he notes, "the great apologetic effort called forth by this disaffection itself narrowed its focus so drastically. It barely invoked the saving action of Christ, nor did it dwell on the life of devotion and prayer, although the seventeenth century was rich in this. The arguments turned exclusively on demonstrating God as Creator, and showing his Providence."[13] What we get in the name of "Christian" defenses of transcendence, then, is "a less theologically elaborate faith" that, ironically, paves the way for exclusive humanism. God is reduced to a

9. Ibid., 223.
10. Ibid., 224.
11. Ibid., 229.
12. Ibid., 226.
13. Ibid., 225.

Creator and religion is reduced to morality.[14] The "deism" of providential deism bears many marks of the "theism" that is often defended in contemporary apologetics. The particularities of specifically *Christian* belief are diminished to try to secure a more generic deity—as if saving *some* sort of transcendence will suffice.[15]

When Taylor broached this theme earlier, he specifically noted that the "religion" that is defended by such apologetic strategies has little to do with religion in terms of *worship*: "The eclipse of certain crucial Christian elements, those of grace and agape, already changed quite decisively the centre of gravity of this outlook. Moreover, there didn't seem to be any essential place for the worship of God, other than through the cultivation of reason and constancy." What we see, then, is the "relegation of worship as ultimately unnecessary and irrelevant."[16] This is the scaled-down religion that will be rejected "by Wesley from one direction, and later secular humanists from the other."[17]

There is also an important epistemological concession already at work in apologetic responses to immanentization. This mode of "Christian" apologetics bought into the spectatorish "world picture" of the new modern order. Rather than seeing ourselves positioned within a hierarchy of forms (in which case we wouldn't be surprised if "higher levels" are mysterious and inscrutable), we now adopt a God-like, dispassionate "gaze" that deigns to survey the whole. In this mode, the universe appears "as a system before our gaze, whereby we can grasp the whole in a kind of tableau."[18] And it is precisely in this context, when we adopt a "disengaged stance," that the project of *theodicy* ramps up; thinking we're positioned to see everything, we now expect an answer to whatever puzzles us, including the problem of evil. Nothing should be inscrutable.

But this apologetic project—particularly with respect to the "problem" of evil—is taken up in a way that is completely consistent with the "buffered self";[19] while earlier the terrors and burdens of evil and disaster would have cast us upon the help of a Savior, "now that we think we see how it all works, the argument gets displaced. People in coffeehouses and salons [and philosophy classes?] begin to express their disaffection in reflections on divine justice, and the theologians begin to feel that this is the challenge they must meet to fight back the coming wave of unbelief. The burning concern with theodicy is enframed by the new imagined epistemic predicament."[20]

14. Ibid.
15. Taylor notes that specifics of Christology also recede in importance in light of this: "Insofar as the figure of Christ, as divine, stands behind claims to sacral authority, while the issue of whether Jesus was God or simply a great prophet or teacher is not relevant to the question whether God is the Designer of the order of mutual benefit, there is a temptation to abandon either the question or the doctrine of Christ's divinity, to slide towards Socinianism, or Deism; or else to adopt a skeptical stance towards such questions" (238).
16. Ibid., 117.
17. Ibid., 226.
18. Ibid., 232.
19. Ibid., 228.
20. Ibid., 233. It's very difficult for me to resist recognizing how much of the "industry" of Christian philosophy and apologetics today remains the outcome of these shifts. Just compare Christian responses

Here's where Taylor's "irony" comes into play: What's left of/for God after this deistic shift? Well, "God remains the Creator, and hence our benefactor . . . but this Providence remains exclusively general: particular providences, and miracles, are out."[21] In other words, God plays a function within a system that generally runs without him. "But having got this far," Taylor concludes, "it is not clear why something of the same inspiring power cannot come from the contemplation of the order of nature itself, without reference to a Creator."[22] The scaled-down God and preshrunk religion defended by the apologists turned out to be insignificant enough to reject without consequence. In other words, once God's role is diminished to that of a deistic agent (*by his defenders*, we should add), the gig is pretty much up: "And so exclusive humanism could take hold, as more than a theory held by a tiny minority, but as a more and more viable spiritual outlook. . . . The points at which God had seemed an indispensable source for this ordering power were the ones which began to fade and become invisible. The hitherto unthought became thinkable."[23]

### The Next Step: The Politics of "Polite" Society

"But not yet thought," Taylor concedes.[24] Think*able*. For exclusive humanism to become a "live option," there also had to be a *political* shift, one that mirrors or parallels the theological shift. Just as we noted the move to a "less theologically elaborate" (i.e., less determinate, specified, embodied, *practiced*) religion, so also the political order will be liberated from any particular magisterium. The "modern moral order," as Taylor often calls it, which amounts to an ordering of society for mutual benefit ("economy"), will come to reflect the generic nature of this religion. Unhooked from the specifics of Christian doctrines and tethered to a more generic deistic god, the modern moral order is independent of any specific—and hence contestable—claims about this god. If the generic religion of the apologists is "independent from ecclesiastical or particular-doctrinal authority," then the state and political life can be similarly liberated. "This didn't have to mean,

to the "new atheists" that, in a similar way, have already conceded the game to exclusive humanism by playing on their turf. Or consider how much "Christian" philosophy is content to be "theistic" philosophy. That said, in a way, my colleague Stephen Wykstra's work on skeptical arguments from evil has pushed back against just this epistemic expectation of being able to "see" everything. See, for example, Stephen J. Wykstra, "The Humean Obstacle to Evidential Arguments from Suffering: On Avoiding the Evils of 'Appearance,'" *International Journal for Philosophy of Religion* 16 (1984): 73–93; Wykstra, "Rowe's Noseeum Arguments from Evil," in *The Evidential Argument from Evil*, ed. Daniel Howard-Snyder (Bloomington: Indiana University Press, 1996), 126–50.

21. Taylor, *Secular Age*, 233.

22. Ibid., 234.

23. Ibid. In this context, Taylor cites Michael Buckley's classic study, *At the Origins of Modern Atheism* (New Haven: Yale University Press, 1990).

24. Taylor, *Secular Age*, 234.

of course, independence from religion; because one could easily conceive of the modern moral order in a providentialist framework, as God's design for humans, as I have described it above. But this just strengthens the point: to see the order as God's design gives it an authority which cannot be overturned by the deliverances of any magisterium, nor set aside in the name of any doctrine particular to one or other denomination."[25] What we have, in other words, is the making of a "civil religion," rooted in a "natural" religion, which can allegedly transcend denominational strife. (Welcome to America!) The ultimate and transcendent are retained but marginalized and made increasingly irrelevant. Our differences about the ultimate fade in comparison to the common project of pursuing the "order of mutual benefit."[26]

What emerges from this is what Taylor describes as "polite society," a new mode of self-sufficient sociality that becomes an end in itself.

> Polite civilization, and the moral order it entrenches, can easily become lived as a self-sufficient framework within which to find the standards of our social, moral and political life; the only transcendent references admitted being those which underpin the order and do not justify infringing it. On the social and civilizational level, it fits perfectly with, indeed expresses, what I called above the "buffered identity," the self-understanding which arises out of disenchantment. Otherwise put, it is a social and civilizational framework which inhibits or blocks out certain of the ways in which transcendence has historically impinged on humans, and been present in their lives. It tends to complete and entrench on a civilizational level the anthropocentric shift I described in the previous section. It builds for the buffered identity a buffered world.[27]

On the one hand, Taylor regularly describes these moves as reductive: shrinking, scaling down, lowering the bar, and so on. On the other hand, such "shrinking" is not experienced as a subtraction, as if we are left with less. To the contrary, the scaling down to immanence actually amplifies its importance. The immanent sphere—the this-worldly plane—swells in importance just to the extent that the eternal and the transcendent are eclipsed. So there's no lament here; if anything, there is new confidence, excitement, and celebration. Look what we can do!

25. Ibid., 237. Those forms of religion that refuse to play by these rules will be those that continue to hold an "ideal of sociality" and "sacral authority" identified with the Catholic Church or "high" interpretations of authority in the Church of England. (Which would also anticipate how uneasily some forms of Islam would sit within this imaginary.) "The actual coming-to-be of a range of non-Christian and anti-Christian positions, ranging from various forms of Deism and Unitarianism to exclusive humanism, can best be understood within this field of potential and frequently actualized conflict" (238).

26. An honest assessment of this would have to reckon with the fact that this Hobbesian and Lockean strategy did seem to alleviate the "wars of religion" that beset early modern Europe. For an argument of this point, see Ephraim Radner, *A Brutal Unity: The Spiritual Politics of the Christian Church* (Waco: Baylor University Press, 2012).

27. Taylor, *Secular Age*, 238–39.

The epistemic Pelagianism we noted above (the confidence that *we* can figure everything out) is now complemented by a civilizational or cultural Pelagianism: the confidence that *we* make *this* world meaningful. "Once the goal is shrunk," Taylor observes, "it can begin to seem that we can encompass it with our unaided forces. Grace seems less essential."[28] And now we can begin to see how exclusive humanism might arise: "The stage is set, as it were, for its entrance." But the negative permission (we don't seem to need grace anymore) does not seem a sufficient condition for its emergence. There also needs to be a constructive push, "the positive move that moral/spiritual resources can be experienced as purely immanent. . . . We need to see how it became possible to experience moral fullness, to identify the locus of our highest moral capacity and inspiration, without reference to God, but within the range of purely intra-human powers."[29] It is the order of mutual benefit that provides this mechanism. The order of mutual benefit offered a moral goal that was experienced as an obligation but was at the same time achievable—and achievable under our own steam, so to speak.

Here Taylor the Hegelian argues that, even though it rejects Christianity, exclusive humanism was only possible having come *through* Christianity. The order of mutual benefit is a kind of secularization of Christian universalism—the call to love the neighbor, even the enemy. If Christianity renounced the tribalisms of paganism, exclusive humanism's vision of mutual benefit takes that universalizing impulse but now arrogates it to a self-sufficient human capability. We *ought* to be concerned with others, we *ought* to be altruistic, and *we* have the capacity to achieve this ideal. Thus, once again, Taylor describes this as an "immanentizing move": "The main thrust of modern exclusive humanism has tried . . . to immanentize this capacity of beneficence." We need to appreciate "the way in which modern humanisms innovated in relation to the ancients, drawing on the forms of Christian faith they emerged from: active re-ordering; instrumental rationality; universalism; benevolence. But of course their aim was also to reject the Christian aspiration to transcend flourishing. Hence only the self-giving which conduced to general flourishing as now defined

---

28. Ibid., 244.

29. Ibid., 244–45. Taylor's notion of "fullness" has been a matter of critique. See, for example, Jonathan Sheehan, "When Was Disenchantment? History and the Secular Age," in *Varieties of Secularism in a Secular Age*, ed. Michael Warner, Jonathan VanAntwerpen, and Craig Calhoun (Cambridge, MA: Harvard University Press, 2010), 217–42, at 229–31. The critique is generally that the category of "fullness" smuggles in a specific religious notion under the guise of a general or universal concept. In his afterword, Taylor clarifies his intention, without backing away from the universalism of his claim: "I wanted to use this as something like a category term to capture the very different ways in which each of us (as I claim) sees life as capable of some fuller, higher, more genuine, more authentic, more intense . . . form. The list of adjectives is indefinitely long, because the positions we may adopt have no finite limit. Why do this? Because I think that it is valuable to try to grasp a position you find unfamiliar and even baffling through trying to bring into focus the understanding of fullness that it involves. This is particularly the case if you want really to understand it, to be able to feel the power it has for its protagonists, as against simply dismissing it." *Secular Age*, 315. To get a sense of what phenomenon Taylor is trying to name, consider Hubert Dreyfus and Sean Dorrance Kelly's notion of the "whoosh," a "wave" that overwhelms. *All Things Shining: Reading the Western Classics to Find Meaning in a Secular Age* (New York: Free Press, 2011), 199–202.

was allowed as rational and natural, and even that within reasonable bounds. The rest was condemned as extravagance, or 'enthusiasm.'"[30] What exclusive humanism devotes itself to as the "moral fullness" possible within immanence will turn out to be an "agape-analogue" that is dependent on Christianity.[31] Indeed, Taylor's (rather Hegelian) claim is quite strong: "It would probably not have been possible to make the transition to exclusive humanism on any other basis."[32]

"So exclusive humanism wasn't just something we fell into, once the old myths dissolved or the 'infamous' ancien régime church was crushed."[33] Exclusive humanism is an *achievement*: "The development of this purely immanent sense of universal solidarity is an important achievement, a milestone in human history."[34] Indeed, discovering immanent resources for fullness and meaning in this way will become "the charter of modern unbelief."[35]

## Religion for Moderns

The anthropocentric shifts we've just noted find mirror images in shifts in religion itself. In chapter 7 of *A Secular Age*, Taylor tracks this corresponding "change in the understanding of God." Once again, Taylor is interested in the ways that, in the Latin West, Christianity was both an unwitting progenitor *and a reflector of* the new modern social imaginary, even as it was trying to resist it.

What becomes increasingly distasteful (the word is chosen advisedly) is the notion of God's *agency*, and hence the personhood of God. Sometimes dismissed as a feature of gauche "enthusiasm," at other times seen as a threat to an ordered cosmos, there would be an increasing interest in jettisoning the notion of "God as an agent intervening in history. He could be agent *qua* original Architect of the universe, but not as the author of myriad particular interventions, 'miraculous' or not, which were the stuff of popular piety and orthodox religion."[36] Such an active God would violate the buffer zone we have created to protect ourselves from such incursions. And so the "god" that governs the cosmos is the architect of an *im*personal order. In short, we're all Masons now.

But to reject God's personhood and agency entailed rejecting an entire fabric of Christianity that revolved around the notion of religion as *communion*.[37] According

---

30. Taylor, *Secular Age*, 247.

31. Ibid., 246. The agape-analogue, of course, is very different from Christian agape precisely because of its immanentization and hence refusal of grace. This is why it must reflect "an activist, interventionist stance, both towards nature and to human society."

32. Ibid., 247. And "the transition didn't have to happen," he adds on 248.

33. Ibid., 255.

34. Ibid.

35. Ibid., 257.

36. Ibid., 236.

37. Taylor sees Christianity summed up in the theme of communion: "The central concept which makes sense of the whole is communion, or love, defining both the nature of God, and our relation to him" (279).

to historic, orthodox Christian faith, "salvation is thwarted to the extent that we treat God as an impersonal being, or as merely the creator of an impersonal order to which we have to adjust. Salvation is only effected by, one might say, our being in communion with God through the community of humans in communion, viz., the church."[38] To depersonalize God is to deny the importance of communion and the community *of* communion that is the church, home to that meal that is called "Communion."

So it is not surprising, then, that the "religion" of this impersonal order is also de-Communion-ed, de-ritualized, and disembodied. Taylor helpfully describes this as a process of *excarnation*. In contrast to the central conviction of Christian faith—that the transcendent God became *in*carnate, en-fleshed, in Jesus of Nazareth—*ex*carnation is a move of disembodiment and abstraction, an aversion of and flight from the particularities of embodiment (and communion). This will be a "purified" religion—purified of rituals and relics, but also of emotion and bodies[39]—of which Kant's "rational" religion is the apotheosis. With the body goes the Body; that is, with the abandonment of material religion we see the diminishment of the church as a communion as well. The "Deist standpoint involves disintricating the issue of religious truth from participation in a certain community practice of religious life, into which facets of prayer, faith, hope are woven."[40]

We might describe this as "deistic" religion—if it didn't look like so much contemporary Protestantism.[41] And we might be tempted to identify this with the "liberal" streams of Protestantism—if it didn't sound like so many "progressive" evangelicals. Taylor sees this as an open door for exclusive humanism and atheism; it is a pretty straight line from excarnation to the vilification of religion[42]—which raises important questions for Christianity in the new millennium.

But let's keep this in mind: to this point, Taylor has only got us to something like the seventeenth century! There's a lot of the story to come. But in closing part 2, Taylor offers a helpful summary of his analysis and argument thus far:

> So putting this all together, we can see how a certain kind of framework understanding came to be constituted: fed by the powerful presence of impersonal orders, cosmic, social, and moral; drawn by the power of the disengaged stance, and its ethical prestige, and ratified by a sense of what the alternative was, based on an elite's derogatory and somewhat fearful portrait of popular religion, an

38. Ibid., 278–79.
39. Ibid., 288.
40. Ibid., 293.
41. Taylor is quite unapologetic about this later in the book when he claims that "the direction of this Reform was towards a far-reaching excarnation" (614) and that "the development of Reformed Christianity worked to sideline the body" (611). Indeed, he says this is "one of the main contentions of this book" (614). However, this should be tempered if we note—however ad hoc—an increased attention to embodiment, ritual, and the aesthetic among Protestant evangelicals.
42. Ibid., 293–94.

unshakeable sense could arise of our inhabiting an immanent, impersonal order, which screened out, for those who inhabited it, all phenomena which failed to fit this framework.[43]

It turns out it's not so hard to see ourselves four hundred years ago; it's as if we're looking at childhood photos of our contemporary culture.

---

43. Ibid., 288.

# 19

## Natural Theology, or a Theology of Creation?

### Stanley Hauerwas

If what Christians believe about God and the world could be known without witnesses, then we would have evidence that what Christians believe about God and the world is not true. All that is, all that is creation, is a witness to the One alone who is capable of moving the sun and the stars as well as our hearts. If we and the world existed by necessity, then no witness, no story of creation, would be required. But God did not have to create, much less redeem; yet we have it on good authority that God has created and redeemed. Creation and redemption constitute the story necessary for us to know who we are. Such knowledge comes only through the telling of this story.

Calling attention to the necessity of witnesses suggests to many people, particularly those of the philosophical bent, the end of argument. For Christians, however, "witness" names the condition necessary to begin argument. To be a witness does not mean that Christians are in the business of calling attention to ourselves but that we witness to the One who has made our lives possible. Witness, at least the witness to which Christians are called, is, after all, about God and God's relation to all that is.

Originally published in "The Necessity of Witness," in Stanley Hauerwas, *With the Grain of the Universe: The Church's Witness and Natural Theology* (Grand Rapids: Brazos, 2001), 205–41, here pp. 207–15, 232–40. Copyright © 2001. Used by permission.

To speak of witnesses, then, is not the end of argument; however, what Christians believe about God and God's relation to the world requires that the form and manner of our arguments have a particular shape. For example, Bruce Marshall observes that "Christian theologians have long maintained, that there is no hope of generating what William James calls 'coercive arguments' for the church's chief convictions (though the Christian community expects that it will be able, at least in the long run, to meet almost any argument which is brought against these beliefs, by showing that objections to them are not rationally coercive either)."[1] According to Marshall, the Spirit's work is to teach us how to believe and judge all things in accordance with claims whose denial will always be rationally plausible.[2] In other words, it is the work of the Spirit to teach Christians that their claims about the way things are, though always susceptible to being refuted on rational grounds, are not without persuasive power and/or the support of argument.

That there can be no "coercive arguments" for Christian convictions is but an elaboration of Aquinas's discussion of whether sacred doctrine is a matter of argument. Against those who argue that doctrine is not a matter of argument, Aquinas quotes from Paul's letter to Titus, which states that a bishop should "embrace that faithful word which is according to doctrine, that he may be able to exhort in sound doctrine and to convince the gainsayers."[3] Aquinas explains that just as other sciences do not argue in proof of their principles but from their principles to demonstrate other truths in the sciences, so proceed arguments from doctrine. Accordingly, doctrines, which are the articles of faith, do not argue in proof of their principles but from them go on to prove something else. Aquinas notes, however, that "it is to be borne in mind" that inferior (philosophical) sciences "neither prove their principles nor dispute with those who deny them" but leave such

---

1. Bruce Marshall, *Trinity and Truth* (Cambridge: Cambridge University Press, 2000), 181. Of course, one of the great failures of Christians in modernity has been, as Alasdair MacIntyre observes, to offer the atheist less and less to disbelieve. See Alasdair MacIntyre with Paul Ricoeur, *The Religious Significance of Atheism* (New York: Columbia University Press, 1969), 24. Christians owe it to themselves and their neighbors to put descriptions of the world that presume that God does not exist into what MacIntyre calls "epistemological crisis." The great failure of Christians in modernity is our willingness to make peace with the world.

2. "Judge all things" and "the way things are" may be regarded as stand-ins for the more philosophical notion of existence. As Aidan Nichols suggests, the habit of theology entails the willingness to be stimulated by appropriate objects. Such objects can be arranged in three concentric circles: (1) "existence," (2) "sacred history," and (3) "the Bible." "Existence" is the largest of the circles, which often leads some people to think that it is the most important "object," which in turn means that theology depends on the development of an adequate metaphysics. Nichols, however, suggests that "existence" is but shorthand for "anything you care to mention." Unfortunately, theologians have too often thought that by developing an account of being qua being—that is, an account that mimics the mistaken view that philosophy has a subject peculiar to itself called "being"—they can avoid having to come to terms with "anything you care to mention." Precisely as a way of avoiding this mistake, I have enlisted colloquial phrases like "the way things are." See Aidan Nichols, *The Shape of Catholic Theology* (Collegeville, MN: Liturgical Press, 1991), 18.

3. Thomas Aquinas, *Summa Theologiae* I.1.8, trans. the Fathers of the English Dominican Province (Westminster, MD: Christian Classics, 1948). Thomas is quoting Titus 1:9.

proofs and disputes to the highest science in philosophy, which is metaphysics. Metaphysics, however, is not the highest science, for higher still is what Aquinas calls the divine science.

According to Aquinas, if an opponent in a dispute concerning the first principles of a science will make some concession, then an argument is possible; but if the opponent concedes nothing, there can be no dispute, though the science "can answer his objections." Therefore,

> Sacred Scripture, since it has no science above itself, can dispute with one who denies its principles only if the opponent admits some at least of the truths obtained through divine revelation; thus we can argue with heretics from texts in Holy Writ, and against those who deny one article of faith we can argue from another. If our opponent believes nothing of divine revelation, there is no longer any means of proving the articles of faith by reasoning, but only of answering his objections if he has any against faith. Since faith rests upon infallible truth, and since the contrary of a truth can never be demonstrated, it is clear that the argument brought against faith cannot be demonstrations, but are difficulties that can be answered.[4]

These remarks are not meant to be a protective strategy to insure that Christian doctrine can evade objections that may be brought against it.[5] Rather, Aquinas assumes that he is simply providing an account of the conditions necessary to have an argument, not only in theology but in any subject. Nothing in Aquinas's

4. Ibid. Aquinas's claim that first principles are necessary for argument is, of course, not widely accepted by contemporary philosophers. For a defense of Aquinas's (and Aristotle's) understanding of first principles, see Alasdair MacIntyre, *First Principles, Final Ends, and Contemporary Issues* (Milwaukee: Marquette University Press, 1990). MacIntyre argues that the contemporary philosophical habit of ignoring first principles is closely related to the exclusion of a *telos* necessary to describe the activity of particular beings. According to MacIntyre: "Genuine first principles can have a place only within a universe characterized in terms of certain determinate, fixed and unalterable ends, ends which provide a standard by reference to which our individual purposes, desires, interests and decisions can be evaluated as well as badly directed" (7). MacIntyre notes that first principles are analytic, but that does not mean that they can be known to be true a priori; rather, first principles are judgments grasped intellectually through participation in the activity in which they are embedded. MacIntyre's understanding of first principles is crucial for understanding his account of how traditions of inquiry can, when confronted by alternative accounts of the way things are, be put in an "epistemological crisis." Such a crisis is but a reminder that theoretical achievements are rooted in practices that entail narrative display. My emphasis on witness as a constitutive aspect of Christian convictions is an attempt to display how theological inquiry works, if, indeed, MacIntyre's understanding of inquiry is, as I take it to be, correct.

5. On the notion of a protective strategy, see Wayne Proudfoot, *Religious Experience* (Berkeley: University of California Press, 1985); and Matthew Bagger, *Religious Experience, Justification, and History* (Cambridge: Cambridge University Press, 1999), 103–4, 133–34. Bagger, following Proudfoot, characterizes a protective strategy as one designed by philosophers of religion to exclude critical inquiry from outside religion. Put differently, it is the attempt to sustain accounts of religious experience and/or belief by showing that they can be neither justified nor falsified. Though I think Bagger is right to criticize this "strategy," he does appreciate why it is so tempting for theologians in modernity, namely, because of the natural presumption, which has no particular warrant, that theological claims bear the burden of proof. "Protective strategies" are often attempts to resist that presumption.

remarks commits him to the view that the Christian faith is just another set of beliefs incapable of justification. Christians do not seek to justify what they believe out of fear that it may not be true. Rather, justification is inherent in the material convictions that constitute what Christians believe exactly because they are required by what they believe to be witnesses.[6] The witness of Christians may or may not take the form of argument at different times and places, but if the Holy Spirit does not witness to the Father and Son through the witness of Christians, then Christians have no arguments to make.[7]

Christian argument rests on witness, and both argument and witness are the work of the Spirit. Thus, as Marshall argues, acquiring a Christian view of the world

> calls for a persistent willingness to overturn the epistemic priorities (though not the totality of belief) we would otherwise be inclined to have. In at least this sense, ordering one's beliefs such that Jesus Christ has unrestricted epistemic primacy requires a change of heart and not simply a change of mind. The gospel of Jesus Christ, it seems, proclaims a truth which cannot be known unless it is also loved (see 2 Thess. 2:16).[8]

6. Marshall rightly notes that the martyr's blood may provide evidence for others of the truth of his or her beliefs, but that cannot be true for the martyr. The martyr "dies because he believes the gospel and loves the gospel's God, not in order to believe it. So participationist versions of the pragmatic thesis end up in a paradox: the more excellently or successfully a person participates in the church's practices, the less need he has to treat those practices as evidence for the church's beliefs (or would have, were practice susceptible of being treated this way in the first place). Whatever epistemic bearing the saint's life has—and it surely, as the New Testament insists, has one—is for others, and not for the saint; however the saint comes by his convictions, it seems not to be by way of his own sainthood" (*Trinity and Truth*, 190–91). One might object that I am confusing issues of justification with the question of truth, but given my purposes, I have not thought it necessary to maintain a strict distinction between justification and truth. Marshall, however, provides a helpful account of the difference between a justified and a true belief (*Trinity and Truth*, 7–9, 105–6, 223–26). For an extraordinary confirmation of Marshall's account of martyrdom, see Brad Gregory's *Salvation at Stake: Christian Martyrdom in Early Modern Europe* (Cambridge, MA: Harvard University Press, 1999). Gregory notes that martyrdom exposes many of the methodological shortcomings in recent accounts of religion just to the extent such accounts assume everyone willing to die because they believe what they believe is true must be "vocational." He notes that "Nietzsche is not so shocking; he is passé. Meanwhile, the aftermath of indifference has helped embed atheistic assumptions so deeply in the status quo that skepticism and unbelief are mistaken for neutrality. Institutionally and intellectually, our world is one that committed early modern Christians scarcely could have imagined. I am certain they would not have wanted to live in it" (352).

7. James McClendon entitles the third volume of his "systematic theology" *Witness* because this last volume deals with issues traditionally associated with missiology, that is, with the delineation of the mission field and the strategy and tactics of the mission to that field. Accordingly, he takes up questions once associated with the relation of Christianity and culture, as well as questions about how Christian convictions can be justified. I think McClendon has it just right; issues of justification are, indeed, a subset of Christian witness. See, in particular, the last chapter of McClendon's book, which is entitled "A Theology of Witness" and offers a wonderful account of how and why "witness" is tied to the Christian understanding of our place in the world. James W. McClendon, *Systematic Theology*, vol. 3, *Witness* (Nashville: Abingdon, 2000).

8. Marshall, *Trinity and Truth*, 181. Marshall's qualifier, "though not the totality of belief," is extremely important. No one can doubt all one's beliefs at once. The gospel does not require that we doubt everything

That the truth of Christian convictions requires witnesses is but the "pragmatic" display of the fact that the God who has created and redeemed the world has done so from the love that constitutes the life of the Trinity. That is what it means to say that witness and argument are the work of the Spirit, and that truth involves the heart as well as the mind. The truth of Christian convictions can be known only through witnesses because the God Christians worship is triune. If the truth of Christian convictions could be known without witnesses, then that truth would no longer be the work of the Trinity, and those who espoused it would no longer be Christians.[9] William James rightly thought that lives matter. Unfortunately, he too often failed to understand how the people who lived the lives he thought mattered actually meant what they said about the God who had made their lives possible. In other words, James did not understand that the lives he admired were the lives of witnesses, and that there can be no witnesses without the One to whom they witness.

---

we believe but that everything we believe be reordered. Marshall, like anyone dealing with these matters, has to fight linguistic habits that seem to suggest that "beliefs" can be isolated from "changed hearts." The truth that is loved is not a "belief" that provides the basis of a subsequent love. Rather, the love that changes hearts is knowledge. Appreciative as I am of Marshall's work, I think his commitment to the account of truth conditions set forth by Alfred Tarski and Donald Davidson appears as though he believes that propositions and/or sentences can be judged apart from the speaker. To his credit, Marshall is well aware of this problem: "A Tarski-Davidson approach cannot by itself be adequate for a theological account of what truth is because it gives us no clue about how to connect truth to a person as its bearer" (245). Marshall makes this comment as he explores the necessary theological claim that Jesus Christ is the truth.

Fergus Kerr also questions Marshall's use of Tarski-Davidson, just to the extent that their account of truth may fail to acknowledge Aquinas's ontological understanding of truth. Kerr notes that for Aquinas truth is found not only in sentences and in formal identity between thoughts and things, but also in the relationship of the world to God. Therefore, for Aquinas, even if there were no human minds, things would still be "true" in relation to God's mind: "Thus, while 'the way of truth for us' is indeed 'demonstrated' in Christ our Savior, Thomas supposes that logically prior to that any truth whatsoever is brought about by a mind/world identity, which is grounded in the participation of created beings in God's own being." Fergus Kerr, "Book Symposium: Bruce D. Marshall, *Trinity and Truth*," *Modern Theology* 16, no. 4 (October 2000): 503–9. In his response to Kerr, Marshall says that he doubts whether Thomas holds that any truth, including the truth that creatures have by virtue of their likeness to God, is logically (or ontologically) "prior to the way in which Jesus Christ is the truth." Bruce Marshall, "Theology after Cana," *Modern Theology* 16, no. 4 (October 2000): 517–27, esp. 524. I do not share Marshall's judgment that the Tarski-Davidson account of truth is "the best philosophy available to us," though he may be right that this account does not exclude the kind of ontological claim to which Kerr calls attention. On the other hand, I do share what I take to be Marshall's "Barthian" reading of Aquinas. Marshall rightly argues that Barth's great achievement was to see that Christian talk of the Trinity is not a metaphysical proposal about divine unity but a way of calling attention to what Christians are talking about when they speak of God. Talk of the Trinity is not, according to Marshall, a theological stipulation about what Christians ought to believe "but an empirical judgment warranted by an analysis of public Christian practices." As I intimated in "The Faith of William James," in *With the Grain of the Universe*, 43–64, James displays how such judgments work for helping us understand what we do when we say as Christians what we believe is not only what we believe but what we believe is true.

9. To put it as forcefully as I can, if there were a "knockdown" argument capable of demonstrating the truth of what Christians believe about God and the world that made witness irrelevant, then we would have evidence that what Christians believe is not true.

Witnesses must exist if Christians are to be intelligible to themselves and hopefully to those who are not Christians, just as the intelligibility of science depends in the end on the success of experiments. Indeed, Marshall argues that the Christian martyr's willingness to die for his or her faith in Christ is similar to the scientist's commitment to experimental results, though any pragmatic similarity that can be drawn between science and theology is inexact. Thus, martyrs—who are but the most determinative display of what being a witness entails—go to their deaths convinced that the gospel is true, but scientists do their experiments in order to become convinced that a hypothetical set of beliefs is true. Moreover, for the scientist the failure of predicted results may disconfirm the theory that shaped their experimental designs; but Christians believe that they should trust the gospel even when they fail to live lives congruent with it, and even when such trust requires that they die.[10] Christians behave in this way because they understand themselves to have become characters in the story that God continues to enact through the ongoing work of the Holy Spirit. Lives that seem like failures do not disconfirm the gospel, because Christians learn to confess their sins by being made part of the work of the Spirit.

Still, like scientists, Christians can never deny that successful Christian practices must remain open to explanations other than the ones given by those who engage in those practices. Marshall notes that Christians have no grounds to deny, for example, that the martyrdom of St. Maximilian Kolbe, a Catholic priest who voluntarily took the place of a condemned prisoner at Auschwitz, might be open to a nontheistic account of Kolbe's action. Such an account could acknowledge that Kolbe thought the beliefs that led him to his martyrdom were true, but deny that such beliefs are in fact true. Christians must be open to such alternative explanations, but, like scientists, they also must be able to distinguish when such explanations have completely altered what they were trying to describe in the first place. As Marshall notes, alternative accounts of the practices of Christians often cease to be descriptions of Christian practice.

Alternative accounts of Christian practice often fail to do justice to events because such accounts divorce practice from belief. Marshall argues, for example, that psychoanalytic accounts of actions like Kolbe's often diminish "the inextricability of practices and their description from the larger web of belief in terms of which practices are described."[11] In other words, to say that St. Maximilian's

---

10. Marshall, *Trinity and Truth*, 185–86.

11. Ibid., 188. The "inextricability of practices and their description from the larger web of belief" has been the animating center of how I have tried over the years to "do ethics." Ethics, as a theological discipline, but names for me the attempt to make the connections Christians need to make if our lives are to be located within the story that is the gospel. Accordingly, I have tried to do little more than elicit simple questions, such as: "If Christians come to think that abortion is morally acceptable, what does that mean for our understanding of Mary's 'Here am I, the servant of the Lord; let it be with me according to your word'"? I am not suggesting that Mary's response should determine everything that Christians have to say about abortion, but it is surely a good place to start.

death is rightly described as martyrdom, that is, as an act by which one shares in the self-sacrificial love the Triune God shows to the world through the cross, is a description not only of that act but also of a complex set of beliefs about God and how God acts in the world. Therefore, whether the description of St. Maximilian's death is rightly described as martyrdom involves questions of how that description fits in the larger web of beliefs. According to Marshall, then, the description of *a* practice alone cannot be decisive for an epistemic assessment of the larger system of belief.[12] Put differently, the truthfulness of Christian convictions cannot be abstracted from the politics that supports the practices necessary "to fix the meaning of the community's most central beliefs."[13]

According to Marshall, a "pragmatic thesis," that is, the view that "successful practice on the part of the Christian community and its members helps to *justify* the community's central beliefs," seems entailed by fundamental Christian convictions.[14] The idea that the practices of a community justify its beliefs may suggest that Christianity functions according to a "pragmatic definition of truth," that is, Christians can make the world anything they want it to be if they just work hard enough at it. But Marshall's pragmatic thesis in fact suggests something else.

The work of the Spirit is not to create evidence for the truth of what Christians believe, because there can be no "evidence" for beliefs beyond the totality of beliefs to which any contested claims might be brought. Thus, the Spirit does not, as Marshall puts it, "persuade by adding something to the totality of belief, by giving us reasons or evidence we do not already have, but by eliciting our assent to a way of structuring the whole."[15] In other words, that martyrs die for their faith does not *prove* that Jesus is risen; on the other hand, that some people have assented to a totality of belief that includes the belief that Jesus is risen surely means that martyrs will die for their faith.[16]

To put Marshall's pragmatic thesis in the idiom of this lecture: Christianity is unintelligible without witnesses, that is, without people whose practices exhibit

12. Ibid.

13. Ibid., 202. Marshall elaborates: "The Spirit instructs the church—and thereby also the world—in the meaning of its own beliefs by his total mastery of the practical situations in which the community and its members (and indeed all human beings) speak. Since the Spirit creates and rules the total situation in which the relevant utterances are made, the meaning of those utterances depends primarily on the action of the Spirit himself, and only secondarily on the free human agents who make them. As the immediate agent of the unitary action of the Trinity in the world, the Spirit is the total cause of all that is not God: of, as the Nicene Creed says, 'all things, visible and invisible.' 'All things' presumably includes the free acts of human beings as well as occurrences which have other sorts of causes; God, transcending the distinction between causes which produce their effects with necessity and those which produce them contingently, is free to create what exists in its totality, including the manner (necessary or contingent) in which each thing is" (203). For an elaboration of Marshall's position along the lines I am developing, see Nicholas Healy, *Church, World, and the Christian Life: Practical-Prophetic Ecclesiology* (Cambridge: Cambridge University Press, 2000), 115–28.

14. Marshall, *Trinity and Truth*, 182.

15. Ibid.

16. Ibid., 188.

their committed assent to a particular way of structuring the whole. That such witnesses exist, however, cannot and should not be sufficient to compel others to believe what Christians believe. Witnesses are not evidence; rather, they are people whose lives embody a totality of beliefs and, accordingly, make claims about "how the world is arranged."[17] To understand what the church believes is to know what the world is like if these beliefs are true. Just to the extent that witnesses such as Maximilian Kolbe live as if these beliefs are true, they show us what the world is like.

That Christians come to hold beliefs that the world is structured in a certain way depends, as Marshall puts it, "on the attractiveness and the habitability of the world they describe." But as attractive as a world created and redeemed in love may be, such an attraction is not and, more important, should not be sufficient to convince anyone that such a world exists. Attractive worlds can often turn out to be no more than fantasies. The needed incentive not just to entertain but to live Christian convictions requires the display of a habitable world exemplified in the life of the Christian community. As Marshall puts it: "Communal success at holding these beliefs and living accordingly—the encounter with actual public willingness to suppose that the world described by these beliefs is not simply desirable but real—encourages and prompts its like."[18]

Marshall's account of the relationship between Christian belief and practice reminds us that when Christians get their theology wrong, they cannot help but get their lives and their accounts of the world wrong as well. Or rather, more accurately, Christians often get their theology wrong because they have gotten their lives wrong. In part, Barth refused to use natural theology as a way of attracting those not already convinced by Christianity because he understood that, for Christians, everything is related to everything else and that, therefore, the only truthful way to make Christianity attractive is through witness. Barth understood that to get our theology right, we have to have our lives in order. For Barth, Christianity is not a "position," just another set of beliefs, but a story at once simple and complex that encompasses all that is. Christians, therefore, are people who, via a community called church, witness to the Creator of all that is.

· · · · · · · · · · · · · · · · · · ·

By directing attention to the university as a site where Christians might rediscover the difference that being Christian makes for claims about the world, I do not mean to overvalue the importance of universities for Christians. Given the character of the modern university, we should not be surprised that the most significant intellectual work in our time may well take place outside the university.[19]

17. Ibid., 194.
18. Ibid., 205.
19. In particular, I am thinking about Wendell Berry, who quite self-consciously stands apart from the university. He does so because the modern university is organized to divide the disciplines in a manner that insures that the university need pay little or no attention to the "local and earthly effects" of the work

Moreover, the Christian practice of hospitality embodied by Dorothy Day and the challenges of church unity that have been central for John Paul II are more important for the Christian understanding of the habitability of the world than our ability to maintain universities.[20] Nonetheless, by attending to the university, I can at least suggest how Christians and non-Christians can discover useful disagreements. And it should become clear as I proceed that the question for me is not whether a university can be Christian, but whether a church exists sufficient to sustain a Christian university.[21]

---

that is done in them. According to Berry, if the university sponsored authentic conversation between disciplines, the college of agriculture would have been brought under questioning by the college of arts and sciences or medicine. Berry confesses that he has no wisdom about how the disciplines might be organized but observes only that at one time, a time when the idea of vocation was still viable, the disciplines were thought of as being useful to one another. However, once the notion of vocation is lost, the university has no other purpose than to insure that the rich or powerful are even more successful. Berry wryly notes he does not believe that a person was ever "called" to be rich or powerful. The hallmark of the contemporary university is, of course, the professionalism whose religion is progress, and "this means that, in spite of its vocal bias in favor of practicality and realism, professionalism forsakes both past and present in favor of the future, which is never present or practical or real." Wendell Berry, *Life Is a Miracle: An Essay against Modern Superstition* (Washington, DC: Counterpoint Press, 2000), 129–30. Berry's criticism could fruitfully be compared to John Paul II's understanding of the culture of death. For example, Berry observes that the story that dominates our age is the story of freedom from reverence, fidelity, neighborliness, and stewardship. Strikingly, he suggests that the "dominant story of our age, undoubtedly, is that of adultery and divorce. This is true both literally and figuratively: The dominant *tendency* of our age is the breaking of faith and the making of divisions among things that were once joined" (133).

20. Hospitality and questions of the church's unity, however, do have everything to do with the ability of Christians to maintain a culture of excellence that includes the work of scholars. Christianity, by its very nature, requires that some people be set aside to think hard about our faith. The work of those so set aside will differ in different times, but part of such work requires those who do it to struggle to understand their relation to the work done in the past. It is sometimes assumed that the radical accounts of Christian convictions represented by people like John Howard Yoder, Dorothy Day, and Peter Maurin provide no space for such work. That is simply not the case. Peter Maurin, for example, loved nothing more than a good argument and was deeply committed to the life of the mind. In his essay entitled "Back to Newmanism," he joined President Hutchins of the University of Chicago to complain that students no longer knew the "great books of the Western World." Maurin quoted Newman: "If the intellect is a good thing, then its cultivation is an excellent thing. It must be cultivated not only as a good thing, but as a useful thing. It must not be useful in any low, mechanical, material sense. It must be useful in the spreading of goodness. It must be used by the owner for the good of himself and for the good of the world." Maurin, *Easy Essays* (Chicago: Franciscan Herald Press, 1977), 126–27. Maurin's attitude toward the modern university was quite similar to Wendell Berry's critique of the curriculum of the contemporary university (see the previous note).

21. My reflections on the university are informed by James McClendon's last chapter in *Witness*: "Theology and the University," 387–420. I believe McClendon is right to note that what we need is not Christian universities or secular universities but universities that are identified by the beauty of their practices. McClendon identifies such practices: (1) conflict resolution, (2) interethnic inclusiveness, (3) economic leveling, (4) a division of labor based upon acknowledgment of vocation, and (5) a voice for all (403–6). Such universities would not feel the need to exclude theology, according to McClendon, but would discover that, just to the extent that they are universities, they *cannot* exclude theology. See also John Milbank's "Theology and the Economy of the Sciences" in *Faithfulness and Fortitude: In Conversation with the Theological Ethics of Stanley Hauerwas*, ed. Mark Thiessen Nation and Samuel Wells (Edinburgh:

It is not surprising that John Howard Yoder and John Paul II refuse to accept the relegation of Christian knowledge to the "soft side" of the university. For example, Yoder argues that if the relationship between the obedience of God's people and the triumph of God's cause is not a relationship between cause and effect but one of cross and resurrection, then it must surely be the case that how history is done by Christians will be different than how it is done by those who assume that God has nothing to do with our lives.[22] Therefore, history must be taken back from the grasp of military historians and chroniclers of battles and dynasties so that a society's character will be described and thus judged by how those "without a role in history" were treated. Thus, Yoder asks: "Instead of reading history as proof of a theory of political science, i.e., the definition *sine qua non* of the state as its monopoly of physical coercion, could we study the story with some openness to the hypothesis that genuine power is always correlated with the consent of the governed or legitimized in some other way?"[23]

Yoder does not mean to suggest that Christian historiography should be done in isolation from how others conceive of and write about history. He is not recommending a state of affairs in which Christians get to say, "You have your story, and we have ours." Rather, he is suggesting that if Christian witness is to be faithful, then how Christians tell their story, as well as how they tell the stories of others, cannot be based upon the presumptions that govern non-Christian historiography. Furthermore, only by writing history on their terms can Christians learn to locate the differences between the church and the world. Of course, it may be the case

---

T&T Clark, 2000), 39–57. Milbank argues a stronger position than the one I take—namely that unless the "other disciplines are (at least implicitly) ordered to theology (assuming that this means participation in God's self-knowledge as in the Augustinian tradition) they are objectively and demonstrably null and void, altogether lacking in truth" (45).

22. The first part of this sentence is a paraphrase of a passage from John Howard Yoder, *The Politics of Jesus: Behold the Man! Our Victorious Lamb*, 2nd ed. (Grand Rapids: Eerdmans, 1994), 238, and the second part is from Yoder, "Christ, the Hope of the World," in *The Royal Priesthood: Essays Ecclesiological and Ecumenical* (Grand Rapids: Eerdmans, 1994), 208.

23. Yoder, "Christ, the Hope of the World," 208. Yoder is not equating the "consent of the governed" with democracy, nor does he assume that democracies are intrinsically less violent. See, for example, John Howard Yoder, "The Christian Case for Democracy," in *The Priestly Kingdom: Social Ethics as Gospel* (Notre Dame, IN: University of Notre Dame Press, 1984), 151–71. In "Christ, the Hope of the World," Yoder provides a fascinating example of the kind of historiographical practice for which he is calling. He contrasts the response of the natives of North America to the European invasion with that of the natives in Latin America. The North American natives fought and were defeated, with the result that their culture was degraded; the Latin American natives, lacking the means to defend themselves, were rolled over, with the result that they not only saved much about their lives but shaped the resulting culture (213). I am sure Yoder would not want too much to be made of this example, as it obviously needs to be "thickened" with detailed descriptions of the similarities and differences between the North American and Latin American invasions. His point, however, still stands, as is increasingly clear by the development of so-called subaltern histories of the colonial period. See, for example, Dipesh Chakrabarty's extraordinary book *Provincializing Europe: Postcolonial Thought and Historical Difference* (Princeton: Princeton University Press, 2000). Chakrabarty observes that the "time" of modern history is "godless, continuous and, to follow Benjamin, empty and homogeneous" (73).

that Christians will discover deep continuities between their account of events and the accounts of others, but this is simply evidence that the church does not exist in isolation from the world. Given the God we worship as Christians, we should not be surprised when evidence of that God shows up in work that assumes our God does not exist.

Yoder's position—which may seem quite challenging to Christian and non-Christian alike—pales in comparison to the stance John Paul II takes toward philosophy in his encyclical *Fides et Ratio*, though just how radical the pope's stance is may not be apparent immediately.[24] John Paul II asserts that in spite of the various meanings of the term "philosophy" and the variety of philosophical systems, there exists a core of philosophical inquiry in which Christians have a stake. For example, he asks us to consider

> the principles of non-contradiction, finality and causality, as well as the concept of the person as a free and intelligent subject, with the capacity to know God, truth and goodness. Consider as well certain fundamental moral norms which are shared by all. These are among the indications that, beyond different schools of thought, there exists a body of knowledge which may be judged a kind of spiritual heritage of humanity. It is as if we had come upon an *implicit philosophy*, as a result of which all feel that they possess these principles, albeit in a general and unreflective way. Precisely because it is shared in some measure by all, this knowledge should serve as a kind of reference point for different philosophical schools.[25]

Accordingly, John Paul II claims that the church cannot help but value philosophy as that which names the activity through which our lives are rendered more worthy. Indeed, he goes so far as to claim that "the Church considers philosophy an indispensable help for a deeper understanding of faith and for communicating the truth of the Gospel to those who do not know it."[26]

None of this seems radical, but John Paul II goes on to say that because the church is confident of its competence to bear the revelation of Jesus Christ, and because the Second Vatican Council insisted that the bishops are a "witness of divine and catholic truth," criticism must be leveled at philosophy that, "rather than voicing the human orientation toward the truth, has wilted under the weight of so much knowledge and little by little has lost the capacity to lift its gaze to the heights, not daring to rise to the truth of being."[27] From John Paul II's perspective, modern philosophy has made a philosophical mistake by trying to develop epistemologies that insure that our knowledge is true. In the process, modern

24. John Paul II, *Fides et Ratio* (Boston: Pauline Books and Media, 1998).
25. Ibid., 12–13, par. 4. It is fascinating to wonder what Barth would have made of these claims about philosophy. I think it is a mistake to assume that he would have dismissed them outright. After all, the pope is not suggesting that philosophy can give us knowledge of Jesus Christ.
26. Ibid., 13, par. 5.
27. Ibid., 14, par. 5.

philosophy has forgotten that existence is prior to knowledge and thus determines how we know what we know.[28]

At the end of the twentieth century—a century that at least in the Northern Hemisphere had become increasingly secular—we find the pope, of all people, defending the activity of reasoning. Moreover, we find him honoring the good of philosophy as a discipline. Yet we also find him arguing that although the results of reasoning may be true, they "acquire their true meaning only if they are set within the larger horizon of faith: 'All man's steps are ordered by the Lord: how then can man understand his own ways?'" (Prov. 20:24).[29] In other words, the truths discovered through philosophy must be tested and judged by the truth known through revelation; for the latter is not the product or consummation of arguments devised by human reason but comes to us as the gift of life, Jesus Christ. That gift gives purpose to the work of reason by stirring thought and seeking acceptance as an expression of love.[30]

John Paul II, therefore, assumes that how philosophy is done in Catholic universities may well be different from how it is done in more secular institutions. Of course, much of what Catholic philosophers do will be indistinguishable from philosophy done by non-Catholics. Indeed, Catholic philosophers will have much

28. It would be an extremely instructive enterprise to compare John Paul II's account of modern philosophy and MacIntyre's account in *First Principles, Final Ends, and Contemporary Philosophical Issues.* MacIntyre suggests that philosophers who are committed to a Thomistic-Aristotelian mode of philosophy, that is, a view that by training we can be made adequate to understand the way things are, must approach contemporary philosophy in a manner akin to a Nietzschean genealogist. Genealogists try to explain why their antagonists have come to an impasse and why they cannot recognize or extricate themselves from the impasse on their own terms. Accordingly, a Thomist must try to show that the predicaments of contemporary philosophy, both analytic and deconstructive, are the result of the long-term consequences of rejecting the Aristotelian and Thomistic teleology at the threshold of the modern world (59).

29. John Paul II, *Fides et Ratio*, 32, par. 20.

30. Ibid., 26, par. 15. Later in the encyclical, John Paul II suggests that the best way to conceive of the relationship between theology and philosophy is that of a circle: "Theology's source and starting point must always be the word of God revealed in history, while its final goal will be an understanding of that word which increases with each passing generation. Yet, since God's word is Truth (cf. John 17:17), the human search for truth—philosophy, pursued in keeping with its own rules—can only help to understand God's word better. It is not just a question of theological discourse using this or that concept or element of a philosophical construct; what matters most is that the believer's reason use its powers of reflection in the search for truth which moves from the word of God toward a better understanding of it. . . . This circular relationship with the word of God leaves philosophy enriched, because reason discovers new and unsuspected horizons" (92–93, par. 73).

It would be fascinating to compare MacIntyre's understanding of the relation of philosophy and theology to John Paul II's understanding of that relation. I am sure that MacIntyre would accept the pope's account in general, although the claim that theology not only judges philosophy but adds content to the subject of philosophy seems to go beyond what MacIntyre has said explicitly. John Paul II identifies exemplars of his understanding of philosophy and theology: St. Gregory of Nazianzus, St. Augustine, St. Anselm, St. Bonaventure, and St. Thomas, and, more recently, John Henry Newman, Antonio Rosmini, Jacques Maritain, Étienne Gilson, and Edith Stein—a list, I suspect, that MacIntyre would approve. What is interesting, however, is that most of the people named made no hard-and-fast distinction between philosophy and theology.

to learn from their non-Catholic counterparts. The pope clearly respects the kind of specialization in philosophy and in other disciplines that makes it difficult to locate a strong difference between Catholics and others. But what he refuses to accept is the fragmentation of the curriculum characteristic of modern universities. This fragmentation is but an expression of our cultural presumption that there is no order to what we know, nor to how we know it.[31] From John Paul II's perspective, philosophers have a particular responsibility for the intellectual work necessary for the ordering of our knowledge and, thus, of the curriculum.

Given this understanding of the relation of faith and reason, it comes as no surprise that John Paul II thinks that a university can and should be fully Catholic without in any manner compromising its activity as a university.[32] In *Ex Corde Ecclesiae*, he makes it clear that not only does the church have a stake in the work of the university, but the work of the university is best done when the Truth, who is God, is acknowledged. In other words, the university has a stake in the church. Thus, Catholic universities are called to continuous renewal both as universities and as extensions of the Catholic Church, for the very meaning of the human person is at stake in their common task. Theology must play a particularly important role in Catholic universities because "it serves all other disciplines in their search for meaning, not only by helping them to investigate how their discoveries will affect individuals and society, but also by bringing a perspective and an orientation not contained within their own methodologies."[33]

31. In a number of his essays, MacIntyre has noted that one of the characteristics of modern life that makes the moral life, at least the moral life as conceived by a Thomistic-Aristotelian, impossible is the compartmentalized character of our lives. The fragmentation of the university curriculum at once reflects and reproduces this compartmentalization. As a result, education cannot do what an education should do, that is, transform the desires students bring to their studies. Of course, the modern university does, in a certain sense, provide moral training, just to the extent that the fragmentation of the curriculum reinforces the fragmentation of student lives, making it impossible for students to think of their lives as whole. This kind of training is justified insofar as the university is expected to produce the kind of "personality type" necessary to sustain liberal democracies, that is, people who believe that in the name of fairness they are capable of understanding and appreciating without prejudice any and all people and positions. For MacIntyre's account of compartmentalization, see "Social Structures and Their Threats to Moral Agency," *Philosophy* 74, no. 289 (July 1999): 311–29.

32. Put more strongly, I suspect that John Paul II assumes that any university that has the ambition to be a university, whether it is officially sponsored by the church or not, cannot help but exhibit the characteristics of a Catholic university, which may mean that only Catholic universities in our time have the potential to be universities just to the extent that they are committed to the rational possibility of giving a coherent account of themselves. As Reinhard Hütter has suggested: "God matters for the university because only a university in and for which God matters can be an enterprise that can give a comprehensive account of what it is all about" (personal correspondence). The Catholic university should be capable of such a witness to the extent that it gains its intelligibility from the witness that is the church.

33. John Paul II, *Ex Corde Ecclesiae*, in *Origins* 20, no. 17 (October 4, 1990): 269. John Paul II also observes that interaction with other disciplines enriches theology by making theological research more relevant to current needs. I have no intention of entering the debates surrounding questions concerning the implementation of *Ex Corde*. For the text of the implementing document, see "Ex Corde Ecclesiae: An Application to the United States," in *Origins* 30, no. 5 (June 15, 2000): 65–75. As a Protestant, I can only

In the last chapter of *Three Rival Versions of Moral Enquiry*, MacIntyre suggests that the modern university confronts the Thomist with a problem. Any attempt to embody Thomism "requires both a different kind of curricular ordering of the disciplines from that divisive and fragmenting partitioning which contemporary academia imposes and the development of morally committed modes of dialectical enquiry, for which contemporary academia affords no place."[34] Therefore the Thomist, particularly a Thomist like John Paul II, cannot avoid asking what the modern university is for, as well as what particular goods the modern university serves. But those are just the questions, according to MacIntyre, that the modern university must repress in order to preserve the illusion that the university transcends conflict. Like James's famous hotel corridor, the modern university has become all things to all people (who have money) by looking away, as James puts it, from "first things, principles, 'categories,' supposed necessities; and [by] looking towards last things, fruits, consequences, facts."[35]

In contrast, MacIntyre argues that universities ought to be where "conceptions of and standards of rational justification are elaborated, put to work in detailed practices of enquiry, and themselves rationally evaluated, so that only from the university can the wider society learn how to conduct its own debates, practical or theoretical, in a rationally defensible way."[36] Accordingly, MacIntyre suggests that we need, as an alternative both to the premodern university of enforced and constrained agreements and to the modern university of alleged unconstrained agreements, a university of constrained disagreements.[37] MacIntyre's university

---

stand in awe at the clarity with which the pope seems to understand the challenges before the modern university. He is not about to let theology be relegated to "ethics" or, even worse, to "values." John Paul II thinks that theology and philosophy involve claims about the way things are that have implications across the curriculum. Julie A. Reuben's *The Making of the Modern University* (Chicago: University of Chicago Press, 1996) could serve as a commentary on what happens when theology is no longer thought to entail claims about the way things are and is reduced at best to "morality."

34. Alasdair MacIntyre, *Three Rival Versions of Moral Enquiry: Encyclopaedia, Genealogy, and Tradition* (Notre Dame, IN: University of Notre Dame Press, 1990), 220.

35. William James, *Pragmatism and the Meaning of Truth*, intro. A. J. Ayer (Cambridge, MA: Harvard University Press, 1996), 32. George Marsden uses this quotation from James to justify the possibility as well as the existence of Christian scholarship in the university; see Marsden, *The Outrageous Idea of Christian Scholarship* (New York: Oxford University Press, 1997), 45–46. Many people think that Marsden's defense of "Christian scholarship" is radical. From my perspective, Marsden is not nearly radical enough, as his use of James's image makes clear. Christians do not desire just a place at the "table," particularly a table that has been set by the modern university. Christians do not want a place at the table; they want both to build and set the table itself. See, e.g., Mike Baxter, CSC, "Not Outrageous Enough," *First Things* 113 (May 2001): 14–16.

36. MacIntyre, *Three Rival Versions of Moral Enquiry*, 222.

37. Ibid., 230–31. MacIntyre acknowledges that some people might think his suggestion utopian, but he asks those who would do so to consider that "the degree to which it is difficult to envisage the restructuring of the university so as to make systematic debate concerning standards of rational justification between such points of view as the genealogical and the Thomistic a central preoccupation of our shared cultural and social life, is also the degree to which the structures of present society have exempted themselves from and protected themselves against being put in question by such systematic intellectual

would have faculties of encyclopedists, genealogists, and traditionalists, that is, all of the various options for serious inquiry would be included. In time, this arrangement might well result in the establishment of a set of rival universities. Such a result would present to the wider society rival claims, as each university advanced its own inquiries on its own terms and secured agreements to ensure the progress of its inquiries by its own set of exclusions and prohibitions.[38]

MacIntyre's analysis of the character of the modern university makes clear why what Yoder says of history and what the pope says of philosophy are not simply curricular suggestions. Rather, both Yoder and the pope are making claims about what Christian practice entails if we are rightly to know our world. Moreover, both Yoder and the pope are making the claim that such knowledge can be rationally sustained only by a politics called church. The question is not whether Christian claims about the way the world is make it impossible for Christians to enter debates with those who hold alternative views. Instead, the question is whether the church can produce people capable of sustaining the arguments that Christians and non-Christians so desperately need to have with one another. From this perspective, Christians and non-Christians alike should despair when it becomes difficult to distinguish the church from the world. Of course, for Christians, despair is a vice that robs us of our ability to see what is before our eyes—that is, lives with names like John Howard Yoder, John Paul II, and Dorothy Day.

---

and moral enquiry. What are accepted as the de facto standards of argumentative justification in the established forums of political and bureaucratic negotiation are to a remarkable degree now protected against subversive challenge because the legitimacy of any particular challenge is measured by those self-same standards" (235).

I should hope that MacIntyre's university of constrained disagreements would have a place, as the University of Notre Dame did, for John Howard Yoder in the Department of Theology.

38. Ibid., 234. MacIntyre knows that such encounters are always dangerous just to the extent that "knowing how to read antagonistically without defeating oneself as well as one's opponent by not learning from the encounter is a skill without which no tradition can flourish" (233). Those people the church sets aside to do this kind of work obviously must be formed by the virtues necessary to have their souls so tested.

# 20

## Science, Stories, and Our Knowledge of the Natural World

### ALASDAIR MACINTYRE

**I**

What is an epistemological crisis? Consider, first, the situation of ordinary agents who are thrown into such crises. Someone who has believed that he was highly valued by his employers and colleagues is suddenly fired; someone proposed for membership of a club whose members were all, so he believed, close friends is blackballed. Or someone falls in love and needs to know what the loved one *really* feels; someone falls out of love and needs to know how he or she can possibly have been so mistaken in the other. For all such persons the relationship of *seems* to *is* becomes crucial. It is in such situations that ordinary agents who have never learned anything about academic philosophy are apt to rediscover for themselves versions of the other-minds problem and the problem of the justification of induction. They discover, that is, that there is a problem about the rational justification of inferences from premises about the behavior of other people to conclusions about their thoughts, feelings, and attitudes and of inferences from premises about how individuals have acted in the past to conclusions expressed

Originally published as Alasdair MacIntyre, "Epistemological Crises, Dramatic Narrative and the Philosophy of Science," *The Monist* 60, no. 4 (1977): 453–72. Published by Open Court Publishing Company, Chicago, Illinois. Reprinted by permission.

as generalizations about their behavior—generalizations which would enable us to make reasonably reliable predications about their future behavior. What they took to be evidence pointing unambiguously in some one direction now turns out to have been equally susceptible of rival interpretations. Such a discovery is often paralyzing, and were we all of us all of the time to have to reckon with the multiplicity of possible interpretations open to us, social life as we know it could scarcely continue. For social life is sustained by the assumption that we are, by and large, able to construe each other's behavior—that error, deception, self-deception, irony, and ambiguity, although omnipresent in social life, are not so pervasive as to render reliable reasoning and reasonable action impossible. But can this assumption in any way be vindicated?

Consider what it is to share a culture. It is to share schemata which are at one and the same time constitutive of and normative for intelligible action by myself and are also means for my interpretations of the actions of others. My ability to understand what you are doing and my ability to act intelligibly (both to myself and to others) are one and the same ability. It is true that I cannot master these schemata without also acquiring the means to deceive, to make more or less elaborate jokes, to exercise irony and utilize ambiguity, but it is also, and even more importantly, true that my ability to conduct any successful transactions depends on my presenting myself to most people most of the time in unambiguous, unironical, undeceiving, intelligible ways. It is these schemata which enable inferences to be made from premises about past behavior to conclusions about future behavior and present inner attitudes. They are not, of course, empirical generalizations; they are prescriptions for interpretation. But while it is they which normally preserve us from the pressure of the other-minds problem and the problem of induction, it is precisely they which can in certain circumstances thrust those very problems upon us.

For it is not only that an individual may rely on the schemata which have hitherto informed all his interpretations of social life and find that he or she has been led into radical error or deception, so that for the first time the schemata are put in question—perhaps for the first time they also in this moment become visible to the individual who employs them—but it is also the case that the individual may come to recognize the possibility of systematically different possibilities of interpretation, of the existence of alternative and rival schemata which yield mutually incompatible accounts of what is going on around him. Just this is the form of epistemological crisis encountered by ordinary agents, and it is striking that there is not a single account of it anywhere in the literature of academic philosophy. Perhaps this is an important symptom of the condition of that discipline. But happily we do possess one classic study of such crises. It is Shakespeare's *Hamlet*.

Hamlet arrives back from Wittenberg with too many schemata available for interpreting the events at Elsinore of which already he is a part. There is the revenge schema of the Norse sagas; there is the renaissance courtier's schema; there is a Machiavellian schema about competition for power. But he not only has the problem of which schema to apply; he also has the other ordinary agents' problem: whom now to believe? His mother? Rosencrantz and Guildenstern? His father's ghost? Until he has adopted some schema he does not know what to treat as evidence; until he knows what to treat as evidence he cannot tell which schema to adopt. Trapped in this epistemological circularity the general form of his problem is: "What is going on here?" Thus Hamlet's problem is close to that of the literary critics who have asked: "What is going on in *Hamlet*?" And it is close to that of directors who have asked: "What should be cut and what should be included in my production so that the audience may understand what is going on in *Hamlet*?"

The resemblance between Hamlet's problem and that of the critics and directors is worth noticing, for it suggests that both are asking a question which could equally well be formulated as: "What is going on in *Hamlet*?" or "How ought the narrative of these events to be constructed?" Hamlet's problems arise because the dramatic narrative of his family and of the kingdom of Denmark through which he identified his own place in society and his relationships to others has been disrupted by radical interpretative doubts. His task is to reconstitute, to rewrite that narrative, reversing his understanding of past events in the light of present responses to his probing. This probing is informed by two ideals, truth and intelligibility, and the pursuit of both is not always easily coherent. The discovery of a hitherto unsuspected truth is just what may disrupt a hitherto intelligible account. And of course while Hamlet tries to discover a true and intelligible narrative of the events involving his parents and Claudius, Gertrude and Claudius are trying to discover a true and intelligible narrative of Hamlet's investigation. To be unable to render oneself intelligible is to risk being taken to be mad, is, if carried far enough, to be mad. And madness or death may always be the outcomes which prevent the resolution of an epistemological crisis, for an epistemological crisis is always a crisis in human relationships.

When an epistemological crisis is resolved, it is by the construction of a new narrative which enables the agent to understand *both* how he or she could intelligibly have held his or her original beliefs *and* how he or she could have been so drastically misled by them. The narrative in terms of which he or she at first understood and ordered experiences is itself made into the subject of an enlarged narrative. The agent has come to understand how the criteria of truth and understanding must be reformulated. He has had to become epistemologically self-conscious and at a certain point he may have come to acknowledge two conclusions: the first is that his new forms of understanding may themselves in turn come to be put in question at any time; the second is that, because in such crises the criteria of truth, intelligibility, and rationality may always themselves be put in question—as they are in *Hamlet*—we are never in a position to claim that now we possess the truth or now we are fully rational. The most that we can claim is that this is the best account which anyone has been able to give so far, and that our beliefs about what the marks of "a best account so far" are will themselves change in what are at present unpredictable ways.

Philosophers have often been prepared to acknowledge this historical character in respect of scientific theories, but they have usually wanted to exempt their own thinking from the same historicity. So, of course, have writers of dramatic narrative; *Hamlet* is unique among plays in its openness to reinterpretation. Consider, by contrast, Jane Austen's procedure in *Emma*.

Emma insists on viewing her protégée, Harriet, as a character in an eighteenth-century romance. She endows her, deceiving both herself and Harriet, with the conventional qualities of the heroine of such a romance. Harriet's parentage is not known; Emma converts her into the foundling heroine of aristocratic birth so common in such romances. And she designs for Harriet precisely the happy ending of such a romance, marriage to a superior being. By the end of *Emma* Jane Austen has provided Emma with some understanding of what it was in herself that had led her not to perceive the untruthfulness of her interpretation of the world in terms of romance. *Emma* has become a narrative about narrative. But Emma, although she experiences moral reversal, has only a minor epistemological crisis, if only because the standpoint which she now, through the agency of Mr. Knightly, has come to adopt is presented as though it were one from which *the* world as it is can be viewed. False interpretation has been replaced not by a more adequate interpretation, which itself in turn may one day be transcended, but simply by the truth. We of course can see that Jane Austen is merely replacing one interpretation by another, but Jane Austen herself fails to recognize this and so has to deprive Emma of this recognition too.

Philosophers have customarily been Emmas and not Hamlets, except that in one respect they have often been even less perceptive than Emma. For Emma it becomes clear that her movement toward the truth necessarily had a moral dimension. Neither Plato nor Kant would have demurred. But the history of epistemology, like the history of ethics itself, is usually written as though it were not a moral narrative, that is, in fact as though it were not a narrative. For narrative requires an evaluative framework in which good or bad character helps to produce unfortunate or happy outcomes.

One further aspect of narratives and their role in epistemological crises remains to be noticed. I have suggested that epistemological progress consists in the construction and reconstruction of more adequate narratives and forms of narrative and that epistemological crises are occasions for such reconstruction. But if this were really the case then two kinds of questions would need to be answered. The first would be of the form: How does this progress begin? What are the narratives from which we set out? The second would be of the form: How comes it, then, that narrative is not only given so little place by thinkers from Descartes onward, but has so often before and after been treated as a merely aesthetic form? The answers to these questions are not entirely unconnected.

We begin from myth, not only from the myths of primitive peoples, but from those myths or fairy stories which are essential to a well-ordered childhood. Bruno Bettelheim has written: "Before and well into the oedipal period (roughly, the ages between three and six or seven), the child's experience of the world is chaotic. ... During and because of the oedipal struggles, the outside world comes to hold more meaning for the child and he begins to try to make some sense of it. ... As a child listens to a fairy tale, he gets ideas about how he may create order out of the chaos that is his inner life."[1] It is from fairy tales, so Bettelheim argues, that the child learns how to engage himself with and perceive an order in social reality; and the child who is deprived of the right kind of fairy tale at the right age later on is apt to have to adopt strategies to evade a reality he has not learned how to interpret or to handle.

"The child asks himself, 'Who am I? Where did I come from? How did the world come into being? Who created man and all the animals? What is the purpose of life?' ... He wonders who or what brings adversity upon him and what can protect him against it. Are there benevolent powers in addition to his parents? *Are* his parents benevolent powers? How should he form himself, and why? Is there hope for him, though he may have done wrong? Why did all this happen to him? What will it mean to his future?"[2] The child originally requires answers that are true to his own experience, but of course the child comes to learn the inadequacy of that experience. Bettelheim points out that the young child told by adults that the world is a globe suspended in space and spinning at incredible speeds may feel bound to repeat what they say, but would find it immensely more plausible to be told that the earth is held up by a giant. But in time the young child learns that what the adults told him is indeed true. And such a child may well become a Descartes, one who feels that all narratives are misleading fables when compared with what he now takes to be the solid truth of physics.

Yet to raise the question of truth need not entail rejecting myth or story as the appropriate and perhaps the only appropriate form in which certain truths can be told. The child may become not a Descartes, but a Vico or a Hamann who writes a story about how he had to escape from the hold which the stories of his childhood and the stories of the childhood of the human race originally had upon him in order to discover how stories can be true stories. Such a narrative will be itself a history of epistemological transitions, and this narrative may well be brought to a point at which questions are thrust upon the narrator which make it impossible for him to continue to use it as an instrument of interpretation. Just this, of course, happens to Descartes, who, having abjured history as a means to truth, recounts to us his own history as the medium through which the search for truth is to be carried on. For Descartes and for others this moment is that at which an epistemological crisis occurs. And all those questions which the child has asked of the teller of fairy tales arise in a new adult form. Philosophy is now set the same task that had once been set for myth.

1. Bruno Bettelheim, *The Uses of Enchantment* (New York: Alfred A. Knopf, 1976), 74–75.
2. Ibid., 47.

## II

Descartes's description of his own epistemological crisis has, of course, been uniquely influential. Yet Descartes radically misdescribes his own crisis and thus has proved a highly misleading guide to the nature of epistemological crises in general. The agent who is plunged into an epistemological crisis knows something very important: that a schema of interpretation which he has trusted so far has broken down irremediably in certain highly specific ways. So it is with Hamlet. Descartes, however, starts from the assumption that he knows nothing whatsoever until he can discover a presuppositionless first principle on which all else can be founded. Hamlet's doubts are formulated against a background of what he takes to be—rightly—well-founded beliefs; Descartes's doubt is intended to lack any such background. It is to be contextless doubt. Hence also that tradition of philosophical teaching arises which presupposes that Cartesian doubts can be entertained by anyone at any place or time. But of course someone who really believed that he knew nothing would not even know how to begin on a course of radical doubt; for he would have no conception of what his task might be, of what it would be to settle his doubts and to acquire well-founded beliefs. Conversely, anyone who knows enough to know *that* does indeed possess a set of extensive epistemological beliefs which he is not putting in doubt at all.

Descartes's failure is complex. First of all he does not recognize that among the features of the universe which he is not putting in doubt is his own capacity not only to use the French and the Latin languages, but even to express the same thought in both languages, and as a consequence he does not put in doubt what he has inherited in and with these languages, namely, a way of ordering both thought and the world expressed in a set of meanings. These meanings have a history; seventeenth-century Latin bears the marks of having been the language of scholasticism, just as scholasticism was itself marked by the influence of twelfth- and thirteenth-century Latin. It was perhaps because the presence of his languages was invisible to the Descartes of the *Discours* and the *Meditationes* that he did not notice either what Gilson pointed out in detail, how much of what he took to be the spontaneous reflections of his own mind was in fact a repetition of sentences and phrases from his school textbooks. Even the *Cogito* is to be found in St. Augustine.

What thus goes unrecognized by Descartes is the presence not only of languages, but of a tradition—a tradition that he took himself to have successfully disowned. It was from this tradition that he inherited his epistemological ideals. For at the core of this tradition was a conception of knowledge as analogous to vision: the mind's eye beholds its objects by the light of reason. At the same time this tradition wishes to contrast sharply knowledge and sense-experience, including visual experience. Hence there is metaphorical incoherence at the heart of every theory of knowledge in this Platonic and Augustinian tradition, an incoherence which Descartes unconsciously reproduces. Thus Descartes also cannot recognize that he is responding not only to the timeless demands of skepticism, but to a highly specific crisis in one particular social and intellectual tradition.

One of the signs that a tradition is in crisis is that its accustomed ways for relating *seems* and *is* begin to break down. Thus the pressures of skepticism become more urgent, and attempts to do the impossible, to refute skepticism once and for all, become projects of central importance to the culture and not mere private academic enterprises. Just this happens in the late Middle Ages and the sixteenth century. Inherited modes of ordering experience reveal too many rival possibilities of interpretation. It is no accident that there are a multiplicity of rival interpretations of both the thought and the lives of such figures as Luther and Machiavelli in a way that there are not for such equally rich and complex figures as Abelard and Aquinas. Ambiguity, the possibility of alternative interpretations, becomes a central feature of human character and activity. *Hamlet* is Shakespeare's brilliant mirror to the age, and the difference between Shakespeare's account of epistemological crises and Descartes's is now clear. For Shakespeare invites us to reflect on the crisis of the self as a crisis in the tradition which has formed the self; Descartes by his attitude to history and to fable has cut himself off from the possibility of recognizing himself; he has invented an unhistorical self-endorsed self-consciousness and tries to describe his epistemological crisis in terms of it. Small wonder that he misdescribes it.

Consider by contrast Galileo. When Galileo entered the scientific scene, he was confronted by much more than the conflict between the Ptolemaic and Copernican astronomies. The Ptolemaic system was itself inconsistent both with the widely accepted Platonic requirements for a true astronomy and with the perhaps even more widely accepted principles of Aristotelian physics. These latter were in turn inconsistent with the findings over two centuries of scholars at Oxford, Paris, and Padua about motion. Not surprisingly, instrumentalism flourished as a philosophy of science, and Osiander's instrumentalist reading of Copernicus was no more than the counterpart to earlier instrumentalist interpretations of the Ptolemaic system. Instrumentalism, like attempts to refute skepticism, is characteristically a sign of a tradition in crisis.

Galileo resolves the crisis by a threefold strategy. He rejects instrumentalism; he reconciles astronomy and mechanics; and he redefines the place of experiment in natural science. The old mythological empiricist view of Galileo saw him as appealing to the facts against Ptolemy and Aristotle; what he actually did was to give a new account of what an appeal to the facts had to be. Wherein lies the superiority of Galileo to his predecessors? The answer is that he, for the first time, enables the work of all his predecessors to be evaluated by a common set of standards. The contributions of Plato, Aristotle, the scholars at Merton College, Oxford, and at Padua, the work of Copernicus himself at last all fall into place. Or, to put matters in another and equivalent way: the history of late medieval science can finally be cast into a coherent narrative. Galileo's work implies a rewriting of the narrative which constitutes the scientific tradition. For it now became retrospectively possible to identify those anomalies which had been genuine counterexamples to received theories from those anomalies which could justifiably be dealt with by ad hoc explanatory devices or even ignored. It also became retrospectively possible to see how the various elements of various theories had fared in their encounters with other theories and with observations and experiments, and to understand how the form in which they had survived bore the marks of those encounters. A theory always bears the marks of its passage through time, and the theories with which Galileo had to deal were no exception.

Let me cast the point which I am trying to make about Galileo in a way which, at first sight, is perhaps paradoxical. We are apt to suppose that because Galileo was a peculiarly great scientist, therefore he has his own peculiar place in the history of science. I am suggesting instead that it is because of his peculiarly important place in the history of science that he is accounted a particularly great scientist. The criterion of a successful theory is that it enables us to understand its predecessors in a newly intelligible way. It, at one and the same time, enables us to understand precisely why its predecessors have to be rejected or modified and also why, without and before its illumination, past theory could have remained credible. It introduces new standards for evaluating the past. It recasts the narrative which constitutes the continuous reconstruction of the scientific tradition.

This connection between narrative and tradition has hitherto gone almost unnoticed, perhaps because tradition has usually been taken seriously only by conservative social theorists. Yet those features of tradition which emerge as important when the connection between tradition and narrative is understood are ones which conservative theorists are unlikely to attend to. For what constitutes a tradition is a conflict of interpretations of that tradition, a conflict which itself has a history susceptible of rival interpretations. If I am a Jew, I have to recognize that the tradition of Judaism is partly constituted by a continuous argument over what it means to be a Jew. Suppose I am an American: the tradition is one partly constituted by continuous argument over what it means to be an American and partly by continuous argument over what it means to have rejected tradition. If I am a historian, I must acknowledge that the tradition of historiography is partly, but centrally, constituted by arguments about what history is and ought to be, from Hume and Gibbon to Namier and Edward Thompson. Notice that all three kinds of tradition—religious, political, intellectual—involve epistemological debate as a necessary feature of their conflicts. For it is not merely that different participants in a tradition disagree; they also disagree as to how to characterize their disagreements and as to how to resolve them. They disagree as to what constitutes appropriate reasoning, decisive evidence, conclusive proof.

A tradition then not only embodies the narrative of an argument, but is only to be recovered by an argumentative retelling of that narrative which will itself be in conflict with other argumentative retellings. Every tradition therefore is always in danger of lapsing into incoherence, and when a tradition does so lapse, it sometimes can only be recovered by a revolutionary reconstitution. Precisely such a reconstitution of a tradition which had lapsed into incoherence was the work of Galileo.

It will now be obvious why I introduced the notion of tradition by alluding negatively to the viewpoint of conservative theorists. For they, from Burke onward, have wanted to counterpose tradition and reason and tradition and revolution. Not reason, but prejudice; not revolution, but inherited precedent; these are Burke's key oppositions. Yet if the present arguments are correct, it is traditions which are the bearers of reason, and traditions at certain periods actually require and need revolutions for their continuance. Burke saw the French Revolution as merely the negative overthrow of all that France had been, and many French conservatives have agreed with him, but later thinkers as different as Peguy and Hilaire Belloc were able retrospectively to see the great revolution as reconstituting a more ancient France, so that Jeanne D'Arc and Danton belong within the same single, if immensely complex, tradition.

Conflict arises, of course, not only within, but between traditions, and such a conflict tests the resources of each contending tradition. It is yet another mark of a degenerate tradition that it has contrived a set of epistemological defenses which enable it to avoid being put in question or at least to avoid recognizing that it is being put in question by rival traditions. This is, for example, part of the degeneracy of modern astrology, of some types of psychoanalytic thought, and of liberal Protestantism. Although, therefore, any feature of any tradition, any theory, any practice, any belief can always under certain conditions be put in question, the practice of putting in question, whether within a tradition or between traditions, itself always requires the context of a tradition. Doubting is a more complex activity than some skeptics have realized. To say to oneself or to someone else, "Doubt all your beliefs here and now," without reference to historical or autobiographical context is not meaningless, but it is an invitation not to philosophy, but to mental breakdown, or rather to philosophy as a means of mental breakdown. Descartes concealed from himself, as we have seen, an unacknowledged background of beliefs which rendered what he was doing intelligible and sane to himself and to others. But suppose that he had put that background in question too—what would have happened to him then?

We are not without clues, for we do have the record of the approach to breakdown in the life of one great philosopher. "For I have already shown," wrote Hume,

> that the understanding, when it acts alone, and according to its most general principles, entirely subverts itself, and leaves not the lowest degree of evidence in any proposition, either in philosophy or common life. . . . The intense view of these manifold contradictions and imperfections in human reason has so wrought upon me, and heated my brain, that I am ready to reject all belief and reasoning, and can look upon no opinion even as more probable or likely than another. Where am I, or what? From what causes do I derive my existence, and to what condition shall I return? Whose favour shall I court, and whose anger must I dread? What beings surround me? and on whom have I any influence? I am confronted with all these

questions, and begin to fancy myself in the most deplorable condition imaginable, inviron'd with the deepest darkness and utterly depriv'd of the use of every member and faculty.[3]

We may note three remarkable features of Hume's cry of pain. First, like Descartes, he has set a standard for the foundations of his beliefs which could not be met; hence all beliefs founder equally. He has not asked if he can find good reasons for preferring in respect of the best criteria of reason and truth available some among others of the limited range of possibilities of belief which actually confront him in his particular cultural situation. Second, he is in consequence thrust back without any answers or possibility of answers upon just that range of questions that, according to Bettelheim, underlie the whole narrative enterprise in early childhood. There is indeed the most surprising and illuminating correspondence between the questions which Bettelheim ascribes to the child and the questions framed by the adult, but desperate, Hume. For Hume by his radical skepticism has lost any means of making himself—or others—intelligible to himself, let alone, to others. His very skepticism itself becomes unintelligible.

There is perhaps a possible world in which "empiricism" would have become the name of a mental illness, while "paranoia" would be the name of a well-accredited theory of knowledge. For in this world empiricists would be consistent and unrelenting—unlike Hume—and they would thus lack any means to order their experience of other people or of nature. Even a knowledge of formal logic would not help them; for until they knew how to order their experiences, they would possess neither sentences to formalize nor reasons for choosing one way of formalizing them rather than another. Their world would indeed be reduced to that chaos which Bettelheim perceives in the child at the beginning of the oedipal phase. Empiricism would lead not to sophistication, but to regression. Paranoia by contrast would provide considerable resources for living in the world. The empiricist maxims "Believe only what can be based upon sense experience" or Occam's razor would leave us bereft of all generalizations and therefore of all attitudes toward the future (or the past). They would isolate us in a contentless present. But the paranoid maxims "Interpret everything which happens as an outcome of envious malice" and "Everyone and everything will let you down" receive continuous confirmation for those who adopt them. Hume cannot answer the question: "What beings surround me?" But Kafka knew the answer to this very well: "In fact the clock has certain personal relationships to me, like many things in the room, save that now, particularly since I gave notice—or rather since I was given notice . . . —they seem to be beginning to turn their backs on me, above all the calendar. . . . Lately it is as if it had been metamorphosed. Either it is absolutely uncommunicative—for example, you want its advice, you go up to it, but

3. David Hume, *Treatise of Human Nature*, ed. L. A. Shelby-Bigge (London: Oxford University Press, 1941), 1.4, 1.7 (pp. 267–69).

the only thing it says is 'Feast of the Reformation'—which probably has a deeper significance, but who can discover it?—or, on the contrary, it is nastily ironic."[4]

So in this possible world they will speak of Hume's Disease and of Kafka's Theory of Knowledge. Yet is this possible world so different from that which we inhabit? What leads us to segregate at least some types of mental [illness] from ordinary, sane behavior is that they presuppose and embody ways of interpreting the natural and social world which are radically discordant with our customary and, as we take it, justified modes of interpretation. That is, certain types of mental illness seem to presuppose rival theories of knowledge. Conversely every theory of knowledge offers us schemata for accepting some interpretations of the natural and social world rather than others. As Hamlet discovered earlier, the categories of psychiatry and of epistemology must be to some extent interdefinable.

## III

What I have been trying to sketch are a number of conceptual connections which link such notions as those of an epistemological crisis, a narrative, a tradition, natural science, skepticism, and madness. There is one group of recent controversies in which the connections between these concepts has itself become a central issue. I refer, of course, to the debates which originated from the confrontation between Thomas Kuhn's philosophy of science and the views of those philosophers of science who in one way or another are the heirs of Sir Karl Popper. It is not surprising therefore that the positions which I have taken should imply conclusions about those controversies, conclusions which are not quite the same as those of any of the major participants. Yet it is perhaps because the concepts which I have examined—such as those on epistemological crisis and of the relationship of conflict to tradition—have provided the largely unexamined background to the recent debates that their classification may in fact help to resolve some of the issues. In particular I shall want to argue that the positions of some of the most heated antagonists—notably Thomas Kuhn and Imre Lakatos—can be seen to converge once they are emended in ways toward which the protagonists themselves have moved in their successive reformulations of their positions.

One very striking new conclusion will however also emerge. For I shall want to reinforce my thesis that dramatic narrative is the crucial form for the understanding of human action, and I shall want to argue that natural science can be a rational form of enquiry if and only if the writing of a true dramatic narrative—that is, of history understood in a particular way—can be a rational activity. Scientific reason turns out to be subordinate to, and intelligible only in terms of, historical reason. And if this is true of the natural sciences, *a fortiori* it will be true also of the social sciences.

4. Letter to his sister Valli in *I Am a Memory Come Alive*, ed. Nahum N. Glatzer (New York: Schocken Books, 1974), 235.

It is therefore sad that social scientists have all too often treated the work of writers such as Kuhn and Lakatos as it stood. Kuhn's writing in particular has been invoked time and again—for a period of ten years or so, a ritual obeisance toward Kuhn seems almost to have been required in presidential addresses to the American Political Science Association—to license the theoretical failures of social science. But while Kuhn's work uncriticized—or for that matter Popper or Lakatos uncriticized—represents a threat to our understanding, Kuhn's work criticized provides an illuminating application for the ideas which I have been defending.

My criticisms of Kuhn will fall into three parts. In the first I shall suggest that his earlier formulations of his position are much more radically flawed than he himself has acknowledged. I shall then argue that it is his failure to recognize the true character of the flaws in his earlier formulations which leads to the weakness of his later revisions. Finally I shall suggest a more adequate form of revision.

What Kuhn originally presented was an account of epistemological crises in natural science which is essentially the same as the Cartesian account of epistemological crises in philosophy. This account was superimposed on a view of natural science which seems largely indebted to the writings of Michael Polanyi (Kuhn nowhere acknowledges any such debt). What Polanyi had shown is that all justification takes place within a social tradition and that the pressures of such a tradition enforce often unrecognized rules by means of which discrepant pieces of evidence or difficult questions are often put on one side with the tacit assent of the scientific community. Polanyi is the Burke of the philosophy of science, and I mean this analogy with political and moral philosophy to be taken with great seriousness. For all my earlier criticisms of Burke now become relevant to the criticism of Polanyi. Polanyi, like Burke, understands tradition as essentially conservative and essentially unitary. (Paul Feyerabend—at first sight so different from Polanyi—agrees with Polanyi in his understanding of tradition. It is just because he so understands the scientific tradition that he rejects it and has turned himself into the Emerson of the philosophy of science; not "Every man his own Jesus," but "Every man his own Galileo.") He does not see the omnipresence of conflict—sometimes latent—within living traditions. It is because of this that anyone who took Polanyi's view would find it very difficult to explain how a transition might be made from one tradition to another or how a tradition which had lapsed into incoherence might be reconstructed. Since reason operates only *within* traditions and communities according to Polanyi, such a transition or a reconstruction could not be a work of reason. It would have to be a leap in the dark of some kind.

Polanyi never carried his argument to this point. But what is a major difficulty in Polanyi's position was presented by Kuhn as though it were a discovery. Kuhn did of course recognize very fully how a scientific tradition may lapse into incoherence. And he must have (with Feyerabend) the fullest credit for recognizing in an original way the significance and character of incommensurability. But the conclusions which he draws, namely that "proponents of competing paradigms must fail to make complete contact with each other's viewpoints" and that the transition from one paradigm to another requires a "conversion experience," do not follow from his premises concerning incommensurability. These last are three-fold: adherents of rival paradigms during a scientific revolution disagree about what set of problems provide the test for a successful paradigm in that particular scientific situation; their theories embody very different concepts; and they "see different things when they look from the same point in the same direction." Kuhn concludes that "just because it is a transition between incommensurables" the transition cannot be made step by step; and he uses the expression "gestalt switch" as well as "conversion experience." What is important is that Kuhn's account of the transition requires an additional premise. It is not just that the adherents of rival paradigms disagree, but that *every* relevant area of rationality is invaded by that disagreement. It is not just that threefold incommensurability is present, but rationality apparently cannot be present in any other form. Now this additional premise would indeed follow from Polanyi's position, and, if Kuhn's position is understood as presupposing something like Polanyi's, then Kuhn's earlier formulations of his positions become all too intelligible, and so do the accusations of irrationalism by his critics, accusations which Kuhn professes not to understand.

What follows from the position thus formulated? It is that scientific revolutions are epistemological crises understood in a Cartesian way. Everything is put in question simultaneously. There is no rational continuity between the situation at the time immediately preceding the crisis and any situation following it. To such a crisis the language of evangelical conversion would be appropriate. We might indeed begin to speak with the voice of Pascal, lamenting that the highest achievement of reason is to learn what reason cannot achieve. But of course, as we have already seen, the Cartesian view of epistemological crises is false; it can never be the case that everything is put in question simultaneously. That would indeed lead to large and unintelligible lacunas not only in the history of practices, such as those of the natural sciences, but also in the personal biographies of scientists.

Moreover Kuhn does not distinguish between two kinds of transition experience. The experience which he is describing seems to be that of the person who having been thoroughly educated into practices defined and informed by one paradigm has to make the transition to a form of scientific practice defined and informed by some radically different paradigm. Of this kind of person what Kuhn asserts may well on occasion be true. But such a scientist is always being invited to make a transition that has already been made by others; the very characterization of his situation presupposes that the new paradigm is already operative while the old still retains some power. But what of the very different type of transition made by those scientists who first invented or discovered the new paradigm? Here Kuhn's divergences from Polanyi ought to have saved him from his original Polanyi-derived conclusion. For Kuhn does recognize very fully and insightfully how traditions lapse into incoherence. What some, at least, of those who are educated into such a tradition may come to recognize is the gap between its *own* epistemological ideals and its actual practices. Of those who recognize this some may tend toward skepticism and some toward instrumentalism. Just this, as we have already seen, characterized late medieval and sixteenth-century science. What the scientific genius, such as Galileo, achieves in his transition, then, is not only a new way of understanding nature, but also and inseparably a new way of understanding the old science's way of understanding nature. It is because only from the standpoint of the new science can the inadequacy of the old science be characterized that the new science is taken to be more adequate than the old. It is from the standpoint of the new science that the continuities of narrative history are reestablished.

Kuhn has of course continuously modified his earlier formulations and to some degree his position. He has in particular pointed out forcefully to certain of his critics that it is they who have imputed to him the thesis that scientific revolutions are nonrational or irrational events, a conclusion which he has never drawn himself. His own position is "that, if history or any other empirical discipline leads us to believe that the development of science depends essentially on behavior that we have previously thought to be irrational, then we should conclude not that science is irrational, but that our notion of rationality needs adjustment here and there."

Feyerabend, however, beginning from the same premises as Kuhn, has drawn on his own behalf the very conclusion which Kuhn so abhors. And surely if scientific revolutions were as Kuhn describes them, if there were nothing more to them than such features as the threefold incommensurability, Feyerabend would be in the right. Thus if Kuhn is to, as he says, "adjust" the notion of rationality, he will have to find the signs of rationality in some feature of scientific revolutions to which he has not yet attended. Are there such features? Certainly, but they belong precisely to the history of these episodes. It is more rational to accept one theory or paradigm and to reject its predecessor when the later theory or paradigm provides a standpoint from which the acceptance, the life story, and the rejection of the previous theory or paradigm can be recounted in more intelligible historical narrative than previously. An understanding of the concept of the superiority of one physical theory to another requires a prior understanding of the concept of the superiority of one historical narrative to another. The theory of scientific rationality has to be embedded in a philosophy of history.

What is carried over from one paradigm to another are epistemological ideals and a correlative understanding of what constitutes the progress of a single intellectual life. Just as Descartes's account of his own epistemological crisis was only possible by reason of Descartes's ability to recount his own history, indeed to live his life as a narrative about to be cast into a history—an ability which Descartes himself could not recognize without falsifying his own account of epistemological crises—so Kuhn and Feyerabend recount the history of epistemological crises as moments of almost total discontinuity without noticing the historical continuity which makes their own intelligible narratives possible. Something very like this position, which I have approached through a criticism of Kuhn, was reached by Lakatos in the final stages of his journey away from Popper's initial positions.

If Polanyi is the Burke of the philosophy of science and Feyerabend the Emerson, then Popper himself or at least his disciples inherit the role of J. S. Mill—as Feyerabend has already noticed. The truth is to be approached through the free clash of opinion. The logic of the moral sciences is to be replaced by *Logik der Forschung*. Where Burke sees reasoning only within the context of tradition and Feyerabend sees the tradition as merely repressive of the individual, Popper has rightly tried to make something of the notion of rational tradition. What hindered this attempt was the Popperian insistence on replacing the false methodology of induction by a new methodology. The history of Popper's own thought and of that of his most gifted followers was for quite a number of years the history of successive attempts to replace Popper's original falsificationism by some more adequate version, each of which in turn fell prey to counterexamples from the history of science. From one point of view the true heir of these attempts is Feyerabend, for it is he who has formulated the completely general thesis that all such attempts were doomed to failure. There is *no* set of rules as to how science *must* proceed, and all attempts to discover such a set founder in their encounter with actual history of science. But when Lakatos had finally accepted this, he moved on to new ground.

In 1968, while he was still a relatively conservative Popperian, Lakatos had written: "The appraisal is rather of a *series of theories* than of an isolated *theory*." He went on to develop this notion into that of a research program. The notion of a research program is of course oriented to the future and there was therefore a tension between Lakatos's use of this notion and his recognition that it is only retrospectively that a series of theories can be appraised. In other words what is appraised is always a history; for it is not just a series of theories which is appraised, but a series which stand in various complex relationships to each other through time which is appraised. Indeed what we take to be a single theory is always "a growing developing entity, one which cannot be considered as a static structure."[5] Consider for example the kinetic theory of gases. If we read the scientific textbooks for any period, we shall find presented an entirely ahistorical account of the theory. But if we read all the successive textbooks, we shall learn not only that the kinetic theory of 1857 was not quite that of 1845 and that the kinetic theory of 1901 is neither that of 1857 nor that of 1965. Yet at each stage the theory bears the marks of its previous history, of a series of encounters with confirming or anomalous evidence, with other theories, with metaphysical points of view, and so on. The kinetic theory not merely has, but is a history, and to evaluate it is to evaluate how it has fared in this large variety of encounters. Which of these have been victories, which defeats, which compounds of victory and defeat, and which not classifiable under any of these headings? To evaluate a theory, just as to evaluate a series of

---

5. Richard M. Burian, "More than a Marriage of Convenience: On the Inextricability of History and Philosophy of Science," unpublished paper, 38.

theories, one of Lakatos's research programs, is precisely to write that history, that narrative of defeats and victories.

This is what Lakatos recognized in his paper "History of Science and Its Rational Reconstructions."[6] Methodologies are to be assessed by the extent to which they satisfy historiographical criteria; the best scientific methodology is that which can supply the best rational reconstruction of the history of science, and for different episodes different methodologies may well be successful. But in talking not about history, but about rational reconstructions, Lakatos has still not exorcised the ghosts of the older Popperian belief in methodology, for he was quite prepared to envisage the rational reconstruction as "a caricature" of actual history. Yet it matters enormously that our histories should be true, just as it matters that our scientific theories make truth one of their goals.

Kuhn interestingly and perhaps oddly insists against Lakatos on truth in history (he accuses Lakatos of replacing genuine history by "philosophy fabricating examples"), but yet denies any notion of truth to natural science other than that truth which attaches to solutions to puzzles and to concrete predictions. In particular he wants to deny that a scientific theory can embody a true ontology, that it can provide a true representative of what is "really there." "There is, I think no theory-independent way to reconstruct phrases like 'really there'; the notion of a match between the ontology of a theory and its 'real' counterpart in nature now seems to me illusive in principle."[7]

This is very odd because science has certainly shown us decisively that some existence-claims are false just because the entities in question are *not* really there—whatever *any* theory may say. Epicurean atomism is not true, there are no humors, nothing with negative weight exists; phlogiston is one with the witches and the dragons. But other existence-claims have survived exceptionally well through a succession of particular theoretical positions: molecules, cells, electrons. Of course our beliefs about molecules, cells, and electrons are by no means what they once were. But Kuhn would be put into a very curious position if he adduced this as a ground for denying that some existence-claims still have excellent warrant and others do not.

What, however, worries Kuhn is something else: "In some important respects, though by no means in all, Einstein's general theory of relativity is closer to Aristotle's mechanics than either of them is to Newton's."[8] He therefore concludes that the superiority of Einstein to Newton is in puzzle solving and not in an approach to a true ontology. But what an Einstein ontology enables us to understand is why *from the standpoint of an approach to truth* Newtonian mechanics is superior to Aristotelian. For Aristotelian mechanics as it lapsed into incoherence could never

6. I. Lakatos, "History of Science and Its Rational Reconstructions," in *Boston Studies in the Philosophy of Science*, vol. 8, ed. Roger C. Buck and Robert S. Cohen (Dordrecht, Holland: D. Reidel, 1974).

7. Thomas S. Kuhn, *The Structure of Scientific Revolutions*, 2nd ed. (Chicago: University of Chicago Press, 1970), 206.

8. Ibid., 206–7.

have led us to the special theory; construe them how you will, the Aristotelian problems about time will not yield the questions to which special relativity is the answer. A history which moved from Aristotelianism directly to relativistic physics is not an imaginable history.

What Kuhn's disregard for ontological truth neglects is the way in which the progress toward truth in different sciences is such that they have to converge. The easy reductionism of some positivist programs for science was misleading here, but the rejection of such a reductionism must not blind us to the necessary convergence of physics, chemistry, and biology. Were it not for a concern for ontological truth, the nature of our demand for a coherent and convergent relationship between all the sciences would be unintelligible.

Kuhn's view may, of course, seem attractive simply because it seems consistent with a fallibilism which we have every reason to accept. *Perhaps* Einsteinian physics will one day be overthrown just as Newtonian was; perhaps, as Lakatos in his more colorfully rhetorical moments used to suggest, all our scientific beliefs are, always have been, and always will be false. But it seems to be a presupposition of the way in which we do natural science that fallibilism has to be made consistent with the regulative ideal of an approach to a true account of the fundamental order of things and not vice versa. If this is so, Kant is essentially right; the notion of an underlying order—the kind of order that we would expect if the ingenious, unmalicious god of Newton and Einstein had created the universe—*is* a regulative ideal of physics. We do not need to understand this notion quite as Kant did, and our antitheological beliefs may make us uncomfortable in adopting it. But perhaps discomfort at this point is a sign of philosophical progress.

I am suggesting, then, that the best account that can be given of why some scientific theories are superior to others presupposes the possibility of constructing an intelligible dramatic narrative which can claim historical truth and in which such theories are the subject of successive episodes. It is because and only because we can construct better and worse histories of this kind, histories which can be rationally compared with each other, that we can compare theories rationally too. Physics presupposes history and history of a kind that invokes just those concepts of tradition, intelligibility, and epistemological crisis for which I argued earlier. It is this that enables us to understand why Kuhn's account of scientific revolutions can in fact be rescued from the charges of irrationalism leveled by Lakatos and why Lakatos's final writings can be rescued from the charges of evading history leveled by Kuhn. Without this background, scientific revolutions become unintelligible episodes; indeed Kuhn becomes—what in essence Lakatos accused him of being—the Kafka of the history of science. Small wonder that he in turn felt that Lakatos was not a historian, but a historical novelist.

A final thesis can now be articulated. When the connection between narrative and tradition on the one hand, and theory and method on the other, is lost sight of, the philosophy of science is set insoluble problems. Any set of finite observations is compatible with any one out of an infinite set of generalizations. Any attempt to show the rationality of science, once and for all, by providing a rationally justifiable set of rules for linking observations and generalizations breaks down. This holds, as the history of the Popperian school shows, for falsification as much as for any version of positivism. It holds, as the history of Carnap's work shows, no matter how much progress may be made on detailed, particular structures in scientific inference. It is only when theories are located in history, when we view the demands for justification in highly particular contexts of a historical kind, that we are freed from either dogmatism or capitulation to skepticism. It therefore turns out that the program which dominated the philosophy of science from the eighteenth century onward, that of combining empiricism and natural science, was bound either at worst to break down in irrationalism or at best in a set of successively weakened empiricist programs whose driving force was a deep desire not to be forced into irrationalist conclusions. Hume's Disease is, however, incurable and ultimately fatal, and even backgammon (or that type of analytical philosophy which is often the backgammon of the professional philosopher) cannot stave off its progress indefinitely. It is, after all, Vico, and neither Descartes nor Hume, who has turned out to be in the right in approaching the relationship between history and physics.

# 21

## Science for the Church

### Natural Sciences in the Christian University

Jonathan R. Wilson

Every day I receive five to ten messages in my email box from a service that monitors news items and events that concern the relationship between "science and religion." After becoming interested in this dialogue, I began collecting books on the topic, a collection that now fills an entire bookcase. With this much activity in one area of scholarship, one might think that the issues and positions would be fairly well worked out. But that is not the case. The conversations go on separate from one another, positions are taken but seldom engaged, and the "relationship" threatens to become a prime example of incommensurability.

These discussions about "science and religion" are undisciplined and confused for several reasons. The most obvious and frequently recognized reason is that "science" and "religion" are reifications and abstractions. There is no one thing called "science" and no one thing called "religion" except as they are created by the work of a particular scholar or set of scholars. But that bare acknowledgment is about as far as the discussion gets—if it gets to this point.

What is needed, if we are to consider "the place of the natural sciences in an ecclesially based university," is a more articulate account of this relationship,

Originally published as Jonathan R. Wilson, "The Place of the Natural Sciences in an Ecclesially Based University," in *Conflicting Allegiances: The Church-Based University in a Liberal Democratic Society*, ed. Michael L. Budde and John Wright (Grand Rapids: Brazos, 2004), 128–39. Copyright © 2004. Used by permission.

greater attention to the doctrine of creation in the church, and unremitting *local* arguments and practices about "the place." First, I turn to an articulation of this "place" rooted in Alasdair MacIntyre's presentation of institutions, practices, narratives, traditions, and virtues.[1]

## Institutions

If we are to engage this question fruitfully, one of the aspects that we must recognize is that we are dealing with *institutions*. The sciences are institutions; the ecclesially based universities are institutions.

To say that the sciences are institutions is to recognize that sciences exist in networks of relationships that concern training, hiring, approving, advancing, and financing the work of the sciences. This institutionalization of sciences determines much of what goes on in particular science departments. For a college to have a "respectable" science department, say, a physics department, the faculty members in that department must have standing within the institution of physics—degrees from recognized programs, approved research projects, funding for the projects, and students to work on the projects.

This institutionalization of physics in most cases (in all that I know) overwhelms the college as an institution, so that no one would even think of the physics department as primarily identified with this or that university. The physics department is institutionally determined by physics; it happens to be located within this or that school. If it is known as the "physics department" at Wilson University, it is known as such because the institution of physics has recognized it, not because Wilson University thinks so highly of it.

Or consider the chemistry department whose curriculum is set by the American Chemical Society. According to discussions in which I have participated, the ACS curriculum sets the boundaries for a chemistry department. If a college wants to have a credible chemistry major, the other curricular requirements must not intrude on the units needed by the chemistry department. Thus, the ACS—one institutionalization of one science—sets limits for the college's curriculum.

At the same time that we recognize the institutionalization of sciences, we must also recognize that colleges are institutions—institutions of higher education. In that very identity, church-related colleges entangle themselves in other institutions—such as the sciences. For the ecclesially based university to form, survive, and thrive, must it be intertwined with other institutions? I think that it must. So what I suggest is a strategy of subversion. This strategy ultimately depends upon people, a point to which I will later turn. In the meantime, three suggestions for institutional subversion: First, accept the curricular impositions of institutionalized sciences, then work within those courses to change their character

---

1. Alasdair MacIntyre, *After Virtue: A Study in Moral Theory*, 2nd ed. (Notre Dame, IN: University of Notre Dame Press, 1984).

by including instruction on the aims of that science within an ecclesially based university. Second, provide required cocurricular seminars that regularly break down the disciplinary boundaries not only among the sciences but between the sciences and other disciplines. An ecclesially based university is the one place this may been done with regularity. My own college does this with an ongoing natural science seminar and with "Pascal Society" lectures on the relationship between sciences and the Christian faith. Finally, the sciences at an ecclesially based university need to be creative in seeking funding, looking beyond (but not overlooking) traditional sources, so that projects may be pursued that are integral to the school's institutional identity.

But let's take a more radical step, a thought experiment beyond subversion to replacing the sciences. What would the sciences at an ecclesially based university look like if they thought of themselves as belonging, through the university, to the church? What if their shapes, their practices, their research programs were determined more by their place in the body of Christ than in the American Association for the Advancement of Science? I don't know the answers. I don't know whether the question can even be pondered at our present moment in history—we may be lacking the requisite ecclesiology and practices.[2]

## Practices

In addition to being institutions, sciences are also practices. Among the many descriptions of the sciences as practices, I will focus on sciences as practices of apprenticeship. In our cultural moment, this seems to be an apt description.

Several summers ago I was talking to one of my colleagues who teaches science. He began telling me about the research project he was working on that summer with three students from our college. I asked what granting agency was funding his project, expecting to congratulate him on a National Science Foundation grant, or something similar. No, his funding was a regular line item in the department budget, funded by the college. "After all," he informed me, "that's the only way you can really teach science—to three or four students at a time."

This practice takes place within a Christian college that at the time required four courses in Christianity. (It has since reduced that requirement to three courses, but the description that follows remains accurate.) Those classes average between fifty-five and sixty-five students each. Of course, one can teach Christianity to that number of students, but no one would dare to think of "really" teaching science to more than a few students at a time. Sciences are practices; Christianity is . . . ?

This anecdote seems to me revelatory of the place of the natural sciences in a Christian college today. That place quite simply reflects the place of the sciences

2. See Jonathan R. Wilson, *Gospel Virtues: Practicing Faith, Hope and Love in Uncertain Times* (Downers Grove, IL: InterVarsity, 1998); and Wilson, *Why Church Matters* (Grand Rapids: Brazos, 2006).

in the culture of late modernity. Sciences are entrusted with the providential care of our society and the redemption of our lives. We want to be certain that our scientists really know what they are doing.

Over against sciences as apprenticeship stands Christianity as discipleship. As the ecclesially based college pours enormous resources into science apprenticeship, does it recognize its betrayal of the call to discipleship? Apprenticeship in sciences forms students deeply. How can their formation as Christian disciples be as deep when so many more resources are poured into the sciences? Do ecclesially based universities even recognize this contrast as a problem for their mission? Or have they so accommodated to liberal democratic society that they have no resources for even recognizing this as an issue? (I can imagine raising this question at my own institution and being met with a collective "Huh?")

These practices of apprenticeship in the sciences are so deeply embedded in our Christian colleges that most administrators, professors, and students never perceive the incongruities between the practices and the propaganda. Science departments are more expensive than most other departments; the other expensive program at our college is studio and theatre arts. In the sciences we have regularly scheduled labs, so that students learn to do science. We have lab assistants alongside the professors so that our students get individual attention. And all of this is simply an accepted part of the fabric of educational excellence.

What if we actually practiced the Christianity that we profess? What if our Bible classes had discipleship sessions scheduled in the afternoon so that students learn to do Christianity? What if a doctrine class had assistants alongside the professor, so that students received individual attention in their quest to live the doctrine?

Has this rant taken us away from the sciences in an ecclesially based university? Not at all. The practices of the sciences should continue, but so also should countervailing practices in Christianity. Indeed, let's again take another step and think about reconceiving the practices of scientific apprenticeships in the ecclesially based university. What if the dominant context and purpose of such apprenticeships were training in Christian discipleship? That is, what if the practices of the sciences overcame our present fragmentation, instead of enshrining the separation of sciences and Christianity as my earlier suggestion may tend toward? On this model, professors in the sciences would then say, "After all, that's the only way to teach people to do science as Christians—just a few at a time." Such professors would also find their own identity first in the church as disciples of Jesus Christ who express that discipleship in their science.

## Traditions

I must begin this section by confessing that the traditions of the sciences are so variegated that any account of the place of the natural sciences in an ecclesially based university must move very cautiously. In the next section I will consider one approach to the narratives that form these traditions. Here I will consider the traditions themselves.

With that confession and warning as a starting point, I move to a series of observations and questions. We are mistaken if we think that we can helpfully speak of "science" as if it were a clearly identifiable, coherent, clearly bounded tradition. It is certainly possible to map relationships among the "sciences," and we can find overlaps and similarities. But even those may be drawn in different ways. A theoretical physicist may share more in common with certain mathematicians than with other physicists. A biologist studying the brain may have more to talk about with some psychologists than with other biologists. Those who work in labs, whatever their "discipline," may have concerns that cross disciplines.

Therefore, when we try to think about the place of the sciences in the ecclesially based university, we must be local and particular in our concerns.[3] The first step along this path is simply to learn to talk to one another and spend time together. I learned something about this from a friend, a scientist who has taught at a Christian college for almost twenty years, has had many close friends outside his own field, and is very well read in theology. He told me recently that he has finally begun to understand what we theologians do. I congratulated him, then realized that I am not certain that I could say the same about my understanding of his work.

If traditions are "socially embodied arguments," then the traditions of the sciences are embodied by the scientist across campus or on the next floor. (Doesn't architecture reveal interesting things about our institutions and traditions?) Certainly, the traditions are not individualistic (unless the scientist in question is a "maverick"), but they are embodied by individuals. Moreover, there are similarities among the scientists at different levels and with different terms of comparison. But for us to know how these all take their places in the ecclesially based university, we must do the hard work of developing friendships across disciplines within the context of our common end.

## Narratives

Although it is possible to identify "traditions" common to various natural sciences, and even within one of the natural sciences, there is an identifiable "tradition" that marks the sciences in relation to the concerns of the ecclesially based university. This tradition has been narrated as one of conflict or warfare. In spite of the fine historical work that has been done to overthrow that tradition, many persist in it. One can easily imagine that those who persist in the face of a well-founded counternarrative do so because the perpetuation of the conflict tradition serves

3. One contribution to the discussion that reflects some recognition of this differentiation is Nancey Murphy and George F. R. Ellis, *On the Moral Nature of the Universe: Theology, Cosmology and Ethics* (Minneapolis: Fortress, 1996).

the institutional and practice dimensions of the sciences. As long as science has cultural hegemony or cultural capital, one or the other will be used to suppress and disempower those institutions that represent potential threats. Those of us who decry the state of the church may perhaps take some small comfort from the apparent danger that "sciences" still perceive in the church. Alternatively, we may regard that perception as a measure of how little understanding of the church there is within the tradition of the sciences. If they only knew how weak we really are . . .

Can the ecclesially based university narrate a different tradition that places the sciences within the church's own narrative? Possibly. Some historical work has been done, but most of it presumes a Constantinian church. What would a narrative placing of the sciences look like if they were placed within the tradition of the church as a disciple community rather than church as Christendom? Such a task is vitally important to placing the natural sciences in the ecclesially based university. Some have proposed a "theistic science," but such a proposal is still Constantinian and falls short of the narrative of good news in Jesus Christ.

It seems to me that to place the sciences properly we must develop a *cruciform* narrative for the sciences. Such a narrative would acknowledge the world as creation, but it would also recognize that to claim the world as creation is to presume also its redemption. And as followers of Jesus Christ, we recognize that the redemption of the world is accomplished by the crucifixion of Jesus. So "cruciformity" does not name some abstract principle or pattern, but the very event that gives the world its meaning.

Creation, in this view, is not a doctrine that can be separated from the cross, though Christianity has often made this mistake. If the world finds its significance, even as creation, in the cross, then creation does not provide a "Christian" or "theological" basis for sciences unless it is understood to carry with it Christ's work of redemption.

Since this will seem so contrary to much conventional Christian thinking, it is important to elaborate this view. To claim the world as "creation" is to make the claim that what we now have is not God's original creation nor is it all that ever will be. The Old Testament confession of God as Creator and this world as creation is made by a people—Israel—who had come to know God's redemptive work in a chaotic, violent, unjust world. By God's redemptive work, they then came to realize that the God of the exodus was not invading some other god's territory, nor was Israel's Redeemer come to rescue them from this world. Rather, they came to know that the God of the exodus is the Creator and Redeemer of this world. Thus, they confess this world as "creation." Such confession makes no sense in this world as it is, but it makes cosmic, eternal sense if God is bringing God's original work to its final end: the new creation.

That redemption finds its climactic revelation and action in the cross of Christ. That sacrifice is what it took to redeem this world. Thus, we learn that the world we live in is a cruciform creation. Sciences that expect peace and orderliness in this world are mistaken. Those that seek orderliness are mistaken about our place in history. Those that use the absence of peace and orderliness to argue against God and Christ are likewise mistaken. Violence, chaos, breakdown within a particular kind of "order" are precisely what we should expect of a creation that is not yet fully redeemed.

I have struggled to say briefly here what would take at least a book to make clear. I am concerned that most attempts to make the sciences "Christian" misappropriate doctrine. The doctrine of creation, as it is typically presented, cannot provide guidance for the sciences, because, except in rare cases, creation is usually understood separately from the cross and its revelation of our sin.[4] We do not live in the world that God created. We live in the world for which and in which Christ died. More, we live in the world that put Christ to death. Thus, it is not enough to call for a "theistic" science as some general nod in the direction of "the supernatural." The God of Christianity is the God of Jesus Christ, the one who died on the cross to save the world. This is the narrative of creation that provides us with guidance for the place of the natural sciences in the ecclesially based university.

## Virtues

The questions of the virtues requisite to the sciences and to the ecclesially based university are seldom addressed, but the issues should loom large in our consideration and return us to the question of persons that I noted earlier. What kind of person is drawn to the sciences and formed by them? Is that formation conducive to life in an ecclesially based university?

In his marvelous study *Exiles from Eden*, Mark Schwehn considers Max Weber's account of *Wissenschaft* and concludes that "in Weber's account, the process of knowledge formation, if conducted rationally, really does favor and cultivate the emergence of a particular personality type. And this personality type does exhibit virtues—clarity, but not charity; honesty, but not friendliness; devotion to the calling, but not loyalty to particular and local communities of learning."[5] This description embraces all *Wissenschaften*, but in so doing it includes the sciences that are our special concern here. If this list of virtues accurately reflects the "scientific character," then we can readily see the challenge presented by the ecclesially based university.

---

4. Two notable exceptions are Jürgen Moltmann, *God in Creation: A New Theology of Creation and the Spirit of God* (San Francisco: Harper & Row, 1985); Moltmann, *The Way of Jesus Christ: Christology in Messianic Dimensions* (San Francisco: HarperSanFrancisco, 1990); Moltmann, *The Coming of God: Christian Eschatology* (Minneapolis: Fortress, 1996); and Colin E. Gunton, *Christ and Creation: The 1990 Didsbury Lectures* (Exeter: Paternoster, 1993); Gunton, *The One, the Three, and the Many: God, Creation and the Culture of Modernity* (Cambridge: Cambridge University Press, 1993); Gunton, *The Triune Creator: A Historical and Systematic Study* (Grand Rapids: Eerdmans, 1998).

5. Mark R. Schwehn, *Exiles from Eden: Religion and the Academic Vocation in America* (New York: Oxford University Press, 1993), 8.

I must confess, however, to some suspicion about Weber's characterization. It may be the Weberian "ideal," and it may characterize many in the sciences. But I also know many in the sciences who are far from this ideal type. Certainly, some have been powerfully formed to value and seek clarity, honesty, and devotion, not charity, friendliness, and loyalty, as proper to the sciences. But I do know some in the sciences who value that latter list more highly. And what is true of those in the sciences is true also of those in other traditions of *Wissenschaft*.

For those formed, in spite of Weber, in charity, friendliness, and loyalty to a local and particular community, I suspect that the account of their science and character is better found in an account like Michael Polanyi's. To further shape the virtues of those in the sciences (and other traditions of scholarship), I urge that more attention be paid to Polanyi, especially the neglected question in Polanyian scholarship of the formation of the virtues requisite to "personal knowledge."[6] Such an account would have to be tied closely to a renarration of the institutions, practices, and traditions of the sciences.

Such a counteraccount of the virtues and renarration is required by the identity of the ecclesially based university. That community is determinative of the virtues of its citizens. What is required, then, is a commitment to that community and its proper virtues on the part of its citizens; then, following from that commitment, a reconception of the sciences (and other scholarly traditions) that enables the pursuit of those virtues.

## Telos

The *telos* is the goal, aim, end toward which a particular community is living. It gives coherence to the life of the community. It is expressed in and furthered by the community's narrative. The *telos* is extended by the tradition that is socially embodied in the community. The practices of a community are that community's attempt to participate in its *telos*. The virtues identify the character necessary to the proper life of the community.

Without a clear identification and continual reaffirmation of a community's *telos*, the life of the community loses its coherence and meaning. Without a clear *telos*, the way of life in a particular community becomes confused. The practices and virtues seem to have no purpose. The narrative and its tradition appear to be arbitrary. Since most of us live among many competing communities, the most coherent community or the community with the most cultural capital rules our lives in other communities.

In considering the place of the natural sciences in an ecclesially based university, we must face the reality that the sciences are typically more coherent communities with more cultural capital than ecclesially based universities. And when the

---

6. I refer, of course, to the seminal work by Michael Polanyi, *Personal Knowledge: Towards a Post-critical Philosophy*, 2nd ed. (London: Routledge, 1962).

differences between these two come into conflict, the university may exercise some power—in the granting of tenure, for example—but when it does so, there is seldom a coherent, persuasive account given.

In this "confrontation" between the sciences and the ecclesially based university, we are encountering a particular instance of the fragmentation of our time.[7] The world in which we live is not a pluralistic world, made of coherent, competing communities; rather, it is a fragmented world, made of incoherent, incomplete, largely incommensurable communities that live in uneasy toleration.

Thus, when two communities actually confront one another, it is a double affront: to our commitment to tolerance and to our denial of fragmentation. If this is true, it explains why the topic of this chapter is so difficult for us to untangle. Here is one of the places where we may be forced to admit our condition. The ecclesially based university, as it is imagined by most of the contributors to this volume,[8] does not exist, though I will qualify this claim in my concluding section. The sciences, however, do exist as powerful, formative social institutions. And although the sciences take an ateleological, even antiteleological, approach to "nature," they are profoundly teleological in their social organization. As a result, the ecclesially based university finds itself relatively powerless in its "placing" of the natural sciences. In other words, it seems that the title of this chapter should question how the natural sciences "place" the ecclesially based university. Before I elucidate the meaning of "seems" in that previous sentence, I must add one more element to my account.

### Nature versus Creation

One of the biggest challenges to "placing" the "natural" sciences in the ecclesially based university, rather than the opposite, is the theological abdication of the doctrine of creation. It seems to me that this abdication began shortly after the rise of modern science and became complete in the nineteenth century. This abdication took one of two forms. Either theology retreated to inferiority—the pietist turn—or theology submitted to the strictures of science—the rational turn. Of course, these two turns are not mutually exclusive; we find a bit of both in Immanuel Kant.

In the first case, the pietists turn to an account of inwardness as the basis and form of theology. This is an explicit or implicit retreat from the threats of science to a place of safety. My inwardness, my experience, is immune to the challenges of science. Thus, theology becomes an elucidation of my experience of the world, not an elucidation of the shape of the world according to the gospel. In this work the doctrine of creation has little, if anything, to contribute.

---

7. See my argument for this fragmentation in Jonathan R. Wilson, *Living Faithfully in a Fragmented World* (Valley Forge, PA: Trinity Press International, 1997), 24–38.

8. Editor's note: this is referring to *Conflicting Allegiances: The Church-Based University in a Liberal Democratic Society*, where this chapter originally appeared.

In the second case, the rationalists submit their theology to screening by the sciences. Theology then says only what it is permitted to say by the sciences. The doctrine of creation reduces to a translation into religious language of the discoveries of the sciences. At this point, theology becomes redundant: we have no need for a doctrine of creation since it tells us in less precise and persuasive language what the sciences have already produced.

Given this surrender of the doctrine of creation, the tradition of the ecclesially based university lacks a robust, well-developed, highly articulated doctrine of creation. Yes, we have the controversies over creation and evolution. Yes, we have ecological theologies. But none of these rests on highly developed, thick theological discourse about the doctrine of creation.

As a result, the ecclesially based university has only some recently developed doctrinal resources to draw upon.[9] Even the discussions of the relationship between science and religion that lurk throughout this essay are relatively immature in most of their manifestations—not because the protagonists are immature, but because the doctrinal discourse on creation is still immature. The challenge facing us is to develop this tradition in the midst of controversy and confusion. But that is where most doctrinal development takes place. What we must be careful to recognize is the relative absence of any resources in the last three hundred years and the "false humility" that has become the habit of theologians in the midst of an age of scientific reasoning.[10]

We now face the challenge of building a thick theological discourse about creation in the midst of much confusion and babble. As I noted earlier, any Christian account of creation will be cruciform, because it submits to the revelation that, in Jesus Christ, the Creator became a participant in creation and died on a cross so that the world might be saved.[11] So, let the conversation begin.


## Hope

My assignment for this chapter was to describe "the place of the natural sciences in the ecclesially based university." However, convinced that our present circumstances provide neither the resources nor the warrant nor a model for such a project, I have instead sought to describe some elements of a *process* by which

9. See note 3 above for one suggestion.

10. In addition to the work of Gunton and Moltmann that I noted earlier (n. 4), I am also intrigued by the possibilities that I discern in the work of Karl Heim, *Christian Faith and Natural Science*, trans. Neville Horton Smith (London: SCM, 1953); Heim, *Jesus the World's Perfecter: The Atonement and the Renewal of the World*, trans. D. H. van Daalen (Philadelphia: Muhlenburg, 1959); Heim, *The World: Its Creation and Consummation; The End of the Present Age and the Future of the World in the Light of the Resurrection*, trans. Robert Smith (Philadelphia: Muhlenburg, 1962).

11. For a daring account of how such a claim is the truth about this world and thus the basis for any discourse about the nature of the world, see Stanley Hauerwas, *With the Grain of the Universe* (Grand Rapids: Brazos, 2001).

we might form an ecclesially based university that could, with coherence and integrity, welcome the natural sciences.[12]

I am pessimistic about such formation taking place within our present civilization. Our fragmentation is too advanced, the culture of late capitalism is global, and *technē* rules over us.[13] Therefore, I propose instead ecclesially based communities of scholars in the sciences, as well as other disciplines, who are committed to the formation that I have sketched in this chapter. These scholars would form a new kind of monasticism—after all, the monasteries were the repositories of learning for several centuries. This new scholarly monasticism would not be defined by geographical proximity. It would, rather, be spread throughout the world and be located within many kinds of institutions. These new monastics would have to be creative in finding ways within those institutions and across their geographical distances to form communities. Examples might be provided by the Society of Christian Philosophers and the Christian Theological Research Fellowship. In the sciences a model might be the Association of Christians in the Mathematical Sciences. Some of these professional associations meet along with a larger professional society (the CTRF convenes during the annual meeting of the American Academy of Religion); others are supported well enough to sponsor their own conferences. The purpose of these societies would be to "countercultivate" scholars who have been (mal)formed by their disciplines and want to be transformed by their discipleship to Jesus Christ.

This strategy seems to me to be the embodiment of hope—not an optimism rooted in a historical trajectory but a hope rooted in the knowledge of God who acts to create and redeem. This is the God in whom hope never fades. This is the God whose redemption is the *telos* of the world. This is the God to whom we are called to witness in all the times, tasks, and places of our lives.

---

12. Let me emphasize here a point that I have made earlier in this essay: the sciences present *particular* challenges to this project, but any area of scholarly inquiry does so. What is unique about the sciences is not the challenge, but the particular shape that the challenge takes.

13. In this sentence I am referring, in order, to MacIntyre, *After Virtue*; Frederic Jameson, *Postmodernism, or the Culture of Late Capitalism* (Durham: Duke University Press, 1988); and Jacques Ellul, *The Technological Society*, trans. John Wilkinson (New York: Knopf, 1964).

# Index